The Hand that Rocks the World

An Inquiry into Truth, Power and Gender

DAVID SHACKLETON

Take2Now Inc., Ottawa, Ontario, Canada

www.take2now.com

Published by Take2Now Inc., Ottawa, Ontario, Canada.

www.take2now.com

ISBN: 978-0-9947453-0-9

Contents

Acknowledgements

Compiling a list of people who contributed to this book is complicated by the fact that it has been a work in progress for fifteen years; undoubtedly some names have been overlooked and I apologize sincerely to those inadvertently omitted.

For moral support, my thanks to Maureen Geddes, Robert Grantier, Kaia Nightingale and Katherine Willow. For author coaching, I appreciate and recommend Willa Silver. For critical feedback on portions or drafts of the manuscript, I am indebted to Bryan Alford, Peter Allemano, Robert Bly, Fayerweather Douglas, Jeffrey Duval, John Everingham, Maureen Geddes, Herb Goldberg, Tim Goldich, Rick Goodwin, Michael Kaiser, Maraya Loza-Koxahn, Greg Scammell, Kimana Soni, Steven Svoboda, Char Tosi, Bill Unitt and Woodrow Willow. I am pleased with the cover design and grateful to the designer, who does not wish to be named.

Above and beyond all of these, I am hugely grateful to my wife, Christine Eberl, who has been unwavering in her support and enthusiasm for my work in pursuit of real gender equality for the whole of the twenty years we have been together. Without her, this book would probably not exist.

Chapter 1 – The Puzzle of Life

"A good puzzle, it's a fair thing. Nobody is lying. It's very clear, and the problem depends just on you." – Erno Rubik

"While physics and mathematics may tell us how the universe began, they are not much use in predicting human behavior because there are far too many equations to solve. I'm no better than anyone else at understanding what makes people tick, particularly women." – Stephen Hawking

"If you look for truth, you may find comfort in the end; if you look for comfort you will not get either comfort or truth only soft soap and wishful thinking to begin, and in the end, despair." – C. S. Lewis

"Seeing reality for what it is is what we call discernment. The work of discernment is very hard." – Lewis B. Smedes

"People like to say that the conflict is between good and evil. The real conflict is between truth and lies." – Miguel Angel Ruiz

"Many people, especially ignorant people, want to punish you for speaking the truth, for being correct, for being you. Never apologize for being correct, or for being years ahead of your time. If you're right and you know it, speak your mind. Speak your mind. Even if you are a minority of one, the truth is still the truth." – Mahatma Gandhi

I remember a time in my school years when I had a daydream, a kind of fantasy. I was in class, maybe eleven years old, and the teacher was writing math equations on the blackboard. I had been thinking about the nature of the world, and especially about how to know what is true. My classmates all had different ideas about the world and how to be in it. Some were aggressive, bullying. Some were friendly and open. Some were shy and timid. Some lied and denied it; others lied, admitted it and argued for its utility. It was very confusing.

In the daydream, I imagined the teacher writing "$2 + 2 = 5$" on the board, and I imagined the chalk smoking and falling off the chalkboard, the incorrect equation vanishing from the board and the world, destroyed for all to see by some cosmic force aligned against falsehood. In that moment, I realized that I wanted to live in a world where what was true was self-evident and obvious, where an untrue statement was a kind of violation of the laws of nature, repudiated by the very essence of the universe.

I have come to terms with the fact that none of us live in that kind of universe, where knowing what is true and real is easy. But the hunger for the true and the desire to know *how* to discover truth that I first glimpsed in that daydream has been a constant in my life and has guided much of my life's journey. It has led me, in my 61st year, to the publishing of this book.

Life is a puzzle. Each of us arrives into a world already formed into complex patterns of rules, stories, expectations and behaviors – political patterns, social patterns, moral patterns – and we must decide what to do and what to say in each moment. Choosing a response, choosing an action requires us to solve the puzzle of life, at least partially. In order to know how to be and what to do, we have to decide what is true and what is false about the world, which stories are genuine and useful and which are mistakes or illusions. We can decide unconsciously, by what feels right, or we can bring our thinking to bear on the problem as well.

We have help with this, of course. Our culture, the contemporary stories we tell and believe about what is true and how to live, are solutions to the puzzle of life. They may not be optimum solutions, or even correct solutions, but they provide answers that it is difficult to get in any other way. Our families, friends and teachers guide us in interpreting the cultural answers in light of specific life problems. Usually, we put together a solution that works well enough, and hold it for much if not all of our life.

But a problem remains. Our solution to the puzzle of life, what we believe to be true and false about the world, differs from the solutions that others have chosen. In almost every area – religion, politics, culture, morality – people's beliefs about what is true and what is false, what is right and what is wrong, what is good and what is bad differ, sometimes greatly. The usual response to this problem is to conclude that one's own, personal solution to the puzzle of life is the best answer, the most accurate, and that everyone else is wrong to varying degrees. Most of us don't actually acknowledge it to ourselves quite that bluntly, but that is the essence of what we believe. Usually, we look for and find friends and associates who see things much as we do – peer groups, advocacy societies, associations with similar interests, internet groups – so that we don't feel the loneliness of being out of step with so many in the world.

But it remains a problem that there is so much controversy, so little meeting of the minds in many areas of life. Yet not in all areas. The puzzle of life has two major realms and one is already well understood. The material realm is an area where most of the controversy has ceased or been pushed back into fringe areas. There is not much disagreement these days about how to understand gravity or electricity or the properties of steel. Science has largely discovered the nature of our everyday material reality, and the fact that our material technologies work, that our automobiles and cellular phones and bridges predictably do what we expect, is the proof of our understanding. Mysteries remain at the scale of the very small (subatomic) or very large (cosmology), but at the scale of our normal living we have solved, by means of modern science, much of the puzzle of life, and the evidence of that is that there is little argument about what is true, and our technologies work.

Historians differ about exactly when the modern scientific age began, but it is clear that the 'keystones' of its foundation were laid by Rene Descartes, Gallileo Gallilei, and especially Isaac Newton. Newton's *Principia*,[i] in which he introduced his three laws of motion and theory of gravity, laid the foundations of physics by formalizing mathematically the basic rules by which matter behaves. Upon this foundation has been built, in some 300 years, the edifice of science and material technology which has revolutionized our lives.

However, in the realm of human behavior the situation is quite different. In the fields of politics, economics, psychology, sociology and religion there is very limited agreement about what is true and false, and our 'technologies' (interventions) fail as often as they work. The world of politics is split in many ways, with the traditional "left" and "right" just one of the divisions. Macroeconomic policies are more educated guesses than scientific principles. People may undergo intensive psychotherapy for years

---

[i] The full name is *Philosophiæ Naturalis Principia Mathematica*, which is Latin for "Mathematical Principles of Natural Philosophy."

and yet emerge no happier than when they began. For some reason the science that has been so successful in the material realms of physics, chemistry and biology has not yet managed to penetrate very deeply into these other fields, not deeply enough even to choose between competing theories. Let's look quickly into psychology to get a sense of why this might be.

In 1993 Jungian analyst James Hillman coauthored (with Michael Ventura) a book entitled, *We've Had a Hundred Years of Psychotherapy – And the World's Getting Worse.* What did he mean? He wrote, "You don't attack the grunts of Vietnam; you blame the theory behind the war. Nobody who fought in that war was at fault. It was the war itself that was at fault. It's the same thing with psychotherapy." [1] Hillman argued that psychotherapy itself is in serious error. But what does this mean? We have many different theories of psychotherapy; are they *all* wrong? Let's consider the oldest and still the most influential, that developed by the father of psychoanalysis, Sigmund Freud.

In 1896, Freud published his lecture "The Aetiology of Hysteria," in which he offered clear evidence of repressed experiences of childhood sexual abuse by an adult in every one of his eighteen cases of hysterical illness (six men and twelve women). He wrote,

> "All the singular conditions under which the ill-matched pair conduct their love-relations – on the one hand the adult, who cannot escape his share in the mutual dependence necessarily entailed by a sexual relationship, and who is yet armed with complete authority and the right to punish, and can exchange the one role for the other to the uninhibited satisfaction of his moods, and on the other hand the child, who in his helplessness is at the mercy of this arbitrary will, who is prematurely aroused to every kind of sensibility and exposed to every sort of disappointment, and whose performance of the sexual activities assigned to him is often interrupted by his imperfect control of his natural needs – all these grotesque and yet tragic incongruities reveal themselves as stamped upon the later development of the individual and of his neurosis, in countless permanent effects which deserve to be traced in the greatest detail. Where the relation is between two children, the character of the sexual scenes is none the less of the same repulsive sort, since every such relationship between

children postulates a previous seduction of one of them by an adult." [2]

By careful observation and deduction, this psychotherapeutic pioneer had discovered a deep truth about our culture; the widespread sexual abuse of children within families and how its repression in the child's psyche leads to neuroses which can distort one's entire life. But in uncovering this truth he faced a huge problem. Psychoanalyst Alice Miller describes the situation he had to deal with.

"If we picture [Freud's] readers, the women of the bourgeoisie of that day, with their elegant long dresses that hid their ankles, and the men with the stiff white collars and faultlessly cut suits (for it can hardly be supposed that his books were read by the working class), it is not hard to imagine the outrage and indignation that would have greeted the facts presented above. The indignation would not have been directed against this form of child abuse per se but against the man who dared to speak about it. For most of these refined people were firmly convinced from an early age that only fine, noble, valiant and edifying deeds (subjects) ought to be talked about publicly and what they as adults did behind closed doors in their elegant bedrooms very definitely had no place in print. Satisfying sexual desires with children was nothing bad in their eyes as long as silence was preserved, for they were convinced that no harm would be done to the children unless the matter was discussed with them." [3]

Faced with this massive cultural resistance to the truth about child sexual abuse, Freud chose in 1887 to abandon his trauma theory, which no one could accept, and develop in its place a theory of infantile sexuality and the Oedipus complex – his drive theory – which dominates Freudian psychotherapy to this day. By this means he diverted attention away from the sexually abusive actions of adults onto the child's own supposed sexual fantasies. Instead of exposing the widespread sexual abuse of children within families, he chose to deny this abuse and mislabel the resulting symptoms of mental illness in the lives of the abuse victims as the results of their own nascent psychosexual 'drives.' He declared that the memories of sexual abuse, repressed as children and recovered in therapy, were simply the child's own sexual fantasies.

This may be the most egregious example ever of blaming the victim. By diverting attention away from the truth about child sexual abuse and substituting a false cover story, Freud's incorrect drive theory has undermined psychotherapeutic healing for over a hundred years. Hillman's view that it is psychotherapy itself that is the problem is certainly supported by this example, and there are many more.

I have shared this story because it is emblematic of the difficulty that scientists – and indeed all of us – have when it comes to seeking and speaking truth around human culture and behavior. The puzzle of life may be more complex in the social than in the material realm, as Stephen Hawking suggests in the quotation at the beginning of this chapter, but that is not the major difficulty in solving it. The major difficulty is that *the solutions often seem to implicate us*. They are difficult to discern and to accept and above all to speak about because they have major, personal consequences for our lives.

Politics and psychology, sociology, culture and religion: these are the very things upon which we build the meaning of our lives. They are not comfortably removed and innocuous like the theory of electricity or the properties of steel. We have largely solved the puzzle of life in the material realm mainly because the solutions in that realm do not threaten us; do not implicate us; do not seem to convict us. But in studying culture, psychology and politics we are studying ourselves, and it can take extreme courage to face the truth about ourselves, and even more courage to share that truth with others, especially when society is strongly attached to a mistaken story.

At the beginning of this chapter I offered a quotation from Erno Rubik, the inventor of Rubik's cube. "A good puzzle, it's a fair thing. Nobody is lying. It's very clear, and the problem depends just on you." The realm of material reality is a good puzzle by this description, which is why it was solved first. But the realm of human nature is not a good puzzle, since many people are (usually unconsciously) lying, advocating passionately for their mistaken worldview. This self-deception adds an extra dimension of difficulty to its solution and makes the work of a researcher more like that of a detective seeking to solve a crime. Like criminals trying to hide their guilt, many, perhaps most people are opposed to the truth being discovered, and they actively engage in obfuscation and denial, all the while remaining unaware of their real motivation. This was the problem that caused Freud to turn away from his discovery. For Freud to continue to accept the truth of his trauma theory, he would have had to go against all of his peers, against all of his readers and probably against what felt right to him as well. He would have put his professional reputation at serious risk. Few have this much courage.

Psychiatrist M. Scott Peck has observed that:

> "Truth or reality is avoided when it is painful. We can revise our maps [of reality] only when we have the discipline not to avoid pain and effort. To have such discipline, we must be totally dedicated to the truth, not partially. That is to say, we must always hold truth, as best as we can determine it, to be more crucial, more vital to our self-interest, than our comfort. Conversely, we must always consider our personal discomfort relatively unimportant, and, indeed, even welcome it in the service of the search for truth. Mental health is an ongoing process of dedication to reality at all costs. What does this life of total dedication to the truth mean? It means, above all, a life of continuous and never-ending stringent self-examination and honesty with oneself." [4]

This is a high standard to aspire to. Can we really live a whole life this way? What do we do when we aren't so driven or so idealistic – can we still hope to find truth? Social philosopher Jacob Needleman considered these questions in his book, *Why Can't We Be Good?* He recounts a time in class when he was asked the question, "How do you recognize a real spiritual teacher? How do you tell the difference between someone who really knows something and someone who's just a charlatan?" [5] This is indeed a hard question, and a major part of what we need to know if we are to seek truth successfully. He first offered the standard answer;

> "A spiritual teacher, we are told, seeks only the good of the pupil; he or she uses no seductive methods or tricks that play on human weaknesses such as suggestibility, spiritual pride, or emotional vulnerability. ... And as for the personal qualities of the true spiritual guide, we are told that he or she is tranquil, humble, unconcerned with material things such as money, and is, above all, compassionate and all-loving, never given to egoistic anger or self-serving personal emotions of any kind." [6]

But then Needleman acknowledges,

> "... I never really was able to believe in such an answer. ... I continued, 'All of those qualities of a true teacher – they can all be imitated, obviously. Anyone can say they are authorized; anyone can say they are sent by God; anyone can pretend to be serene and compassionate, at least for a little while and to a certain extent.'" [7]

Needleman has put his finger on the key problem in discovering what is true in the arena of human society and culture, that there are many stories that claim to be true, and many people who claim to possess truth. Probably, most of them are sincere, the way that it seems Freud was, or eventually became, about his drive theory. Virtually all of the people arguing with each other in the comments sections of websites sincerely believe what they are saying. How are we to know who is right and who is mistaken? How can we discover what is really true, in the realm of human culture, values, and meaning? And, very much to the point, how can you, the reader of this book, know whether I, the author, am someone who can be trusted to guide you in these matters?

Needleman continues;

> "'We want to know how to recognize a real teacher, but do we ever ask ourselves in what way we are searching for a teacher, in what way we are searching for truth? Could it be that we only recognize a teacher when we are in a state of need, when real need pours through us and sensitizes our powers of perception? A hungry man looks for food in a very different way than a full man. Need can attract intelligence." [8]

Jacob Needleman suggests that what really matters in a search for truth is how much we want it, how intently we search. It is the same answer as Peck offered when he said, "Mental health is an ongoing process of dedication to reality at all costs." *At all costs!* In other words, we find truth when we make the search for truth our top priority. Isn't this what Jesus of Nazareth said two thousand years ago? "The Kingdom of Heaven is like a treasure that a man discovered hidden in a field. In his excitement, he hid it again and sold everything he owned to get enough money to buy the field." [9] This metaphor speaks to our *attitude*; it suggests that we find truth when we want it more than comfort or reassurance, when we want it more than anything else. American philosopher Henry David Thoreau exhibited this attitude when he said, "Rather than love, than money, than fame, give me truth!"

As I observed earlier, this is a high standard. What do we do if we can't summon that kind of intensity, that kind of deep need to know? Needleman has something to say about this also.

> "But suppose we don't have such a sense of need? Suppose it is too buried? … What do I do? I stay with my uncertainty, which is now sensed as a need. It is not only he or she about whom I now have a question; it is myself who is in question." [10]

Needleman takes too long in answering his own question for me to quote it all here, but his answer is that in this space of holding the question open, one's mind is both creatively open to new insights and simultaneously critical and focused on finding any flaws in those ideas. It is a powerful combination of intentional open mindedness, featuring a determination not to leap to conclusions or settle too early on an answer that might feel right, and critical thinking, featuring a disciplined evaluation of the merit and veracity of each idea.

Notice that the openness and the critical thinking are not just with respect to the abstract truth about the other, but also include oneself; one's possible biases, fears, ego needs and illusions all become part of what is carefully considered and evaluated. Needleman suggests that this combination, this state of mind is the best that we can do in evaluating what is true and in penetrating illusion, and I think that he is right. I will have more to say later about *why* this approach is uniquely powerful.

Not only is this the best that we can do, it is often enough to take us all of the way to truth in these difficult areas of human behavior and interaction. There is joy in it, the joy of deep discovery and of living fully. When we hold the question open, we use our minds in a way that is deeply meaningful, that yields the experience of being fully alive. We cease to skate over the surface of life, moving from one ego pleasure or bodily satisfaction to the next, and instead we engage with the deep, transcendent puzzle of life itself. In some mysterious fashion, we are blessed by this deeper process, this genuine seeking after truth.

These joys help to sustain us in the process, but they are still in the future and unknown when we begin. What is the motivation for beginning this work? After all, it is difficult to remain in the state of not knowing the answer, and there is no way of knowing how long it will take for the answer to become clear. Once again, the motivation can only be the desire for truth, over a more convenient or reassuring story. We have to want the truth enough to search for it, and to wait for it, and throughout the waiting and the searching to continually deny ourselves the comfort of a false but plausible story that would relax the tension of not knowing and feed our ego, or give in to our fears. We have to be determined to find the truth no matter what consequences it may entail for our lives. The consequences may be significant, perhaps as great as they would have been for Freud.

The fifteenth century Indian poet Kabir spoke of these things:

> "Friend, hope for the Guest while you are alive.
> Jump into experience while you are alive!
> Think … and think … while you are alive.
> What you call 'salvation' belongs to the time before death.
> If you don't break your ropes while you're alive,
> do you think ghosts will do it after? …
>
> So plunge into the truth, find out who the Teacher is. Believe in the Great Sound!
> Kabir says this; When the Guest is being searched for, it is the intensity of the longing for the Guest that does all the work.
> Look at me, and you will see a slave of that intensity." [11]

I do not know where this desire for truth comes from, nor do I have any idea how to encourage it in others. Indeed, my attempts to do so have not been notably successful. So for the rest of this book, I will tell my own story. I have, for reasons I know not and claim no credit for, been willing to look hard for truth in certain areas of my life – by no means in all areas, but in some. I have found, at times, the willingness in myself to hold a question open, sometimes for years, while searching for the answer. As a result, I have found some truths about the world and about human nature that I propose to share with you in these pages. I name them as truths because they have been confirmed by the testing that I have done, but what they are really are hypotheses and theories. I offer them for you and others to test.

I suspect, and I hope, that our society may be on the brink of genuine insight into the second realm that I mentioned, the realm of human behavior; on the brink of a deep and genuine and hugely useful true understanding of human nature and human society. This book is my contribution towards that effort. The theories that I will offer are about the fundamental processes of the human psyche and some basic consequences of those processes in contemporary society. If they are true, then I hope that they may provide a small part of the solid foundation that is required for a new, genuinely scientific approach to human nature, in the way that Newton's *Principia* did for the science of material reality some 330 years ago.

Is this possible? Can we discover and understand the unique, genuine nature of human psychosocial reality the way that we have discovered the unique, genuine nature of much of material reality? I am convinced that it is possible, and that we may be ready to begin this journey. It is difficult to predict when society is about to turn in a new direction, but there are signs that indicate such a possibility. The emergence in the last decade of public interest in formal debates between Christians and atheists is a positive sign that people are becoming interested in having these questions explored through rational processes of evidence and reason. The fast growth of new, controversial areas of scientific exploration into human behavior (e.g., evolutionary psychology) bodes well for the readiness of the scientific establishment.

It is clear that we need this understanding urgently – our inability to comprehend and therefore to manage our own behavior and that of our societies has led us to the brink of disaster. Environmental destruction, climate change, economic collapse, fossil fuel depletion, overpopulation – any of these could lead to devastation on a scale we haven't seen in centuries, if ever, and all of them together represent a most urgent call for us to wise up, to grow up, to begin to get a handle on our own behavior on this planet. To begin, in short, to understand ourselves.

We do not lack the technical ability to solve these problems. What we lack is the political will. We don't want it enough. That is, we lack the psychosocial ability to alter our behavior as a society away from dysfunctional and destructive behaviors, toward strategies that will actually work. We lack, in short, the ability to live well.

How will we develop this ability? The first thing that we need is an intellectual foundation, a basic understanding of the deepest, most fundamental elements of our human psychosocial nature. I will suggest the beginnings of such a system in this book. Some of my hypotheses and theories challenge society's story about itself, in the way that Freud's discovery about child sexual abuse threatened the society of his day. Part of my account in these pages will be how I spent years wrestling with that, seeking the courage to stand strongly in what I had found to be true, searching myself for evidence of anger, judgment, arrogance, the dysfunctions that I was accused of by those who disagreed with my conclusions. It has taken me years to come to the place where I feel ready, competent to put these conclusions strongly into the world, confident that they are well tested and true. I will tell some of the story of that personal journey, as an illustration of what it looks and feels like to hold the question open and seek truth that is deeper than one's feeling reactions.

I will illustrate my theories with examples and evidence but will not attempt to prove them; there isn't room for that, and it isn't what matters. Any reader who wants more evidence will find a great deal of it elsewhere. I am attempting something different here, to approach what is real and foundational in a more holistic way, through story and insight, through synthesis of simplicity out of complexity. Oliver Wendell Holmes, Sr., said "For the simplicity on this side of complexity I wouldn't give you a fig. But for the simplicity on the other side of complexity, for that I would give you anything I have." I believe that the concepts, models and theories I will outline here are the simplicity on the other side of complexity.

In some ways, what follows is a detective story in which we seek the truth about certain aspects of human nature and human culture, and we must contend with and move past the distortions in our thinking from our own fears, needs and habits, and from the well-intended, sincere and plausible but mistaken claims of others. I note, however, that detective stories are a major branch of literature, enjoyed by many. Join me as we decipher some aspects of the puzzle of life.

Chapter 2 – Wisdom is Dualistic Balance

"Science is organized knowledge. Wisdom is organized life." – Immanuel Kant (1724 - 1804)

"In the frank expression of conflicting opinions lies the greatest promise of wisdom in governmental action." – Louis D. Brandeis (1856 - 1941)

"One's first step in wisdom is to question everything - and one's last is to come to terms with everything." – Georg C. Lichtenberg (1742 - 1799)

"The truth that makes men free is for the most part the truth which men prefer not to hear." – Herbert Sebastien Agar

"Knowledge can be communicated, but wisdom cannot. A man can find it, he can live it, he can be filled and sustained by it, but he cannot utter or teach it." – Hermann Hesse (1877 - 1962)

"The greater the ignorance the greater the dogmatism." – Sir William Osler (1849-1919)

"None are more hopelessly enslaved as those who falsely believe they are free." – Johann Wolfgang von Goethe (1749-1832)

The aspect of human nature that has the most to do with knowing the truth about ourselves and the world in the field of human behavior (that controversial field that I have suggested includes psychology, sociology, politics, economics, etc.) is wisdom. Several of the above quotations suggest that wisdom has to do with the balancing of opposites. In this chapter I will develop this idea into a clear and useful concept and discover why attaining wisdom is difficult.

Historically, one way that life wisdom was captured and offered to us all was through proverbs. These days, we tend to think of proverbs as simply amusing or interesting sayings, but only those that struck a wide resonance and found a genuine utility survived to become well known catchphrases.[ii]

[ii] A proverb is the wisdom of many and the wit of one. - John Russell

Here's a little known fact about proverbs;[iii] many of them contradict each other. Our ancestors knew that true wisdom is paradoxical, contradictory. For example: "Fools rush in where angels fear to tread." Good advice to take careful consideration before making big decisions. Yet, "She who hesitates is lost." Do it, don't think about it, just do it right away. What can we make of this contradictory advice? Another example: "Two heads are better than one." And its opposite, "Too many cooks spoil the broth." Or the more recent, "A camel is a horse designed by a committee." The realm of proverbs is full of contradictory advice like this. So what use are they?

Proverbs remind us that wisdom cannot be reduced to one-sided advice, to a formula. Right action is circumstantial and situational. To hold the complexity to address any situation, wisdom has to be paradoxical. It is, in a word, balanced. There are times when caution is wise, and times when it should be abandoned. There are tasks for which individuals work best alone, and tasks which are best approached by a team. To be able to make the best of any situation we need to balance *ourselves*, to develop our capacity to work well alone, and also our capacity to work well with others.

The psychologist Carl Jung developed this idea into a formal theoretical system. He proposed that the natural process of adult psychological development is to develop one side of a set of dualities, then switch over to developing the other side, and finally to integrate the two sides into a balanced set. For example, consider the general pattern of human development through childhood and into adulthood. As infants, we are emotionally expressive, moving from joy to rage to tears in moments. We are comfortable with intimacy, with cuddling and touching, and likewise we are comfortable with being dependent on others. Then we enter adolescence, and often find that in this stage we become fiercely independent, unemotional and distant. In the third and most difficult stage, as young adults, we attempt to integrate the opposites of the two earlier opposite stages, to become interdependent, for example – capable of dependence when that is indicated or independence when that is needed. To become emotionally integrated – capable of feeling and expressing

---

[iii] The wisdom of the wise and the experience of the ages is preserved into perpetuity by a nation's proverbs, fables, folk sayings and quotations. - William Feather (1908 - 1976)

our emotions, but able to suppress them also (for instance, in an emergency when lives need to be saved). To become comfortable with intimacy but not needful for it, so that we can be fully our own person, yet enjoy close relationships with others.

It is clear that most adults fail to fully integrate many of these opposites and this is understandable; it is difficult to do. It is difficult *because* they are opposite, challenging to reconcile. But without that integration, we remain on one side or another of all of the dualistic balances, so that only one approach feels right to us, and its dualistic opposite feels quite wrong, mistaken, immature or immoral. This is why, for instance, the political right and left are so hostile to each other, each group convinced that they have the whole of the answer and that the other is quite wrong. In fact, mature politics, wisdom, is an integration of these two partial systems.

We will consider some particular dualities and the difficulty of balancing them in order to get a sense of this issue, beginning with one that offers little difficulty, where most people already are comfortable with both sides.

The first sentence in M. Scott Peck's famous *The Road Less Travelled* is "Life is difficult." Peck explains that once we really get that this is true, and that it *should* be true, it ceases to matter to us that life is difficult. We stop feeling sorry for ourselves that our own lives are difficult and get on with the business of living *well*. In other words, we let go of the concept of *ease* as a major life goal. We come to understand that a life lived in pursuit of ease, avoiding things that are difficult, will be a shallow life of little worth or accomplishment.

That doesn't mean that we stop valuing ease as a worthy part of life. A pleasurable vacation as a break from work or a reward for accomplishment is important. Resting from our labors is vital – but so are our labors in the first place. In short, neither ease nor effort should be made the prime goal of life. Laziness and workaholism – ease or effort carried to excess – are both destructive of a good life. The key is to have a reasonable balance between the two. To achieve this balance, this integration of opposites, we need to become comfortable and competent in both areas, able to work hard and well, and also able to rest and play. Notice that healthy balance between these opposites takes the form of *alternation* between them, periods of effort alternated with periods of rest and recreation. Balance does not mean a middle way, ease mixed with effort in some 50/50 mixture, like warm water is a mixture of hot and cold.

Most of us already appreciate the right relationship between these opposite concepts of ease and effort. We know that, even though ease is pleasurable and effort is difficult, these feelings are not adequate guides for living our lives. We must discipline ourselves to endure some distress as we strive towards a difficult goal, or simply earn what we need to survive. Following our natural inclinations towards ease and away from effort would be to undermine much that makes life worth living, and would ultimately make life impossible.

I have spent time describing a duality that most people already understand because I want to use it as an analogy to bridge to others that are more of a stretch. Let's now move to the concepts of peace and conflict. Peace is like ease and conflict is like effort. A life lived in pursuit of peace and in avoidance of conflict is ultimately as empty and misguided as a life lived in pursuit of ease and in avoidance of effort. Once we really 'get' that this is true and that it *should* be true, it ceases to matter to us that life is conflictual. It ceases to be a problem and becomes just part of life's nature. In other words, we let go of the concept of peace as a main life goal.

This is more challenging. The notion of peace as an ideal state that we should strive towards, and conflict as an unfortunate product of immaturity or dysfunction on somebody's part, is well entrenched in modern culture. We have put a polarized value structure on top of the concepts of peace and conflict: the former is good, the latter at best a necessary evil, at worst totally wrong. I don't want to reverse this value structure, I want to remove it. This common value structure simply represents our natural human inclination to seek ease and avoid stress. Conflict is stressful, it feels difficult. But as we saw in the case of ease and effort, these feelings are *not* good guides to life. They are incompetent guides who will steer us wrong.

What evidence can I present that conflict is a fundamental, inherent and valuable part of life? Consider the nature of the human psyche. It is inherently oppositional. It is oppositional because it is a regulated system, and every regulated system achieves control through balancing opposing energies. For instance, we have a human need for social interaction but also for solitude. We are always in the process of balancing these opposing needs. We need autonomy but also relationship. Our need to go out and discover the fresh and new is opposed to our need for security, for the familiar. And so on.

All major systems of modeling the human psyche reflect this oppositional nature. Freud saw the psyche as tripolar: the natural urges and drives of the id being opposed by the socialized 'conscience' of the superego, with the balance between the two mediated by the ego. Jung's model of the psyche is bipolar, a continual dance of conflict between dualistically opposite psychic energies. The oppositions that he saw as foundational for the personality (popularized in the Myers-Briggs personality typing scheme) are introversion vs. extraversion, intuition (visionary possibility) vs. sensing (factual here-and-now), thinking vs. feeling, and open-endedness vs. closure. The healthy psyche, these pioneering thinkers all affirm, is a psyche in *conflict*, one that embraces and manages the dynamic tension between inherent opposing forces.

What is structural and foundational for the individual human psyche will, of course, also manifest between people. As individuals with unique personalities and histories, we choose various solutions, differing rest-points or comfort zones on the oppositional continuum, and we constantly run up against people who have made different choices. Oppositional social dualities such as hawks and doves, conservatives and liberals, represent large groups of people who have made similar one-sided choices about what to value and what to devalue or demonize. Each sees the dualistically opposite group as completely wrong-headed about the issue that divides them. Neither group recognizes that they both have pieces of wisdom, and they both have components of error. In particular, neither group sees that integrated wisdom could be achieved through intense dialogue between them, by debate that is characterized by subordination to truth – in short, by conflict, competition around their differing ideas. Like a healthy psyche, a healthy society embraces and supports conflict and competition in diverse forms, seeking the wisdom that comes from integrating – valuing and accommodating, not eliminating – difference.

Why do we avoid such debate? Why do we prefer the company of those who already agree with us? The answer is not difficult. We see these issues as win/lose propositions, we feel sure that they have just one right answer. Obviously we do not fear to win; that would be great. The other possibility in our imagined scenario is that we might lose. That is what we fear. But this fear must be dysfunctional. Clearly, every time we correct a misapprehension that we hold, every time we discover an error, we improve ourselves. Provided that we are indeed surrendered to truth, losing means that we gain a better, more accurate understanding of life and how to live it. It is better to lose than to win, for only the loser gets to improve his worldview.

By this analysis, we are suffering not from too much conflict in the world today, but too little. Having enshrined peace as the only worthy goal of social progress, and conflict as largely dysfunctional, we are unable to bless ourselves through conflict, to be improved and chastened by it. We have removed its sacred role and vulgarized or demonized it. Most of the conflict that we do have has lost its healthy focus on discovering what is true, and instead has become ego defense, defense of one-sided stuckness, purely dysfunctional. It is hard to see the value in genuine conflict when we are surrounded by such ineffective examples.

In the world's oldest recorded myth, from Mesopotamia (Iraq), the great king Gilgamesh is without peer and therefore lonely. The Gods, seeing his distress, create an equal companion for him, a man called Enkidu. When Gilgamesh and Enkidu first meet, they fight. Why? They fight in order to know each other truly. If you want to know who someone truly is, don't watch them at their ease, in their comfort zone, composed and in control. Anyone can look good under those conditions. To truly know someone quickly and deeply, fighting them is a good strategy.

Note how different this is to our conventional wisdom. In our overvaluing of peace, we see conflict as bad, or at best a necessary evil. We see it as divisive and destructive of relationship. But Gilgamesh and Enkidu fight in order to *build* a relationship, in order to discover if they can become *friends*. And they do indeed become the closest of friends.

This is an aspect of conflict that we have forgotten and have a hard time accepting. We see only the dark side of conflict, where it is about domination, hate or control. We don't see its light side, which is about respect and striving for truth and excellence. We come closest to remembering this in the area of ritualized conflict, i.e., sports. Ask a professional athlete whether they respect the opposing team or athlete – and most will tell you yes. Athletes know how difficult it is to excel at a sport. They know that to win a match or a tournament requires discipline and excellence, and losing athletes usually respect the ability of the team that beat them.

Who doesn't love to see human performance at its best – Olympic competitions, for instance? Some of our best, most intense, most memorably alive moments are when we strive to beat a worthy opponent, or watch others in that striving. Competition can bring out the very best in us. To put it bluntly, we are currently very unwise, meaning unbalanced, about peace and conflict.

In his book *Iron John*, Robert Bly says, "Conscious fighting is a great help in relationships between men and women. Jung said, 'American marriages are the saddest in the world, because the man does all his fighting at the office.'" [12]

Let me be clear here. I am not saying that all conflict is good. I am saying that not all conflict is bad. There is bad, harmful, dysfunctional conflict as well as good, productive conflict, just as there is harmful, dysfunctional peace (for instance, fearful avoidance of confrontation) as well as good, healthy peace. The difference between healthy and unhealthy conflict is whether we are open to truth, which means open to discovering that we are wrong, and whether we are fighting from love, which means in order to build relationship rather than destroy it.

Most of the debate in families or on the internet is ego-motivated, between people whose minds are closed, already made up, and so it devolves into acrimony and frustration – useless, dysfunctional conflict that *is* destructive of relationship. But conflict that is a genuine search for truth is a wonderful thing to see, all parties are enhanced by it. It is in the tension, in the conflict between the competing views, like the tension and conflict between political left and right, that wisdom lies. In workshops that I conduct, I hold space for *sacred conflict*, for intense confrontations between deeply held beliefs and perceptions of men and women, having faith that such conflict is the fertile ground out of which new integrations, new insights, new wisdom can grow.

We are seeing that cultural one-sidedness around dualistic opposites can have huge social consequences. Indeed, our lack of wisdom, of balance around these issues is the most significant cultural dysfunction facing society today. Let's get really clear on this by exploring more examples of dualistic opposites that we tend to see in a one-sided, unbalanced way.

The subjective/objective duality is an interesting one. Most people are relatively comfortable with the concept that there is a subjective realm of internal thoughts and feelings, and an objective realm of objects and phenomena in the outer world. Common distortions of this duality consist of seeing one of these opposites as dominant and the other as a consequence, a derivative of the first. For instance, the new age idea of consensual reality sees the outer, objective world as purely a consequence of people's internal, subjective beliefs. Consider the following writing from a popular website:

"Living Consciously

"Dear Friends,

"To paraphrase Neville: the future becomes the present and is revealed in our inner talking.

"The reason that kind of statement initiates resistance is simple. Most of us do not stay with an inner dialogue on a particular topic long enough to actually set it in motion. We day dream but we do not really get to the feeling of the thing as already being so. Our future then, is a rehash of the past or a hit and miss kind of experience, where we feel we have nothing much to say about the events in our life. We have not had the experience of the power of mind to bring about desired results.

"The key is to assume the Effect is in the Cause and Cause is in our mind. We are not making something happen as much as we are "seeing" the thing done before it appears in the world. It is in this seeing that mind power takes shape as form and substance. Matter follows the direction that Mind takes. Just as the chronic worrier always has something to fear, the chronic affirmer of prosperity always has supply to spare.

"People complain that the emphasis on this Law is misplaced in a spiritual teaching. It is not! The ignorance of it causes people to be in despair or intense anger at the seeming injustices in their world. Despair and anger cause violence, greed, self destructive behaviors, crime, war and ultimately taint the collective unconscious, making dis-ease a reality. Poverty exists because people do not know how to generate prosperity. This causes the rich to hoard, to arm themselves against marauding invaders, to live behind iron gates. This causes the poor to stay poor and/or to hate those who prosper, creating an "us and them" atmosphere which always leads to violence of some kind.

"The world of effects is not the problem. It is the inner world of ignorance that needs to change.

Stay tuned in,

Dr. Carol Carnes" [13]

We can see from these ideas that a coherent, internally consistent worldview can be created entirely around one side of this subjective/objective duality. Dr. Carnes' view of the world, as expressed in this post, is that the objective is subordinate to, is entirely determined by the subjective. As she says, "Matter follows the direction that Mind takes." The recent popularity of the "Law of Attraction" [iv] represents the same elevation of the subjective over the objective, in different words. Here is the blurb from author Rhonda Byrne's website:

"The Secret [the Law of Attraction] has been passed down through the ages... coveted, hidden, lost, stolen, bought for vast sums of money, and known by some of the most exceptional people who ever lived: Plato, Galileo, DaVinci, Beethoven, Edison, and Einstein, to name but a few. *The Secret* book reveals how you can change every aspect of your life. You can turn any weakness or suffering into strength, power, unlimited abundance, health and joy. Everything is possible, nothing is impossible.

[iv] The Law of Attraction is the belief that achievements in the external world, such as success and prosperity, are entirely the consequences of internal states of mind.

> There are no limits. Whatever you can dream of can be yours,
> when you use The Secret." [14]

It is not difficult to discern the attraction of such a worldview – it promises to deliver whatever you desire without the troublesome problems of merit, competence or sustained effort. It is, of course, a fantasy. It is a fantasy that has netted its author millions of dollars (*The Secret* book and film grossed over $300 million and the book remained on the *New York Times* bestseller list for 146 consecutive weeks).[15]

The idea that the objective world can be controlled just by wishing it so is magical thinking at its most obvious – and yet it is believed by millions. Such a worldview will manifest some problems in that it is false-to-fact, but it provides explanations for such difficulties. For instance, a person who believes with Dr. Carnes or Rhonda Byrne that the subjective controls the objective may try many times to get their mind into the right place to create prosperity for themselves – and as long as that result doesn't occur, their worldview will tell them that they must still be harboring negative thoughts that are defeating their purpose, undermining their unity of mind. If at some point their trying meets a matching opportunity in the outer world and they do find some prosperity, they will attribute that success to finally getting their mind into the right place.

The worldview, despite being a serious abbreviation and distortion of reality, has an explanation for everything. Dr. Carnes' short piece of writing above, for example, purports to explain external, objective manifestations of violence, greed, self-destructive behaviors, crime, war, poverty and prosperity all as solely and entirely consequences of the inner, subjective world.

The truth about these dualistic opposites is always the same – both sides have independent existence and equal power. In the case of the subjective/objective duality, the subjective world is independent of the objective, and the objective world is independent of the subjective. This doesn't mean that they have no relationship, no influence on each other; clearly they do. Our thoughts and feelings are affected by what happens in the outer world, and the outer world is affected by our subjective attitudes and decisions. What independence means is that a change in one does not instantly and automatically produce a change in the other. Each side is influenced, but not controlled, by the other.

Consider the famous philosophical question, "If a tree falls in the forest and no one is there to hear it, does it make a sound?" This is a question about the subjective/objective duality. It asks if the objective world has independent existence from the subjective. Behind the question is the obvious fact that we cannot know for sure. Since we can only perceive when we look or listen, then we cannot know by observation what is happening when we aren't looking and listening. If, however, we accept the independence of the objective and the subjective worlds, as suggested by the dualistic balancing model, then the answer is clear. The tree falling in the forest makes a sound, whether or not there is anyone to hear it.

I find this a satisfactory answer because if I invert the question the answer seems obvious. The question about the tree is really asking whether an event in the objective world that has no consequences in anyone's subjectivity is still real. Inverting that question produces this: If a person has a thought or feeling that has no consequences in the objective world, is the thought or feeling still real? The thought or feeling was *experienced*; it seems obvious that it is real. By dualistic balance, I say that the objective and the subjective are both fully real, fully independent, and of equal, balanced power.

What would a worldview look like with the opposite imbalance, one that elevates the objective over the subjective, that sees our thoughts and feelings as simply the consequence of controlling events in the outer world? This is the worldview of religious determinism, which sees people essentially as predetermined puppets of God's plan for the objective cosmos. This worldview is not as common these days as new age consensus reality, but it has had great following in the past. Which side of a duality people gravitate toward varies with cultural and individual factors of the time. What seems to remain constant is that it will be just one side that they choose, while making the other side wrong.

The progress of an individual or a society towards wisdom, then, is progress towards dualistic balance, towards the state where we 'get' both sides, by which I mean that both sides feel right to us, both are in alignment with how we experience and comprehend the world, and both are in full use in our consideration of strategies and solutions for our lives. There are many such dualities; in some we are already well advanced towards balance (like the ease/effort duality we began with), while others are more challenging and most people remain one sided around them. How we move ourselves intentionally towards balance will be the subject of a future chapter. For now let us continue our exploration of current dualistic imbalance in society.

Currently, the most influential and widespread imbalance in society is around thinking/feeling. This duality is fundamental, and a central concern of this book, since it relates to the process by which we decide what is true in our lives and in the world. If we have a bias towards thinking, then we determine what is so by considering evidence and following deductions and inferences towards conclusions. If we have a bias towards feeling, then we judge what is true by what feels right, what fits best with our "gut feel" about life and the world. This latter imbalance in favor of feeling is the dominant psychic dysfunction of our time, so common that it is practically invisible, regarded as completely normal. Most people don't realize that thinking is a learned skill, and that having thoughts about things, which everybody does, is no more thinking than hacking at a piece of wood is sculpture or carpentry. One has to learn how to sculpt and to build, and one has to learn how to think.

However, we don't have to learn how to feel. How we feel about the world presents itself immediately as life goes along, and feels both right and complete, so the fact that one lacks something, the fact that the feeling could be mistaken needs to be deduced from other evidence, and doing so means losing that feeling of complete rightness, at least for a time while one contemplates the possibility that it could be an error. Most people simply refuse to do this, or even to recognize any need for it, until life gives them so much trouble that they begin questioning their basic ideas. For many, probably most, they do not get to this point before death intervenes. Feeling is so powerful, it often overwhelms the psyche, and the certainty that one is completely right needs no more support or confirmation than the feeling of rightness that presents itself ready made and deeply compelling.

For evidence of this one-sided pattern as the basic mode of human psychic interaction these days, consider the three things that everybody knows there is little point discussing – sport, politics and religion. Why is that? Why can't we have a reasonable discussion about these things? I think we know that it is because we are basically not rational, i.e., reasonable – which means, in practice, willing to discover that we are wrong about these issues. In the past I have asked Mormons or Jehovah's Witnesses who came to my door whether there was anything that I could say, any argument that I could make, that might convince them that they were wrong in their beliefs. All told me proudly that there is no such argument, that they know what is true by unshakable faith. They have, it would seem, insulated themselves from reason, indeed from reality. If they are mistaken, they cannot discover it because they will not allow themselves to consider the possibility of error.

What is acknowledged by the religious is often just as true, though unacknowledged, in sports and politics. It is the feeling of rightness that provides the conviction that one is right, and that allows one to simply dismiss any argument to the contrary. Contrary arguments are dismissed on the grounds that they don't feel right, don't feel true, and this is the sole and solitary test of truth for that large majority of us who have a strong bias towards feeling. So let us examine how good a test this is. How well does feeling work in knowing what is true?

Let's start with falling in love. Most of us have experienced this overwhelming human feeling, and it is clearly a form of delicious insanity. Love songs and poems often contain hyperbole insisting that love will last for ever, will never change. Yet we are surrounded by evidence that this is not true – the divorce rate, for starters. What is going on? Clearly we mistake intensity for longevity. The love experience is such an intense feeling that we conclude it *must* last for ever. We *feel* it to be true. How could something so deep, so powerful, be ephemeral? [v]

Yet it is. It changes, it passes. Do we go back and learn from our error, realize how mistaken we were? Not usually. We prefer to hold onto the magic memory of that feeling, to believe that it was true, just that the *lover* has changed, they are not the same person we

---

[v] "Love may start out as a good feeling, but to love someone long-term is an act of the will." - Elizabeth George, *One-Minute Inspirations for Women*.

fell in love with. We prefer not to learn from experience, or rather, we learn the wrong lessons. The power of feeling, the intensity, and the pleasure we gain from feeling right and wise and knowing what is true, leads us to sacrifice real truth for its image, for what feels true.

The falling in love feeling achieves its intensity by being augmented with a host of brain chemicals, dopamine and other drugs dispensed from the body's inner pharmacy. But what of other feelings of rightness, those associated with sports or politics or religion, or just those supporting our worldview? How do they achieve their power to insulate us from reality, to make us deny and dismiss all evidence that they are mistaken?

The psychological answer is "cognitive dissonance". What does that mean in ordinary language? It means that discovering that we are wrong about something is distressful. It hurts. It is embarrassing, it is upsetting, it usually means that we discover we have done harm to others in the past when we acted on our false beliefs, and it always means that we have to revise our picture of reality, our psychic maps. All of these things are difficult, indeed painful to do or even to contemplate. And the longer we have left it since we last made a revision to our worldview, the greater all of these stresses will be and the less practice we will have at tolerating the pain and finding our way through it. For many people, the task becomes impossible in practice and they become completely stuck, deeply wedded to falsehood and determined to defend it to the end.

So we witness the almost universal spectacle of people arguing with each other about what is true in some area, where each side is convinced that they are right and cannot understand why the other side doesn't get what they are saying, doesn't see the truth the way that they do. Read any internet comments page and you will see this in spades. Each side believes as they do because it feels right to them. They present thoughts about their beliefs – sometimes evidence, more usually just repeated assertions of their beliefs. After all, that's enough to convince them – the feeling of rightness that they experience when they hear their own assertions is all that it takes for them to know that they are true. Why doesn't the other person see the obvious? They don't see it, of course, because they don't get the same feelings when they hear the assertions. Rather, they get opposite feelings, feelings of wrongness. People resort to flaming, to personal accusations in these situations because it is so frustrating – one is so sure of one's rightness, because of one's feeling of rightness, that it is clear that the other person must be an idiot, or worse, a subversive of some kind, not to agree with you.

Of course, exactly the same is going on for the other party. There is no possibility of one side convincing the other because each is insulated from reality by their attachment to their personal image of reality, the only image that gives them the feeling of rightness that they need. There is no way that reason can contradict such feelings, since the feelings simply tell us that the reasoning is faulty. Thus we see a proliferation of interest groups, where people with corresponding feelings about what is true align themselves together. The liberal left is one such group; the conservative right another.

There is experimental evidence that confirms the current primacy of feeling. In his book *The Righteous Mind*, psychologist Jonathan Haidt relates how he presented experimental subjects with stories in which something disturbing or disgusting was done, such as eating a deceased family pet or cutting up the national flag, but in which no one was harmed. The subjects of his experiments reliably judged that the action was morally wrong, but didn't know why because they couldn't identify a victim. He found that

> "… even when subjects recognized that their victim claims were bogus, they still refused to say that the act was ok. Instead, they kept searching for another victim. They said things like, 'I know it's wrong, but I just can't think of a reason why.' … These subjects were reasoning. They were working quite hard at reasoning. But it was not reasoning in search of truth, it was reasoning in support of their emotional reactions. It was reasoning as described by the philosopher David Hume, who wrote in 1739 that 'reason is, and ought only to be the slave of the passions, and can never pretend to any other office than to serve and obey them.' [16] I had found evidence for Hume's claim. I had found that moral reasoning was often a servant of moral emotions, and this was a challenge to the rationalist approach that dominated moral psychology." [17]

Where do these feelings come from that provide us such certainty about what is right, what is true? Let us consider a thought experiment. You are walking in your home town, and you see a close friend exit a nearby shop. The friend looks right at you but does not say hello, does not acknowledge you in any way before turning away and hurrying down the street. How could your friend be so thoughtless, to ignore you completely? Perhaps you feel affronted, insulted at your friend's avoidance of you. Perhaps you feel guilty; you must have done something to offend your friend. These feelings arrive ready made, they show up instantly.

You go into the store that your friend was in. The owner recognizes you and says, "You just missed your friend. She had a cell phone call while she was here; her daughter was in a motor accident." Instantly your feelings change; now you understand your friend's behavior and feel compassion for her distress and your earlier feeling of offense vanishes as if it had never existed.

It is clear from such thought experiments that feelings do not come from nowhere; they are built upon our beliefs about a situation, the *meaning* that we give it. They change as soon as our beliefs change. Accurate beliefs give rise to appropriate feelings, like your compassion for your friend. Inaccurate beliefs give rise to inappropriate feelings, like your initial offense at your friend's behavior. Our feelings of rightness or wrongness about what is so are the same – they arise instantly to confirm a description that agrees with our worldview, or to deny one that contradicts it. It's no more complicated than that. Yet most of this process is unconscious, invisible to us. You weren't aware of forming your beliefs, for instance your assumptions about the causes of your friend's behavior in the thought experiment above; it happened instantly and automatically.

What this means in practice is that our worldview actively defends itself from discovering error, by making any statements that contradict it feel instantly wrong to us. If we wish to know whether our worldview contains error, we must tolerate the feelings of wrongness in the knowledge that those feelings might be inappropriate, might be quite wrong themselves. Whether something feels right or wrong to us is not a measure of objective or subjective truth, it is a measure only of how well it aligns with and supports the assumptions we have made, what we already believe.[vi]

A story from my own life illustrates this. At some point in my childhood, I came across the word "misled" in a book. Not knowing how it was pronounced, I made a wrong assumption. I assumed it was the past tense of a verb I hadn't met before, the verb "to misle," pronounced *myzell*, which from the context must mean something like 'to confuse, to lead astray.' I spent the next few years innocently holding a wrong belief about this word, not knowing that the word I believed in didn't actually exist. Of course, my wrong belief gave rise automatically to wrong feelings. The fact that I never once encountered "misle" in the present tense didn't tip me off to my error, since I wasn't looking to check myself about this.

Even today, years after I discovered and corrected my error, the word "misle" still feels right to me, still has the resonance of a real English word in my mind. It was a little piece of meaning construction that was uniquely my own creation – but it *felt* just as valid to me as all of the other words that *are* objectively real.

It's hard to really get just how arbitrary these feelings are, how they can be completely wrong and untrue. They *feel* real, and that feeling is compelling, difficult to doubt. Yet, if we are to discover what is genuinely, really true, we must question such feelings, and doing so begins with recognizing their fallibility.

What could provide the motivation for this arduous process of going against feeling? For some people, it is an accumulation of life problems that finally provides the conviction that something must be wrong, that something new must be tried. For others, there is a point reached when they become ready and eager for a greater level of truth in their lives. But whether it is desperation or determination, it comes down to just one thing: what do we really want? Do we want to know what is really true, or do we want to keep a set of reassuring lies that *feel* true, while telling ourselves the cover story that we want truth?

[vi] "Is it how it feels to do the right things? Because it sucks!" — Susan Vaught, *Big Fat Manifesto*.

For me, a major change in what I wanted occurred during my relationship with my second wife. Throughout my childhood, my mother had used shame to manipulate me into doing what she wanted, into being a 'good boy.' A result of this was that, as an adult, I still needed the key woman in my life to affirm me, to reassure me that I was a worthy man, a good man. Having married my first wife because she was unlike my mother, I now began to live with a woman who was exactly like my mother (though I didn't see it at the time). She alternately shamed and affirmed me, and I was addicted to the pleasure I felt in the moments when she acknowledged that I was right and worthy, or she forgave me and validated me again. I was dependent on her for this sense of personal worth as a man, but I didn't recognize the reality of this dependence, nor did I see how I was a co-creator of the pattern of rejection and reunion that we danced again and again.

We argued frequently and intensely, she accusing me of being responsible for what was wrong in our relationship, and I accusing her. I was sure that I was right, all of my arguments felt completely righteous to me, and I thought that if she would ever just listen to what I was saying and take it in, all of our problems would be solved. But it didn't happen that way. One time, in an argument, she said something about me that I didn't have a ready answer for. I don't remember what it was, but for the first time I found myself considering that she could have a point. It was a brand new experience, and not a pleasant one. I was not used to considering that I could be wrong.

I took to walking around our neighborhood of east Ottawa in the evenings after work, and as I walked I tried to work out what in our complex relationship was my responsibility and what was hers. What were the boundaries between her and me, where was I truly guilty and where not? It took some weeks of nightly solitary walks for me to get clear on the major divisions of responsibility between us, but they did come clear to me. As I discovered my own areas of guilt and looked at my past behaviors with some shame, I acknowledged my guilt to her and apologized for my behavior and for my self-righteousness in previously denying it. There was pain in it, in falling off my pedestal and owning up to guilt, but there was also a sense of something sacred in it, something real and true and powerful. However, the core of my dysfunction, my need for her affirmation, her good opinion of me for me to feel ok about myself, still hadn't been touched.

That came to a head during a vacation to the Maritime Provinces. We were travelling in my truck, and she accused and shamed me relentlessly, for hours. I would argue, but eventually I would break down in tears and could not drive any more. I would get out and sit on the side of the road and cry until I recovered, then get back in and drive some more, and the pattern would repeat. It culminated in a night in a motor camp when neither of us slept at all. She spent the whole night analyzing my every behavior since we had met, and showing me how I had been totally wrong in every way, while she had been entirely the innocent victim.

That evening, I chose to surrender, to cease to argue at all and to look instead for every bit of truth that I could find in her words. I decided to try to see myself through her eyes and to convict myself in every case where it could be done. I don't know why I made that choice, but it was, in hindsight, the most powerful thing I have ever done. In my total humility I became utterly and completely safe for her, and she shared her most intimate judgments and fears of me. I used none of it to judge her, but only to see myself more clearly. In that place and at that time, I surrendered totally to the feminine, to her power to convict me and shame me and judge me unworthy, and I ceased trying to defend myself from her judgments.

I have never suffered worse psychic pain before or since as I did that night. In my humility I accepted my guilt as accused, and apologized and asked for her forgiveness. I think that if she could have met me in that place at all, could have owned any of her projections and her need for innocent victimhood, we might have begun to build a real and honest relationship. But she did not and instead continued to see me as entirely guilty and herself as blameless. Within a month, the distortions and one-sidedness of her perceptions about me became apparent to me, and I returned to balance, to the truth that we both were guilty, and both innocent.

The effect of that ordeal was to heal the deepest part of the shame wound my mother had inflicted on me. By ceasing to defend myself from the accusations of guilt and shame, I was able for the first time to really look at what they said about me. For the first time, I had taken them seriously and considered whether they were true. I let them in and I discovered, to my surprise, that they weren't true. I had guilt, indeed, I had dysfunctional behavior patterns, but I wasn't shameful, I wasn't unworthy as a man. I was, in fact, a good man, one who cared greatly about others and about doing what was right.

What a gift that was! I had been tested in a total shame attack from my intimate partner, and I had survived. More than survived – for the first time I had allowed myself to cease defending my innocence and actually examine the question, put it to the test. Fearing the worst, fearing that I would convict myself, I actually discovered the best, that my fear of unworthiness was a false fear.

The point I want to draw from this is that as long as we deny and oppose the ideas of others when they suggest that we are wrong, we can learn nothing from them. And we have the most to learn exactly where we defend most vigorously. The wise policy is to ignore the feeling that others are wrong in the knowledge that *it*, the feeling could be wrong, and to look carefully for whatever truth can be found in their ideas, especially their ideas about us. The essence of this careful looking is that we seek ways that the other's ideas could be *true*, rather than the more usual, and much easier, search for ways to refute them. This change of attitude is the key to discovering truth. If the ideas of others are found to be wrong after careful examination (and they often will be), we will have lost nothing but a little time. But then we will *know* that they are wrong based on evidence, rather than just assuming it because of our feelings about them. But if we find that they are right, then we will have learned something important and can correct our error. We will be closer to wisdom.

This is, in fact, the description of how to discover truth that was offered in chapter one. By "holding the question open" while simultaneously examining all ideas with careful, critical thinking, by including ourselves and our potential biases in the question and examining those as well, we are in fact integrating two sets of dualistic opposites; the opposites of open-mindedness and critical judgment, and the opposites of self and other. In a word, we are behaving wisely, and that is why this is the most powerful approach available for the pursuit of truth.

Let us end by summarizing the ideas in this chapter. Wisdom is about balancing contradictory opposites, learning that both can be true together, and that both are useful in different circumstances. Examples of such dualistic opposites are ease/effort, peace/conflict, subjective/objective and thinking/feeling. A wise person has learned to accept the validity and utility of both sides of such dualities, and to balance them in their own life. The last example, thinking/feeling, is the most common imbalance in the modern world, with the imbalance in favor of feeling. The way through this imbalance is to tolerate the feelings of wrongness in order to "hold the question open" while we realistically evaluate (i.e. think very carefully about) ideas that contradict our self image or worldview. The essence of this thinking is that we seek the truth of these challenging ideas, rather than seeking to repudiate them.

The supremacy of feeling over thinking in the western world for the last fifty years has had profound influence, yet it is not widely recognized as a basic vehicle of current culture, responsible for most of what we believe and highly resistant to change. In order to see this clearly, we will spend the next chapter looking deeply into this particular dualistic imbalance.

Chapter 3 – Feeling Rules

"since feeling is first, who pays any attention to the syntax of things
will never wholly kiss you;
wholly to be a fool while spring is in the world
my blood approves, and kisses are a far better fate than wisdom." –
e. e. cummings

"In the economy of the body, the limbic highway takes precedence over the neural pathways. We were designed and built to feel, and there is no thought, no state of mind, that is not also a feeling state." – Jeanette Winterson, *Why Be Happy When You Could Be Normal?*

"Justice's medium is empathy, and empathy's medium is more often the melodrama than it is the manifesto." – Charles Paul Freund.[18]

"If you make people think they're thinking, they'll love you. But if you really make them think, they'll hate you." – Don Marquis (1878 - 1937)

"Ignorance more frequently begets confidence than does knowledge." – Charles Darwin

"Where all men think alike, no one thinks very much." – Walter Lippmann

"Pain makes man think. Thought makes man wise. Wisdom makes life endurable." – John Patrick

"That is true wisdom, to know how to alter one's mind when occasion demands it." – Terence (185 BC - 159 BC)

In this chapter I will argue that feeling, and not thinking, is what determines what most people believe to be true about themselves and the world. If this is true, it is also largely unrecognized, and so I must account for this lack of recognition as well. The difficulty facing us in considering the power of feeling lies in getting some distance from it, finding a place to stand to examine it that isn't entirely under its sway. For if the case that I make is dismissed by my readers because it doesn't feel right, then I will have proved my point – but no one will realize it. If my thesis is right, then, I cannot use reason alone to build an argument; I must employ feeling as well. This is a considerable handicap, since words, the medium I am obliged to employ in a book, have direct access only to reason, only to the thinking side of the feeling/thinking duality. We think in words, but we feel in … well, feelings. Feeling predates the learning of language; it is older and more natural than thinking in every psyche. Feeling is more primitive and, for most of us, much more powerful.

First, let's be clear what we're talking about. We're not talking about emotions – fear, anger, sadness, etc. Psychologists call these affect, because they are disturbances from our normal state. The word 'feelings' is sometimes used to refer to emotions, but that is not how I am using it here. So what am I referring to?

Think about a time when you were trying to remember the name of an acquaintance you hadn't seen for some time. Names come to you, but you discard them instantly because none of them feels right. Then the right name occurs to you, and you instantly know that it's right. It just *feels* right, and the power of that feeling is utterly compelling. You just *know* that it's the right name. How do you know? Not by any thinking process. You have no *evidence* that it's right. Rather, it's a *recognition* process; you recognize the correctness of the name the way you recognize a face, by experiencing, by *feeling* the rightness of fit.

That's what I mean by feeling; it is the feeling of rightness or wrongness associated with a name, an idea, a statement, a conclusion or a belief. This feeling comes from experiencing an alignment or misalignment with something with which we are already familiar, a recognition (re-*cognition*). The feeling of rightness or of wrongness tells us that the new thing aligns or doesn't align with our familiar understanding, with what we already hold to be true. That is what it's actually doing - however, our experience of the feeling is quite different. Our experience of the feeling insists that the new thing is right or wrong, absolutely. The objective reality of the feeling is that it is relative to what we already believe, but the subjective experience of the feeling is absolute. This is a vital distinction to get – and we are obliged to get it first intellectually, when it still doesn't feel right.

This feeling process isn't any kind of disturbance from our normal state, it isn't *affect*. Rather, it *is* our normal state. It's so much a part of who we are and how we experience the world that it can be difficult to separate it out and examine it. But it is important that we do just that, so that we can realize that the truth of our feelings is only as good as the truth of what we already believe. If what we believe is mistaken, is false to fact in any way, then our feelings will only affirm our error (and affirm it powerfully); they can never discover it for us. It falls to our thinking to do that, if we are to do it at all. To think about our feelings productively, we have to be able to recognize them as something distinct from ourselves, something that could be mistaken, no matter how "true" they feel.

How can you know if feeling is dominant in your own psyche, as it is in most? What are the signs of this bias? There are several. First, can you discuss any subject without significant anxiety? If there are subjects or positions that offend you when a person argues for them, or if you find yourself getting defensive when your ideas are challenged, that is a strong sign that it is your feelings that are driving your position. The thinking side of the psyche knows that any argument can be made, and thinking is comfortable discovering the merit or lack of merit of an argument. Indeed, it enjoys evaluating the merit of an argument, including an argument that its own current position or ideas are mistaken. People with strong thinking sides love to debate, they enjoy the process the way others enjoy a game, as a puzzle or a battle of wits. If you strongly dislike debates and discussions, it suggests that you may be someone who has feeling dominant in your psyche.

Another sign that feeling is dominant is the speed with which you reach a conclusion about a new idea. I recently suggested to a friend that the reason that modern tunes are less catchy, less "whistle-able" than they were forty years ago is because there are only so many catchy melodies, and many of them have already been discovered, so now we are running out. He reacted instantly against this idea, arguing that the number of catchy melodies is essentially infinite.

I don't know which position is right, but I know that he was reacting from feeling because of the speed of his rejection of the idea. Thinking takes longer, since it involves evaluating an idea's merit. To evaluate the merit of this idea, for instance, one has to consider what the proportion of catchy melodies would be in the infinite population of random series of notes, and how long it might take human culture to make a significant dent in this population. These are not trivial questions, and cannot be estimated in an instant. If you have an instant response to a non-trivial issue that you haven't previously thought your way through to a conclusion, then you can know that it is feeling that is responsible for that response, not thinking.

The third sign that feeling is dominant in a psyche is intransigence. Since feelings about things are not altered by appeals to reason, a feeling dominated person rarely changes their mind, and almost never as a result of a challenge to their beliefs. Their feelings do evolve under the pressures of life experience, by a process that is largely unconscious, but they do not have much experience with actually discovering themselves to be mistaken. Humility is a sign of someone who has developed the ability to think critically about things, and has thus frequently discovered and corrected errors in their opinions. Ironically, humility is therefore a sign of a person who is more likely to hold accurate ideas and opinions.

The thinking/feeling duality manifests differently from the others, because it is more fundamental. One sidedness around the ease/effort, peace/conflict and subjective/objective dualities that we discussed in chapter two manifests by making one side of the duality feel right and the other feel wrong. In other words, feeling is employed to maintain their one-sidedness. This is why realizing the arbitrariness of feeling is the key to the search for wisdom.

But the think/feel duality operates differently. While feeling is implicated in keeping us stuck on one side of the thinking/feeling duality, it does not do so by making thinking feel wrong. People who are dominated by feeling (the vast majority of us) do not judge thinking to be wrong. Rather, we diminish its power in our psyches so that thinking becomes a slave to feeling and is employed only to generate rationalizations to support what we feel to be true – without ever realizing that this is what we are doing. We become unconsciously but powerfully defended against alternative ideas, and use thinking to generate plausible sounding reasons why such ideas are wrong. Even when our thinking fails to come up with an adequate defense, we will typically fail to be persuaded to doubt what feels right to us, as is expressed in the proverb, "A man convinced against his will, is of the same opinion still."

How can I assist you by means of this book to explore beyond what feels right, to explore thinking even (especially) when it conflicts with feeling? I cannot put a feeling onto the page for you to read directly the way I can a thought, but I can tell a story and hope that you will empathize with the situation I describe. In other words, I can try to evoke feelings in you, and then encourage you to analyze, to think critically about those feelings. Let us start with feelings where we might already have achieved some balance.

Most of us can likely remember a time, probably many times in childhood when we were confronted with an adult, usually a parent, who required something of us that we didn't like. Going to bed at a particular time, being home on time, avoiding certain dangerous situations, whatever. Can you remember feeling, and maybe saying to the adult, "You just don't care about me, about what matters to me, about what's important to me"? Can you remember the feeling of certainty you had about that assertion, how right you felt, how sure that the adult just didn't get your side of things at all, didn't care about what you wanted, and didn't see the world the right way?

I am guessing that, assuming you are now an adult; you may by now have found yourself on the other side of that interchange and experienced a different set of feelings about the same situation. As a parent confronted with a child's wants, you know that the child's judgments about your motivations are limited by her or his experience. It's not the case that you don't care about what the child wants; you care a great deal about that. But your caring is balanced by a wider perspective, a concern about the child's health and safety and an awareness of hazards that are dismissed by the child as unreal or insignificant.

You can see that the situation is actually the opposite of what the child feels to be true – it is actually the child who doesn't care about what the adult wants, not the adult who doesn't care about the child's wishes. You can see that the child's feelings are very unbalanced, almost entirely focused on their desire for personal pleasure or autonomy, entirely about their rights and with little felt sense of their responsibilities. You may try to explain your wider perspective, but you quickly see that it's not going to make much impression on the child. You recognize that the power of the child's feelings about the situation overwhelm any attempt to reason with them. It is impossible for you to communicate your more balanced feelings, your wider perspective, in a way that has them feel what you are feeling. That balance, that development of your own feelings is the result of years of life experience that cannot be communicated in words. So you end up having to insist as an exercise of adult authority and accept that you cannot change the child's mistaken feelings about you and your motivations.

Let's spend some time analyzing this scenario. In terms of the thesis about wisdom being dualistic balance that I am developing in this book, the parent's perspective is wiser than the child's because it is more balanced. On the dualistic dimension of rights and responsibilities, the parent recognizes and *feels* the rights and responsibilities of both parties, while the child feels the truth of only his or her rights. On the dualistic dimension of accountability /compassion, the parent has compassion for the child at the same time as holding them to account; the child feels compassion for herself and probably none for the parent, while feeling little accountability for himself and lots for the parent. On the dualistic dimension of power and powerlessness, the child feels that he is powerless and the parent powerful while the parent recognizes both the power *and* the powerlessness of both the child and the parent. The child is powerful in that what the child wants and how he feels really matters to the parent. The child is powerless in that the parent will ultimately decide what will be done. The parent is powerless in that he is unable to communicate his balanced perspective to the child, or to eliminate the threats against which she is attempting to protect the child. The parent is powerful in that she has formal authority over the child.

We can describe the parent's dualistically balanced perspective in this scenario as wise, but is there one word to describe the child's set of unbalanced, unwise feelings? Yes there is: victim. The child feels like a victim. The felt sense of polarized rights without responsibilities, compassion for self without accountability, and powerlessness (with power being seen as possessed solely by some other) is the feeling of victimhood. Indeed, from a stance of dualistic imbalance, lack of balanced wisdom, we see much of the world in the polarized terms of innocent victims and guilty perpetrators. We will introduce a model to explain the psychodynamics of *victim* in a later chapter.

In this scenario, the child feels like an innocent victim and sees the parent as the guilty perpetrator. However, it is clear that this is not the truth; it is an artifact of the child's abbreviated perception of reality, of her or his dualistic imbalance. The parent, who sees more clearly through possessing a more balanced wisdom achieved through life experience, knows that the child isn't a victim, knows that indeed there aren't any victims in the situation at all, and no guilty perpetrators either. The perception of victimhood by the child, though it feels compellingly true, obvious and unarguable, is nevertheless an *illusion*, a distortion of perception. However, the fact that it is illusory does not reduce its power in the psyche of the child. The persuasive power of feeling comes from its deep resonance within the psyche, for feeling comes to us like dreams, direct and immediate from the unconscious mind, entirely bypassing our faculty for reason and reflection.

Let us pause to consider this. I am hopeful that you can feel empathy for both sides of this situation – both a sense of how compelling the child's feeling of victimhood is, and simultaneously a realization that it is a mistaken perception, that the child's feeling is founded in illusion rather than in truth. If you can, then you know that even the most compelling feelings of truth, of correctness, of total assurance, can be mistaken. Now consider; what could you say to the child that might have a chance of persuading them of this? What form of words could you put together that would make any headway at all against the child's conviction of their victimhood in that situation? Is there any formula for opening the child's eyes to a wider perspective, a less polarized, wiser understanding?

If there is, I confess that I have failed to find it in some thirty years of searching. I think, in fact, that there isn't any such form of words that can be expected, guaranteed to do the job – and this is a good thing, for if there were, we would not have ultimate power over our own psyches. If someone could find words so powerful that we could not resist having our eyes opened, then we would no longer be responsible for our own beliefs, and our wisdom would not be our achievement but theirs.

Let us look a little deeper, though. What is it that makes feeling so compelling, especially a common set of feelings like those of self-compassion, rights without responsibilities and powerlessness that make up the composite worldview that we call victimhood? Why is victimhood attractive? People say, "No one would want to be a victim," and there is a way in which that feels right, but on closer examination it is seen to be disingenuous or at best naïve. The primary attraction of powerlessness is that it absolves one of accountability. By definition, a victim is blameless. Indeed, the importance of this is clear in the modern mantra, "Don't blame the victim." Victims are entirely innocent, and this is attractive indeed.

Along with innocence comes moral superiority – victims are morally superior to perpetrators. Along with the notion of being unjustly treated comes the right to retributive justice, to compensation, and to protection from future victimization. Victims receive compassion for their situation, even if only in their own minds. There are a lot of attractive aspects to being a victim, and a huge sense of loss to giving up that status. In other words, if we don't want to live fully, if we don't want to be accountable for our actions, but want instead the illusion of complete innocence, then dualistic one-sidedness is attractive and the balance of dualistic wisdom is unattractive.

It is one thing to examine in the abstract the situation of a child, and to understand from afar their feeling of victimhood. But what happens when we try to bring that home? What happens when we consider our own feelings of victimhood, or other types of dualistic imbalance that we are attached to in our own psyche? Suddenly the feelings become immediate and real, not abstract and impersonal. Suddenly our one-sided feelings begin to fight for their lives, and the intellectual argument that they are one-sided becomes a great deal less persuasive. Objections arise instantly in our minds to repudiate any suggestion that our feelings could be misperceptions. Sure, I get that other people can be mistaken in this way, but not me, I've got it right! It all feels so true, so obvious, and so certain – how can I possibly go against that primal feeling?

Yet, if we really get that these feelings can be mistaken, and if we wish to discover and know what is genuinely true, then we are obliged to attempt it. My own life journey, as I will relate in future chapters, has been a process of discovering hidden truths that felt quite wrong at first; that went against what felt right to me. For some reason, I wanted to find out what was really true, and I wanted it badly enough to tolerate the distress of not knowing, the distress of risking being culpably wrong. I urge you to consider this life path. It is the only one that leads reliably to wisdom, and wisdom gives you power and competence in your life. The distress on the path to wisdom cannot be avoided; like a road that passes through a desert it is an inherent part of the journey, but the distress is temporary, it passes. The gains, however, the wisdom, remains.

We have considered a scenario where, I hope, we had the ability to empathize with the feelings of another while simultaneously recognizing that those feelings were mistaken. So we know it is possible for feelings to be quite wrong. Indeed, it is clear that we are quite comfortable with this knowledge – as long as it is someone else's feelings that are mistaken and not our own.

The process of someone correcting a mistaken view of the world is actually a common theme of literature. I recently watched the 2013 science fiction movie *Oblivion*, in which the whole human race has been conquered by aliens who have brainwashed some humans into tending the machinery with which they are stripping Earth of its resources. The story revolves around the discovery of his brainwashing and awakening to reality by one of these people, played by Tom Cruise. It is exciting to watch someone penetrating illusion and discovering a deeper reality. It is exciting because this is a major theme, a foundational process of human life. We are attracted to wisdom, to discovering truth – and yet we also fear this process, because it is painful to have our world shaken. But is it really better to hold on to illusions, perhaps for a lifetime, as so many do? What is the cost of that choice in terms of missed opportunities, lost potential and pain of a different kind? How many failed relationships, damaged children, and unhappy lives result from the choice not to face painful truths about ourselves or our world? Carl Jung observed a hundred years ago that "The foundation of all mental illness is the avoidance of legitimate suffering."

Let us consider another scenario, one strongly aligned with contemporary adult culture and therefore more of a stretch to see beyond. Before we begin, let us be really clear what we are about here. If there is to be any possibility of balancing the power that feeling holds over our psyche, then we need to reinforce the power of thinking. Thinking is the only faculty we have that can give us a second take on our perceptions and the feelings that arise from them. I will present scenarios, and then analyze them. Probably, at least one of the analyses that I present will feel quite wrong to you. See if you can follow the thinking on its own terms, despite the feeling of wrongness. See if you can evaluate whether the analysis might be solid in terms of correct procedures – is the logic consistent? Is the evidence correctly applied? Do the conclusions follow from the evidence? The key to accurate thinking is correct *procedure*. (This is unlike feeling; since feeling is not procedural, the key to accurate feeling is correct *perception* and correct *assumption*.)[vii]

These two faculties, thinking and feeling, can augment each other in our search for truth, if we allow each to operate independently. But powerful feelings of wrongness arise in us as we consider any analysis which contradicts what we feel to be true. One achievement of maturity is the ability to tolerate those feelings in the knowledge that they could be quite mistaken and misleading. Their intensity is not a sign of their veracity, just as the intense feelings associated with falling in love are not a sign of their longevity. Give yourself the life gift of freeing your thinking from the power of feeling, by practicing following where thinking leads, independent of what feeling may be telling you. Like two opposing witnesses in a court trial, the messages of each must be carefully considered if truth is to be discovered, even though one of them may be shouting at the top of her voice while the other speaks quietly.

OK, enough with the theory, let's consider more scenarios.

There is a story that made the rounds some years ago, an example of racial prejudice. I don't know if it actually happened, but it will serve our purposes whether or not it is true.

> On a British Airways flight from Johannesburg, a middle-aged, well-off white South African lady found herself sitting next to a black man. She called the cabin crew attendant over to complain

---

[vii] To acquire knowledge, one must study; but to acquire wisdom, one must observe. – Marilyn vos Savant

about her seating.

"What seems to be the problem Madam?" asked the attendant.
"Can't you see?" said the woman. "You've sat me next to a kaffir.
I can't possibly sit next to this disgusting person. Find me another
seat!"
"Please calm down, Madam," the stewardess replied. "The flight
is very full today, but I'll check to see if we have any seats
available."

A few minutes later the stewardess returns with the good news,
which she delivers to the lady, who cannot help but look at the
people around her with a smug and self-satisfied grin. "Madam,
as I suspected, both economy and club are full. However, we do
have one seat in first class." Before the lady has a chance to
answer, the stewardess continues, "It is most extraordinary to
make this kind of upgrade, however, and I have had to get special
permission from the captain. But, given the circumstances, the
captain felt that it was outrageous that someone should be forced
to sit next to such an obnoxious person."

Having said that, the stewardess turned to the black man sitting
next to the lady, and said, "So if you'd like to get your things, sir,
I have your seat ready for you." At which point, apparently the
surrounding passengers stood and gave a standing ovation while
the black man walked up to the front of the plane.[19]

This is a story about feelings driving behavior. The white woman is
obviously driven by feelings of racial superiority, but we are
expected to know that those feelings are inappropriate, indeed
outrageously so. The stewardess who orchestrated and the
surrounding passengers who applauded the white woman's
humiliation are acting on feelings of revenge for her racism and her
insult to the black man, and we are expected to empathize with and
share those feelings. The fact that this story has been forwarded by
email for years speaks to its resonance with current feelings within
our culture. This is where many of us are at.

Let's analyze the story in terms of dualistic balance. The white
woman is clearly unbalanced in empathy – she has lots for herself
but little for the black man whom she insults and publicly humiliates
without hesitation – indeed, with satisfaction. But what of the

stewardess and the applauding passengers – are they really so different? They have simply reversed the empathy polarization. They have empathy for the black man, but none for the white woman whom they are pleased and satisfied to see publicly humiliated. The basis for this is that they identify the white woman as a guilty perpetrator (of racism) and the black man as an innocent victim. There is truth in this, there is no doubt that the white woman is a racist, while the black man is presumed to be innocent (we don't actually know much about him, since in the story he never says a word). The story sets up a victim/perpetrator scenario, and then punishes the perpetrator with public humiliation and compensates the victim with public vindication and a seat upgrade to first class.

This is where our culture is at right now; we seek to punish perpetrators and compensate victims. This behavior feels right to us, but it isn't actually wise. We can see this if we put ourselves into the shoes of the white woman for a moment. Can we feel any empathy for her situation? What will she take from the public humiliation she has received? Will it cause her to reflect on her racism, to consider whether it is appropriate? More likely, the total lack of empathy for her from the stewardess and the passengers will make her more defensive; will convince her that she is a victim, more angrily certain that blacks are receiving inappropriate benefits, more stuck in her racism. She treated the black man as subhuman, as not deserving of respect and empathy, but the stewardess did the exact same thing to her, delighting in turning the tables on her. Such polarized processes do not usually deliver healing or insight. Not only are they ineffective, they are also unjust. With all of the empathy saved for the designated victim and all of the accountability assigned to the designated perpetrator, neither party is treated as a full human being.

If I had been a witness to this scenario, a passenger in a neighboring seat, I hope that I would have had the presence of mind to have gone over to the white woman and sat next to her in the seat vacated by the black man. I hope that I would have had the wisdom to say to her something like, "I apologize to you for the way the stewardess treated you. No one should be publicly humiliated in that way. Your racism toward the black man is indeed inappropriate, and I urge you to consider that he is just as human and just as worthy of respect as you are. He didn't deserve the disrespect that you showed him, just

as you don't deserve the disrespect that the stewardess showed you."
If a conversation with the white woman resulted from this
intervention, it would be a conversation grounded in respect for her
as a human being. It would not avoid holding her accountable for
her attitude and her behavior, but it would also have compassion for
her situation. If an opportunity arose or could be created, I would
also be willing to have a similar conversation with the stewardess or
the applauding passengers. Such a conversation has the possibility to
deliver new insight, to encourage growth in perspective towards the
wisdom of dualistic balance, where the contempt implied by the
public humiliation does not. Such a conversation has this possibility
because it is wise itself, it is dualistically balanced between
compassion and accountability, between rights and responsibilities.
It feels and expresses both, for both parties.

I wonder where you are at, dear reader, with all of this. I regret that
we are not face to face, that we cannot have a conversation where I
can see your responses and tailor my words to fit. I feel close to you,
in a strange way, as I sit here in front of my computer screen
struggling to find a form of words that might inform without
offending, that might assist understanding without triggering
rejection. I know what it is to have my feelings rule my worldview
through the strength of their sense of rightness. However, my
personal experience has been that if a robust intellectual argument
can be constructed, it can withstand the pressure of contrary feelings
and serve as a place to stand and observe oneself, a place from which
one can consider whether one's feelings are delivering truth or
illusion. This is the function of thinking, to serve as the partner to
feeling, a partner that, like a worthy spouse, has the independence to
tell us when they think we are mistaken, but to do so lovingly,
without contempt or humiliation. Also by personal experience, I
have discovered that when we uncover errors in our feelings, those
feelings change to reflect the new insight. Just as one's feelings
about the friend's behavior changed in the story in the last chapter,
when it was revealed that their daughter had been in an accident, so
our feelings about things that seem completely solid to us, like race,
gender, religion, politics, all of these can change and become more
balanced, more just, more truth-based when we examine them
through the lens of thoughtful analysis.

The transition can be painful; it hurts to discover that we have been wrong about important matters for much of our lives – but the pain is brief. On the other side, as it fades away, we discover the joy of expanded awareness, new insight, and new competence and wisdom in our lives.

Let us continue with a true story that was told to me in the 1990s by a man who was then in his eighties, whom we can call Johnny. It concerns an incident from his childhood, when he was eight or nine. He was using a public washroom when a man offered him a nickel if he would suck his penis. Johnny considered the proposal, and agreed. When he was done, the man refused to pay him. Johnny went home and told his mother what had happened. She listened to his story and saw that what he was upset about was the man's breaking of his agreement, so she gave him a nickel. She informed the police about the incident, but, Johnny told me, that was the end of it for him.

What is your reaction to this story? Was Johnny a victim? Was he sexually abused? He didn't think so. He was offered an exchange, and he considered it, and he made a deal. He wasn't coerced in any way. He was outraged that the man didn't honor his part of the bargain, so his mother, who *really* listened to him and thought carefully about it rather than just reacting, made it right by giving him the nickel. Eighty years later, in telling his story, Johnny was full of praise for the wisdom his mother displayed in this circumstance, by not getting all upset and seeing him as abused, victimized. Rather, she acknowledged his authority in his own life, his right to make a deal; she treated him like an adult rather than like a child. Was she right?

Now, this is about as challenging as I know how to be. A hundred years after Freud denied the reality of child sexual abuse, we have brought it to light and now see it as hugely damaging, life destroying. Indeed, it can be, when it is coerced, when it is by a family member, when it goes on for years, when it is concealed by means of threats and intimidation. It is good that we have exposed this deeply abusive behavior. But have we gone too far? Has our reaction hardened into feeling alone, into a kind of hysteria, so that we have lost the ability to discern nuances? Our outrage at child abuse feels deeply resonant, unassailably right to most people. This story about

Johnny doesn't disqualify that reaction; it just raises a question that points in the other direction. I have done this here in order to give you, my reader, a strong experience of a fact that doesn't fit what feels true to you.

Of course, I don't know you; maybe you can see and acknowledge the difference that I am pointing to. But if so, you are in a minority. My experience in telling this story has been that most people tend to turn against me with indignation, to judge me as an abuse apologist. If that's your reaction, I'm not saying that you're wrong. I think that you are, but that's not my point right now. Rather, I am suggesting that if you want to get maximum value out of this book, and indeed out of life, the best approach is to tolerate those feelings of wrongness while you carefully examine the analysis for correct procedure. If you really want to find what is true, don't just go with your feeling and turn away. Think about the scenario and the analysis with an attitude of seeking to discover if it is true, rather than an attitude of seeking to disprove it. That's a difficult thing to do, for it will raise strong feelings of fear and self-judgment, guilt and anxiety, but practicing that process is worthwhile on its own, irrespective of the conclusion you eventually reach. Holding the question open, tolerating the feelings of wrongness for as long as it takes to *think* your way through the question is *the* fundamental process for a truth seeker. It is the main highway towards wisdom. (I am aware of the irony in calling it a highway, for it is consistently travelled by only a minority of people. The real, popular highway is the route that aligns with feeling; almost everyone is following that road.)

I was musing a few days ago about what I would say if I were asked to address a graduation ceremony. What could I say that would be relevant and useful to the students as they enter their adult, working life? I concluded that this message about thinking and feeling would be the most valuable thing that I could offer. I would say something like,

> "You can live a whole life being guided solely by your feelings about things. You in the second row; why did you turn and grin at your friend beside you when I said that? It was a feeling that made you do that, the same way that feelings make us do just about everything we do for our whole lives. A good life can be

lived that way, but not an exceptional life. Feelings come out of our biology and our culture; they represent our history and the status quo. If you want to go somewhere truly new and original, if you want to create something which will be genuinely useful, which will move society forward, then feelings cannot guide you to that. Thinking is the only function which can take you to new places. Especially thinking which is opposed to feeling, which challenges and questions what feels right to you and your peers. However, beware – thinking alone, unmediated by feeling, can lead as easily to sociopathy, to criminality, as to healthy creativity. We need the empathy for our fellows and for the natural world that shows up as powerful feelings, in order to constrain ourselves from harmful excess. But if feeling is all we have or all we trust, then we are stuck in a rut, unable to identify our major errors or to seriously consider anything that challenges our beliefs, but completely unaware of our disability. It is in the balance of thinking and feeling that true wisdom lies. For most of us, that balance is biased strongly toward feeling, and it is thinking that needs to be supported and developed. Make it a habit, a practice of discipline, to question what feels right to you and to society, to look behind and underneath the stories that support contemporary culture. Listen to radicals, social outliers and consider their ideas. Many of them are wacky, but hidden among them are some that are right. Ask questions that few are asking, and earnestly seek for true answers, answers that may not feel right at first but can be tested and found to be true. This is the very best that you can do to prepare and empower yourself to make a genuine and worthy contribution to the health and success of our world."

For a final scenario, consider the following story, reported on the FOX40 News website on 2 November, 2014.

"Dad Invites Young Daughter's Alleged Rapist to Dinner, Then Tortures Him to Death

A father is facing murder charges after he invited his 14-year-old daughter's alleged rapist over for dinner, and then burned his genitals with heated tongs before... (According to police, the father turned himself in after strangling the man who allegedly raped his 14-year-old daughter.) fox40.com

Like · Comment · Share: 247,554 like this   56,029 shares"

Here are the first 42 of 22,169 comments:

"[Male] Here in Illinois, few years back, a governor George Ryan was going down on corruption charges, so he had an opportunity to do Something pointedly not political, but simply JUST. He observed that 12 out of 25 individuals on death row here would be exonerated...See More

[Male] Do you really think that the false conviction rate for rape is likely to be less than the false conviction rate for murder? Seriously, folks! And this in a legal system which supposedly respects that ol' presumption of innocence. And y'all want to take that away? Ye Gods!

[Male] You go... hack each other to death. I won' miss ya, and we'll all be better off without ya.

[Male] Oh. So, George Ryan suspended the death penalty, here. It has not been reinstated, to date.

[Male] And if he didn't actually rape his daughter?

[Male] I only hope "Father Knows Best".

[Female] How can anyone 'like' this? Shame on you.

[Male] Good job!

[Female] Super Dad

[Male] well done 1 more jess peado

[Female] Good for him, at least it will be one rapist that we do not need to worry about!!!!

[Male] cool dad, he must be released, given a medal and a case of johnny blue

[Female] And there's a problem with that?

[Male] Did the guy actually rape her though?

[Female] Good job, Dad!!

[Female] Way to go dad that's how it should be an eye for an eye!!!

[Female] Although I hate violence, this man's act should be viewed as saving another child from rape and possible murder. Pedophiles do not rehab...ever. I am sure I would consider the same path if it had been my daughter.

[Male] I think rapists like that should be strung up during half time at the super bowl! I'd bet there would be a lot less rapes and child molestation going on then! If anyone would rape my lil girl I would do the same!

[Female] Hell yeah. He got what he deserved. Good job, dad. If someone would cause this to my daughter I would do worse.

[Male] Works for me! ! !

[Female Well justified

[Male] What's not to like about the Father, My kind of Man.

[Male] Where exactly is the problem and how stupid was the rapist to accept the invite did he expect a pat on the back

[Male] GIVE THIS MAN A MEDAL
let me know when and where to send the check for legal funds.

[Male] Great job dad!

[Male] i guess these people never heard of right to a fair trial but that's none of my business. i mean underage girls never lie about anything....

[Female] Why kill pedophiles......its so much more fun torturing them for a few decades first their victims suffer, so should they and then some.

[Male] He got off easy but at least he's dead. I would have done worse to him, maybe we could nominate the father for the Medal of Honor or Nobel peace prize, regardless I hope his family recovers from,

[Male] Good for dad

[Male] wtg dad

[Female] way to go dad

[Male] So what's problem

[Female] Things would have been worse if it happened to any of my daughters, he got off easy!

[Male] An eye for an eye.....bend over punk!

[Male] Hell Yeah

[Female] He got what he deserved!! More rapists should get the same treatment however I think he should of left him live with his burned genitals and see how many girls he will rape

[Male] How could u do that but he got what he deserved

[Female] Where do I send a thank you card!

[Female] GOOD DEAL!!!

[Female] That dad is a hero

[Female] Good" [20]

I don't know if the rest of the over twenty thousand comments are like this; I didn't read past the first page. But clearly the majority of the first people to comment, both male and female, approved of the father's actions in taking the law into his own hands and deceiving, torturing and finally murdering the alleged rapist. For many of us, it would seem, the hard won legal protections of the presumption of innocence, the right to question one's accuser, the right to be judged by a jury of one's peers, etc., have no legitimacy for someone accused of rape of a young girl.

Where are you on this, dear reader? Are you with the majority who approved of the father's action and would set him free? What kind of a world would we create if we actually did free people who brutally avenged crimes against their loved ones – even alleged, unproven crimes? This is the dark side of being dominated by feeling – it can give rise to ugly mob behavior unmediated by the sober reflection that thinking can offer. The fact that so many people approve of this father's actions is appalling to me, as it suggests that for many of us civilized behavior is merely a thin veneer over base feelings, and that in the right circumstances large numbers of us may resort willingly and self-righteously to primitive savagery. This is how lynch mobs formed in earlier times. I will have more to say about this in future chapters.

At the end of three chapters, I am about to change direction. So far, I have been focusing on persuading you that what feels right to a person, to a peer group, and even to much of the world might yet be mistaken – indeed, might be greatly, dangerously mistaken. Either I have succeeded in that task, or I have not. Either way, I intend now to change my focus, and to begin to present to you some of what I think one discovers if one follows the path of earnestly seeking to know what is true in the realm of human society and behavior. Some of what one finds is not well known – indeed is denied within popular culture, as the reality of child sexual abuse that Freud discovered was denied, with his assistance, for a hundred years. At the end of chapter one, I promised you a detective story, an uncovering of facts hidden and denied beneath contemporary beliefs, assumptions and assertions. That uncovering starts in the next chapter.

We will begin by turning our attention to one very practical aspect of dualism in our culture, namely gender. So far we have referenced gender only in passing; in the next few chapters we will explore it in depth and in detail. For this is a book about dualistic balance, and the balance between male and female is a fundamental manifestation of that principle.

Chapter 4 – Wisdom and Gender

"To understand how any society functions you must understand the relationship between the men and the women." – Angela Davis

 "Men are from Earth, women are from Earth. Deal with it." – George Carlin

"Nobody will ever win the battle of the sexes. There's too much fraternizing with the enemy." – Henry Kissinger

"Male and female represent the two sides of the great radical dualism. But in fact they are perpetually passing into one another. Fluid hardens to solid, solid rushes to fluid. There is no wholly masculine man, no purely feminine woman." – Margaret Fuller (1810 - 1850)

It will not have escaped the reader's attention that one of the fundamental dualities in the world is female/male. It seems to be a basic, foundational split, like those of mind and of matter that we will discuss in a moment, for it divides the entire biological realm, with the tiny exception of the most primitive, single-celled organisms. Indeed, it was gender that first drew my attention to dualism, and I spent twelve years, from 1994 to 2006, editing and publishing a magazine attempting to balance the perceptions around gender. It was the fact that this task was so difficult that persuaded me to think about the universality of dualistic imbalance in the world, and why balanced wisdom is difficult to achieve.

In this chapter we will begin by considering dualism more deeply, and discover that it is built into the very structure and fabric of our universe. We will examine the concept of archetypes and discuss two fundamental archetypes; the masculine and the feminine. Finally we will explore how our current conceptions of gender are polarized and unbalanced, and discover how seriously distorted our perceptions have become around men and women.

How fundamental is this concept of dualism? How deeply does it extend into the nature of reality? I suggest that it goes right to the bottom, to the foundations. A fundamental dualistic split is between mind and matter – many would say that this is the most fundamental dualism, and it seems reasonable to imagine that everything that exists falls on one side or the other of that duality. So let's consider each side in turn, and ask about its basic nature.

Our best understanding of the essential nature of matter is the theory of quantum mechanics. It has been completely verified experimentally, by which I mean that it correctly predicts the outcome of every experiment we have been able to devise. Quantum mechanics says that the fundamental nature of matter is dualistic – matter is composed of particles, and matter is simultaneously composed of waves. Every particle is also a wave; every wave is also a particle. Yet these two concepts appear inherently opposed, completely contradictory. A particle is dense, located at a single point in space, and interacts with other particles through collisions. A wave is diffuse and dispersed, with no single location, and passes through other waves without collisions. How are we to reconcile these two contradictory aspects of reality?

The Copenhagen Interpretation, developed in the 1930s by the theory's originators and accepted by most scientists to this day, says that no meaningful reconciliation is possible. The situation does not admit of a coherent mental image, and it is futile to attempt to construct one. We should simply accept that it is the way it is and that it cannot be interpreted in terms of rational models or pictures.

I think that this inability to make a coherent mental model of dualistic balance is true of all such balances, not just in the case of quantum mechanics. This is part of the difficulty of achieving balanced wisdom: wisdom is non-rational. Not irrational, but trans-rational, beyond rational. Wisdom transcends rationality.

Matter, then, is mysteriously dualistic in its fundamental nature. What of mind, the other side of this most basic duality? Mind, too, appears to be inherently dualistic. Consider the nature of your own mind. You have a part of you that experiences life as a passive observer; that experiences your thoughts, sensations, emotions, memories and imaginings. You also have an active part of you that desires, intends, chooses and acts. What is the connection between them? They are distinct and different in nature, and yet you are also undivided, seamlessly whole. The two sides are intimately connected; your sensations inform your choices, your actions give rise to new experiences, yet the connection is ultimately mysterious.

Like the mystery of the dual nature of matter, the dual nature of mind is intriguing and ultimately beyond rational explanation.

Why is this? Is there a way that we can get some kind of a handle on this, some way of comprehending something of this mystery about deep reality? There is a thought experiment that pleases me, though it is entirely speculative and I make no claim for its rigor. It works by analogy. Consider that you are holding a cylindrical object like a can of beans. If you project the shadow of the can onto a wall, then the shadow will alternately appear rectangular when you hold the can side on to the light source, or circular when you hold the can with its end facing the light. There are, of course, an endless number of intermediate forms that arise from holding the can at an angle, but the circle and the rectangle are the pure forms, known as the "poles". Now these two shapes, a rectangle and a circle, are quite different, indeed opposite in a number of ways. Yet they are both aspects, inherent properties of the same object, the can. The can integrates them both in a non-contradictory way that is not at all mysterious in three dimensions, but which becomes mysterious when the can is abbreviated to two dimensions by means of the shadow projection. The three dimensional can is not dualistic, but its two dimensional image on the wall is.

By analogy, the deep reality of the universe, outside of three-dimensionality, is non-dualistic, and that the dualism enters when it takes form, when its deeper nature is abbreviated into the three spatial dimensions. Matter becomes dualistic in this way and so does mind. So do deep archetypal qualities like love and truth. It is no accident, therefore, that wisdom is also dualistic, involves the balancing of opposites. It is simply a reflection of the basic structure of the universe we live in. This conjecture 'fits' (i.e., feels right) to me, but it is not testable in any rational way, and so I offer it only as an interesting speculation and make no truth claims about it.

I have mentioned the word 'archetype' a couple of times now. It is a key concept, and it is time to define what it means. The dictionary [21] defines archetype as: 1) the original pattern or model from which all things of the same kind are copied or on which they are based; a model or first form; prototype, or 2) (in Jungian psychology) a collectively inherited unconscious idea, pattern of thought, image, universally present in individual psyches. In *King, Warrior,*

Magician, Lover, authors Moore and Gillette define archetypes as "instinctual patterns and energy configurations, probably inherited genetically through the generations of our species," and which "provide the very foundations of our behaviors." [22] I like to think of archetypes in terms of a metaphor. I imagine the psychic world is like a jungle where paths have been trod by people's behavior since the beginning of time. Those paths that many people have walked throughout history (e.g., mother, father, warrior, woodcutter, etc.) have been made wide and easy by the passage of many feet, and efficient by those creative minds that blazed shortcuts that others chose to follow. Such paths are psychically easy to walk, compared to the difficulty of cutting a new path through the jungle or following one seldom-used and overgrown. These paths are archetypes, typical psychological ways of being, and they have an energy that precludes stepping off the path. This metaphor matches Carl Jung's description when he says, "There are as many archetypes as there are typical situations in life. Endless repetition has engraved these experiences into our psychic constitution, not in the form of images filled with content, but at first only as forms without content, representing only the possibility of a certain kind of perception or action." [23]

UK *Guardian* columnist George Monbiot wrote evocatively of the powerful feelings associated with the hunter archetype without, apparently, knowing the word.

> "The foraging had not gone well. We had hoped to find nettles, hawthorn buds, perhaps some spring mushrooms. But it was a cold March and scarcely anything had yet stirred. I pushed through a screen of branches and saw, beside a small stream, a dead muntjac: one of the Chinese barking deer that have proliferated in Britain since they were released by the Duke of Bedford in the early 20th Century. Its eyes were bright; the body was warm. There was no wound or trace of blood.

> I hesitated for a moment, surveying the sleek tube of its body, the small coralline antlers, the fangs protruding from its upper lip, the tiny hooves. Then I gathered up the ankles and heaved it onto my shoulders. The deer wrapped around my neck and back as if it had been tailored for me; the weight seemed to settle perfectly across my joints. As soon as I felt its warmth on my back, I was

overwhelmed by a sensation raw, feral, pungent that I had never experienced before. My skin flushed, my lungs filled with air. I wanted to roar and thump my chest.

I experienced a similar rush of feeling some fifteen years later, while hunting flounders in an estuary in Wales, a couple of summers ago. I was wading with a trident through shallow water as the tide ebbed, hoping to catch the flatfish on their way back to the sea. As I stalked up a channel, my spear poised above the water, trying to detect the minute signs of fish buried in the sand, my concentration intensified until I felt as flexed and focused as a heron.

It is hard to explain what happened next, but I was suddenly transported by the thought – the knowledge – that I had done this before. I do not believe in reincarnation or in the persistence of a soul after the death of the body. Yet I felt that I was walking through something I had done a thousand times; that I knew this work as surely as I knew my way home.

These experiences were both exhilarating and dismaying. The sensations were so powerful and so unfamiliar that I could neither dismiss nor assimilate them. The two events left me with a deep sense of dissatisfaction: I felt I had caught a glimpse of something rich and grand and thrilling, from which I had been excluded.

I believe that in both cases I stumbled upon an unexercised faculty: psychological equipment which was once invaluable, but which is now vestigial. Through the greater part of human existence, while we were still subject to powerful selective forces, we were shaped by imperatives – the need to feed ourselves, to defend and shelter ourselves, to reciprocate and work together, to breed and to care for our children – which ensured that certain suites of behavior became instinctive. Like the innate response which makes a pensioner vault over a five-foot wall just before a truck ploughs into him, they evolved to guide us, alongside the slower processes of the conscious mind." [24]

Monbiot is describing the feeling of an archetype manifesting in an individual mind. However, perceiving these feelings, separating them from your own personal psyche and recognizing them as foreign is an advanced accomplishment. Indeed, archetypes commonly move whole populations in ways of which they are unaware. Carl Jung, who greatly developed the concept, said that "... from within the realm of the subjective psyche ... the archetype presents itself as numinous, that is, it appears as an experience of fundamental importance. Whenever it clothes itself with adequate symbols ... it takes hold of the individual in a startling way, creating a condition of 'being deeply moved', the consequences of which may be immeasurable." [25] James Hillman concurs; "... one thing is absolutely essential to the notion of archetypes: their emotional possessive effect, their bedazzlement of consciousness so that it becomes blind to its own stance. By setting up a universe which tends to hold everything we do, see and say in the sway of its cosmos, an archetype is best comparable with a god." [26] We will have reason to look closely at this power of archetypes to overwhelm reason and seduce the psyche as we examine the compulsive nature of ideologies in later chapters.

Two fundamental archetypes are the masculine and the feminine. Together they divide up the whole psychological realm into complementary pairs of opposites. They are groupings of psychological behaviors that have historically and stereotypically been associated with females and males, but they are *not* equivalent to being male and female, in that individual women and men can and do display varying degrees of masculinity and femininity. It is important to really get this distinction: archetypes are idealized forms and not everyday, practical patterns. The masculine archetype is idealized masculinity, a completely one-sided distillation of the essence of historical manhood, and the feminine archetype is a similarly one-sided and refined formulation of historical womanhood. They are not depictions of modern womanhood or manhood. As idealized forms with psychic resonance, they have great utility for understanding cultural patterns, and that is how we will use them in this book.

The archetypal feminine and masculine are what is known as polar opposites. Carl Jung explained that all psychic life is governed by a necessary opposition and that this opposition is inherent in human nature. For, he said, "the psyche is ... a self-regulating system," and "there is no balance, no system of self-regulation, without opposition." "Everything human is relative, because everything rests on the inner polarity, for everything is a phenomenon of energy. Energy necessarily depends on a pre-existing polarity, without which there could be no energy. There must always be high and low, hot and cold, etc., so that the equilibrating process – which is energy – can take place." [27]

This is an important concept, this idea of oppositional forces, so let me illustrate it with a practical example of a self regulating system with which we are familiar – a thermostat. If we consider the operation of a thermostat in controlling the temperature of a building, what it does is monitor the room temperature until it falls to a preset point, then turns on the furnace. The furnace pushes the room temperature up until the thermostat, continuing to monitor the rising temperature, turns it off at an upper set point. The thermostat achieves temperature control by balancing the opposing forces of heating and cooling. Without those two opposites – the cold entering the building from outside and the heat entering the building from the furnace, temperature control is not possible. The human psyche, indeed the whole human body, works in a similar way, balancing opposing forces or needs for solitude/company, hunger/satiation, work/recreation, and hundreds more.

The whole realm of human behaviors can thus be divided into complementary (opposite) archetypes of masculine and feminine. A few examples of such complementary opposite pairs of behaviors are listed below.

Masculine	Feminine
Competitive	Cooperative
Hierarchical	Consensual
Overt	Covert
Achieve	Receive
Lead	Follow
Autonomy	Relationship
Effort	Ease
Conflict	Peace

Direct	Indirect
Lead	Follow
Truth	Love
Think	Feel
Intellect	Emotion
Objective	Subjective
Physically coercive	Deceptive

It is important to realize that since each pair of complementary opposites consists of different active or evaluative approaches to a situation, they cannot be employed simultaneously, but rather represent alternative strategies or choices. Which strategy will be optimum cannot be determined in general, but depends on the situation. Human psychological wholeness or wisdom can be conceived of as becoming competent in the understanding and use of all such strategies. However, we naturally tend to prefer and overuse those strategies with which we are familiar as individuals or as cultures, and historically most of us, due to reinforcement and conditioning in childhood, embraced first that set of behaviors and attitudes culturally mandated for our gender. Traditionally (less so today), boys tended to absorb and manifest those behaviors and attitudes described above as masculine, and girls tended to value and embrace the complementary feminine set. One consequence of that is that men and women are psychologically drawn to each other. The opposites attract because we unconsciously seek what we lack.

Neither the feminine nor the masculine archetype is either dominant or derivative. Both are equal in power and importance, although our individual and cultural value systems generally elevate and rank one above the other. This equality of the masculine and the feminine is inherent in the dualistic nature of all polar opposites: like day and night, up and down, left and right, they create and define each other. Also, any particular strategy, masculine or feminine, can be used for good or ill, to help or to harm – none are good or bad in essence but only in application and intention. For instance, masculine hierarchy (authority) can be employed to serve or to oppress, feminine cooperation can be used to support or to manipulate. However, again, we tend as individuals and as cultures to group them into categories of right and wrong, good and bad, categories which vary widely from one area to another and which can change, sometimes rapidly, from age to age.

Now we have a theoretical construction to support the power of feeling that was the subject of the last chapter. A few paragraphs ago, I mentioned that archetypes are like gods, they "bedazzle consciousness so that it becomes blind to its own stance." I ask you to consider that your felt reaction to things might be mistaken, might be an artifact of this powerful kind of misperception. I ask you to contemplate the possibility – no, the probability – that you are one sided around some of these dualisms (because just about everybody is), even though your one-sidedness feels right, feels balanced. This is a lot to ask. Felt reactions are so immediate and speak with such authority in our psyches that it is hard to imagine that they could lead us astray. Yet they really can and really do. I have made the case for this in theory – now it is time to work with it in practice.

For instance, I expect that some of the words in the table above, listing archetypal feminine and masculine behaviors, raised your eyebrows if not your ire. It is exceedingly difficult not to jump from archetype to gender, not to take what is said about the feminine as being about women and similarly to conflate men with the masculine. When I say that leadership is in the masculine and followership in the feminine, for instance, I am not saying that women can't lead. They can and do – but they do it by accessing the masculine (not the male) side of their psyches.

However, even this is challenging for many people, who feel that women, or men, come off worse than the other gender because of something that is, or that isn't in their list. There's not a lot I can do about this, though, because I believe that that is the way it is. The archetypes were formed by our history, and our history was what it was. Historically, men tended to lead, women to follow. That didn't make men better, only more prominent. It didn't make women weaker, only less visible. Both leading and following are equally important and equally necessary human behaviors – a wise, dualistically balanced human being has achieved competence and comfort with both. We need to get over our preference for foreground over background, for leaders over followers – this is another dualistic imbalance. Our only choice about reality is whether we surrender to it, or fight it. Assuming, of course, that we can work out what it really is. Fighting reality is ultimately a fool's game – reality will always win in the end.

One of the basic conclusions of this whole book is that men and women are equal, inherently and totally; always have been and always will be. With the polarized (i.e., unbalanced) gender perceptions of today, that is a startling and challenging conclusion. But think – if it's true, isn't it good news? Wouldn't that be a better reality than the idea that one gender has oppressed and dominated the other? Isn't it worth postponing judgment, opening up to the possibility that this could be true? The case for it is strong, as you will see.

I will build my case slowly, piece by piece. I ask that you consider what I offer with an open mind and resist the temptation to decide early that I am mistaken. Sir Arthur Conan Doyle's character Sherlock Holmes said, "Once you eliminate the impossible, whatever remains, no matter how improbable, must be the truth." A lot of what people currently believe, like the idea that the subjective controls the objective that we discussed in chapter two, is actually impossible, but it will take time to work our way through the more widely believed mistaken ideas (e.g., that men have oppressed women) to discover this. Stay with me, it'll be an interesting journey.

Let's begin our journey into the gender archetypes with the famous poem "If" by Rudyard Kipling. It is a celebration of heroic masculinity. As you read, make note of the feelings (e.g., judgments about rightness or wrongness) that arise in you, and any emotions.

If

If you can keep your head when all about you
Are losing theirs and blaming it on you;
If you can trust yourself when all men doubt you,
But make allowance for their doubting too:
If you can wait and not be tired by waiting,
Or, being lied about, don't deal in lies,

Or being hated don't give way to hating,
And yet don't look too good, nor talk too wise;

If you can dream – and not make dreams your master;
If you can think – and not make thoughts your aim,
If you can meet with Triumph and Disaster
And treat those two impostors just the same:.
If you can bear to hear the truth you've spoken
Twisted by knaves to make a trap for fools,
Or watch the things you gave your life to, broken,
And stoop and build 'em up with worn-out tools;

If you can make one heap of all your winnings
And risk it on one turn of pitch-and-toss,
And lose, and start again at your beginnings,
And never breathe a word about your loss:
If you can force your heart and nerve and sinew
To serve your turn long after they are gone,
And so hold on when there is nothing in you
Except the Will which says to them: "Hold on!"

If you can talk with crowds and keep your virtue,
Or walk with Kings – nor lose the common touch,
If neither foes nor loving friends can hurt you,
If all men count with you, but none too much:
If you can fill the unforgiving minute
With sixty seconds' worth of distance run,
Yours is the Earth and everything that's in it,
And – which is more – you'll be a Man, my son!

Rudyard Kipling, 1910

This is the best poetic description of archetypal masculinity that I
know. It illustrates the virtues and strengths of traditional manhood
– courage, duty, perseverance, self-restraint, autonomy – and also its
weaknesses – solitude, stoic invulnerability, and unemotionality.
There is not a word in it about love or joy or peace. It is dualistically
unbalanced, as of course it must be, lacking the presence of the
archetypal feminine.

For example, consider the poem's attitude to work. The first duality that I presented at the beginning of chapter two was that of ease vs. effort; we recognized the need for a balance between work and recreation. Kipling's man has no such balance – he is all work and no rest. "If you can fill the unforgiving minute … with sixty seconds worth of distance run." Reread the last four lines of the third verse for an even more explicit presentation of this imbalance. I present this poem here because it runs against the modern idea that men are oppressive, aggressive, self-interested. It shows the other side, the one that we tend to overlook or deny today. It speaks to the honor, the sacrifice, the service of men. It celebrates men, something that has become unpopular and politically incorrect.

I wondered if, as a demonstration of the gender equality I am talking about, I could write a parallel poem which paid homage to the archetypal feminine, which offered the other side of this duality and spoke to the virtues and strengths of traditional womanhood. I chose to keep the same length, meter and rhyming scheme, i.e., the identical structure as Kipling's original, in order to contrast the different content of the archetypal feminine. Here is the result of my effort, which I call "If for the Feminine." Again, as you read, make note of your judgments and any emotions that arise. I will offer suggestions on how to work with these reactions in chapter six, Seeking Wisdom.

If for the Feminine

If you can keep your heart when all about you,
Are losing theirs in anger, fear and pain,
If you can act from peace and not just shout too,
And soothe their spirits time and time again,
If you can love when loving feels like losing,
Like giving in and letting others win,
And open up your heart to still more bruising,
Feel the pain and really let it in,

If you can speak your truth without defending,
Without attacking and without complaint,
If you can show your hurt without pretending,
And live with joy in freedom or constraint,

If you can love your man through all his blunders,
Support him as he deals with loss and pain,
Believe in him especially when he wonders,
How to face his fear and try again,

If you can find the good in every person,
Nurture it until it comes to flower,
If you can watch a loved one's illness worsen,
And hold them as they suffer hour by hour,
If you can keep your hope and love of living,
When dreams and plans all die and turn to dust,
If you receive no thanks but go on giving,
If you perceive the risk yet choose to trust,

If you can give your body to your husband,
A sacred trust for him and him alone,
Meet his desire with full and matching lust, and
Open to him everything you own,
If you can love your children without limit,
Yet as they find their own way, set them free,
My daughter, life and love and all that's in it,
Is yours – what's more, a Woman you will be!

David Shackleton, 2013

These poems are complementary depictions of heroic archetypal masculinity and femininity. As an exercise, compare your reactions to each. Did either inspire you? Repel you? Move you? What about judgments – did either strike you as inappropriate or simply wrong? The archetypes are what they are, and our reactions to them can tell us a lot about where we are on our journey to balanced wisdom. (A suggestion: ignore the last line of each poem – the archetypes are about components of our psyches and aspects of our culture, not men and women. Every person, female or male, has both masculine and feminine aspects and potentials.)

The masculine and the feminine are equally worthy, equally heroic, equally admirable, and equally powerful. They are also equally dangerous, equally self-interested, and equally capable of evil. They are inherently equal – yet completely different. The masculine has a solitary focus on accomplishment and conquest; its highest value is truth. The feminine has an interpersonal focus on relationship and nurturing; its highest value is love. Equal in this case means equal in worth, equal in power, as in the phrase "equal before the law," it does not mean identical. A fully balanced reaction to the two poems would also be equal, seeing both the merit and the shortcomings in each archetype. For the feminine and the masculine are two sides of the same coin, two halves of a complete and balanced psyche. We need both for life, we need truth *and* love. Life itself continues only through sexual reproduction which needs both male and female. The masculine archetype alone leads to death by destruction, the feminine alone to death by stagnation.

The feminine and masculine archetypes are inherently balanced and equal – but not so our perceptions of them. We can and do elevate one over the other in our estimation, both as individuals and as cultures. Today, in the Western world, the feminine is generally seen as morally superior to the masculine. Consensus is better than hierarchy as a decision making process. Cooperation is better than competition. Empowerment is better than authority. These preferences are cultural biases, expressions of our imbalance around the masculine/feminine duality. They feel right to us, because when we are archetypally unbalanced, both our thoughts and our feelings are aligned with our bias – indeed, they are what our bias consists of.

To get a sense of how this happened, consider our recent history. Until about 1960, the masculine archetype was seen as preferable, superior. A popular TV program from 1954 to 1960 was *Father Knows Best*. Imagine the reception a program like that would receive today! Only twenty years later, we had *All in the Family* (rated #1 from 1971 to 1976) and a few years after that *The Simpsons*, (the longest running American sitcom, 1989-2015) where fathers became figures of ridicule, bigots and idiots. What happened?

What happened was that there was a great upwelling of archetypal feminine energy in the 1960s. Civil rights, feminism, hippies. "Make love not war," flowers in your hair, "peace, man!" Our perceptions shifted in just a few years from overvaluing the masculine archetype to overvaluing the feminine. A hit song of the time expressed this one-sidedness perfectly – "All You Need is Love" by the Beatles, 1960. We are still there, more than fifty years later. But the iconic TV program of the 2010s is *Keeping up with the Kardashians*, a show which displays some of the dark side of the feminine archetype – a preoccupation with image, with consumption, with fame. Are we starting to tire of feminine one-sidedness? Could it be that the time is approaching for us to move past our current overvaluing of the feminine and towards cultural balance, towards a general recognition of the equal value of the masculine and the feminine, and a consequent realization of the inherent equality of women and men? I fervently hope so.

But at present we are still in the era of biased perceptions, in which women are seen as victims of men who have been their oppressors. Since it is likely that most readers of this book will share that perception, I have an obligation to show evidence of its falsehood. However, this is not primarily a book about gender, but about wisdom, about how to discover and know what is true and how to understand what is happening in the area of human society, and so I do not have space to provide a full and comprehensive rebuttal. In any event, that task has been done competently a number of times, most recently by Tim Goldich in his excellent *Loving Men, Respecting Women; The Future of Gender Politics*,[28] and any reader who wants to explore the literature of genuine gender equality will find a recommended reading list in Appendix A.

What I will do is provide some counterexamples, historical events which, if considered carefully, disprove the feminist thesis of general oppression of women by men and suggest instead a more nuanced and balanced power relationship between men and women.

We begin in 1912, with the maiden voyage of the Titanic. Some of the richest, most famous and powerful men in the world were on that ship. If it's true that men have oppressed women, if it's true that men have had the power and control, if it's true that men's lives have been valued more than those of women, then surely when the ship foundered, those powerful, valuable men would have been the first into the lifeboats. Were they?

Encyclopedia Britannica records the survival figures. First and second class children: 100%. First and second class women: 93%. First and second class men: 21%. In other words, women were more than four times as likely to survive as men. Benjamin Guggenheim, realizing that death was inevitable, donned evening dress in order to "die like a gentleman." John J. Aster, the richest man in the world, wealthy enough to buy ten Titanics, was impotent to command a single seat in a tiny lifeboat. Those patriarchal, oppressive, capitalist men went down with the ship in order to save "powerless, oppressed" women and children.

Why did they do it? They did it for honor, because of their deep, abiding belief that good men protect women and children, even unto death. A belief shared by the majority of men in every civilized society, then and now. Yes, men had social power roles, but they also had serious social responsibilities that came with them, responsibilities to protect and provide for women and children, even unto death if necessary. It is quite certain that oppression never looked like this.

Let's consider it carefully and be very sure. When it came to the acid test, the lives of men – all men, including the wealthiest and most 'powerful' – were judged of lesser worth than those of women and children. John Aster's life was judged of lesser worth not only than his wife, but also than his female servants.

This is no trivial exception to a general pattern; this is life and death! This is where the truth about any relationship can no longer be disguised and is most authentically displayed, when the stakes are the highest. Has there ever been a time in history when oppressors have died to save the oppressed? I mean, even one? Think of the 18th century slave ships sailing from Africa to the new world – that was indeed oppression. When one of those ships foundered, do you think for a moment that the crew would have gone down with the ship so that the slaves could live? Of course not, the idea is ridiculous. But that is what the male crew members of the Titanic did, and the male passengers as well.

I described in the previous chapter how feeling is often more powerful than thinking in our psyches, and that it takes a disciplined effort to think our way through issues. This is a perfect example. The notion that historically men have oppressed women is one that feels right to most of us. That feeling has allowed us to hold on to this mistaken idea and make it the basis of our gender law and policy for over fifty years now. But, if one thinks carefully about what happened with the Titanic, it disproves that thesis all on its own. The claim that men have oppressed women is a general claim about the fundamental relationship between men and women. But if it were true, then what happened on the Titanic could not have happened. Oppressors do not feel or act upon obligations of honor to save the lives of the oppressed at the cost of their own. If we allow ourselves to think carefully about this scenario, we can reach no other conclusion. We don't yet know what the historical relationship between men and women has really been (I will address that in the next chapter), but we now know that it wasn't oppression. More precisely, we know that it wasn't oppression of women by men.

I know that this is huge. It's hard to take in. The feelings that arise when we consider that we, and the world, could have been wrong about something so basic for fifty years are difficult to tolerate. This is where the rubber meets the road. This is where we find out what we really want. Do we really want the truth, at any cost? If we do, and only if we do, we will choose to go through the pain of acknowledging our error and revising our worldview.

The women who survived were rightly proud of the men on the Titanic who sacrificed their lives. In 1931, after fundraising for nineteen years through the First World War and the Great Depression, the "women of America" erected a memorial inscribed, "To the brave men who perished in the wreck of the Titanic, April 15, 1912. They gave their lives that women and children might be saved." The memorial was erected in downtown Washington, DC, but was removed in 1966 and re-erected without ceremony (without ceremony!) – notice the year, post 1960 when we stopped honoring men) in 1968 on a more obscure site on the Potomac in a residential part of town. At first, there was a program of annual wreath laying on the anniversary of the disaster, in the spirit of "lest we forget". But the wreath laying has stopped. We have forgotten about men's service, men's honor. We have stopped praising men, as men, for what they do for women and children. We are telling ourselves a different story now.

More recently, in 1982, the Vietnam War Memorial was erected in Constitution Gardens, Washington, DC, listing the names of all those who died in that war. The memorial represents all occupations and all branches of the military. Over 58,000 men's and eight women's names are listed. Of those eight women, most succumbed to sickness; only one died from enemy fire. Yet feminists argued that the women who served in Vietnam deserved a separate memorial, one for them alone. The Vietnam Women's Memorial was erected in 1993 on the same site. The American Legion helped them build it. It praises women alone and uniquely, even though they were included in the first memorial anyway, and even though only eight lost their lives, compared to 58,000 men. Does this seem as strange to you as it does to me? Is this evidence that women have been oppressed by men, or that their lives are valued *more* than those of men?

More recently still, a series of memorials have been erected across Canada to the memory of "women killed by men". Vancouver, Calgary, Edmonton, Winnipeg, Toronto, Ottawa and Moncton are some of the cities that have seen fit to do this. These memorials go beyond separating out women specifically for honor apart from men, to something uglier. They explicitly shame men. When a society begins to erect public monuments that *shame* a particular group, we are in a very dark place.

In order to see that this is what these monuments are about, we need to ask a pointed question – are women killed by *women* not worth remembering? Women killed by women are still women who have been murdered – why are they excluded from these memorials? The answer must be that it is important to name men as the murderers on the monuments. They are not so much about remembering murdered women as they are about indicting men. Clearly, this is toxic. We didn't do this even in the aftermath of two massive world wars, with all of the anger, fear and hate that war engenders. To the best of my knowledge, no war memorials have been dedicated to those of our citizens killed "by Germans" or "by the Japanese." We know as a society that this would be wrong, would be unhealthy and inappropriate. Why, then, have feminists argued for monuments to be erected that shame men? Why have we allowed it?

I will end with a true story from popular culture. The story is told by Fred Hayward, founder of Men's Rights Inc., about a time when he was on the Oprah Winfrey show representing men's gender issues.

> "The first time I was on her show, she threw me off. We got off on the wrong foot right from the start. Her introduction was – these are not her exact words, but it was something to the effect of – 'We all know men don't have any serious problems, but this

guy's job is talking about them anyway. Please welcome our guest, Fred Hayward.'

I don't know why I reacted the way I did, because talk show hosts do that all the time, especially with someone who's talking about men's issues. They don't play devil's advocate to women, but they do to men because they're trying to cater to the women who are watching. So I said to her, 'You know, the black population in prison is eight times as high proportionately as the rest of the population. Why do you think that is?' So now I've pressed her buttons and she's thinking, 'Not only is he a sexist, but he's a racist too.' She gave the stock response of how blacks have more serious problems than the rest of the population and the high incarceration rate is a symptom of that. So I had her. I said, 'Well, OK, blacks are eight times as likely to be in prison as the rest of the population and you're saying that's a symptom that they have serious problems. Men [at that time] are *twenty-four* times as likely to be in prison as the rest of the population. Isn't that an even bigger symptom that we do have something here to talk about?' They cut right to a commercial and asked me to leave. The producer said to me, 'I'm sorry, this isn't going the way we planned.' … So they made me leave. They had a chef standing by, I guess for just such emergencies, and they did chicken recipes for the rest of the show. This is all live, you know." [29]

Let's take this apart. First of all, let's consider Hayward's argument. He clearly had some awareness of cultural dualities. He knew that, in modern culture (unlike years ago) we are now in touch with the victimhood of African Americans. We can and do empathize with their suffering. Hayward knew that Oprah would likely offer the argument that the high relative incarceration rate of African Americans is a symptom of their extreme difficulties, of the discrimination and disadvantages that they suffer. Clearly there is truth in this argument. He then attempted to make an analogy to men, offering the statistic that the disproportion in incarceration rates between men and the rest of the population (i.e., women) is even higher than that for African Americans, and observing by analogy that this must mean that men have severe problems and disadvantages with respect to women.

Is this a valid analogy? It's not perfect; because of dualistic gender archetypes there are more differences between the genders than there are between the races – the fact that men have some cultural expectations to deal with the violence in society, while women do not, for instance. But these are subtle distinctions. There is no question, no question at all, that he had raised a valid discussion point, one highly relevant to the question of men's gender issues that the program was ostensibly about.

But he was immediately ejected from the show. Why? The answer is clear from what the producer told him. "This isn't going the way we planned."   They didn't plan for Hayward to raise solid, persuasive points in favor of men having real issues. The way that they planned for the show to go was signaled by Oprah's introductory comments; "We all know that men don't have any real problems ..." Hayward was invited as a straw man, his expected function on the show was to be knocked over, shown to be wrong in his contentions. When he presented a solid argument in support of his case, one difficult to refute or ridicule, he was expelled.

Notice the nature of this "knowledge" that men don't have any real problems. It is shared between Oprah and her (mostly female) audience, as she acknowledges with her words, but it is clear that it is not to be challenged in any serious way by counterarguments. It is not to be subjected on the show to the test of reality, to debate, to any strong challenge. It is to be felt, but not to be thought about. A show purporting to examine men's gender issues actually turns out to be determined *not* to examine them in any serious way, but rather to reinforce the existing beliefs of its audience. Troubling facts are specifically unwelcome, and in fact the planned show was completely terminated rather than suffer the difficulty of dealing with a single awkward fact.

I may sound judgmental here, but I'm not actually making a moral argument. My position is empirical; I am simply noticing human behavior. I am observing how blatantly a preoccupation with what feels right operates to suppress contrary evidence. In contemporary society, it feels right to hold men accountable, but it doesn't feel right to have compassion for them as a class.

I don't imagine that Oprah, her producer, or the vast majority of her TV audience spent time wondering about the fact that a men's advocate had been silenced because he was too challenging, too insightful, too persuasive. The feeling of righteous innocence which is associated with following one's feelings of rightness is resilient. Hayward was known to be wrong from the start, anything he said needn't be taken seriously because he was on the wrong side; he had incorrect ideas, no matter how craftily he might manage to present them. Oprah was quite right that virtually everyone in her audience knew that men don't have any real problems, so silencing a troublesome advocate was simply avoiding an unpleasant red herring, a confusing irrelevancy. This is how a felt reality acts to dominate our psyches and suppress contrary evidence. Like moving the Titanic memorial away from downtown Washington DC into a residential district, we just move the uncomfortable facts away to a place where they are no longer prominent and can be easily ignored.

The basic difficulty for Oprah and her producer was simple dualistic imbalance of feeling over thinking. The story that Oprah told about how the higher incarceration rate of African Americans is due to their special difficulties is a story that feels right. Most of us have become able, over the last few decades, to empathize with the victimhood of racial subgroups. However, almost all of us are still unable to perceive any victimhood in men as a group. We assign gendered victimhood entirely to women, and hold men to be accountable, to be perpetrators, not victims.[viii] So when an analogy is made which aligns the situations of people we feel to be victims (African Americans) with people we feel to be perpetrators (men in prison), it jars. It puts our thinking side, which recognizes the

---

[viii] For an explicit illustration of this, consider that in 1997 President Clinton apologized for the racism – but not the sexism – of the now infamous 1932-1972 Tuskegee experiment on 399 syphilis infected black men. The racism could be seen (i.e., felt), but the sexism could not, since the victims were men and not women. This now infamous experiment involved 399 black men who were suffering from syphilis, and who were left untreated in order to study the effects of the disease. They were not informed that they had syphilis, in order to ensure their cooperation. The data for the experiment was to be collected from autopsies after their deaths. The 1997 presidential apology specifically noted the racism in performing this unethical experiment only on blacks, but overlooked the sexism involved in performing it only on men. See http://en.wikipedia.org/wiki/Tuskegee_syphilis_experiment

validity of the analogy, into conflict with our feelings. The response of most people confronted with this dissonance is to quickly turn away and avoid it, returning promptly to what feels right, and this was indeed the response of the show's producer.

What is going on at a deeper, unconscious level is the need to defend one's basic beliefs from critical scrutiny, from challenge. The fact that the show was stopped, the fact that Hayward was silenced shows that in fact he was powerful, too powerful to be permitted to remain. If in fact he was truly known to be wrong, to be mistaken, then he would not have been powerful and there would have been no reason to eject him for there would be no threat; he could be shown to be wrong on the show. At that deeper level, the psyches know that they are fooling themselves; they know that they are perpetuating a cover story and hiding from the truth. But this knowledge remains unavailable to the conscious mind, eclipsed behind a reassuring cover story; it has to be deduced from the behavior.

Deduction is a function of the thinking, not the feeling mind. This is why a conscious effort has to be made to seek earnestly for the truth, while tolerating strong feelings of fear and anxiety, or of outrage. It feels to most of us as if the truth would reveal itself to us and that we would be completely open to it, but this feeling is a delusion. Rather, since our feelings are a recognition process where what feels right to us is that which aligns with what we already believe, they can never show us the errors in what we believe. Anything that goes against what we already believe, even the total objective truth, will feel to us to be wrong. The result is that, contrary to how we feel, we are actually strongly defended against the truth in many areas of our lives, while remaining completely unaware of the existence and the operation of those defenses. In a curious fashion, we can often see such defenses operating in others, while remaining blind to their power in our own lives.

In chapter one I observed that a major reason we hide from the truth is because we fear that it would convict us. Here you see an example of that. Oprah and her audience believe that as women they are the unique victims of gender discrimination and disadvantages, and that belief is valuable to them for reasons we will examine closely in later chapters. If men have major disadvantages just from being men, and women receive major advantages just from being women, then important parts of Oprah's audience's identity and worldview collapse. The feeling that Hayward is completely wrong and that he can be readily dismissed and silenced without any injustice being done, is how they preserve that worldview and defend against discovering that it may be mistaken.

We are in the grip of something very powerful and prejudiced, something very unbalanced and unwise, something that is severely distorting our feelings of right and wrong around gender. I mentioned the power of psychological archetypes to possess and blind whole populations – that is what we are seeing here. But naming it in this way is not enough. We need to understand it in detail; how it works, what the mechanism is. We will develop that detailed understanding in the next chapter. But this chapter is entitled "Wisdom and Gender." Let us end it by considering what a wise stance with respect to men and women would look like.

We have seen that moving toward wisdom involves moving toward dualistic balance, adding the balancing side to the one that we already get, the side that we already feel to be true. The duality that is relevant to two groups in contention, indeed to any situation where an "us and them" attitude has developed, is accountability/ compassion. Steven Pinker said, "In any dispute, each side thinks it's in the right and the other side is demons." The natural human tendency is to empathize with us, the in group, while judging *them*, the out group. We have compassion for our side, while holding their side accountable. It is difficult to hold both attitudes with respect to the same group. Yet, it is so powerful to do so. How would it change things, do you think, if the parties in a dispute struggled to empathize with each others' issues, to see things from each others' perspectives?

Feminism, which arose to public prominence in the sixties with the upwelling of archetypal feminine energy I described earlier, is polarized in this way. It holds compassion for women, the 'in' group in feminism, but no accountability (which is perceived, and named, as blaming the victim). It holds men, the 'out' group, accountable without compassion (patriarchal oppressors and perpetrators). In this time of feminine archetypal dominance, all of this feels right to most of us, or at least not wrong enough that we are inclined to argue against it.

I do not take issue with the holding of men accountable, this is necessary and important. I take issue that it is done without compassion, so that all men have become stereotyped as perpetrators. I do not take issue with having compassion for women, this is necessary and important. I take issue that there is no holding of women accountable so that all women have been stereotyped as victims. It is the polarization that is the problem, the lack of balance, the lack of wisdom.

There was a time, years ago, when I was outraged by these one-sided perceptions, angry that men were being judged so guilty and women held so innocent. Since this book is about wisdom, it is important to ask, what is a wise stance with regard to willful blindness and one-sidedness of the kind that feminism has given us? Can we say that people *should* be wise, *should* be more balanced? Can we expect it, and judge them for their failure?

The wise answer is dualistic; it is yes – and no. It is, of course, accountability *and* compassion. We recognize feminists' power, their choice and their accountability for it. We simultaneously recognize their powerlessness, their huge fear and the pain that drives their denial. For me, this balance is founded in human freedom. I really get, I feel that people are genuinely, intrinsically free. That includes the freedom to lie to ourselves for a whole lifetime, the freedom to make choices that injure ourselves and others. This is an absolute.

Yet, this freedom isn't itself free, it comes at a price. We have the choice, but we are responsible for the choices we make. Not guilty, responsible. What's the difference?

Guilt carries the implication that we *should* have done something else. But saying that we should have done something else denies our freedom. More than that, it is impossible to know for anyone else. If I say to you that you should have done a certain thing, what I am really saying is that if I were in your shoes I would have done that thing. But this is impossible to know. I can never weigh the influence of someone else's life experience, the things that shaped their choices. I can never know that I would have done 'better' than they did – such a claim amounts, in fact, to a simple assertion of moral superiority, to my saying that I am better than you, a claim that, given the same life experiences as you have had, I would still have chosen differently. This is impossible to know, and therefore illegitimate to claim.

So we cannot attribute guilt. But responsibility, accountability, that is different. Responsibility says that we have obligations flowing from the choices that we make. Our choices are free, but if they injure others we have obligations to acknowledge this, obligations to remorse, obligations to attempt to make things right. We must try to heal the hurt we have caused.

This, then, is the position that I take with regard to feminism and all of the other mistaken us-and-them isms in the world. Feminists are free to hold their mistaken, one-sided ideologies, free to attribute guilt to men and innocence to women. They are not guilty because of this, but they are responsible for the hurt they have caused in doing so, and they have caused a great deal. The fact that they repudiate this responsibility, seeing it as misapplied, as blaming the victim, does not change the reality of the situation. One day, when we wake up to the wrongheadedness of this whole ideological system, we can begin to acknowledge these responsibilities, to feel remorse for so much harm done, to apologize and to heal the injuries.

What will it be like when we move past the us and them, good girl/bad guy thinking of today, to the wiser perception of gender that has no us and no them? When we hold women accountable as well as with compassion? When we offer men compassion as well as accountability? Does it sound like something that you want to see? What does that look and feel like?

The 1995 movie *Dead Man Walking* starred Shawn Penn as a death row inmate convicted of murdering a young couple, and Susan Sarandon as a nun who seeks to support him emotionally as his execution approaches. The dramatic climax is the man's execution, and the movie imagery alternates between a grisly re-picturing of the brutal murder and the nun stretching out her hand to him as he dies. We see his accountability and his humanity side by side, the ultimate accountability of a death sentence and simultaneously the loving compassion of human dignity. If this balance, this wisdom is achievable for such an extreme case, if a movie audience can empathize with it for a male character who truly is a murderer, what makes it so difficult for us to find balanced empathy for the good men and women who comprise the majority of our citizens?

What would that balanced empathy look and feel like? What would a healthy gender movement look and feel like? I think that it would start with gratitude, with honoring both men and women. We would hold front and center in our minds our respect, indeed our love for men and for women. We would say to men, especially from women, thank you for thousands of years of work in creating and maintaining social order, in defending home and hearth, in working in field and factory to support wives and children. Thank you for thousands of years of discovery of new frontiers and new knowledge. Thank you for companionship and love. You have done well.

We would say to women, especially from men, thank you for thousands of years of birthing and nurturing our children. Thank you for thousands of years of taking care of the basic business of living; cleaning and cooking and mending and teaching. Thank you for companionship and love. You have done well. And then we would, in partnership, seek to articulate a vision of where we want to go together, how we want to change and develop our roles and our lives.

I feel tears in my eyes as I write these words, for I want this kind of a healthy gender movement so much – and what we have instead is bitter, judgmental, acrimonious and terribly ineffective because of these flaws. Perhaps you think that what I am holding up here is idealistic and impractical, impossible for one reason or another. But it is what gives me hope, hope that the dysfunctional, unbalanced gender movement we have today can grow up and become healed, become healthy and effective. I refuse to let that hope die. I will speak to what is wrong, but I will do so with compassion. We are all, men and women, human beings together. We are in the same boat. We are truly equal, in all the ways that really matter. Let us be thankful that we have each other, equal but fascinatingly different, worthy companions for the journey of life.

But at the moment, the hope and dream that I describe above is still just that, a hope and a dream. There is a detailed psychological pattern that gets in our way around gender, a pattern that keeps us attached to a cover story of female innocence and male guilt. We will discover that pattern and the hope for healing it in the next chapter.

Chapter 5 – Gender Codependence

"Re-examine all you have been told … dismiss whatever insults your own soul." – Walt Whitman, from the preface to *Leaves of Grass*.

"Codependents are reactionaries. They overreact. They under-react. But rarely do they act. They react to the problems, pains, lives, and behaviors of others. They react to their own problems, pains, and behaviors." – Melody Beattie

"We live in a world of denial, and we don't know what the truth is any more." – Javier Bardem

"I think the greatest illusion we have is that denial protects us. It's actually the biggest distortion and lie. In fact, staying asleep is what's killing us." – Eve Ensler

"The capacity for people to kid themselves is huge. Living on illusions or delusions, and the re-establishing of these illusions or delusions requires a big effort to keep them from being seen through." – James Hillman

"You cannot continue to victimize someone else just because you yourself were a victim once – there has to be a limit" – Edward W. Said

We saw in the last chapter that real gender equality involves offering both compassion and accountability to both women and men, and that feminism has focused on compassion alone for women and accountability alone for men. In this chapter we will explore what is behind this imbalance, how to understand the fact that it ruled the minds of the women (and men) who developed feminist theory, and why it has completely dominated society's understanding of gender for over fifty years now. This was quite a journey of discovery for me, over twenty years ago. I choose to offer it here in the form of a story, the intimate story of how I thought and felt as various events unfolded and my determination to understand, to get to the bottom of the gender conundrum moved me over a period of four years until finally I saw the wheels and levers of the psychological mechanism below the surface and worked out what was going on.

I offer it in this way for three reasons. Firstly, I want you to know me, because unless you know me, why would you trust what I say about these challenging issues. Secondly, the events that led me to the development of a new model of gender relations are useful to consider, for they showed me the deeper reality beneath the surface story. I am hopeful that relating them might help you to see it as well. Thirdly, I am inviting you to take a similar journey. The journey toward wisdom is necessarily one of some turbulence and stress, it takes dedication, patience and persistence in seeking what is true. By showing you my own journey from the inside, I hope to encourage you to a similar effort. Here is my story.

It feels like a regular evening as I walk into the Glebe Community Centre for the monthly meeting of the Ottawa/Hull Men's Forum. I have no inkling of the life-changing event that is about to happen.

It is February, 1990, two and a half years since my first wife left me, to my huge surprise. No, it wasn't that I thought we had a great marriage, only that I was completely unconscious of her truth or mine. But I am awake now and feeling strong. I have started a men's group and done a lot of work on myself in the last year. With the wonder of a small child, I have begun to see that the world is very different than I had thought, and that most men are still lost in the labyrinth of the male role. I am starting to see myself as a potential leader of the fledgling men's movement. I have begun attending regular meetings of the Ottawa/Hull Men's Forum, described as a male-positive, safe space for men growing out of stereotypes of masculinity.

The organizing group of the OHMF has arranged for this meeting to be about male violence against women. Three women from the Ottawa Rape Crisis Centre have been invited to lead the group in an exploration of this issue. I arrive early: only a few men and the three women are present, sitting on chairs arranged in a circle. It is unusual to have women at the men's forum, and so I ask them, "Are you leading the discussion tonight?" In a sign of things to come, the women sigh and exchange despairing glances, and one of them turns to me and says scornfully, "Hierarchy already! No, we're not going to *lead*, we're going to *facilitate*!"

Rebuked, I sit quietly. More men arrive, we introduce ourselves, and the women are invited to begin their facilitation. They say that violence against women is a part of male behavior that men must help to eliminate. I certainly agree with that. They propose a debate and offer the contention: "Although not all men commit violence against women, all men benefit from it." At first, we are divided arbitrarily into two groups, for and against the contention. After a while, we are permitted to 'cross the floor' if we wish, in order to take the position on the issue that feels right to us. The debate is orderly and also passionate. I do not need to cross the floor, as I am already in the group that I feel has the right of the matter.

I think about how men's violence against women has affected my life. I remember that when my wife left me, she did so secretly, saying that she was taking our dog to the vet. I asked her later why she did it that way, why she didn't tell me she was leaving, indeed why she never said that she was even considering such an action. She said, "I was afraid you would be violent." I couldn't understand that. I could scarcely believe it. I had never hit her, raised my hand or threatened her, or even imagined myself doing so. In fact, I haven't hit anyone in my entire adult life. I felt sure that she must have been poisoned by the general perception that men are violent. I felt like I had lost a great deal through men's violence against women and gained nothing if even after nine years of living together my wife did not feel safe with me. How many years would it have taken, I wondered, for her to see me and not the prejudice? How much had that fear, never before expressed, kept her from really trusting me, kept us from coming closer? I think of the two or three times when I lost my temper and shouted at her. Was she thinking that I could begin using my fists at any moment?

I imagine a world in which men are never violent against women. It seems to me that, comparing that world to this, there is not a man in it that would not be better off. More trusted, more loved, more respected, more honored, more happy, more seen and understood. Less feared, less ashamed, less defensive, and less insecure. I know which world I would want to live in. There is no question that I feel diminished rather than advantaged by the violence of men against women.

The debate proceeds and some men have begun crossing the floor. To my surprise, they are crossing in both directions. Some are actually choosing the group that is arguing that they benefit from men's violence against women. I begin listening more carefully, more seriously to what they are saying. I had thought that this issue was obvious.

They are saying that they benefit from having their partner afraid of them. That someone in fear is like a slave, willing to obey them and reluctant to take a stand against them. They get to have their way much more often than is fair, because she is afraid to offend. I wonder what these men want from their relationships with women. Are they actually attracted to a relationship of fear? What about intimacy? What about happiness? Have they said these things to their wives? I cannot imagine that men in recovery, in the men's movement, should feel that they would benefit from fear on the part of their intimate partner. Yet it is so. For the first time, I sense a profound divide within the Ottawa men's movement.

The debate is over. It has been a valuable experience for me. I have much to think about.

But wait. The women have more to say. They stand up together and move to the centre of the room. To my group, to the men who do not believe that they benefit from men's violence against women, they say this: "You men are worse than the men who beat their wives, the guys in the strip clubs and using prostitutes. You are pretending to be deconstructing masculinity, you are pretending to be growing into new and more whole, more conscious and responsible men, yet you are denying the very benefits you get from the violent, patriarchal system that you are a part of. You should be ashamed."

My God! I am reeling from this. I didn't see it coming. My heart is pounding and I can't think. What can I say? What can I do?

A man talks about his pain, about the way that he is also injured by the patriarchal system. The women interrupt him. "Don't tell us about your pain. Your pain is insignificant. You are the oppressor!"

Another man speaks of his experience with his ex-wife. "She accused me of sexually abusing my three-year-old daughter. How could I prove my innocence?" he asks with tears in his eyes. "I haven't been allowed to see my children for three years." "A woman would never lie about such an issue," he is told.

We seem helpless in the face of the angry accusations of these women. I have recently read Warren Farrell's *Why Men Are the Way They Are*,[30] and I try to describe some of his ideas about the equality of men and women, how men are victims of violence more often than women are. Even as I speak, however, I feel guilty and ashamed of the anger that I am feeling and that is probably in my voice, and I am ignored by the women.

Another man speaks more eloquently. "Your pain is real and needs to be heard," he says to the women, "but so is our pain. We do not deny your pain as women; please do not deny ours as men." He too is shamed in response.

The situation is incredibly charged. The women are clearly feeling unheard and angry, their worst fears about the men's movement confirmed before their eyes. The men are feeling shamed and devalued, accused by women who will not listen. We close the meeting in great awkwardness, with stiff thanks for the facilitation. The women leave in silence, obviously hugely offended. Some men huddle and talk in low tones, others leave quickly. I feel abandoned, the naughty boy standing in the corner, sent to bed without my supper, punished and feeling guilty for not being how I 'should' be. I compliment those men that I think spoke well, and leave.

I know that something pivotal has happened for me. I see that I am far from healed, far from secure and strong in my manhood. I don't know the nature of the wound I am carrying, but I know that it disqualifies me from leadership. I am not ready. I must withdraw from a public role in men's issues while I heal myself.

The Forum was never able to heal the divide that was exposed that evening. The drama played itself out over the next weeks and years. The women sent a letter to the Forum, protesting the way that they were 'abused.' The organizers responded with a formal apology, promising that they would make sure that it never happened again. They renamed the Forum "The Ottawa/Hull Men's Forum Against Sexism" and declared it actively pro-feminist. Men not of that persuasion were subtly (or not so subtly) unwelcome. The Forum continued for another three years, never again attracting the numbers it once had, before ceasing to operate from lack of attendance and lack of energy among the organizers. An offer from a new group to restart it on an unaligned, non-ideological basis was rejected by the holders of the name and the mailing list, who felt that they could not allow it to continue as other than specifically pro-feminist. It died, and has never revived.

I am either blessed or cursed with a passion to get to the bottom of things. Most days I think it is a blessing. For years I struggled to understand what happened that day. It seemed pivotal to the gender debate, as if the vast forces that move us had risen for a moment to the surface, like a great sea monster from the depths.

Gradually, some things became clear to me. First was that the three women in that room were anything but powerless. In that encounter, they were both the formal leaders of the program and also the emotional and moral centre of the experience. They controlled all of the structure of the event. They felt to me like unshakeable rocks against which I and the other men battered ourselves in vain. Yet, as I replayed it over and over in my mind, I realized that they were sincere in their belief that they were victims, being abused even as they were defining the terms of the debate and overpowering the protests of the men. They did not experience their power over us as a feeling of power. I knew that this was important. They were incredibly powerful to us, yet they felt powerless and abused even as they exercised that power. How could this be, I wondered?

Slowly, I realized that I was the same. As I listened to women talk about men's power, about the oppression of women and the patriarchal advantages I had as a man, I saw that I didn't experience them as power. Indeed, my position that evening had been the denial that men's violence against women gave them any advantages at all. Yet clearly, the fear of violence seemed to dominate a lot of women's lives, and they saw violent men as very powerful. I began to get an inkling that power, between the genders at least, is very much in the eye of the beholder, and that this is very contrary to the way it *feels*. But I still didn't have an explanation for these facts. Nor did I have any sense of why this issue carried so much energy for me, why I experienced the accusation of those women as so powerful in my life. How could their shaming of me remain so devastating when I didn't agree with it, didn't think that they were right about me? What was the nature of their power over me?

In 1991, at a ten-day experiential, personal growth workshop, I found a piece of the answer. It was my first experience with people dedicated to discovering the truth about themselves, undistracted, over several days. For the first few days I risked little, but watched very carefully. I learned that when people dropped their guard and confessed their fears and failings, they were not shamed, but rather supported and held through the experience. What's more, they seemed to emerge stronger and with more self-respect, not less.

On about the sixth day, we did an exercise involving shadow fighting with opponents from within the group. We chose partners and mimed fighting, with or without imaginary weapons, and then changed partners and did it again. After several changes, I noticed a pattern. When my opponent was a man, I would fight energetically, striving to win. When I was in conflict with a woman, however, I would be more anxious and more restrained, and try strenuously to ensure a draw. I remember a moment of astonishment when I discovered myself fighting with a sword in my left hand. I am right handed, but I had taken an imaginary sword in my left hand, because my female opponent had done so. Why was I allowing her to choose the weapons and the rules? I had never before had any awareness that my behavior was so different with women than with men.

On about the eighth day, the workshop leaders hauled three mattresses into the middle of the room and said, "OK, each of us is going to have a tantrum." "Right," I thought, "you've got to be kidding." I couldn't imagine myself doing such a thing at thirty eight years old. I made sure that I was toward the end of the line that formed around the wall. But, as I watched, I saw that people were really getting into it. One by one, they opened a door into their rage and kicked and screamed and wept. I decided that when it came to my turn I would give it a try and see what happened. I had no notion of any anger in me that needed to come out, but I had moved myself into a willingness to discover what might be there instead of a fear-based denial of there being anything in me that I didn't already know about.

As I ran out to the mattresses, I felt sure that I would end up feeling foolish. But almost immediately I found myself kicking and pounding the mattresses, and words began to pour out of me. Over and over I cried, "It's not fair, it's not fair." There was huge emotion in the words and a great sense of release. "It's not fair." I knew that what I was shouting was my outrage from my childhood, when I would argue with my mother and not once over many years (and still to this day) did she acknowledge to me being responsibly wrong about anything. Instead, if the argument began to go against her, she would end it with an unanswerable phrase like "You'll see when you grow up." Or, "You can't understand because you're not a woman." Or worse, "You're always completely unreasonable, there's no sense arguing with you." At one level, I was dreadfully afraid that she was right, that what seemed right to me was totally wrong, that I was self-centered and arrogant and unworthy, as she claimed. At another level, I knew that this was her defense because she knew that she was on shaky ground. Her unwillingness to ever admit it drove me crazy. I was incensed at her dishonesty. For twenty years I had carried that anger inside me, not suspecting its existence, but unable to really trust a woman because I expected her to turn against me, and to deny all responsibility for her words or her actions.

The next day brought a new exercise. A rolled up blanket, tied with cord, was brought into the room. One by one, we were invited to have the blanket be whomever we wished, and to say and do what we needed to. Each person's session was contained within a formal ritual designed by the leaders, to identify the action as sacred space, as symbolic and not something that could or should occur in the real world, with the real person. This was deep psychological work.

My heart was pounding with fear as I contemplated what I wanted to do. I knew, now, that I had a great deal of rage at my mother. I knew also that I had never really expressed it to her, because of the power that she had over me, the fear that she would abandon me and throw me out of our home. (When I was four, because I refused to run with her for a bus, she got onto the bus alone and left me crying in fear at the bus stop. Unknown to me, she got off at the next stop and watched me crying. She waited until she thought I had learned my lesson before coming back to reclaim me. I always ran after that.) So I had never allowed myself to win a fight with her, but contained my anger and held back my rage, as I had shown myself so eloquently in the shadow fighting exercise. Could I give myself permission to say and do what was in my heart? Was I ready to go past my fear of abandonment, still real in me twenty years after leaving home?

I still didn't know as I walked out to begin my work. For a while I just walked around the blanket, looking at it lying on the floor, trying to find the courage to speak my truth and unshame my anger. I started talking to it, asking questions like "What did you think you were doing to me? Why did you never hug me or kiss me? Why couldn't you tell me you loved me?" Gradually, I began to feel my anger. I began to shout. "Don't you know how much that hurt me? Couldn't you see how afraid I was?" I began kicking the blanket and screaming, "I hate you. I hate you." I kicked it across the room, picked it up and slammed it down on the floor. I kicked it so high it lifted one of the ceiling tiles. With tears rolling down my cheeks, I stomped my mother's head into the floor. For the first time in my life, I experienced my anger without shame. At thirty eight years old, after spending my life till then unconsciously circling around her, I killed my mother and began the process of setting myself free and growing myself up.

The process of discovering the source of one's shame and recovering from it is not trivial. It involves looking deep into one's soul and learning to love what one finds there. It is fearful because what one expects to find is guilt, is unworthiness, is inferiority, is everything shameful. It can only be accelerated through intensity, through the passion with which we pursue it. Sometimes, if we are willing, life brings us to moments when we are able to go very deep and return richly blessed.

My journey of understanding continued. Further insight came when I discovered the field of addiction recovery. I began to recognize my own codependence and the denial patterns with which I had concealed myself from myself. Over the course of a year, in 1992, I read voraciously about addictive behaviors, attended a weekly twelve step self-help group called Adult Children Anonymous, entered weekly therapy with a Jungian analyst, and intensively studied my own behavior in my current relationship. I began to see the patterns, the ways that my new partner, her family and I were all codependently intertwined and interlocked, and the layers of rationalizations with which we hid the real nature of our relationships from ourselves and each other. As I did, I stopped my part of the dance, the deception. I confess that although all of the literature had warned me, still I thought that I would be able to reach them, to help them to see and share the truth that I was discovering.   What happened instead was that I was rejected. But, for the first time, I had the strength not to take it personally.

The final piece of the puzzle came to me in the spring of 1994, during a workshop on community building. On the first evening, a man took a major risk in talking about his need for emotional support in caring for his disabled daughter. A woman responded by shaming him for not dealing with his emotional needs as she had dealt with hers. Her attack was halted by several people who spoke of their distress with her action, but the woman defended herself throughout the weekend. On the last day she privately asked my opinion why her words were taken so seriously, when other things that had been said (e.g., one man saying to another, "When you said that, I felt like ripping your face off!") were not challenged.

Sometimes I learn something by explaining it. I told the woman that men have a great fear of being shamed by women. I realized that *men's fear of being shamed by women is of similar magnitude to women's fear of being physically abused by men.* I suddenly understood that mixed workshops need to have two fundamental rules: no violence and no shaming. The two are of equal importance for ensuring safety: one limits men's power in order to ease women's fear, and the other limits women's power in order to reduce men's fear.

The woman thanked me for my explanation, and we parted on good terms. I mention this because what happened next was remarkable. In the next workshop session, the same woman immediately declared that she was about to leave the workshop because a man whom she had asked for help in understanding something had verbally abused her, and she felt so devastated that she had to leave. For the next hour and a half, virtually all of the men (and one or two women) assured her that what had happened would not happen again, and pleaded with her to stay. Not a single one questioned her story; her interpretation was accepted without question. I sat in the circle in stunned amazement, watching a woman take over the workshop agenda so that it all revolved around her, while feeling and expressing complete powerlessness and victimhood. It didn't seem important to anyone to discover what really happened – the woman's story was accepted as fact, and my guilt was presumed. What mattered was that a woman was offended and felt victimized, and it seemed that the men felt a deep need to fix it, to make her feel ok again. After an hour and a half of support and reassurance, the woman consented to remain and the room finally relaxed. I had received another clear and unmistakable lesson about the power of women, their inability to feel that power, and the deep need in men to try to fix things for them.

I spoke at the end about the group dynamic that I thought I had seen and I noted that no one had wondered whether the woman had described what happened accurately. I told my own version of our interaction to the group and commented that something very important to understand about the power relationships between men and women had happened in that room. I spoke pretty strongly, and I described the device of threatening to leave the group as "emotional blackmail." My heart was pounding and I felt the negative judgments of just about everyone there.

At 6am the following morning, after a night of intense and dynamic dreams, I found myself pacing my room with a new model of gender relations churning in me. I had somehow assembled the full answer about what was going on that evening back in 1990 at the Ottawa/Hull Men's Forum, what was going on in the workshop right where I was, and what is still going on at the deepest level between most men and women in our society. I developed what I call the "Gender Codependent Matrix", a model which identifies women's personal and social power as equal to that of men, but less visible because of its different form. At that workshop, my mind finally found its way to the simple underlying mechanism, the model that explains gender power in personal relationships and in society, and which we will explore for the rest of this chapter.

Key to understanding this model is the notion of codependence, which is a form of addictive relating. We are codependently engaged with someone when we transact with them to get our needs met, but hide the truth about our transactions from ourselves and each other with rationalizations, stories that preserve a reassuring but false picture of ourselves. A trivial example might be a husband who "has a shell around him" and a wife who "nags". The wife will explain her behavior by saying, "It's because he has a shell around him that I have to repeat and emphasize everything in order to get through to him." The husband will report, "I wouldn't have a shell around me if

I didn't need it to cope with her nagging." Each is entirely sincere at a conscious level, each believes their own story, but the mutual codependence can be seen in the fact that each escapes from guilt, each makes the other responsible for their own behavior. Therefore, neither feels powerful. The structure is dysfunctional in that it is dishonest, but it provides something each needs – a way to escape from responsibility and a kind of stability, perhaps a defense against the vulnerability of real intimacy. The pathology lies in the fact that both parties are (unconsciously) lying to each other and to themselves, and each feels powerless, each feels that their behavior is determined by the other.

The Gender Codependent Matrix, like much of the material in this book, is challenging. It is a fundamental reframing of our modern understanding of gender relations. The usually accepted feminist theory of gender relations is a theory of one-sided oppression of women by men, a model in a moral system of right and wrong, guilt and innocence. The Gender Codependent Matrix is a theory of codependence, a model in a *health* system, not a moral system. It is a *disease* model of addictive, dysfunctional behavior which is nevertheless completely understandable in terms of underlying psychological needs and constraints. Achieving this understanding, however, requires us to undo the moral polarization of the feminist model, to take women off the pedestal of innocent victimhood and redeem men from the basement of moral indictment. It requires that we see men and women as simply human beings, equally guilty and equally innocent, but stuck in a compulsive, largely unconscious pattern that is about trying to get our needs met.

The Gender Codependent Matrix came to me about four years after the events at the Ottawa Hull Men's Forum that I described at the beginning of this chapter. It took four years of holding the question open, struggling to understand what was really going on between men and women. Four years of fairly intense personal work for me to get myself to the place where I could hold women accountable as well as have compassion for them, and have compassion for men as well as hold them accountable. I do not want you to underestimate the difficulty of such pioneering journeys of personal growth and discovery. You, dear reader, are probably one of those pioneers, or you wouldn't be (still) reading this book. It is important for you to know that healthy social transformation on this scale is not an impractical dream. It has happened before. Moving from a system of moral judgment to one of balance is actually part of the process of human maturation, as we will see when we consider the path of wisdom development in chapter 6. This is precisely what was achieved by Alcoholics Anonymous in its remarkable development of the twelve step recovery program.

Until about eighty years ago, alcoholism was seen as a moral failing. Not just by the sober, but by drinkers as well. Organizations like the Women's Christian Temperance Union and the Anti-Saloon League exhorted drinkers to reform themselves. Churches, psychologists, social workers, upright citizens, all were active but nothing really worked. Then a couple of self-confessed drunks started something that came to be known as Alcoholics Anonymous – without doubt the most effective social healing movement of the twentieth century. For the first time, significant numbers of alcoholics began to recover – and to stay recovered.

AA's basic accomplishment was the *reframing* of alcoholism from moral failure to disease. They stopped *blaming* drunks. AA had no quarrel with people who wanted to drink, but if you wanted to stop and were finding it difficult, AA would help you. Drinkers could stop seeing themselves as moral degenerates, let go of their shame and begin to *heal*. Not to get *better* (notice how moral terms still contaminate our language about sickness), but to *recover*, to become *healthy*. It was also discovered that the disease of alcoholism affected more than just the designated drunk. The modern notion of codependency, of addictive and enabling behaviors that all the family engages in, has shown us that the polarized, "He's the drunk, she's the victim" thinking actually undermined the efforts to reform. Of course it was difficult for him to recover on his own – he was but a part of a larger, addictive family and social system. Today we "get it"; our culture has embraced and understood the disease model of alcoholism to the point where it *feels* right – of *course* that's the way it is.

However, when it comes to gender, we are still deeply wedded to polarized moral thinking, to finding guilty male perpetrators and innocent female victims. Consequently, what we are doing to improve things isn't working well at all. Our programs for domestic violence, for instance, are founded on *reforming* men who are seen as morally deficient, exercising their patriarchal power to oppress and control women. These programs overlook the family-wide, culture-wide codependent patterns that give rise to violence as just one of their symptoms. With a false and mistaken formulation, domestic violence programs usually fail to produce real or lasting change, despite the frequently sincere efforts of all concerned.

Modern gender politics is founded on this 'men bad, women good' moral judgment. Feminism, as an ideology of oppression, is *inherently* chauvinistic, in that it defines a class of innocent victims and a class of guilty oppressors. The good guy/bad guy, morally superior/morally inferior foundation of such a model undermines from the start the notion that it is about equality. Check it out. From sexual harassment to zero tolerance on male violence against women, from "no means no" sexual consent legislation to the bias against fathers in family court, we live today in a world which tends to see women as morally superior and men as morally deficient, while simultaneously paying lip service to gender equality. For most of us, men as well as women, this feels right. Indeed, addiction can be defined as that state in which our thoughts and our feelings lie to us about what is true. To an alcoholic, his drinking *feels* right; it feels like it will solve her problems and remove her anxiety. What's more, his thoughts agree with his feelings: one drink won't hurt, she tells herself. AA calls these rationalizations "stinking thinking". They *feel right* to the addict. But they aren't right, and they don't lead to right action or to recovery. To find something that will *work*; that will stand a chance of restoring health, we must reframe the issue.

Here is my vision of how it will look and feel when we move to a health model of gender. We will lose our obsession with who is right and who is wrong, who is the victim and who the perpetrator. These are not categories that make sense when thinking about a disease. Instead, we will recognize symptoms and patterns of dysfunction. We will give people responsibility for their personal recovery, without shaming them for moral failure or protecting them like children behind a blanket of innocent victimhood. We will celebrate with them every step forward into greater health. Perhaps best of all, men and women will work *together* to heal, rather than accusing and shaming from morally defended positions.

OK, that's the vision – so what's the model? What does the gender codependent matrix look like? Here it is.

	Reward	**Punish**
Men's Power (External) - *Physical* - *Economic* - *Political*	Protect Provide Represent	Attack Abandon Oppress
Women's Power (Internal) - *Moral* - *Emotional* - *Sexual*	Honor Nurture Favor	Shame Abuse Reject

Gender Codependent Matrix

In codependence, we transact unconsciously around needs, trying to manage the other party who has something we need by either supplying (reward) or denying (punish) their needs. In the larger gender dynamic, the codependent exchange of responsibilities has occurred as follows. In general, men have had what we can call external power, i.e. physical (greater personal strength and military might), economic and political. Women have had internal power: moral, emotional and sexual. We are in the strange situation today in which men's power has been well-articulated by the women's movement, while women's equivalent and balancing power remains unrecognized.

Note that feminism focuses on just one quarter of the pattern shown above, the box at top right. The major feminist concerns are all there – male violence against women ('attack'), women's economic struggles after divorce and in the workplace ('abandon') and lack of political power ('oppress'). The gender codependent matrix doesn't deny the reality of these concerns; it says rather that they represent only a quarter of the whole picture. It asks us to expand our understanding to include women's power to 'oppress' men, and men's and women's powers to reward each other as well. This is a common development in the physical sciences, where a later theory expands our worldview and shows us a more complex and complete fundamental reality underlying our previous view. Einstein's theory of relativity did this to Newtonian mechanics, for instance, as did quantum mechanics to classical particle physics.

The areas of physical, economic and political power held mainly by men are familiar to us. However, women's power areas have not been sufficiently articulated by either women or men, and so merit discussion.

Women have moral power over men. It has been recognized throughout history that women are the protectors of morals. Alexis de Tocqueville observed this in his 1834 tome *Democracy in America,* [31] and it was specifically noted by the conference that arguably launched the women's liberation movement, in Seneca Falls [32] a hundred and sixty years ago (although that document incorrectly described the power as being given to women by men). But what is moral power? This is the power to say whether an action or a person is OK, is worthy, is right or wrong. As I see it, this power balances men's superior physical strength and military might. It is the honor code by which society has traditionally tried to ensure that the violence of the warrior is used only against the enemy, and never against the women and children he is supposed to protect. The most devastating thing that a can be done with moral power is to use it to shame someone, to assert that they are morally deficient, flawed, unworthy.

Sociopsychologist Howard Schwartz recognizes the power of shame in his *Revolt of the Primitive: An Inquiry into the Roots of Political Correctness.*

> "How does political correctness get its power over its opposition? The stands taken as politically correct are often quite radical and have a great deal of opposition to them among more traditional elements of the university. These traditional elements are often rapidly and decisively overcome. They often stand quite mute in

fact. How does that happen? Much of the answer may be found in an understanding of the way the PC University mobilizes the power of shame through public humiliation. … [U]nder the aegis of university administration, such practices have become the norm." [33]

Ironically, the existence of feminism itself is perhaps the best evidence against its claims. If men really were the oppressors of women, why would they ever have allowed all of the legislation against their interests, such as equal pay, sexual harassment or violence against women laws? Feminists correctly point out that men are more numerous and thus appear to be in control in the legislature, the courts, the media, the police and the universities. Why haven't men exercised this power and defeated feminist initiatives at every turn? It is because we are ashamed, and we are ashamed because women have told us that we should be. Feminism itself is an exercise of women's moral power to define what is right and what is wrong, what is morally important and what should be done about it, and to coerce men, through shame, into prioritizing women's gender issues and ignoring their own.

This power has operated throughout history, although it has not often been specifically recognized and noted. Philosopher Ferrel Christensen writes that "In the [1900s] the women's 'purity crusade' created laws against pornography, prostitution, and male homosexual acts. Without a single vote, the women involved were able to shame male legislators into doing what the crusaders perceived as being in their own best interests as women." [34]

The roots of this power lie in infancy, when the mother was the source of moral authority, the one who decided when we were good and when we were bad. Our fathers may have carried out the sentence, but for most of us mother was both judge and jury. Today most men still give this authority to women. This was why I could not stand up to the women at the Ottawa Hull Men's Forum, this was why I was devastated by their shaming of me, even though I had only met them that evening. They were *women*; I gave them the power to judge me and I felt unable to refute their judgment.

It is not comfortable to admit this about myself, but it is necessary because it is true. If you can contemplate the possibility that this might be universally true for most men, then you have an alternative explanation for feminism, that it is a *power play* by women in the ancient gender dance of codependence.

The notion that women are powerful as individuals and as a group is difficult to absorb, since it is hard to reconcile with their claimed and obvious vulnerability and victimhood. Let me illustrate it.

Sociopsychologist Howard Schwartz offers us this, in his *The Revolt of the Primitive*.

> "Thus, we find, on the one hand, that the image of the woman as passive, helpless victim is ubiquitous in our society, with whole classes of institutions having been created to protect these victims. On the other hand, and indeed partly through the manipulation of this image, women have manifested enormous power in the transformation of almost every aspect of society.

> … An example of this contrast occurred at the University of Michigan in 1992. This case involved a sophomore student in an introductory Political Science course. The student, in a paper criticizing telephone polling, invoked a hypothetical Dave Stud, who, while knowledgeable about a certain area of taxation, refused to answer a pollster's question because he was busy entertaining three beautiful ladies in his penthouse. This male student's female teaching assistant responded this way in the margin of the paper: 'This is ludicrous & inappropriate & OFFENSIVE. This is completely inappropriate for a serious political science paper. It completely violates the standard of non-sexist writing. Professor Rosenstone has encouraged me to interpret this comment as an example of sexual harassment and to take the appropriate formal steps. I have chosen not to do so in this instance. However, any future comments, in a paper, in a class or in any dealings w/me will be interpreted as sexual harassment and formal steps will be taken. Professor Rosenstone is aware of these comments & is prepared to intervene. You are forewarned!' (*The Michigan Review*, 1993)

> The disparity here between the frail, vulnerable woman, grievously damaged by the merest mention of male sexuality; and the powerful woman, capable of mobilizing the full weight of the University of Michigan against a hapless sophomore, is breathtaking." [35]

The clear conclusion, paradoxical and therefore difficult to embrace as is most wisdom, is that women are both powerless *and* powerful, simultaneously. Of course, the corresponding truth is that men are both powerful *and* powerless, simultaneously. When we realize this, the inherent equality between men and women becomes much easier to see. However, when we embrace only one side of the truth and deny its opposite, we do a disservice to both genders.

In 1992, under pressure from feminist groups, the Supreme Court of Canada, in a unanimous decision, defined obscenity in terms of what harms women! Not what harms people, or what harms society, but what harms women. Our highest court could not see the blatant one-sidedness of this decision (or, seeing it, could not oppose it, for shame). Even the extreme external power and success possessed by Supreme Court judges does not remove or compensate for their subjection to the moral power held by women. The fact that women sincerely deny this power, the fact that they genuinely do not feel it, does not mean that they lack it. That is the purpose of the codependent cover story, to hide and deny the reality of uncomfortable facts. The uncomfortable facts are that in this area of moral shaming, women are powerful and men are powerless. Women are also perpetrators, men are also victims.

In a similar way, women hold emotional power over men. By emotional power, I mean that women have had the role of emotional provider, doing the emotional work for the family in a similar way to that in which men have done the economic work. Thus, in general, grieving, nurturing, excitement, love and passion have fallen to women to feel and express, while men have been "stoic" and unfeeling, and "held the fort". Because of fifty years of feminist rhetoric, we are liable to see this as yet another cross for women to bear, but it is in fact a power area just as much as is the economic power of men, because men, through social conditioning and stigma, cannot readily do this emotional work. Since psychological health requires that emotions be expressed, vicariously if not personally, this male incompetence gives women a significant power over men. (If it seems that this power is overstated, consider that in the two years after a marriage failure men commit suicide at ten times the rate that women do. What have they lost that is so devastating?)

Finally, let us examine sexual power. I am not saying that men's and women's physiological sex drives are different: the evidence suggests that they are not. Yet, to men, women have the sexual "goods"; men need the sexual favors of women in a way that women do not need from men. At a deeper level, what men really need is the approval, the validation of women, expressed most fundamentally and unmistakably through their consent to access to women's bodies. After all, a woman doesn't open her body to just anyone. Men know that this is the acid test, the real thing. When a woman shares her body with a man, she is risking pregnancy (or used to be, when these cultural mores evolved). So she is selective – usually highly selective. Men, hungry for the validation, the approval implicit in being thus selected, strive to 'score' with a woman. (The word 'score' itself is very revealing – as in sports, the motivation for scoring is the adulation, the validation of one's skill, prowess, worth.) Thus sex is a "seller's market", and women, with the ability to accept or reject, possess the primary power. Thus in the dating dynamic the man takes risk after risk as he initiates each increment of sexual intimacy, and at each step the woman can favor him, refuse, or postpone. The sexual power lies with her.

An aspect of this could be referred to as 'beauty power,' and a number of authors (e.g., Warren Farrell) have explored this dynamic in depth. Robert Bly speaks to this in his *Iron John:*

> "I remember a man telling me of a summer he spent at fifteen working as a busboy in a Catskills resort. He and the other boys were doing all right until one day a tall, blond, beautiful self-contained, high-cheekboned sixteen-year-old girl walked into the dining room. It was all over in a moment. The fifteen-year-old boy sank under the waves, bubbles came up; he was lost.

> "It is interesting that neither he nor his equally moved friends ever talked to her. Instead they spent hours after work discussing who spoke to her today, what she wore at breakfast, whom she walked up with, who sat at her table. Her face and its beauty, which seemed inaccessible, or invulnerable, made them all feel like hicks, inarticulate clods of earth, hopelessly matter-ridden louts. She was above matter.

> "For three weeks the obsession went on; they woke up every morning feverish. Then the summer ended; she left, that was it.

There was only one event in the summer, that one. ...

> "The girl, on her side, is equally confused. She may in reality be lacking in self-esteem, be insecure, shamed, even victimized, but on the outside, in the radiance from her face, she is queenly, self-possessed, golden and invulnerable." [36]

Do you see, do you feel the codependence here? Remember that codependence, addiction, is a spiritual disease, one in which we worship the wrong gods. There is indeed an aspect of worship in the boys' relationship to the beautiful girl. They put her on a pedestal, make an idol of her. Yet, although she is so immensely powerful in their lives, she probably experiences little or none of this power *as* power. In codependence, no one is really powerful, since everyone is dependent on another. Still, there is an asymmetry; the power that there is belongs to her, the boys worship her and not the other way around. At some unconscious level (remember, this is a dance of unconsciousness), she knows this.

Boys grow out of this inarticulate beauty-worship, of course. One way is that, as they begin to *achieve,* to become competent providers or potential providers on the world's terms, they begin to feel a little more equal, that they have something to offer, something to trade that might be worth the shining value of a woman's beauty and sexual favors. But the basic dynamic, the power of female beauty and sex to compel men's attention and inflame their desire continues. Women can and do trade on their beauty power, on their sexual power, to get things that they want. A beautiful woman almost always marries above the social class of her origin; this is so common that it is iconic, we expect it.

Of course, if a woman is too punishing in the dating dynamic, she risks the man resorting to one of his own power areas – physical force, for example, and so she doesn't experience her power over as a feeling of power. Instead, like him, she feels anxious rather than secure. This feeling of powerlessness on both sides is a major symptom of codependence, and completely misleading since it seems obvious on each side that the other holds the power that matters.

Recall the observation made earlier of the power wielded by the women in the Ottawa Men's Forum, even as they felt themselves to be powerless and abused. This false feeling of one-sided power and oppression by the other party completely explains feminist analysis of male power, and also explains why it totally overlooks the other side of the pattern, namely men's powerlessness in the face of women's power. So, for example, women have used their moral power to identify date rape, i.e., women's experience of men's power, as the important dating issue, while most men remain afraid or ashamed to acknowledge (perhaps even to feel) their own powerlessness in the same dating dynamic. When they do speak up about their own fears, e.g., about how devastating a false accusation of rape can be, they are often shamed in response. The dance of codependence is complex and confusing. For the moment we have oversimplified it by privileging women's experience over that of men, because of our ability to empathize with women, but hardly at all with men.

Dissident feminist Camille Paglia writes,

> "When I was young, I thought teenage boys were the most awkward, miserable, antsy, bratty, scuzzy, snickering creatures on God's green earth. Now at midlife and, as it were, *hors de combat,* I see them quite differently. Watching them rampage on the street or at the shopping mall; I find them extraordinarily moving, for they represent the masculine principle struggling to free itself from woman's cosmic dominance.

> "Teenage boys, goaded by their surging hormones (at maximum strength at this time), run in packs like the primal horde. They have only a brief season of exhilarating liberty between control by their mothers and control by their wives. The agony of male identity springs from men's humiliating sense of dependence upon women. It is women who control the emotional and sexual realms, and men know it." [37]

What Paglia describes here is not the whole story of teenage male behavior; it is just an overlooked piece. It is overlooked today because it is sympathetic in tone towards men. It recognizes male *powerlessness,* and so contradicts the one-sided story of our time. Paglia has learned to empathize with boys, to see deeper than they do into their souls (they do not know in any conscious sense, or course, about their own dependence on women), into their issues and their challenges, and to feel for them. It is a rare gift in our present climate, from either men or women, and it is received by this male with gratitude.

Let us pause to recap. I have presented an alternative theory of gender relations and some basic supporting evidence. I have told at some length the story of how I came to this theory, twenty years ago. My experience since that time has confirmed the validity of the model, but also the difficulty of communicating it. Codependence, as an addiction, has enormous power over both our thoughts and our feelings – and what else do we have with which to discern what is true? The feeling associated with codependence is one of victimhood, of being oppressed because one perceives the other party as having the power that matters. So women, who got in touch with their powerlessness first, have told a story of oppression by men. They remain codependently unaware that it is their moral power, their ability to shame men that is driving our whole society to address women's issues and deny men's issues. They are exerting enormous power in an unbalanced, dysfunctional way even as they continue to feel victimized and righteously innocent.

Since the Gender Codependent Matrix derives from traditional patterns of relating between men and women, the feelings that it gives rise to match the historical relationship. So feminists, like conservatives, see women as needing protection from men even as they declare that women are the equal of any man. They see women as victims of male power even as they talk about girrrl power and female empowerment. The rhetoric is about equality, but the feeling is more like Victorian moral chasteness, which is why they will never *feel* equal, no matter how much legislation and policy addresses their issues. The problem they have identified is being addressed in the outer world, because that is where they feel it to be, but that is not where the problem actually lies. The real problem is internal, the codependent addictive relationship and cover story of denial, and that is where the only real solution lies as well. More of us must move into recovery.

I am aware from personal experience that there is pain in admitting that one has been addicted and moving into recovery. Yet some do it, and from the other side they report joy and no regrets. For each individual, it comes down to what we really want. If we want to know what is true, we find it. It may take persistence and courage, but we really do find it. Conversely, if we stay addicted, then that is what we want. At the deepest level, the level that lies beneath our cover story of innocence or ignorance, we know what is true and we are in control and responsible.

If we wish to stay addicted, if we choose to remain codependent, then we need do nothing, for that is the path of least resistance. However, if we want to recover, if we decide that we want the truth, if we really do want to move towards wisdom, what do we do? How do we proceed? Are there maps or tools for that journey? That is the subject of the next chapter.

Chapter 6 – Seeking Wisdom

"We don't receive wisdom; we must discover it for ourselves after a journey that no one can take for us or spare us." – Marcel Proust (1871 - 1922)

"We could never learn to be brave and patient if there were only joy in the world" – Helen Keller

"The gift of willingness is the only thing that stands between the quiet desperation of a disingenuous life and the actualization of unexpressed potential." – Jim McDonald

"It may actually be more healthy to be disturbed, confused, or searching than confident, certain, and secure." – Mark Scandrette

"Any transition serious enough to alter your definition of self will require not just small adjustments in your way of living and thinking but a full-on metamorphosis." – Martha Beck

"No price is too high to pay for the privilege of owning yourself." – Friedrich Nietzsche

"Know well what leads you forward and what holds you back, and choose the path that leads to wisdom." – Buddha

We have seen that wisdom is dualistic balance, and we have looked at how imbalance produces distorted perceptions and poor life decisions. How, then, does one move towards balanced wisdom?

In this chapter I will present a map of the journey through dualistic imbalance to personal wisdom, and discuss the nature of the terrain that one travels on that journey, what it looks and feels like. I will examine the attractions of imbalance, including addiction, a particularly compulsive form of imbalance. Finally, I will present a method of self-assessment for determining one's stage of development towards wisdom for any issue or area of one's life.

The content of people's lives varies greatly; different circumstances, different experiences, different beliefs, different attitudes. If a map or model of the journey of life is going to serve and fit them all, it must focus at a deeper level than that surface complexity, it must identify a single, simple underlying process that is common to everyone and that is basic to the experience of being human. That common underlying process is the creation of meaning.

Meaning is not intrinsic, it is our own creation. We saw in chapter two in the story about the person who received a cell phone call about their daughter's accident that the meaning you give to someone's behavior is your own construction or interpretation – it can alter without any change in the facts or the experience. The meaning that we give to everything in life, what it means that we live and then die, that there is suffering, that life is capricious – these are all our own creation. Often we accept meanings from the culture or from human subgroups (e.g., religions), but it is our choice which sets of prepackaged meanings we believe. In the past I have used the word 'spirituality' to describe this process, and I have offered the definition, "Spirituality is the process of creating and maintaining life meaning," but this word is troublesome for some people. If you bear in mind that I am not in any way referring to religion or talking about God or the divine, then perhaps we can employ the word to mean something like "deep psychology".

However, we have not got to simplicity yet – the meanings that people give to life also vary greatly. It turns out, though, that there are basic structural patterns that are common to everyone. One is now familiar to us – whether the meaning structure is dualistic or not. If we organize our world around good and bad; men/women/Jews/Blacks/Whites/Muslims/etc. are good, or are bad, that is a dualistic meaning structure. In fact, most of the "isms" are dualistic. Feeling like a victim in your life is dualistic; feeling responsible for everything is the opposite side of the same duality. So one basic meaning structure is whether you see yourself and the world dualistically or not.

So far, we have spoken only of dualistic balance or imbalance. But what happens when we *are* dualistically balanced, when we see and value both sides equally? What happens is that the duality disappears; we see it as just two aspects of the same substance. When we see that men and women are truly equal, then the whole issue of better/worse, right/wrong, guilty/innocent stops being relevant. They are just different kinds of people where the differences don't matter, don't alter their basic status. The name for this unity of substance, this "opposite" of dualism is monism. We discussed in chapter four that the deep reality of the universe is that it is of one substance, like the can of beans that nevertheless shows up as dualistic when abbreviated into two dimensions. Dualism, then, is abbreviated perception, but deep reality is monistic.

So monism/dualism is one deep, fundamental pattern of meaning creation. Another is conscious/unconscious, whether we are creating and maintaining meaning by a conscious process of observation and learning, or by an unconscious process based (usually) on avoiding what we fear.

I developed the map of personal growth towards wisdom by plotting these two dimensions of meaning creation against each other.

	Monistic	**Dualistic**
Unconscious	*Stage 1* Innocence ⟶	*Stage 2* Denial
Conscious	*Stage 4* Wisdom ⟵	*Stage 3* Recovery

The four stage path to wisdom.

We are born into stage 1, unconscious monism. Monism is defined by *Webster's Encyclopedic Dictionary* as "the view, common to various philosophical systems, which reduces all reality to a single principle or substance." [38] Psychologists tell us that infants have no sense of self-identity, no concept of boundaries between themselves and all that they perceive. They haven't yet put themselves, as a separate entity, into their picture of the world. Indeed, they do not yet possess a concept of "self" at all. Their world is all of one substance, undifferentiated. And stage 1 is *unconscious* monism because the infant is not aware of its own process of meaning construction, is not the intentional author of that developmental task. Rather, in a similarly unmanaged fashion to that by which we learn language, the complex set of meanings associated with life (what boys and girls *do,* what adults are for) are assembled out of what we see going on around us.

At some point, a major transition happens; we form a 'self' and begin to spend some of our time in stage 2. Unfortunately this great, first act of self creation will always be a result of psychic distress.[ix] No matter how loving the parents, they cannot anticipate or relieve all pains. Fear, hunger, physical discomforts are all a part of our experience as an infant, and our inability to control pain, to turn off distress simply because we don't like it, speaks loudly in our psyches. We suffer as infants, and our suffering does not answer to our will. Moreover, we are weak and powerless, unable to control anything that happens to us, and we are surrounded by people who are powerful, who can move around and who have complete power over us. Thus we conclude, as the basic act of self-creation, that there is something wrong with us. How else is an infant psyche to account for the horrible, intimate, irresistible facts of suffering and powerlessness? And since the folk around us are powerful and aren't suffering (we know this because we don't feel their pain), then *whatever is wrong with us makes us inferior to them. We are not an OK person, we are flawed and inferior.*

Note what has happened here. It is profound. In order to make sense out of suffering and powerlessness, in order to give meaning to a world that includes pain and impotence, the infant psyche has created a dualistic moral system out of nothing at all! It is an act of pure meaning creation, and on it will be built the massive dualistic moral edifice of good/bad, right/wrong, guilty/innocent, victim/perpetrator,

---

[ix] "... when someone steps on my foot, only I feel the pain. The basis of the self is not thought but suffering, which is the most fundamental of all feelings. While it suffers, not even a cat can doubt its unique and uninterchangeable self. In intense suffering the world disappears and each of us is alone with his self. Suffering is the university of egocentrism." — Milan Kundera, *Immortality*

etc. that provides the foundational meaning structures in the psyches of virtually everyone alive today. We human beings disagree widely about the content, about *what* is right and what is wrong, but we don't disagree that this right/wrong dualistic picture is the right way to view the world. Yet it is an artifact of pure error, a manufactured idea that has no intrinsic or essential place in the world and that actually causes a great deal of suffering.

This conclusion that "I am inferior" is drawn even in the best of family circumstances. However, in a dysfunctional or abusive family, it is reinforced with implicit or explicit messages of 'not-OK-ness' directed toward the child, as parents and siblings try to reassure themselves that *they* are OK by making the child wrong.

The self that is created in this way is a (dualistically) divided self. The two parts are a deeper self that believes that it is not OK, and a surface self that is dedicated to denying that belief. 'I am inferior' is so painful a conclusion that it *must* be denied, which is why I call stage 2 of the model 'Denial'. It takes time to develop sufficient ego strength to tolerate the raw pain of the acceptance of inferiority, so we hide it below conscious awareness, and in its place we construct a system of meanings, an interpretation of the world and our place in it, that is carefully designed to reassure us of our worth. To deny our inferiority, we fill our dualistic world-view with content that proves our superiority. The pain of a belief that we are flawed is known as shame; as a defense against that shame, the surface self clothes itself in moral superiority, in righteousness.

Here lie the roots of all the one-upmanship ego games, all the 'us and them' moral classification systems in the world. Whether we choose to found our personal superiority on gender (men/women are better than women/men), race, politics, religion, social status, macho posturing, feminine beauty, a combination of all of the above, or whatever, will depend on the details of our life. We choose some way of grouping or classifying people, with ourselves categorically in the morally superior group, and we defend it vigorously against any suggestion that it is wrong. We *must* defend it; our very identity and self-worth depends on it. But, because at root we are defending against ourselves, against ever discovering that we believe we are not OK, our defense must be convoluted so that it fools us as well. *In stage 2, we sincerely believe our own cover story, and compulsively find ways to explain away every hint that it might be mistaken.*

This deep and universal fear that we are flawed was revealed in a classic experiment by Asch. [39]

> "In that experiment subjects were required to make the simple perceptual judgment of whether lines were the same or different lengths. They were confronted with the question in a group situation in which the other members of the group had already unanimously made their judgments in an erroneous way. Unknown to the subject, the other members of the group were confederates of the experimenter. The question was whether the real subject would contradict the clear evidence of his senses and go along with the group, or whether he would go along with his senses and differ from the group. Strikingly, most of the subjects – approximately three quarters – conformed.

"Scheff,[40] analyzing this experiment, argues that the response which occasioned the conformity, a response felt, incidentally, both by those who conformed and those who did not, was shame: 'the fear that they were suffering from a defect and that the study would disclose this defect.'" [41]

Let me share a story to illustrate how this internal shame gets started and reinforced. Some years ago, on Christmas Eve, I went with family to a Toronto church. At one point in the service, young boys and girls are called up from the congregation into a group at the front and questioned about Christmas by a young woman with a microphone. She begins, "How do you feel?" A boy replies, "Fine." On to the next child; "What about you, how do you feel?" "Fine." This isn't going where the woman wants. "It's Christmas Eve," she says. "Isn't anyone excited?" A chorus of "Yes" and "I am." The children are getting the drift now. "What are you excited about?" the woman asks. This time there is no response. Silence.

I know what they're excited about, of course. These are children aged four to twelve. It's Christmas Eve. What they are excited about is the gifts they are expecting to receive tomorrow morning. But not one of them says so. Why not? Well, they know that although the questions seem to be asking about their feelings, about their truth, that's not what's really wanted. They know, at some level, that they are expected to perform, to pretend to be other than they are; that our approval of them depends on it. They are waiting for more direction so they can figure out the right answers.

The woman gives them a hint. "What's special about Christmas? What's Christmas about?" An older child thinks she knows the answer. "Compassion," she says. The young woman with the microphone is visibly relieved. "That's right," she says. "And what is compassion?"

The conversation continues; I look around the church. I am looking to see if anyone other than me is disturbed by this. Among 200 parishioners I see only smiles of pleasure; parents and other adults enjoying the cuteness of the children. Perhaps they are telling themselves how wonderful children are, how much they love them. I experience a profound loneliness and despair. For I know that what I am witnessing is child abuse, in church, by good, honest, upright folk. And I fear that I am the only one who sees it.

Let's look carefully at what was going on. We adults in that church, and I include myself since I did not challenge it, were seeking to have the children say the 'right,' virtuous things about Christmas; that it is about love and giving and compassion and selflessness. Perhaps we wanted to hear these things from the innocent mouths of our children so that we could be reassured in our pious belief that those are the important virtues. We wanted the children to be 'excited' about those virtues – perhaps because we weren't very excited about them ourselves any more. I don't know. But I do know this. We were using the children as objects for our own selfish purposes. We didn't care to hear their real feelings, but only the ones we wanted from them. What's worse, we wanted them to fake it for us, to pretend that what they gave us *were* their real feelings. The stick with which we coerced these lies was our conditional approval. And of course it worked, as it usually does.

I looked at their faces as the children walked back to their seats. Some were excited, presumably at having spoken over the microphone. Some were subdued. None looked angry. What had happened was unremarkable; it happens every day, a hundred times a day, to every child and to every adult. It's our way of life. It's completely and totally normal. And it's utterly abusive. I don't know how to express my horror at the universality and the destructiveness of this subtle form of abuse and our almost total blindness to it. We have taught children to be ashamed of who they really are, and to substitute instead a false self for our approval. This deep, essential shame is what I call the shame wound.

These archetypally feminine (not female) forms of child abuse are hard to recognize. They are covert, indirect, manipulative and deceptive; the cover-up is built into the crime. To make it even more difficult, we have little empathy for this form of suffering, because we are all caught up in it ourselves. When it was done to us as children under the guise of righteousness, we hid our pain from ourselves. Now, still hiding and in denial of our pain, we fail to recognize the abusiveness of these forms of manipulation and control of others. Failing to recognize them, we perpetuate them.

We injure our children this way. We undermine their natural pride and authenticity, and leave shame and insecurity, a false self in its place. It isn't done maliciously, in anger or cruelty, but rather covertly, hidden from our awareness and theirs as well. It is done unconsciously, under a cover story that it is all for their own good. Nevertheless, the children's behavior proved that they knew, at some level, that who they really were wasn't valued, wasn't loved. The fact that they, like we, hid that knowledge from themselves doesn't make it less harmful, less abusive. On the contrary, by forcing self-deception on top of the manipulation, it makes it worse, more convoluted, more difficult to recognize. We get trapped into the conspiracy of the cover up, all of us pretending that what we are doing is loving. Is it any wonder that stage 2 is so difficult to find our way out of?

The majority of people in the world spend most of their lives in stage 2. It is a stage of *spiritual* development because it is defined by the way that we construct *meaning* in our lives. It is an *unconscious* stage because we remain unaware of the real purpose of this activity – the meanings that we *are* aware of are fake, untrue, are actually a cover story. It is dualistic because we have constructed two camps, the OK and the not-OK, with us (according to our cover story) solidly and demonstrably in the 'good' camp. Our spiritual (i.e., meaning-maintaining) life is dedicated to a defense against the truth, which we are sure will convict us, and so we live in fear and anxiety, which we interpret as coming from 'out there' since *we* are just and righteous, at least in the ways that *matter.* We thus cast ourselves as victims, since we are not responsible for the suffering we are enduring; it is all the fault of those unrighteous 'others.'

The experience of victimhood is characteristic of this stage. If we can find a way to establish the good guys as morally superior and righteous by definition, as a matter of identity (e.g., whites for a white person who chooses racism as a defense mechanism, or women for a feminist), so much the better for ensuring that our goodness is unassailable, is beyond challenge.

Here lies the genesis of almost all war, most crime and violence, most seeking for power and control and status, almost all of the social ills of our world. What is worse, virtually everything done to address these problems is done from within stage 2, and so does not actually improve things. For instance, suppose that a stage 2 man is telling a sexist joke, in order to reinforce his belief that as a man he is superior to women (which is itself a defense against his unconscious fear that he is inferior to women). Then shaming him for his sexism, (i.e., reversing the duality on him by implying that he is inferior to us because he is sexist) may make us feel superior and thus reinforce our own defenses, but is in fact (i.e., in its essential *meaning*) no different than the behavior we were criticizing. For the sexist man, it attacks him by asserting what he unconsciously fears – his inferiority – so that he is more afraid and wounded than before, and more desperately needs to find ways to convince himself of and demonstrate his superiority.

Similarly, in the story we encountered in chapter three about the racist woman on the airplane, the actions of the stewardess and the applauding passengers all came from stage 2, making the white woman morally inferior. In this way, all interactions that flow out of stage 2 beliefs are win/lose zero-sum games that don't significantly move people towards health or maturity, and don't actually solve the problems that they ostensibly address. How could they; they aren't actually aimed at those problems at all, but are really attempts to prove one's own righteousness or worthiness under a purported but sincerely believed guise of doing good or improving the world. Stage 2 is a place of continuous, usually repressed anxiety and constant self-deception. It is truly an awful place to live.

A personal story from my adolescence, when I was still living my life entirely from within stage 2, may give a sense of how our shame operates to distort our lives. It was December, 1972, and I was 19 years old. There was a fruit pie sitting on the front seat of the car I was driving — my parents' car. The pie was a gift from Mum and Dad, for my lunch. It was late spring in New Zealand, a fine day, and I was hungry. I wanted to take a bite from the pie. While driving through the downtown core of Lower Hutt, my home town, I eased the pie out of its paper bag and crumpled the bag into a ball. I opened the driver's side quarter-light window and tried to push the paper ball out of the car. My attention shifted from the road to the window. Suddenly the car rocked: I had left the road and mounted the curb! I swung the wheel wildly to return to the road, but wham! My head hit the roof and the car stopped dead, its front pushed in over a foot by a lamp post that I hadn't even seen.

What a disaster! My parent's car was badly damaged (it was later written off), and it was entirely my fault. I felt intensely ashamed, completely stupid and unworthy. I had no ability to accept more of these feelings about myself; I had to find an excuse, a mitigating circumstance, a culprit. I had to divert some of the soul-destroying shame that I was pouring at myself in a torrent. But how to do it; there was no one but me involved. My parents' car was wrecked, I possibly injured, but my shame demanded my attention and overwhelmed all other considerations.

I crossed the road to a restaurant where I called my parents. My father answered the phone. I told him about the accident. He was calm and asked the right questions: "Is anyone hurt? Is the lamp post damaged?" I lied about what happened. I said that the fruit pie began to slip off the front seat, and I grabbed for it by reflex, and that was how I ran the car off the road. The lie seemed to assuage my shame a little – my unconscious reflexes, not my conscious littering and careless inattention, were to blame.

Back at the car, a passing police officer had stopped to check things out. I explained to him what had happened, including my lie about the falling pie. He peered into the car. The pie was in several pieces, mashed into the front parcel shelf – clearly it had been on the seat and not the floor when the car hit the post. I started to backfill and embroider my lie, explaining that I had managed to grab the pie and put it back on the seat. He looked at me and I could see he knew I was lying, but I saw him decide; 'What does it matter, there's nobody else involved, it's his fault no matter what story he tells.' He shrugged his shoulders and moved on to other things: insurance, towing details.

I concealed that shame-inspired lie from my parents for over twenty five years, until January, 1998 when I published a story about it and sent them a copy along with a letter apologizing to them for my deception. It was good for me to get it off my chest: part of one's stage 3 process involves making amends and apologizing for one's guilt. But, you might say, it wasn't entirely your fault; your shame was at least partly a result of your parents' treatment of you. Yes, of course, but that's stage 2 victim thinking. I had already spent all of that currency of holding myself blameless and holding others responsible, during my long stay in stage 2. Stage 3 is about searching for all the ways that one is guilty and responsible, and ignoring the (equally true) ways that one is blameless. Only then can the accounts be *balanced,* so that you get, in total, a true picture of personal responsibility. Inevitably, as we embrace and grieve our guilt, we discover its practical limits. Indeed, we discover eventually that the whole notion of our – or anyone's – guilt is entirely mistaken. Let such a discovery come naturally; if it is sought too early it will sabotage the whole process as we use it to avoid the pain of guilt, to return to stage 2 and let ourselves off the hook again.

The spiritual journey is a about growth; each stage has a purpose. The purpose of stage 2 is to insulate the psyche from unendurable pain behind the walls of denial, while it tries to grow the ego strength to move to the next stage, that of recovery. If sufficient strength can be achieved (many do not reach this point before their death intervenes), the birth into stage 3 can take place.

Birth is a good metaphor for what happens at this time. Expelled from the insulated, womb-like state of denial, the psyche begins to experience all the meanings that had been hidden. The pain of birth can be overwhelming. The grief of the repentant sinner, the remorse of the recovering alcoholic or drug addict, the guilt of the now contrite abuser or philanderer. Yet it is a glorious event. The newly aware soul courageously seeks a relationship of truth, of reality rather than of denial. Thus, as in physical childbirth, it is *conscious* for the first time. The pain that had been buried is acknowledged and felt. In stage 3 we accept our guilt and no longer hide from it. The pain of shame is experienced as a wound in the psyche (which it is), and is gradually recovered from through grief, which is the psychic process of letting go of parts of our identity construction. Yet this stage is still dualistic; the 'good' and 'bad' classifications remain. What has happened is that the old, false world view has been abandoned, and a new one, an attempt to find the true worth of one's soul and one's real place in the cosmos, has begun.

It takes time to undo a world view. The rationalizations of years of denial must be painstakingly deconstructed and the truth with which they will be replaced must be discovered. This process is like childhood. It is a time of learning and adventure and discovery, and also of pain and confusion. I first entered this stage at 7pm on December 6, 1988. My experience was one of new (in)sight – "I was blind, but now I see" – as I began to re-evaluate all of the meanings I had given to the world. My process of recovery, of discovering true and authentic rather than self-serving meaning, continues to this day.

Like all who have begun the conscious part of their spiritual journey, I started by embracing the shadow side of my supposed superiority, which is, of course, my supposed inferiority. It is painful work, and humbling, as we own our guilt and apologize to friends and family for our shortcomings, previously denied. Yet there is also joy in it, the joy of being truly alive, of *feeling* the pain rather than numbing it away with self-serving stories of blamelessness. The joy of ceasing to hide from our own soul, of healing the split in our psyche, previously divided into a light half which we could safely acknowledge and a shadow side which ruled us from the dark, unexamined depths of our unconscious. The joy of healing, of 'whole-ing,' of becoming integral and complete and emotionally uncrippled. The wondrous joy of seeing that, yes, there are answers, and they are comprehensible and accessible. The Universe is not hostile, judgmental or perversely enigmatic as we had believed, but clear, benign and understandable.

What of spiritual maturity? What of stage 4 – wisdom? Parts of me now spend time in that place, although other parts still live in other stages. The essence of the transition to stage 4 is to apprehend again what was lost when we moved out of stage 1, the mystical unity and perfection of the Universe, but this time with power and competence rather than in powerless innocence. As we balance the dualistic meanings we had constructed in stage 2 by exploring their opposite side, they become less structural in our psyches. As we integrate the opposites, we see that the dualism itself was a misperception; we begin to apprehend the deeper, non-dual reality. If there is good and bad, guilt and innocence on both sides, then what use is the good/bad split? Can you imagine letting go of duality, seeing that there is no right or wrong, no good or bad, but only stages that we pass through? Our wanting the world to be different from what it is, the violence to stop, or the wars, or the environmental destruction, is just an expression of our own need to have the world meet our expectations rather than expressing its own nature. It's like wanting a three-year-old to understand calculus. From the perspective of stage 4, that isn't wrong either. It's just a dualistic stage, an abbreviated world view that has its moment in our spiritual evolution.

The world is perfect; social immaturity is a phase, not a crime, and not a defect. A child of three is not less than an adult, but perfect as he or she is; lack of calculus knowledge is appropriate to that stage. All the wars, violence and suffering in the world are simply age-appropriate (more precisely, stage-appropriate) behavior. Easy to say and to understand intellectually; in stage 4 we *feel* it, we know and understand and accept it. We know that the world is perfect as it is, yet still there is a vital task for us. Life has a direction that we can assist or oppose. Children grow into adults, not to improve themselves or to fix something that is wrong, and not because it's better to be an adult, but simply because that is the nature and direction of life. Effective parents assist rather than oppose the process; they guide and support the maturation of their children. In the same way, the task of the spiritually mature is to assist the growth of others, not to make them better or to fix anything, for nothing is wrong, but just for the joy of being in harmony with the cycle of life, for the wonder of seeing the unfolding of the flower that is a human being or a human society or a living ecosystem.

That's what stage 4 is like – but how does one get there? We have to dismantle duality, to recognize that it is an illusion, an abbreviated perception of reality. When we are in stage 2 or 3, our perceptions are shaped by the dualistic meaning structures that we have built to divide the world into good and bad. Not only our thoughts, but our feelings too are entirely aligned with these divisions. What we have decided is wrong both *feels* wrong and is *thought* to be wrong. All of our ideas about why it is wrong are instantly available to us. In a word, we are prejudiced in favor of those ideas, classes, people, objects that we have classified as good or superior, and against those that we have defined as bad or inferior. To use a metaphor, we have trashed all the 'bad' ideas. The work of moving ourselves towards stage 4 is the work of rooting around in our psychic trash cans. It's dirty, disturbing, fearful and painful work. But it's worth remembering that all of that psychic trash is our own garbage. From the perspective of stage 4, duality, right and wrong, good and bad; none of these exist, other than as immature methods of meaning construction that we now see with compassion. So there is a kind of psychic economy, a coming full circle, involved in picking through our own trashed concepts and reintegrating our values. It is difficult work, but it is rewarding.

In stage 4 we have transcended duality, but before we transcend it we first have to balance it by living both sides of the duality.

I recommend this work to readers. In the questions of gender, prejudice and working for social change, we need to be clear thinkers and clear visionaries, to know that what we are working towards is indeed worth pursuing and that the personal and social changes we are seeking will genuinely improve matters. Picking through our own prejudice trash can is the only way of knowing this about our chosen strategy. We have the example of feminism to caution us about the risks of pursuing social change without looking deeply into our own motivations, without carefully examining both sides of an issue.

One aspect of stage 4 work is that it is usually misunderstood, just as children frequently mistake the motivations or vision of their parents. No matter; the spiritually mature have the soul-strength to do what is called for no matter what others think they see. Living and working in the same world as those whose lives are built around denial, they sometimes outrage or offend. In particular, they will at times confront denial and expose the pain behind it, injecting a momentary antidote to the tranquilizer and anesthetic that the denial provides. To those in denial, it seems that the pain was *caused* by the intervention, which is seen as violent, abusive or uncaring. That is why, earlier in this chapter, I was careful to say that *most* of the violence, *most* of the abuse in the world is stage 2 people acting out their control needs. Some of what is seen as evil and wrong is actually a projection of stage 2 judgments onto necessary spiritual surgery. Recall that sages and spiritual leaders throughout history have been the targets of hatred as well as love.

I want to emphasize that these stages are not phases that we pass through, never to return. I still spend time in the stage 2 space of judging others in order to feel morally superior, while hiding from myself the awareness that that is what I am doing. Then I often move to stage 3 and judge myself for doing so and apologize for my error. I even return to stage 1 at times; the 'falling in love' experience of oneness with the lover, the self-indulgent high of a drug trip or glorying in a personal achievement are all forms of return to the lost innocence and joy of monistic stage 1. We move among the stages from moment to moment.

I described this model as a *map* of the spiritual journey. It is vital to remember that the map is not the territory. Having a map does not remove the need to make the journey, nor does it reduce the effort of traversing the terrain. However, a map does have two valuable uses. First, it gives a picture, a sense of the whole territory, the "lay of the land" as it were. We can gain an impression of what the whole journey looks like and might involve, and even make some plans about how to travel. Second, a map is useful for identifying where we are right now on our journey. Placing oneself on the map is not difficult. For whatever is on your mind right now (for instance, your relationship with your spouse, or your boss, or your child, or the state of the world or the environment), consider first whether you see it dualistically, in terms of things or issues or people that are right and wrong. If so, then you are definitely in stage 2 or 3 on this issue or relationship. If you see it dualistically, is it the other or others that you see as wrong? Then you are in stage 2. Or do you see yourself as the one who is wrong and needs to change? Then you are in stage 3. (Note, you can be in both stages at the one time, seeing both things 'out there' that are wrong, and also things about yourself that you judge to be wrong.)

I encourage you to use the map to plot your path to the next stage, wherever you find yourself. If you are in stage 2, imagine how it would feel to let go of the need to have others be wrong, and look at what you are doing to cause or maintain the situation you are judging to be bad. Turn the judgment onto yourself for projecting out your internal wounds. If you are in stage 3, consider whether you can let go of the need to see the situation in terms of right and wrong at all. Through grieving your woundedness, you can forgive yourself entirely for your guilt. From stage 4 you see it simply as a dance, as a stage of our evolution through life, and you will be content to dance it as well as you can.

I will relate a story from my own life which illustrates how the stages look and feel as one moves through them, for our authentic feelings can be a guide to what is going on in us, to what stage we are in. In August 1994 I began a six week, six hundred kilometer solo canoe trip down the Missinaibi River in northern Ontario, as a part of the process (I didn't realize this until later) of initiating myself into manhood. From the first day, I found myself reacting strongly to the presence of litter on the campsites. Now, I am used to litter in city streets, on roadside picnic areas, even in provincial parks. But this was remote wilderness, much of it reached only after days of paddling and portages, some over a mile long. I discovered that my expectations about wilderness campsites needed serious adjustment. "I can't believe it!" I raged. "These people carried full beer cans on their backs for miles, and now can't be bothered to carry out the empties, which weigh less than an ounce each. These folk came all this way to get *away* from civilization, to get into unspoiled wilderness. And here they are, *SPOILING* it!" I was *so* indignant, so righteous, so angrily superior. I felt the ugly pleasure of my rage, of my moral superiority to those cretins, those jerks. Not just men either, I saw with satisfaction; the area around the campsites was filled with carelessly discarded tampons and panty liners. I was really projecting my judgment. Pure stage 2. In my solitude, unconcerned about how I would be seen or how I might affect others, I let my feelings flow more freely than usual. As in an experiential workshop, the intensity of my emotions allowed them to do their work swiftly, and within a few days I found myself moving into another space.

I began to realize that my moral superiority was on fairly shaky ground if I wasn't doing anything about the litter that surrounded me.

"If you're not part of the solution," I told myself, "you're part of the problem." I began getting up an hour earlier each day and picking up litter. If I arrived early at a campsite, I would do it before retiring. I burned combustibles in a campfire and collected the glass and cans in garbage bags. But I was still full of judgment, and I resented my actions. "I wouldn't have to be doing this," I raged, "spoiling my vacation with this shitty work, if it weren't for those inconsiderate louts, those self-centered party animals. They haven't even bothered to bury their own shit and toilet paper!" Still stage 2, but with 'good works' added to bolster my superiority. I was now a politically correct wilderness camper, not only leaving the campsite as I found it, but cleaning up after others as well. I was morally unassailable, sure of my righteous superiority. But I wasn't enjoying my trip. I wasn't happy. These feelings: righteous anger, resentment, and unhappiness are characteristic of stage 2.

Over the next few days, something remarkable happened. I began to identify with the 'louts'. I realized that I too had spread garbage around; I had just done it in different ways. In school, when 'the lads' got together and partied, I wasn't invited. I wanted to be, but I was the nerd, the kid at the top of the class who liked to show how smart he was, and I was ostracized. I developed a compensating, 'better than you' attitude that was pure psychic garbage, and I spread it around. "But what if I *had* been 'one of the lads'," I asked myself for the first time. "Wouldn't I have chucked my litter around just like they, to demonstrate my macho, who-gives-a-shit attitude, so necessary for acceptance?" Instead, from the rejection I fashioned the attitude of a rebel, bolstering my self-esteem by telling myself that I was better than that low-life rabble, the party crowd. My litter may have been psychic rather than literal; it was no less toxic.

I grieved my lost acceptance, the fact that I was not and could never return to be 'one of the lads'. My daily litter pickup and my portaging of the growing weight of non-combustibles became a kind of penance, a balancing of the books, an atonement for the guilt of my unconsciousness. I had reversed the duality, previously in my favor, and now saw myself as guiltier than the litterers, rightfully employed in picking up the garbage. For the first time, I began to enjoy the work. I saw it as a gift, as helping to heal nature and the world through selfless service. My daily ritual became a metaphor for the kind of spiritual healing work I might do in the future. As I combed my fingers through the ashes of past campfires for lumps of glass or metal, I imagined I was combing through the psychic garbage of people's lives, the trash left by them and by others, helping them to sort out what to keep and what to discard. In the dust and dirt of the campfire ashes I found a kind of purpose, a holy goal of restoration and healing of a wounded planet. It felt like worthy work, and I was proud to do it. I had moved into stage 3 of my journey with litter. These feelings: sorrow, sadness, humility – and some joy – are characteristic of stage 3.

I stayed in that space for two or three weeks. Toward the end of my trip, however, my attitude changed again. I realized, looking at the litter scattered through the trees around a campsite, that nature wasn't hurt by this at all. Nature didn't need me to help 'heal' her, she could process the litter her own way, and what did it matter whether it took two hours or two centuries? It was only my sense of aesthetics, of 'rightness' that was offended by the litter; nature was not offended. Nothing was wrong, and nothing needed healing. I became free to choose, without emotional attachment. I chose to continue my daily ritual of picking up the litter, only now it wasn't a duty or a holy calling (I smiled at my arrogance) or even an improvement. It was just what I, an autonomous being, chose to do with my time. Neither good nor bad, neither worthy nor unworthy, no different in moral terms from the choice made by those who tossed the litter in the first place. That too was their free choice, and they were just as free as me. Now, I found myself able to really enjoy the litter ritual, for it was something I was doing for me, as an affirmation of my power of choice, of my spiritual freedom and autonomy. I was choosing to align myself with a direction that seemed harmonious with nature's direction. In that time and for that task, I moved myself into adult spirituality, conscious monism, stage 4. The feelings of stage 4 are peace and joy.

I arrived at the end of my journey down the Missinaibi River at Moosonee, Ontario at the bottom of James Bay in October with an accumulation of sixty pounds of unburnable litter. As I dumped it into the town trash cans, it felt like the completion of a major process, a journey of intellectual, emotional and spiritual growth.

My map of the journey of spiritual growth, from stage 2 stuckness in righteous victimhood, through the grief and growth that comes from taking responsibility for one's life in stage 3, recovery, to the destination of dualistic balance in stage 4, wisdom, is a simple, rational description because that has been my life quest, to discover simple underlying structures and mechanisms to human psychology and society. For a more mythological perspective on the same process, read *The Maiden King; The Reunion of Masculine and Feminine*, by Robert Bly and Marion Woodman.[42] The book is their commentary on a Russian folk tale in which Ivan, a young man who neglected his betrothed, now must seek her at the end of the earth. It is a story of seeking wisdom through descent, through trial and trouble, which is the way that it must be sought. At one point Ivan encounters Baba Yaga, a fierce old wise woman, who asks him, "Are you here by your own free will or by compulsion?" If he answers that he comes by free will, she will eat him. If he answers that he is compelled, she will eat him. In other words, if he remains stuck on either side of the duality, he dies.

This is a wise and powerful message, for stage 2 is indeed a kind of death. There is no change, no growth, no wisdom, no reality there; only illusion ossified into one-sided dogmatism. But Ivan has grown through his journey, and he answers, "Largely of my own free will, and twice as much by compulsion." His answer is both dualistically balanced – and also irreverently irrational. He has learned that wisdom transcends rationality, and the witch lets him live.

Let us summarize what we have covered in this chapter. The development of an individual or a society towards wisdom is fundamentally about the evolution of life meaning. This evolution can be modeled in four stages, by plotting the dimension of monism/dualism against the dimension of unconscious/conscious meaning structures. Dualism, seeing things as good or bad, right or wrong, is characteristic of stages 2 and 3, while stage 4, wisdom, is the experience of conscious non-dualism which is achieved by integrating both sides of many dualistic opposites.

This chapter has focused primarily on how an individual grows towards wisdom. But what of a society, a culture? The next chapter will consider where we are, primarily in North America, on the path towards wisdom, and how individuals can assist the process of collective maturation.

Chapter 7 –Wisdom in Society

"I claim that human mind or human society is not divided into watertight compartments called social, political and religious. All act and react upon one another." – Mahatma Gandhi

"Any lazy or biased fool can have opinions; making judgments is the hard work of responsible and compassionate people." – Lewis B. Smedes

"The opposite of courage in our society is not cowardice, it is conformity." – Rollo May

"The saddest aspect of life right now is that science gathers knowledge faster than society gathers wisdom." – Isaac Asimov

We have covered a lot of ground in six chapters, and introduced a fair amount of theory. I have suggested that wisdom is dualistic balance and outlined a map of the journey towards wisdom, a journey that moves into one side of dualism, then the other side, and finally integrates the two sides. I have argued that the feminist model of gender relations, namely general oppression of women by men, is mistaken, and I have suggested an alternative theory which better fits the facts and simultaneously explains how and why the flawed theory of feminism has been accepted as true by society for fifty years.

At the end of six chapters, we now have a set of ideas, theories that could be the simple foundation of a consensus that we need in the psychosocial realm that is at present so contentious, as we noted in chapter one. There are three basic, interlocking components to this synthesis of ideas: dualistic balance as the basis of human psychological maturity, the map of the four stage personal and societal journey toward that maturity and the special difficulty of stage 2 of that journey where most people are today, and finally the particular way that this stage has manifested in gender relations as codependence. I am hopeful that this simple synthesis of philosophy and meta-psychology could serve as an ecumenical platform, a place where different schools of thought could meet and find common ground.

But even in our relative unconsciousness, we have made genuine movement towards balanced wisdom in some areas of society, and I want in this chapter to look at this progress, for it is something that we can be proud of, and it will give us a sense of what progress in this realm looks and feels like. I also want to point to the areas where we seem to be retarded in this progress, where we remain stuck in a dysfunctional imbalance that is doing great harm.

If dualism is so central and foundational a part of our universe and of our human nature, as I argued in chapter four, then it should show up everywhere, in all aspects of society. Why isn't it more visible to us? There are two reasons. First, we often don't see the balance because of our own dualistic imbalance. We don't see political left and right as dualistic equals, for instance, because we see one as correct and wise and the other as wrong, one as the answer and the other as the problem. We see the opposition but not the equality. Similarly, we don't see the dualistic balance, the moral equality between men and women because we are unbalanced around gender, focused on the innocence of women and the guilt of men. The second reason that it isn't more visible is that dualistic balance is often built into the structure of social institutions, and it takes awareness of the theory to see past the surface content to the balanced symmetry of the underlying structure.

For instance, consider democracy. At the basic, structural level, democracy is a synthesis of two dualistically opposite approaches to government decision making – the feminine mode of consensus, and the masculine mode of hierarchy. At its most basic, democracy gives *hierarchical* power (government authority) to the biggest social *consensus* (winning party or coalition). Because of this synthesis of archetypally opposite modes, it is structurally superior to, wiser than the one-sided alternatives of simple hierarchy government (dictatorship or monarchy) or full consensus government (government by referendum, which has been too inefficient to be seriously contemplated, but which modern technology could soon make possible). Even while governing, the winning party or coalition must accept the presence in the decision chamber of the opposition parties, who are naturally motivated to seek and publicize any flaws in proposed legislation. This structural balance of opposites promotes wise government – even while (take note) it often feels hideously inefficient and quite wrong to the individuals being challenged.

Another example is our criminal courts. The basic split into prosecution and defense is a pure dualistic structure. One side argues strenuously and exclusively for innocence, for acquittal, while the other side argues vigorously for guilt, conviction. The intention of the dualistic structure is to hold the question open throughout the trial – right up until the end, new evidence could sway the verdict in a different direction. This is, structurally, a wise process, and it is a major social accomplishment that it has been put so solidly into place and entrenched by law and custom (presumption of innocence, right to cross-examine one's accuser, right to judgment by one's peers, etc.). I feel proud that our ancestors had the wisdom to turn away from being ruled by the strong, one-sided feelings that usually flow around a crime (wish for vengeance, fear of reprisal, need to defend accused loved ones, etc.) and put in place a process that explicitly gives time and space for reflection and sober second thought, and that is dedicated to finding the truth about what happened and dealing with it justly. Even when people bring strongly one-sided perceptions to the trial arena, the fact that they must submit to a balanced structure greatly improves the chances of a wise outcome.

It is where stakes are highest and feelings are most extreme that we most need the wisdom of dualistic balance, and a criminal trial is a good example of that. For the very worst, most desperately challenging human issues, such as genocide or widespread and longstanding societal abuse, we have created what is arguably the wisest mainstream process on the planet, a process which is explicitly dualistically balanced and which is known as "truth and reconciliation." There have been truth and reconciliation processes in South Africa to deal with the aftermath of apartheid, in Rwanda after the genocide, and in Canada to come to terms with the abuses of the residential school system for Aboriginal Canadians. I will explore this last project in some detail in order to illustrate how it works.

From the 1870s to 1996, 150,000 aboriginal children were forcibly taken from their families across Canada and sent to residential schools, where they were alienated from their community, language and culture and where many endured physical or sexual abuse as well. The Indian Residential Schools Truth and Reconciliation Commission (TRC) was established on June 1, 2008 and on June 11 of that year the Prime Minister of Canada made a Statement of Apology[43] to former students of Indian Residential Schools, on behalf of the Government of Canada.

Here is the Introduction from the Mandate of the Truth and Reconciliation Commission of Canada.

> "There is an emerging and compelling desire to put the events of the past behind us so that we can work towards a stronger and healthier future. The truth telling and reconciliation process as part of an overall holistic and comprehensive response to the Indian Residential School legacy is a sincere indication and acknowledgement of the injustices and harms experienced by Aboriginal people and the need for continued healing. This is a profound commitment to establishing new relationships embedded in mutual recognition and respect that will forge a brighter future. The truth of our common experiences will help set our spirits free and pave the way to reconciliation."[44]

The power of this process is its inherent dualistic balance, in that it integrates both truth and reconciliation. Both are required for genuine healing. It is easy to stay stuck on truth telling as accusation and victimhood and never get to forgiveness. It is easy to pretend to a pseudo reconciliation that papers over the issues without acknowledging their import. Telling the truth about abuse makes reconciliation difficult, and wanting a good relationship makes telling the truth difficult. Integrating these dualistic opposites, owning up to the harm that was done and genuinely moving beyond it into a restoration of good relationship, that is the stuff of real human maturity, and I am proud that Canada has tried to meet this challenge fully and honestly. Indeed, the balanced nature of this process was explicitly recognized in the Commission's mandate. The following is from the FAQ page of their website"

> "Will the focus of the TRC [Truth and Reconciliation Commission] be on Truth or Reconciliation? The TRC's mandate activities focus on both truth and reconciliation. Truth will be addressed through statement gathering, research and public education. Reconciliation is an overall objective of the TRC. The Commission views reconciliation as an on-going individual and

> collective process that will require participation from all those affected by the IRS [Indian Residential Schools] experience. We will move towards achieving reconciliation through activities such as public education and engagement, commemoration and recommendations to the parties." [45]

I love that we live in a world where such aspirations can take form. The structure built by this Truth and Reconciliation Commission was genuinely balanced, truly wise. To be sure, this is no guarantee of success, since structure is not content; people bring their own baggage to the process, and many remain stuck on one side or another, failing to reach truth or failing to reconcile. Such a process asks a lot of us, it asks us to rise above our one-sided stuckness in self-righteous victimhood and blame, or in "let's just all get along" or "get over it" denial of the injuries. Many fail to rise to the challenge. But asking for and expecting the best of each other within a structure that is itself dualistically balanced is the very best that we can do.

Even the ubiquitous *Roberts Rules of Order* [46] demonstrates the wisdom of dualistic balance. Robert's Rules work because they balance the rights of the individual or the minority against the rights of the organization or the majority, an example of balance in the dualities of self/other and one/many. In his philosophy book *Lila; An Inquiry Into Morals*, Robert M. Pirsig summed up this balance in two sentences. "No minority has a right to block a majority from conducting the legal business of the organization. No majority has a right to prevent a minority from peacefully attempting to become a majority." [47]

All of these are examples of structural balance, dualistic wisdom built into the structure of major, mainstream social institutions. This is a genuine accomplishment of which we can be justly proud. But structure can only take us so far; what of content? What examples can we find of balanced wisdom in action in society? What does that look and feel like, how do we recognize it?

There are a multitude of examples toward the fringes of society, such as the books from which I have quoted (*The Road Less Travelled* by M. Scott Peck[48] or *Why Can't We Be Good?* by Jacob Needleman[49]) which demonstrate and even teach dualistically balanced wisdom, though they don't usually call it that. But everything can be found at society's fringes, including truly crazy ideas; this is no measure of our general progress toward enlightenment. What about mainstream culture; widely popular literature, art, movies, tv programs, websites, etc.? The news is good – there *are* wise, balanced cultural products that are also widely popular. Let's look at a few, to see what distinguishes them from the rest.

Perhaps the most basic duality in literature is the moral dimension, the good/bad continuum. Unbalanced cultural products divide this realm into idealized good guys and bad guys, heroes and villains, and feed our prejudices by encouraging us to identify with the good guys and feel righteously superior to the bad guys. But wise, balanced creations will transcend this dualism, showing us the humanity of the villain and the failings of the hero, who might even be the same person. Perhaps the iconic example of this is what is probably the most famous play in the world, *Hamlet* by William Shakespeare.

Hamlet, the Prince of Denmark, pretty much destroys his own court by his vacillation, his inability to come to clarity and take strong action when his father is assassinated. He is simultaneously the hero and the villain; we see and identify with his aspirations, his struggle to do the right thing, and at the same time we empathize with his weakness, his fears, his paralyzing doubts. Shakespeare shows us Hamlet's humanity, and it is this that makes the play truly great. We see that terrible consequences can flow even from good intentions and earnest struggle to do right, and this is a vital, human lesson. Prince Hamlet is simultaneously good and bad, strong and weak, just and unjust, like most of us, and in seeing this illustrated in dramatic fashion we are moved a little towards self-acceptance and acceptance of others – in short, towards wisdom.

Some modern and well-received productions also display this balanced wisdom. I have mentioned the 1995 movie *Dead Man Walking*, starring Shawn Penn and Susan Sarandon, which boldly asks us to empathize with a convicted criminal, a death row inmate guilty of rape and murder – a remarkable cinematic achievement of human wisdom. I have been fascinated by the career of Clint Eastwood, who started by starring in some of the most unbalanced, good guy/bad guy movies of the time (*Dirty Harry*) but moved on later to direct and produce some of the best empathic, balanced movies I have seen (*A Perfect World, Letters from Iwo Jima*).

Contrast these movies with the more common moral idealization of James Cameron's 2009 film *Avatar*. In *Avatar* the aliens are the good guys and they are pure victims: innocent, passionate, beautiful, articulate. They are idealized goodness. The humans are perfect bad guys: corrupt, greedy, deceitful, violent and insensitive. They have no redeeming features at all. The movie is a battle between them, and we are supposed to feel happy and vindicated when the good guys win and the bad guys are defeated.

What I felt was disappointment at the moral infancy of the plot, at the abbreviation of characters into one-dimensional stereotypes designed to serve as projection screens for our adulation or contempt. Yet *Avatar* is, as I write in 2014, the highest earning film of all time in the USA and Canada. Clearly a lot of people still find this kind of stage 2, black and white moral oversimplification satisfying.

There are other dualistic dimensions where we could look for balanced wisdom in society. Indeed, the progress of society, though slow, is trending toward greater wisdom on a lot of different fronts. Consider, for example, some recent social trends. The advance of democracy around the world represents a movement towards the balancing of centralized, hierarchical power and distributed, social power. Similarly, the growing acceptance of multiculturalism is an advance in the balance between us and them, an expansion of our ability to empathize with others who are culturally different to our tribe. The overall trend is positive, though very slow.

Once we become aware of the conceptual framework of dualistic balancing as progress towards wisdom, we see examples of it everywhere. Indeed, the concept of wisdom as dualistic balance and the four stage model of human progress toward it can bring a useful clarity and insight to understanding and evaluating the degree of health or wisdom of almost any human endeavor. Let's consider an example. Recently I discovered the acapella singing group Pentatonix, and in researching their background I downloaded Season 3 (2011) of *The Sing Off*, a US television show in 12 episodes of a musical competition between 16 acapella groups for a $200,000 grand prize and a recording contract – a competition that Pentatonix ultimately won. The format of the show is that each week every group creates and performs an arrangement from a particular musical genre. Their performances are ranked by three resident judges and at the end of each episode the lowest ranked group is eliminated from the competition.

One thing that struck me about the show was that as the eliminated group left the auditorium for the last time, singing their swan song, members of the remaining groups were often moved to tears. I think that this is remarkable. Despite the fact that these groups were fiercely competitive with each other for the grand prize (this was clear from the interviews they gave before each performance), they could still empathize deeply with the pain of the loser. Their applause for the performances of their competitors was both sincere and enthusiastic. This is a wonderful example of dualistic balance, where the intensity of competition did not damage the empathy that the groups felt for each other or their ability to appreciate each other's excellence. These singers did not fall into the us-and-them dualistic polarization along the self/other dimension. Because of this, I am sure, the experience was enhanced for all, winner and losers alike.

How was this balance, this transcendence of us-and-them, achieved in the show? Part of the answer, I am sure, is that the beginning of every episode featured a mass acapella number with all of the (remaining) groups singing together and sharing the limelight to present a common spectacle. I suspect that rehearsing and cooperating to learn coordinated dance steps, lyrics and harmonies helped greatly in having the groups come together, get to know each other and empathize with each other's struggles. The groups were in it together, as well as individually competitive – they lived and experienced both sides of the cooperation/competition duality.

I think that for a number of dualistic dimensions we are already quite advanced towards wisdom. I mentioned in chapter two that most of us already get the ease/effort duality, that both are vital components of a well lived life. Some others, such as leader/follower are not far behind – we have probably all enjoyed musical productions or musical jamming, where first one person then another steps in front, shifting easily from follower to leader and back again as someone else takes the lead. Most of the business world understands this duality – every manager in a business hierarchy alternates between the roles of leader of his own group and follower of his superiors.

Others, such as accountability/compassion, subjective/objective and self/other are more challenging, and probably none of us have achieved full dualistic balance across the entire range of dualisms. Perhaps the moral dimension of good guy/bad guy and think/feel are the most challenging of all.

Some areas or subcultures within society seem to be more advanced or delayed. The field of politics seems particularly retarded. We have observed that gender politics remains mired in men-as-oppressors/women-as-victims imbalance. Just an hour ago, as I was writing this chapter, I had a telephone call from a local man who told me he was running for the City Council seat for my district. I asked him if the incumbent was running again, and his answer was awkward. It became clear when I enquired further that he was refusing to say the current Councillor's name – that's how the game is played, he told me. I told him that that was infantile, and that he had lost my vote with that statement. This is an example of an immature structure, where the 'rules of the game' of politics are wedded to a good guy/bad guy structure, where it's bad form to ever say anything good about your opponent, or even mention his name. Nobody is helped by this distortion of reality and good manners.

In the field of politics, gender politics is probably the most unbalanced, as we have noted. This imbalance is made more pernicious by the fact that it is denied behind a public cover story of gender balance and equality. To give an illustrative example of what is happening in gender politics, and of how the black-and-white, stage 2 nature of gender ideology operates in society and why actions based on this understanding cannot work well, I will describe and analyze in detail a Canadian program for men who have been judged guilty of "domestic violence" as it is currently understood in terms of men assaulting women.

The "Confronting Abusive Beliefs" program was developed in 1995 by Family Services of Greater Vancouver under their Family Violence Intervention Program, and subsequently recommended by Family Service Canada for use by family service centers across the country. I am aware that this program is now twenty years old: I am choosing to analyze it rather than a more recently developed program simply because it did us the service of publishing its tenets. More modern programs usually keep their formal policies hidden, but the basic assumptions, the stage 2 perspectives, are the same. Also, several future chapters of this book will focus specifically on feminism, and part of what I want to show is that it hasn't changed significantly in all of the fifty years since its rise to prominence in the 1960s. I will thus select information and examples from throughout that period to build my case.

The foundational principles or tenets of the program are as follows: [50]

1. 100% belief in women's account of abuse.

2. 100% responsibility of men for abuse.

3. Abuse is an act of choice based on ideas of entitlement and privilege.

4. Abuse is defined by impact, and understanding impact is necessary for meaningful change. Questions about impact are therefore a central reference point.

5. Worker positions self as advocate for women's safety. Questions about woman's experience and perspective are therefore central, and questions about what woman might see as evidence of safety are also central.

6. Questions about privilege/status are more relevant than psychological experience/accounts.

7. Work with women for their safety:

     - provide information nights

     - provide ongoing confidential risk assessment

     - workers must be responsive to women's questions about risk and safety.

8. Central assessment question is: "How does it work for a woman's safety to have a man in the group?" rather than "Will he respond to treatment?" or "Will he change?"

9. Confidentiality policy: We will exchange information about men with women and/or police and/or service providers based on our best judgment of what is safe. Therefore, the contract is: "Are you prepared to work with us, with the understanding that we will not agree to any exceptions or disclaimers about confidentiality when women and children's safety is at risk?" Contacts with women are

always confidential; information exchange is for the purposes of facilitating risk assessment for those experiencing impact, namely, women and children.

10. Move from self-focus to other-focus, and ask men: "So, this is your account/experience/view, what would your partner's be?"

11. Intention is irrelevant: impact is key.

12. Deconstruct explanations for mutuality/equality of responsibility/abusiveness by examining impact.

Before analyzing these points, let me insert some context by elaborating the characteristics of stage 2 thinking.

Stage 2 is an immature and unsophisticated stage of moral development. Since the underlying motive is to reassure oneself that one is blameless, it produces very black-and-white, polarized moral structures where all guilt is projected onto the other party. In this regard, it is similar to the moral simplicity of fairy tales like *Snow White and the Seven Dwarfs, Cinderella, Sleeping Beauty*, and *Little Red Riding Hood*. The issues of good and evil in such tales are clear and simple, separated 100% into individuals; Red Riding Hood, Snow White and the Prince (good); the evil Queen and the wolf (evil). There is no moral complexity or ambiguity. And when in the end good triumphs over evil, one feels real satisfaction, a sense that all is right with the world. We know that fairy tales are fantasy, but if the world isn't like this, our feelings seem to tell us, it should be.

Fairy tales, in their moral idealization of life, leave out a lot that is significant. For one thing, they give no explanation for the origin of good or evil in the lives of their characters. Snow White and Cinderella are just 'naturally' good, with a kind of cheerful, brave and simple innocence that, like their beauty, shows no sign of being the result of any effort on their part. The good male characters, like *Sleeping Beauty*'s Prince or the woodcutter in *Red Riding Hood*, are more potent (though less central) characters in that they seem to have some strength in the face of evil – the Prince in his perseverance, the wood cutter in his swift action to kill the wolf. But, again, the story gives no hint of how this moral strength was acquired.

For the evil characters, their evil seems to be either as natural as is the contrasting goodness (e.g., the wolf), or to have some genesis which can serve as the justification for our moral judgment (vanity for the evil Queen of *Snow White*, envy in the case of Cinderella's ugly sisters). But, again, there is no hint in the story of the characters having waged a battle against evil and lost, or of having any remaining vestige of goodness in them. No, they are entirely, willfully and irredeemably committed to the forces of darkness, and the tale usually ends with either their death or their banishment.

In short, these stories are grossly oversimplified as representations of the real nature of men and women, or of good and evil. Their picture of morality is highly abbreviated, hugely attenuated. They capture the immature moral understanding of spiritual stage 2 and entirely ignore or deny the more complex, nuanced and accurate perspectives that one achieves in stage 3 and especially in stage 4.

There is real danger when we take this idealized world of fairy tale and attempt to overlay its polarized moral separation onto the real world and the people in it. We can get, if we do this, very clear, unambiguous, black-and-white moral structures which have the virtue of great simplicity. This is attractive. I confess that it is attractive to me, and that I am continually on my guard against its seductive fascination. Albert Einstein, who gave us the power of the atom with the simple equation $E=MC^2$, cautioned us; "Everything should be made as simple as possible, *but not simpler*." [emphasis added] When we separate people in the real world into good and evil groups, into innocent victims and guilty perpetrators, we do harm to everyone. A primary focus of this book is to encourage awareness of this danger, to teach how to recognize it and to guard against it. In that endeavor, our greatest asset is the ability to think critically and through careful analysis to see clearly – even (especially) when our feelings are still wedded to the black and white moral polarization. Let's look at the principles of this program point by point, and see what critical analysis can reveal to us.

1. 100% belief in women's account of abuse. The assumption seems to be that women, or at least abused women, cannot tell a lie, or even have a one-sided, self-serving perspective, and that a man, if he says anything that contradicts the account of the woman, is lying. For the man, this isn't "innocent till proven guilty." It isn't even "guilty till proven innocent." It is "guilty by definition, with no admissible defense." For the woman, it is "innocent, absolutely and without question – no admissible prosecution."

2. 100% responsibility of men for abuse. Here the operating assumption is clearly that responsibility is a zero-sum game (i.e., for every increment of responsibility that she accepts, he becomes an increment less responsible). This is not how responsibility works, although it is a common error. Consider an argument proposed by Camille Paglia.[51] If you drive to New York City and leave your car keys on the hood of your car, then a thief who steals your car should be caught and punished. But at the same time, the police have a right to say to you, "You stupid idiot, what were you thinking?" Your actions in leaving the car keys in plain sight do not lessen the responsibility of the thief; he or she is still 100% responsible for theft. But you are not free of responsibility if your actions contributed to what happened. This is the complexity of the real world that feminists and many others often deny and avoid dealing with.

A better model of responsibility, and quite appropriate for an intimate relationship, is that it is like a joint bank account. If I have a joint account with you, the money doesn't belong 50% to you and 50% to me, or any other set of numbers that add up to 100. No, because I can spend 100% of it at any time, and so can you. It all belongs to me, and it all belongs to you. If this seems more complex than you would like, well, I agree with you, but I don't believe that any good comes from substituting something simpler in order to avoid the complexity.

So, to return to point 2, the fundamental error here is in assuming that if the woman looks at the ways that she might have contributed to the abuse, then this is "blaming the victim" and she is somehow "letting him off the hook". Not so, he remains 100% responsible for his actions. But if she has no responsibility at all, contributed nothing to the situation, then she also has no power to affect it and is totally dependent on him to change. No wonder she is afraid. This program is keeping her entirely powerless, and him entirely powerful, in order to preserve her moral innocence. Is it worth it?

3. Abuse is an act of choice based on ideas of entitlement and privilege. Here is the basis for the moral judgment of the man; he is entirely a free agent, and reprehensible because he wants to dominate and subordinate his wife. Like "rape is an act of power and not of sex", this is a cornerstone of modern feminism, repeated endlessly in order to keep the complexity of real life at bay. Is it true? Yes – and no. Yes, in some circumstances, for some men, to some extent. No, in other circumstances, for some men, to some extent. What do we hear if we listen to the men? They tell of feeling powerless, of feeling compelled, of feeling provoked and attacked and controlled. Are these stories true? Yes – and no. One thing is very clear and unambiguous, however. When a particular side of a polarity has gained sway and the other side is being silenced, then what is needed is to elevate what is not being heard. Oppression does exist, and it can take many forms. Hitler, Stalin, McCarthy, all justified (sincerely, though mistakenly) their oppressive actions in the name of freedom and social progress.

4. Abuse is defined by impact and understanding impact is necessary for meaningful change. What this says is first that whether, and the extent to which, a man has abused a woman is determined by (and only by) how abused the woman *feels* (impact). If she feels abused, then that is it, she has been abused. What if the man feels abused? It doesn't count, see point 9. Secondly, it says that he will change only by understanding her pain, her fears and her sense of the situation. He is to suppress his own feelings and concerns as invalid (see point 10) and irrelevant (point 11) and focus on her perceptions alone.

This is the kind of attention that parents try to give to children. This kind of absolute, unconditional and unidirectional empathy is the passive pole of self-sacrificing parental love. (The other pole is that of loving challenge; "You can do better, go for it"). Is it appropriate in an intimate relationship between adult spouses? Again, occasionally, at those times when one party is most broken and the other is strong. But as a form, as a mandate, and in one direction only (the man to the woman), it infantilizes her and overextends him. It does not move either of them toward a healthy relationship of equals.

5. Worker positions self as advocate for women's safety. The woman needs an advocate, and her safety is important. However, once again, the man has no advocate. This is ostensibly a program for *him,* yet it is clear that *she* is the client. Even people charged with heinous crimes are given legal advocates in court. How powerful do we think this man is, if even giving him an advocate would make him too strong?

6. Questions about privilege/status are more relevant than psychological experience/accounts. This is really a strengthening of point 3. Men's stories and experience are subordinated to the "fact" of their privilege. This privilege is absolute, and completely independent of circumstance. It depends only on his gender as a man, and there is not a man in Canada that does not have it, at all times, in relation to his wife. It doesn't matter whether she is wealthier than he, or more successful, or healthier, or older, or more articulate, or stronger, has more friends or self esteem. Whether he experiences this privilege in any meaningful way at all is irrelevant; he has it, and she does not. This is, in fact, the most blatant sexism.

7. Work with women for their safety. This is important, and needs to be attended to. Given the extreme prejudice against men displayed by this program, and the absolute unwillingness to listen at all to their issues, then I suspect that the safety issues are very real. I cannot imagine how men who have already shown that they have a problem with violence, would be other than further shamed, humiliated and 'wound up' by a program that is so completely hostile to them. What are they expected to do with their anger? Where is the safety, the understanding and empathy that would allow them to speak about it and be heard? This is an example of how the policies pursued from a stage 2 perspective are always ineffective, and usually worsen the problem that is being addressed.

8. Central assessment question is: "How does it work for a woman's safety to have a man in the group?" rather than "Will he respond to treatment?" or "Will he change?" With the focus entirely on the woman's issues and story, and an unwillingness to listen empathically to his experience, I fail to see how a realistic assessment of his progress or potential for further abuse can be made.

9. Confidentiality policy: We will exchange information about men with women and/or police and/or service providers based on our best judgment of what is safe. Contacts with women are always confidential; information exchange is for the purposes of facilitating risk assessment for those experiencing impact, namely, women and children. Another black and white policy; the men in this program have no rights, not even the right to confidentiality.

Correspondingly, the women have all the rights and no responsibility at all. It is worth noting that in a court of law; even a condemned criminal preserves the right to confidentiality with their lawyer.

10. *Move from self-focus to other-focus, and ask men: "So, this is your account/experience/view, what would your partner's be?"* This is an elaboration of point 4. His account, if listened to at all, is dismissed as of no value, he is immediately directed to focus on her experience. Again, there is no corresponding expectation placed upon her.

11. Intention is irrelevant: impact is key. It doesn't matter what the man was trying to do; if she didn't like it, it was abuse. If you brought home flowers to your wife as a gesture of your love and goodwill, and she decides that it was patronizing or manipulative, then that is what it was, and you have abused her again. You have no recourse, since her experience (impact) is the only one that matters.

12. Deconstruct explanations for mutuality/equality of responsibility/ abusiveness by examining impact. Here is where the argument that I made in my discussion of point 2 above is dismissed. There is no mutuality or equality of responsibility, since there is no mutuality of impact. There is no mutuality of impact, since only the woman's experience of pain or abuse counts. It doesn't matter what you, as a man, are experiencing, you cannot be abused, and she cannot be responsible. Note that the policy doesn't say "Explore explanations . . ." No, the man's explanations are to be *deconstructed*, since they have no validity anyway. I guess that if the man commits suicide, they will see that as his being so attached to his denial structures that he chose "the easy way out." The idea that he might have been in pain and that they might have had something to do with that, will not occur to them.

When I first received this program description, I became angry. I wrote to Maggie Feitz, Chief Executive Officer of Family Service Canada, quoting the program tenets, and asking for her comment on the bias and sexism it represented. She replied,

> "Family Services of Greater Vancouver is indeed a member
> agency of Family Services Canada. I am aware of the program
> "Confronting Abusive Beliefs" and in fact, Family Service

> Canada has encouraged this program's use in service organizations across Canada. This particular program may appear to be extreme to you. However, the men this program is intended for are men who have severely abused women – some have been convicted by the courts. When such abuse occur[s], extreme positions must be taken to stop abuse and ensure the safety of women and children. You can quote me on this." [52]

I felt like writing to my Member of Parliament, going and picketing Family Service Canada, or shouting about it over the internet. (I even did some of the last.) But I know where that energy leads. It leads to the kind of stage 2 one-sidedness that I want to lead away from. It leads to a reinforcement of the very thing that I think I am fighting against.

The policy itself is evidence of what I am saying. There is no evidence that women are more truthful than men in describing domestic violence, yet the policy says that women must always be believed, and men disbelieved. Such a policy is deeply and blatantly sexist. Yet it has been developed and implemented under the banner of feminism, which claims (and believes) itself to be founded on the elimination of sexism. Furthermore, it is highly abusive toward men, yet it purports to be about ending abuse. That is how far wrong we can go when we allow stage 2 judgment to drive our politics, when we go solely by our feelings about what is right action and avoid (indeed, disqualify) any thoughtful reflection. When we avoid the complexity of the real world and substitute the black-and-white simplicity of a fairy tale world of pure innocents and evil villains, our errors can grow to the size of the evil we abhor.

We considered how some social institutions, like democracy and law courts, have dualistic balance built into their structure. This program, in contrast, has dualistic *imbalance* built in at the structural level. We see here how perniciously an imbalance in feeling, in this case an attenuated empathy with the pain of men and an exaggerated empathy with the pain of women, operates to make such a sexist structure yet feel right to us. It feels right because when we listen to women tell of their experience of domestic violence; we empathize with what they say as long as they speak about their victimhood, as they usually will. We believe them. When men speak of their feelings of victimhood in the same situation, what they say feels wrong to us; it feels like denial of accountability. We disbelieve the men unless they speak of their guilt, their responsibility. The sexism, the dualistic imbalance, the lack of wisdom is in *us*.

Why are we so dysfunctional, so unwise, so screwed up around gender – much more than in any other area? I think it goes back to our codependence, and that codependence goes back to biology. Because gender is so intimately associated with sex and reproduction, it has been the subject of evolutionary pressure for millions of years. Evolution doesn't care about why we do things, the reasons we tell ourselves, it just needs the behavior to support reproductive success. The simplest way to get people to repeat certain behaviors that are evolutionarily successful is to have those behaviors feel right, feel good to us. That is why sex is physically pleasurable, of course. That is why the whole mating and child raising process has been hung around with strong feelings about what is right behavior, feelings that our minds have invested with cultural cover stories. The people, in short, who were most appropriately 'addicted' to the other gender, in the culturally approved ways, were the most evolutionarily successful.

This 'baggage' is built into our minds now, reinforced by evolution over thousands of generations in which the less successful (freer from compulsion, more rational about sex and child raising) people were weeded out because they had fewer children. That addictive pattern of what feels right to us around gender roles is what I have labeled the "gender codependent matrix." The matrix provides the framework and the context within which modern gender politics is playing out. It explains, for instance, why feminism wants power for women without accountability – accountability doesn't feel right; that's where the feeling of victimhood comes in to let women off the hook, because what worked for evolutionary success for millions of years was that women felt good about being dependent on their husbands and men in general, because they needed protection by those men. It explains why men feel good about offering that protection. It explains why feminism has been able to create a moral polarization around gender, because evolution gave women moral power over men in order to balance men's physical power over women. So now this moral polarization – bluntly, men bad/women good – runs entirely through the structure of feminism, beneath the cover story that it is about gender equality.

Feminism is not even remotely about equality. Consider that feminism has brought two new words into current usage. One is a female word, feminism, and it stands for everything good, our vision for the future, the way the world should be. The other is a male word, patriarchy, and it stands for everything bad about the way the world has been in the past and still is today. The moral polarization is absolute, and it is foundational.

It's difficult to get past these feelings because they are so compelling, but it's possible, and some have done it. They do it principally by thinking critically about the whole cover story, about what feels right and feels wrong to them. They do it, in general, by growing their dualistic wisdom towards stage 4 as described in the previous chapter.

Feminism, as an expression of sexist imbalance, has become deeply harmful to our society – we will explore just how harmful in future chapters. It is also a movement of great ideals and much energy, and in need of healing itself, rather than judgment. But healing begins with diagnosis, and that is how my description here is intended, not as moral judgment but as a diagnosis of a social disease. It is a disease that is not our fault, but is our responsibility. It is my hope that this book may play a part in that healing.

Compare the moral polarization we see in feminist programs with the balanced gender treatment of the 2008-2012 TV series *Flashpoint*, in my opinion the very best TV drama series that Canada has ever produced. Set in Toronto, Ontario, it is the fictional story of a police tactical response unit. In each episode, the team deals with a different emergency, from hostage takings to bomb threats to murder/suicide attempts. There is violence, but the violence is always a last resort, interpreted as a failure of the team to de-escalate the situation. Best of all, we see what a mature balance between compassion and accountability looks like in practice, in extreme situations. Whether a hostage taker or a bomber is male or female makes no difference in the show, both are treated the same. In each case, there is an earnest search for background, for information that would explain why they have made such extreme choices. We are shown the powerlessness, the desperation of criminals, as well as their accountability for their actions. They are cared about and respected, not just judged. This is compassion *and* accountability.

This is so good, so balanced that it usually moves me to tears. It is so amazing to me to see a mainstream, popular TV show with this level of mature wisdom, that I usually find myself weeping with joy and gratitude by the end of the show. It is truly beautiful to see people operating at this level. This is what stage 4 looks like. I urge you to acquire the show and watch it yourself. It is truly unique; I know of no other TV production which even comes close to demonstrating this level of human maturity.

So where are we at with all of this? Clearly there is a mainstream market for dualistically balanced cultural productions, and has been for several hundred years. There is a fair amount wisdom in society around some of the dualistic dimensions, which I judge to mean that a significant minority of people have moved into stages 3 and 4, but there remains also a great deal of stage 2 moral judgment which supports the large number of simplistic good-guy/bad guy productions that are still the most common media and political format. And there remain issues and areas, such as gender politics, that we are dreadfully confused about, where we are hypocritical and deluded and dysfunctional and where what we are doing is at best unhelpful and at worst horribly harmful.

I encourage you to look for these dualistic imbalances in society, and to help to balance them. Most of my conservative friends, for instance, think that I am a liberal because when we discuss politics I seek to present the other side to their conservative political position. I also spend time affirming the (partial) correctness of their conservative ideas, but what they remember are my arguments against those positions. Similarly, most of my liberal friends think that I am a conservative, for the parallel reason. In gender politics I follow a similar strategy. With feminists I argue against the one-sided feminist position by pointing to the features that they are denying, the power of women and the powerlessness of men. But with angry men's rights advocates I can often be found emphasizing the validity of women's issues and suggesting that lashing out in anger isn't the answer – even to injustice.

For years I felt lonely in such circumstances; always misunderstood, always misperceived and misjudged. That was me holding on to stage 2 self-righteousness; I was stuck in victimhood. The essence of stage 4 is that it has come to terms with reality. If you find yourself resenting any aspect of reality, any aspect at all, then you haven't finished the grief work that is a central task of stage 3. Grief takes time; it isn't finished until it's finished. When it is finished and you have moved fully into stage 4, I have no more advice to offer you. You are a spiritual adult, you know what to do with your life, and you have the strength to do it. The world will be blessed by your life and your work.

Chapter 8 – Extending the Theory

"There is no wisdom without love." – N. Sri Ram

"Honesty is the first chapter in the book of wisdom." – Thomas Jefferson

"The words of truth are always paradoxical." – Lao Tzu

I have suggested that the concepts and models that I have introduced in this book might comprise the beginning of a formal foundation for the realm of psychosocial science. If that is true, then eventually a whole edifice of structured thought – definitions, theories and concepts – will be constructed on this foundation, providing formal definitions for all of the key aspects of human relating. A key achievement of this system will be a clear and cogent understanding of wisdom, the nature of human conscious enlightenment. In this chapter, I want to offer a glimpse of what this might look like, by showing how the concepts of dualistic balancing and four stage human development can be extended to provide useful definitions and descriptions for some common concepts that are often seen as beyond formal definition.

Let's start with love and truth. I have suggested that love is the highest or deepest value of the feminine archetype, and that truth is the corresponding foundational value of the masculine. If wisdom is indeed built on a dualistic balance of opposites, then these fundamental qualities, in their fully developed, wise form, must also be dualistic. Of course, this means that their definitions will be dualistic, since a good definition must capture all significant dimensions of a phenomenon.

What is the common conception of love today? It is that love is unconditional care and acceptance. We call it unconditional love. This is indeed a part of love, but only the feminine pole, the feminine side of the duality. We have explored the idea that following a great upsurge in feminine energy in the 1960s, our conception of ideal human behavior moved towards the feminine and remains there today. We now prefer cooperation over competition, consensus over hierarchy, empowerment over authority, peace over conflict, etc.

No, that isn't strong enough; we don't just prefer the feminine modalities, we judge them as superior, the right way to be. Under the influence of the feminine archetype, unconditional love feels like what love *should* be, and *all* it should be.

But something is missing. If only unconditional care and acceptance is loving, how do we do masculine things like setting boundaries, maintaining standards and judging behavior? Are these things now all to be seen as unloving? Consider what M. Scott Peck says on the matter. "The path of love is a dynamic balance of opposites, a painful creative tension of uncertainties, a difficult tightrope between extreme but easier courses of action. Consider the raising of a child. To reject all its misbehavior is unloving. To tolerate all its misbehavior is unloving. We must somehow be both tolerant and intolerant, accepting and demanding, strict and flexible. An almost godlike compassion is required." [53]

Clearly, a full and complete definition of love must somehow include both of these contradictory aspects. Here is my definition of love. First, the feminine part: *I affirm and accept you totally, exactly the way you are.* Then the masculine part: *I challenge you to become all that you can be.* As always in duality, these two poles seem to be in tension, to contradict each other. Love is that monistic quality that represents the seamless integration of these dualistic opposite poles.

In practice, of course, one must choose one or the other pole at any one moment, since *behavior* is confined to form. Suppose your daughter comes home from school one day with a 'C' on her report card. How do you respond? If you are able to come from a space of love, you consider what this means for her. Is a C in this subject a great accomplishment, a stretch for her? In that case, praise her for her accomplishment. Does it represent a failure of effort on her part? Then challenging her to do better is the loving thing to do. Is she feeling like a failure because of the mark? Reassure her of her unconditional worth to you, that the failure doesn't change how you love her. And so on.

We always have to walk the line between opposites, and no formula can help us much. Staying in either pole, either extreme, is bound to be wrong. The *evidence* of love is in the effort made to sustain this tension, in the work done on the other's behalf to discern what right action in the moment is. This work is always required, since the right decision cannot be reduced to a formula. The *capacity* for love is in the ability you have (or don't have) to remove yourself (e.g., your ego need to have an intelligent child, or a hardworking child, or to be *seen* as a good parent, etc.) from the picture, and make your action entirely about her or his needs, support or development. This capacity and ability is, of course, partly the result of being truly loved by others in the first place. However, we are not victims of our destiny, but can choose to love ourselves and thus grow our own capacity to love.

Love, as the highest value of the feminine archetype, is relational because that is the focus of that archetype. So the definition takes the form of "I accept you," "I challenge you," etc. Truth, on the other hand, as the highest value of the masculine archetype, is not relational but absolute. It is dualistic in that there are two distinct and independent fields of truth – the inner or subjective world where the goal is authenticity, and the outer or objective world where the goal is accuracy. As with love, we can approach and discover genuine truth in either field only to the extent that we can remove ourselves, our ego needs, our biases and prejudices from the picture and surrender to what *is*. As we discussed in chapters one and three, this is difficult; our feelings, especially, tend to overwhelm our ability to perceive either our own motivations or events in the outer world. Because we fear, usually without conscious awareness, that the truth will convict us, we reinterpret what we experience internally and what we perceive externally in ways that reassure us, usually by making them confirm whatever we already believe. This is known as confirmation bias, and numerous studies have affirmed its power and presence in the human psyche.

We see that both the expression of real love and the search for real truth are difficult; they involve the application of disciplined effort or courage, or both – which is why they are both still quite rare in the world. A story from feudal Japan will illustrate what I mean. A Zen monk is working in a field when he is approached by a warrior. The warrior asks, "Explain to me what is heaven and what is hell." The monk regards him for a moment, then says, "Get away from me, you barbarian, and stop wasting my time." The warrior is furious. He has humbled himself and asked a real question, seeking knowledge, and the monk has rejected him and insulted him as well. He draws his sword and raises it high to kill the monk, and the monk says quietly, "That is hell!" The warrior pauses, and realizes that the monk, a stranger, has actually risked his life in order to give a real answer, a true and full answer to his question. Instantly his emotion changes and he feels deep respect and love for the monk. The monk says, "And that's heaven."

In the story, the monk chooses to take a major personal risk for the sake of giving a deeply true answer to the warrior. He accepts and respects the warrior in his question, the feminine pole, and also challenges him to rise above his momentary anger and see truth, the masculine pole. Note that the initial form of the response from the monk is highly disrespectful of the warrior – but that is just surface form. The underlying strategy is deeply respectful, as becomes apparent to the warrior after a moment of reflection. This non-alignment of surface form with deeper essence, with truth, is very common in the world, although it more usually takes the opposite form of outward respect covering over a lack of love in truth, in essence. As I described in chapter one, the task of the truth seeker is to look past the surface forms in order to discover the hidden truth below. When enough people are engaged in this journey, I think that we will see a real consensus emerge about what is true in the area of human society and culture, a genuine 'scientific' (meaning submitted to critical thinking, subordinated to genuine reality testing) understanding of the phenomena of individual and collective human behavior.

My definition of truth, like that of love, is dualistically split – in this case between subjective and objective truth. What is truth really about? It is, essentially, conformance with reality. And so a formal definition is that truth is conformance with subjective and objective reality. In the last fifty years, under the influence of the feminine archetype ascendant, we have seen the feminine, subjective pole of truth grow dominant in various ways. Post-modernism, a new, unbalanced, archetypally feminine branch of philosophy, has suggested that there is no unique, objective truth, but only culturally privileged stories and viewpoints. The New Age has argued that objective reality is actually an artifact of collective subjectivity, a consensual reality. Currently popular ideas like the Law of

Attraction[x] are founded in this notion of the subordination of the objective to the subjective. Once we understand the inherent equality of both poles of a duality and the operation of one-sided cultural biases such as the current dominance of the feminine, we can readily see through such cultural stories to the truth.

The highest value of the feminine is love. The highest value of the masculine is truth. Are they in conflict, or do they somehow support each other, do they integrate seamlessly? How do we marry them in practice? If we keep them clear, if we don't get them tangled together, they do indeed integrate in non-contradictory ways.

Let's start with the love side, since feminine energy is more prominent, more readily accessed these days. We are familiar with the phrase "unconditional love". What we mean by it is that we can and should love each other no matter what. Specifically, no matter what we do. Healthy parents know that no matter what their child might do, even if she breaks the law and ends up in prison, even if he fails at everything he attempts, this will not diminish their love for their children or their acceptance as part of the family. This is what we mean by unconditional love.

Notice, however, that this isn't unconditional forgiveness. There are, and should be, consequences for bad behavior, for failure. A son who spends everything he has on gambling will still be loved, but will remain responsible for his debts and won't be trusted with money.

The masculine side, as always, has a parallel structure. Let's introduce the phrase "unconditional truth." What does it mean? If I make a commitment, for instance to meet someone at a particular time, and I fail to be there at that time, then I have failed my commitment. People try to mitigate the feeling of failure by making excuses: I really tried, I was sick, it wasn't my fault. These may all be true, but they aren't relevant to the *truth* of the failure. The truth is unconditional; you failed to do what you said you would do. Even someone who dies trying to get to a scheduled rendezvous still fails to meet their commitment. Lack of fault does not mean lack of

---

[x] The Law of Attraction is the belief that outcomes such as personal success in the outer world depend entirely and solely on one's attitude and state of mind, that they are direct consequences of subjective states.

responsibility. The party to whom I made the commitment is let down, and it remains my responsibility.

As in the feminine case, the variability, the conditionality shows up in the consequences. Failure after genuine best efforts can usually be simply forgiven without consequences. Failure due to lack of discipline, lack of effort or lack of care is more serious and should result in a loss of credibility. This variability, this need for discretion, is why we have law courts to consider evidence. The judgment is (or should be) about truth; was the crime committed or not? Unconditional. The sentence, however, takes into account mitigating circumstances – attitudes, efforts, stresses, intentions, etc.

This unconditional responsibility as a masculine value is why there is a tradition that the captain goes down with the ship. The foundering of the vessel may have nothing to do with him, it may not be his fault even in the slightest, but it is his responsibility because he had the ultimate authority. In these times when we have shamed most things masculine as abusive, it is well to reflect on the beauty, the selflessness of this masculine code of honor.

With access in our lives to real love and real truth, we can become powerful in the world, wise in both insight and motivation. From this place, what might we do in the world? Here is an essay (slightly edited for this book) that I wrote some years ago to explore this issue.

How do you heal the world?

I wish that I knew the answer to that question. I wish I had the formula, the solution, the path forward, and that I was ready to step out confidently and lead. I wish that people were ready to really hear, that I had more power and influence, that there was a quicker, less painful path to walk towards our vision of gender equality. I wish . . .

I wish that I could let go of my wishes for reality to be different than it is. Wishes like these are romantic fantasies. My mother used to say, "If wishes were horses, beggars would ride." My wishes are the way that I avoid really living in the world, really accepting what is true and real and objective and do-able. They are my personal insanity.

It is ten years now since I realized that, like most of the people in the world, I am insane for much of the time. Every time I think that the world 'should' be different than it is, every time I conclude that someone 'should' behave differently, that something – anything at all – is 'wrong' in the world, I continue and confirm my insanity. I invent a picture of the world, a different world than the real one, and give it more legitimacy, more worth, than what actually *is*. I tell myself that my invented world is superior in that it is, I conclude, the way the real world 'should' be. What arrogance. What insanity! If I have a problem with what *is*, then *I* *am the one who has a problem.*

The fact that this (stage 2) insanity is virtually universal, that almost all of us live this deluded, judgmental existence for virtually all of our lives, only heightens the tragedy.

Most people cannot even imagine life without such beliefs. "If I didn't think there was anything wrong in the world, then why would I work to change anything?" I am frequently asked. This question presumes a very bleak landscape of human existence, where every action is driven by the need to relieve some distress, some wrongness or some feared consequence. We work in order to avoid starvation or the shame of social assistance, we watch TV to relieve the stress of boredom or loneliness, and we write letters to MPs to express our outrage (i.e., distress) at something we find unjust. And, let us be honest, we fight for our kids after a divorce partly in order to avoid the distress of losing them from our lives. We tell ourselves, and we believe, that we fight because we love them and want what's best for them. But this may be a cover story: what is also true is that we have made our children a part of our identity, and to lose them feels like losing a part of ourselves, and our need to avoid the pain of this is what drives us.

This is not wrong! This bleak landscape, where most people spend most of their lives, simply is. It's a fact. We start by accepting it. Then we say, *"What do I want?"*

You see, that's the missing ingredient. Most of us have forgotten what we *want* to do with our lives, since we've become so busy doing what we have to do. Remember when you were a child? You played games, then, not to avoid the distress of boredom, not to achieve some objective, but for their own sake, for the simple pleasure of playing, because *that was what you wanted to do.* It was a causeless want, not derived from trying to fix some problem, reach some goal, find some answer. No, it sprang full grown of itself, a pure creative act of *wanting to do this thing.*

I have spent years working to recover that state of mind, because from that place we can live lives of power and fulfillment. Paradoxically, by first accepting the world just as it is, we become powerful agents to change the world. Why? Because the act of acceptance is the first act of love. The second act of love is the act of *vision*, of knowing what we *want* for the beloved. Love is the most powerful change agent there is.

But remember, love is always about the *other*, not about us. It is not about avoiding our own distress. Do you remember the Bible story that is told to illustrate the wisdom of Solomon? Two women came before the King, each claiming the same child as her own. The King said, "Let the child be divided in two, and each woman be given a half." But one woman threw herself down before King Solomon and said, "No, Your Majesty, let the child live and I will renounce my claim; he can go to the other woman." In questioning the King's announced decision, this woman was risking her own life. For what? In order to *lose* what she wanted; to *lose* the child to the other woman. Clearly, she was acting out of love; she would risk her life *and* suffer the distress of the loss of the child, in order to keep him alive.

The wise King had found a way to discover not, as is frequently presumed, which woman was the child's mother, but which woman really loved – rather than needed – the child. The King gave the child to that woman.

Let me summarize. It is insane to wish that the world were different than it is, or to think that it 'should' be different. Sanity begins with accepting the world exactly as it is, and discovering our vision, what we *want* to do in the world. What we *want* might well involve trying to change the world. The difference will be that we are trying to change the world from love, rather than needing it to change for our own comfort, to avoid some personal distress. A result of that difference will be that, recognizing at some level that we really are coming from love, the world will be more open to the changes we wish to make.

The summary of the summary? The world changes when we do.[54]

Grief is Relationship Addiction

What is it like to love in this way, free of need? I do not claim to be in this place often, but I hold it as an ideal to move towards. One surprising consequence is that there would be no grief at the loss of a loved one. That sounds horrible; to most of us it sounds like not caring at all. We see grief as the evidence of love. But if we follow the theory carefully, we discover that grief is simply the evidence of need, the withdrawal symptoms of relationship addiction. What do I mean? Consider a thought experiment. The telephone rings and it is a lottery company. They tell you that yours is the winning ticket, you have won the first prize of ten million dollars. They congratulate you and hang up. You are so excited. Immediately you begin making plans for what you will do with the money, maybe a world trip, maybe quit your job, maybe buy a new house, make a major donation to charity, whatever. An hour later, the phone rings again. The lottery company apologizes sincerely to you; they made a mistake. It wasn't your ticket that won after all.

How do you feel? I am sure that you agree with me that you would feel a real sense of loss. It would feel devastating for a while. You would have to go through a grief process as you adjusted to the loss of the $10 million.

But wait a moment. What have you lost, really? You never had the $10 million. Your situation now is exactly the same as it was an hour ago, before you received the first telephone call. You are no worse off, not a cent, than you were then. So what are you grieving? The answer is clear if you think about it. You are grieving the loss of an imagined future. Over the course of just one hour, you imagined a particular kind of future for yourself and attached yourself emotionally to that vision. Now you have to let it all go, and it hurts in exact measure to the pleasure you gave yourself in imagining it.

That's what grief is, and that's all it is, the letting go of an imagined future. After all, when a loved one dies, what has changed? Not the past – that's all exactly the same. All that has changed is the imagined future with that person. But the future is always unknowable, undetermined. By imagining a certain future, and attaching ourselves to it emotionally, taking pleasure from it, we set ourselves up for grief if that future should fail to come to pass. If we were able to live in the moment, enjoying the presence of our loved ones for every moment that they are with us, but not building up expectations for the future, then we would not have anything to grieve if they should leave us. Our grief expresses our need for them, not our love of them. The difference between need and love is this: both need and love enjoy the presence of their object, but only need suffers its absence. Need is another name for addiction.

I am not making grief wrong here. If we have attached ourselves to an imagined future, then grieving is exactly what we need to do when that future changes. Since we almost always do make such attachments, grieving is healthy. The form of love that I am describing, love without need, is very advanced and few in the world are capable of it. I describe it for you because it is helpful to have a picture, a theory to guide our own growth work, to inspire us in our recovery process. Certainly I have found it helpful in my own life. Usually, our own love is mixed with need, and our actions with others are partly about them and partly about serving our own needs. Again, this isn't wrong – it is simply where we are at, and we start by accepting it. Then we set a goal for ourselves – what do we want? That is where the theory comes in; it can help us to set meaningful goals and give us genuine measures of our progress, as I described for the four stage model of spiritual growth in chapter six. Be kind to yourself; the journey of life is difficult enough without beating up on yourself as well.

Masculine and Feminine Modes of Human Healing

Another area that is dualistic at the deepest level is that of human healing. If you accept that just about everyone is codependent in their life, then that means that they have a cover story that is false-to-fact but that they defend because it is their way of feeling ok about themselves. It is usually a story that has them be righteously innocent, one of the good guys in the way that they have constructed the world. For feminists, for instance, their cover story has them be victims of male oppressors. That lets them off the hook for the state of the world; because they had no power, therefore they have no guilt. You can see that it is a defense against guilt when you suggest any tiny degree of accountability, and they react angrily against you.

So what does one do about this? How does one promote healing in others? Here's what I've figured out. I'm still learning and practicing the skills, but the theory is in place.

There are two ways that people in denial can discover, or be shown the truth. One way, what I call the feminine mode of healing, is to make an environment that is so safe, so unthreatening that they feel able to be honest and less defended, to search for and share the truth about themselves voluntarily. This is the basic theory behind virtually all modern therapy, personal growth groups and workshops, etc. It works. As with all feminine modalities, it's consensual.

The feminine mode of healing works through relaxing defenses by making the environment safe and unthreatening, thus encouraging truth to be shared and discovered.

The other way, the masculine mode of healing, is exactly opposite (what a surprise!). It works by making an environment that is so intense that it overwhelms a person's defenses. Truth comes out because the intensity, the complexity is too much to be managed. A cover story is actually quite difficult to maintain, and if it is attacked in a way that a person isn't able to cope with in real time, then they inadvertently show their true face – to others and to themselves, and sometimes they even let themselves see it.

This masculine mode isn't necessarily consensual, it's interventionist. In today's culture, with the elevation of the feminine and the shadowing of the masculine, we don't recognize it often because to most observers it just looks like fighting, like regular ego-driven making people wrong. But it can be motivated by love and managed with skill, and in that case it can lead to real healing, in a different way than the feminine mode.

Let's look at some extreme examples first, to get clear on the concept. Do you remember the movie *Good Will Hunting*? Will Hunting was a young man who was a mathematical genius. A university professor who discovers him also sees that he is very disturbed psychologically, and tries to help him by taking him to therapists. But Hunting is so intelligent and intuitive that he can quickly spot the therapists' issues, and he embarrasses or challenges them in ways that they can't deal with.

Then he is taken to the therapist played by Robin Williams. He spots that Williams' unhealed issue is around his dead wife, and challenges him there. Williams grabs Hunting and pushes him up against a wall, saying, "We won't go there." That was a masculine intervention, and it worked. Hunting was challenged back at an even higher level of intensity, and out of that encounter was built the respect that led to a successful therapeutic process.

Now, what Williams did meets the formal definition of abuse, of assault. You can't do that stuff – or if you do you risk jail. That's what a masculine process can look like; sometimes it has to be sacrificial, you have to take the risk for the sake of breaking through a defended psyche. No, that's not right, you don't have to take the risk, you have the choice to take that risk, and acting from love for the other, sometimes you might make that choice.

Another example. Imagine a military boot camp. A sergeant sees that he has a bully in his group of recruits, a hotshot who thinks he's tough and intimidates the other guys. The sergeant provokes the bully, calls him out – "If you're so tough, come and take me on." He humiliates the bully by beating him in a fair fight in front of all of the other recruits. The bully's cover story, his image of a tough guy is in tatters. Something has to change. Truth has been made evident, he's not as tough as he thought, and everyone knows it. How will he accommodate? Perhaps he will learn a little humility, grow up a bit. If the sergeant is coming from love, from genuine concern for the bully and can speak to him afterward in a compassionate way, then that outcome is assisted. But it took the masculine intervention to create the opening, to overwhelm the bully's defenses and break open his cover story.

These are fairly intense or extreme examples of a masculine intervention – most exercises of the masculine mode of healing are less dramatic. Simply challenging someone on abusive behavior, holding them accountable for their actions or their attitudes are more common examples. Of course, even when such an intervention comes from love, there is no guarantee that the person will acknowledge their error. People are free to respond as they choose. But there are no guarantees in the feminine mode of healing either;

probably the vast majority of people who attend growth workshops or therapeutic sessions use their participation to reinforce their cover story rather than to heal. They tell themselves and others how hard they are working on themselves, with the therapy sessions as their evidence, as a means of avoiding doing any real work or learning anything upsetting about themselves. This is just how we are, we human beings, we will often avoid the pain of real recovery, perhaps for a lifetime, while reassuring ourselves with a cover story that can even be about how much we are growing. We're pretty tricky, that's for sure.

Ideally, the feminine and masculine modes of healing would be employed together, married as it were. The masculine intervention would create an opening, perhaps, and the feminine mode would provide safety and support for the individual to work through the issues brought forward. Or the feminine would be employed first, to create a safe environment in which a stress process, a masculine intervention, would be employed to surface and uncover a person's triggers and shadow issues. This is my vision of how wise, advanced psychosocial healing work might be done. But at present, with the cultural dominance of the feminine archetype and our consequent fear and judgment of the masculine mode, we are mainly limited to feminine processes in therapy. Feminine processes work well for some problems, not so well for others.

I find the analogy of physical healing useful to comprehend this distinction. There are some types of illnesses and injuries for which what comes naturally works quite well. If we have a laceration on our body, for instance, then natural behaviors driven by the pain of the wound – protecting the wound from further injury, keeping it clean and covered – will usually lead to full healing. This is analogous to the feminine mode, in which the safe and unthreatening environment is like the clean and protected wound. Sharing our fears and self-judgments in such an environment leads naturally to healing of those wounds, the way the body naturally heals a laceration.

But some injuries do not respond well to this approach. A broken bone, for instance, if left alone and protected to heal naturally, will typically set in a distorted and crippled fashion. Such an injury requires the bone to be straightened and splinted, an intervention that depends on correct knowledge and good technique. This is analogous to the masculine mode of healing, which depends for success on knowledge and skill (think of the drill sergeant's skill at fighting). Confronting someone about their behavior is a process which depends on skill in debating, judgment about where and how hard to push, ability to read the other's reactions, to spot what the ego defenses are concealing. This knowledge and skill, like that of a surgeon, takes time and discipline to master.

Unfortunately, contemporary culture has elevated the feminine mode of healing, along with all things feminine, and denigrated the masculine mode as abuse. Staying with the physical medicine analogy, it's as if we had lost the ability to see the difference between a skilled surgeon wielding a scalpel to save lives, and a sadistic murderer wielding a knife to torture and kill. In our demonization of the masculine, we would see it all as violent abuse.

To be fair, there are areas of society where we can still make this distinction, where we still see the value of masculine modalities. The military and the police are two institutions where the value of intrusive, non-consensual interaction is still recognized. When it comes to dealing with the threat of physical violence, from other states or from criminals, we recognize the need for intrusive processes. But in the rest of society – in the corporate world, for instance – we have passed laws making behaviors that make a woman feel uncomfortable into acts of sexual harassment, criminal acts. Her subjective feelings are taken as defining the external world as a "hostile work environment" – another example of dualistic imbalance, the subjective dominating the objective that we discussed in chapter two.

How do we deal with this social imbalance? How do we practice wise, balanced human interactions when the masculine mode of healing has been so shadowed, even criminalized in large parts of contemporary society? This situation calls for a part of the masculine archetype that we can call the spiritual warrior.

The Spiritual Warrior
One aspect or component of the masculine archetype is the Warrior. I know that a lot of women and men are uncomfortable with the warrior, rightly believing that we have too much violence in the

world. It is, however, the diminishment, the *loss* of the positive warrior archetype in our culture that is behind the widespread abuse and violence. As always when we are in the grip of our own shadow, the cure lies in the very place we don't want to look. Of course it does – it was by fearing to look there that we created our shadow in the first place. We must resurrect and embrace the warrior part of us.

Some years ago, in a workshop built around the videotapes *Bly and Woodman on Men and Women*, I found myself living what is for me a new aspect of the warrior archetype. I am familiar, as are most men, with the endurance side of the warrior. This is the part we use to face the daily work world, and perhaps also to face the frequent lack of appreciation for our role as providers. We accept that being understood and appreciated is not necessary to get the job done, and we soldier on.

This endurance aspect of the warrior archetype is approved of in our culture. However, we are dreadfully afraid of another part – the willingness to take forceful action against that which is wrong. I experienced this fear in myself during the workshop, when I began speaking forcefully and without qualification about what I saw happening. In response to a man who said, "I have forgiven my mother" I asked, "Have you allowed yourself to feel your anger at her?" He replied, "No, it wouldn't be appropriate; she was doing the best she could." I said without hesitation, "You haven't forgiven her; you have just excused her and suppressed your anger." I didn't say "In my opinion …" or "Check this out and see if it fits …" or other such qualifiers. There was a gasp around the room at my effrontery, but no one challenged me.

Because of the aggressiveness of my confrontation, let me confess that I was trembling. I have seen myself as someone who does not invade the space of others with unrequested judgments about them. Such behavior has always seemed arrogant and abusive – *as it can be!* What I am now realizing is that it isn't *necessarily* abusive; it can be loving. When it is, it is an example of the masculine form of love – loving challenge – most lacking and most desperately needed in our society today.

In contemporary culture we have embraced only the feminine, "I affirm and accept you exactly as you are" form as our ideal of love, calling it "unconditional love." We are suspicious of, even hostile to the masculine form of love, which is about challenge, discrimination and development toward wholeness. But only through the integrity of embracing both forms of love and the tension between them can we achieve personal wholeness and effectively move ourselves and society forward.

Either form alone, without the balance provided by the other, becomes abusive, contrary to spiritual growth. The addictive, compulsive society we live in today can be seen as the result of an overemphasis on the feminine "I accept you totally" and a lack of the masculine "I challenge you." Acceptance without challenge, without stretch, leads to compulsive consumption, addiction, and self-centeredness. It keeps us children, unconsciously focused on our own needs. The growing awareness that most of us are "adult children" (96% in US/Canada according to John Bradshaw) testifies to this.

Robert Bly has noticed this lack of the warrior in men.

> "When I look out at my audiences, perhaps half the young males are what I'd call soft. They're lovely, valuable people – I like them – and they're not interested in harming the earth or starting wars or working for corporations. There's something favorable toward life in their whole general mood and style of living. But something's wrong. There's not much energy in them. They are life-preserving but not exactly life-giving." [55]

Later in the same interview, Bly tells of leading a conference of forty young men in New Mexico for ten days.

> "Often the younger males would begin to talk and within five minutes they would be weeping. The amount of grief and anguish in the younger males was astounding! The river was deep. . . . They had learned to be receptive, and it wasn't enough to carry their marriages. In every relationship something fierce is needed once in a while, both the man and the woman need to have it." [56]

This fierceness is an aspect of the warrior that we fear and therefore repress in our contemporary culture.

In ancient societies – and even today – the warrior is expected to remain strong during peacetime (the endurance aspect) and to intervene forcefully against evil when necessary. In this latter role, the warrior *steps outside of law and convention.* Warriors do not besiege a castle or overthrow a tyrant by operating within the law – they do so *because legal means will not work, or have failed to work.* In our modern, technological, comfort-oriented, pain-avoiding society we have lost sight of the need for this forceful action and have become afraid of force in any form. We have become fearful of masculine strength, mistaking it for violation.

I am not saying that all force is strength; it certainly can be abusive. The loving force of the true warrior is motivated by protection or advancement of society, and is exercised only after rigorous self-examination to ensure spiritual purity and clarity of vision, disciplined and surrendered to a stringent ethical code. Let no one misunderstand me – this is not easy! It requires as much dedication to truth and personal growth as does the feminine pole we call unconditional love, with the additional difficulty that the recipient of loving challenge (similar to what Gandhi called 'soul force') rarely feels thankful at the time. In particular, it requires a genuine freedom from emotional compulsion at the moment of action, as illustrated by a story from feudal Japan.

An overlord had been assassinated, and his samurai had tracked and captured his master's murderer. The samurai drew his sword to execute the man, and at that moment the murderer spat in his face. The samurai, being a true warrior, sheathed his sword and walked away. Why? Because he became *angry.*

No doubt he would return and complete the execution later when he was spiritually grounded again, but he knew that to kill in anger would be to commit a personal act under the compulsion of emotion rather than one surrendered to truth and justice and love. It is the loss in our culture of this tradition of warrior spiritual strength that has led to the current level of abuse – our acts of force and violence are virtually all personal acts born of anger or fear. They are acts of powerlessness, even though they seem powerful to the victim. A *solution* to this issue will only be found in a growth in the real power of both men and women.

A further example. In the workshop mentioned earlier a mother spoke of her fears for her twenty-year-old son, who had just bought a powerful motorcycle. She felt he was not mature enough to ride it responsibly, and had spoken to him but been dismissed with a "Yeah, Mom . . ." that indicated he felt he knew best. She ended by saying "What can I do? It's his money, his life."

I replied that one couldn't know without much more information, but if she carefully examined her soul and determined that her fears were genuinely appropriate (and not, for example, motivated by a false sense of "He's just a child") then she might, from the warrior part of her, take an axe and chop his motorcycle to pieces – and give her son the purchase price for the bike from her own pocket. Her action might result in her son realizing "Wow, my mother really cares about me, and is very serious about this." (Of course, it might not have this result, nothing is certain since people's freedom is absolute.)

I am not insisting that this is right action in every case, or even in this case; only that it is an option. The horror or outrage that we may feel in considering this action speaks to the loss of the warrior in our society, to our sad situation in fearing all forceful action. Note also that right action does not seek to but is willing to transcend law and convention (the mother risks being charged and convicted of willful property damage), a truth that was known and practiced by Emerson, Gandhi and Martin Luther-King, all of whom spent time in jail. The willingness to suffer these consequences, where necessary, for love of truth and of the other, is part of the code of the warrior. Again, I am not arguing for abandonment of law – only that occasionally right action goes beyond or outside what is legal or conventional. It takes the rigorous spiritual discipline of the warrior to discern the need and proceed with confidence and willingly accept the consequences.

I have chosen an extreme example to make my case clearly. It is rare that such circumstances arise. Yet we seem to have lost respect for even the smallest actions of confrontation and intervention, seeing them all as *failures* of love or cooperation. It has become an article of faith that one person can *never* know what is right for another. Yet if we think about it for a moment, we know that this is not so. Who among us cannot remember a time when we were confused, and others knew better than we what we should do?

This is an aspect of the lost masculine in our society that goes beyond the lack of a masculine role model for sons. Both sons and daughters need first the feminine form of love – total validation – to build a secure identity and self-esteem, *and then* the augmenting of that with the masculine form of love – stretch, test, challenge and set limits, to generate strength, discipline and purpose. We have discredited that masculine contribution during the past fifty years. It is not gone, just repressed into our shadow side, where it takes on the dark energy of sudden violence, spouse and child abuse and the cowardly forms of warfare such as terrorism and assassination.

In the wisdom of myth, warriors are those who create a new order out of the old, by destroying what is no longer working in favor of a new vision. They depose the tyrant, defeat the evil forces and so allow the good in society to create a new system of greater health and justice. If ever there was a time when such energy was needed, it is now! Immersed, enmeshed as we are in a polluting, compulsive, consumptive, spiritually barren culture, only the clarity, strength and spiritual discipline of the true warrior energy can save us.

The foe is not some external enemy, but our own weakness, our own addictive natures, the compulsive system in which we live, and the dark source of these forces – the hole in our psyches that is filled with shame. These are strong enemies indeed. To overcome them will require courage, discipline, strength and sacrifice, the very best that we can become and aspire to. We begin by acknowledging our fear of our own strength, of the warrior energy within us. That fear is appropriate, and leads us toward the profound spiritual work that must be done to qualify us to act with power.

We continue by ceasing to shame those who still act out of fear or anger. We attribute consequences to their actions, all the way up to loss of liberty, but we cease having them be *wrong*. They have just chosen actions which we will not permit, as individuals or as a society. This is not easy work; in order to dismantle the part of us that wants to guilt and shame others, we have to look deep inside ourselves to the place where we feel shamed and unworthy, and heal that place. Only then are we able to act with confidence, from a spiritually grounded place, as loving and powerful warriors of the spirit.

I want to own here that I am by no means very good at this myself. I frequently struggle in frustration and confusion, and slip into judgment of those who don't see things my way. As a leader in the movement for gender equality, I sometimes find myself called to speak when I don't feel grounded, don't feel that I have my "shit together." Probably, in the real world, this is far more common than it is to act from a spiritually secure and grounded serenity. At least, it is for me. At such times, I try to own what is going on for me, to confess my confusion and self-judgment in my own advocacy.

In this chapter, we have covered a lot of theory about wisdom as dualistic balance, and how to work on ourselves in order to become strong enough, wise enough to begin to work effectively for social change. In the next chapter we will examine a particular gender issue, probably the most difficult and contentious one there is, and see if we can find our way to a just and practical solution that is fair to all. To do it, we will certainly need access to the warrior part of ourselves.

Chapter 9 – A Practical Exercise in Balanced Wisdom

> "He who learns must suffer.
> And even in our sleep pain that cannot forget,
> Falls drop by drop upon the heart,
> And in our own despair, against our will,
> Comes wisdom to us by the awful grace of God." – Aeschylus ,
> Greek playwright, c. 525/524 BC – c. 456/455 BC

> It is impossible to struggle for civil rights, equal rights for blacks, without including whites. Because equal rights, fair play, justice, are all like the air: we all have it, or none of us has it. That is the truth of it. – Maya Angelou

We have now developed a set of basic theories of human psychosocial development, and looked at where we are in society in terms of our progress towards mature wisdom. We have played with the ideas a little, seeing how they might extend to form a framework of formal definitions for concepts of human behavior and relating. I want to pause in this chapter and work with these theories, to explore what it looks and feels like to use them in a practical application. I have chosen, intentionally, probably the thorniest and most difficult gender issue facing contemporary society, the question of abortion.

This is a central gender issue, and one that calls us to wisdom since the stakes are so high. Just about everyone has a strong opinion about this question, so if we can see how it might be explored honestly and reasonably, with mature, balanced wisdom, that will be a significant accomplishment. What would wise people do, in approaching such a major, high stakes decision? How would they resolve the issues and deal with each other? How can we set up a structure so that people who aren't so wise still might be able to work through to a worthy solution, or at least a better one than without the structure?

It is difficult to reach towards wisdom. Much must be unlearned and let go of, including things that may feel like foundations of one's identity. That is the reason that I chose the quote from Aeschylus to start this chapter, which begins "He who learns must suffer." Carl Jung said, "The foundation of all mental illness is the avoidance of legitimate suffering." The path to wisdom, in anything, proceeds through suffering. The suffering is because as we approach balanced wisdom, we also discover that we have been wrong, one-sided and unbalanced about important issues for most of our life, and this hurts. It is hard to take in. We discover that we must give up coercive or manipulative strategies that have been foundational for us in the past.

Jesus said, "The truth will set you free," and that's true, but that comes later – he didn't mention that first the truth will seem to convict you. The fact that you later discover that you can and should forgive yourself, and that then you really do experience freedom, doesn't reduce the initial pain of the conviction. Indeed, it is that pain that the whole denial system is designed to avoid. The *purpose* of dualistic one-sidedness is the avoidance of pain.

What happens if we don't do this work? Well, nothing very remarkable – our lives stay stuck and ineffective in terms of meaning, wisdom, or having our major decisions work out for us, but we don't notice the lack, or more precisely, we don't recognize our problems as flowing directly from our own choices. Let's consider, as an example, how we would likely work with gender issues from the various stages of spiritual growth. We have seen that feminism is built on a mistaken idea, the notion that the history of gender relations is one of general oppression of women by men, supported by the dualistic imbalance of compassion without accountability for women and accountability without compassion for men. This is because feminism is itself coming from stage 2 on the journey of spiritual growth, where women are believed to be victims and only women's issues are felt to be important. Women's issues *are* real, just as men's are, but feminist analysis privileges women's issues as uniquely important because men are perceived as having the power that matters. How would someone seek to address the imbalance of feminism, to correct this error from the different stages of spiritual growth? (As a memory aid, here is the map of the four stages again.)

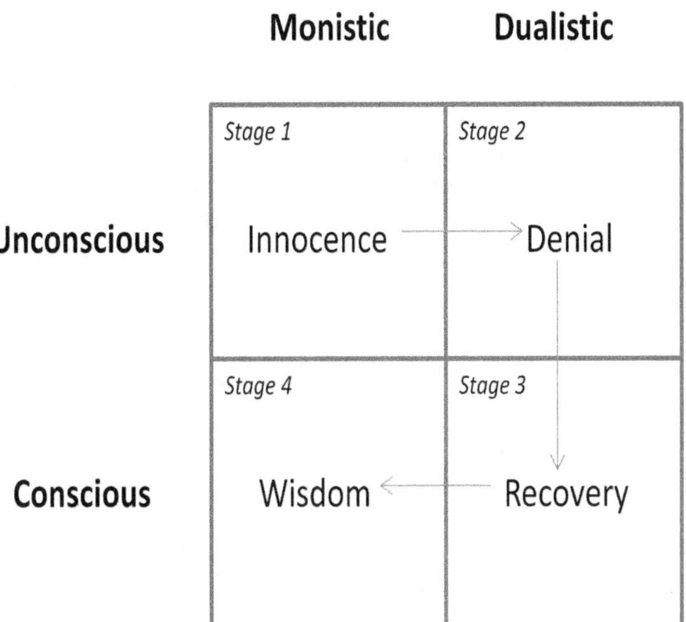

From stage 2, denial, one would hold feminists accountable for this error, but angrily, without empathy for their situation. This is pretty much what Men's Rights Advocates have been doing for years now, and the internet is full of "dialogs" between MRAs and feminists that consist entirely of accusations and counter-accusations, with no meeting of minds. There *can* be no meeting of minds between two groups that are both in stage 2, but with opposite views of the world. In stage 2, one has little empathy to spare for others, since it is entirely applied in favor of one's 'in' group. Indeed, from stage 2 one is convinced that it is *inappropriate* to feel any empathy for the 'out' group, since one has convicted them in one's mind. Each party is righteously certain that any progress depends on a change in the *other* party, while being sure that no change is needed on their own part. This is clearly a stuck situation.

Things improve considerably if one of the parties moves to stage 3, recovery. In stage 3, one looks at one's own responsibility for creating the problems that one experiences, and seeks opportunities to discover what is true and to change oneself if indicated. Such a person can benefit from dialog with just about anyone, since every dialog is an opportunity to discover and explore new facts and information. In fact, stage 2 and stage 3 can be in positive dialog with each other for a while, since their worldviews can match quite well – the stage 2 thinks that all the problems are the fault of the other, and the stage 3 is exploring that very possibility. However, once the stage 3 has learned what they can from the stage 2, there is little juice left. The stage 3 is seeking to discover truth, but the stage 2 is focused on maintaining a false cover story, and so the dialog tends to end fairly quickly. Stage two is stuck and static, but stage three is growing and simply moves on.

Stage 4 is where things get really interesting. At stage 4 a person has integrated and come to peace with the partial truths of the earlier stages and can empathize with all of them, so dialog is not a problem for them with anyone. A stage 4 can be of great assistance to a stage 3, assisting them to grow their understanding like a parent with a child. However, a stage 2 is typically so stuck and so defended that even stage 4 wisdom makes little – or slow – impression on their worldview.

It is clear that people who are largely in stage 2, with perceptions that are both false-to-fact in important ways and highly resistant to reason, present the major difficulty for any negotiation. For example, both of the better-known positions on abortion, called pro-life and pro-choice by their adherents, are dualistically one-sided, stage 2, partial solutions that simply privilege the needs or desires of one party over all the others. Pro-choice advocates believe that the mother's wishes should trump everything else; while pro-life adherents believe that the fetus' right to life overwhelms every other consideration. These completely one-sided positions yet feel exactly right, and powerfully important, to those who hold them. Good solutions, on the other hand, attempt strenuously to address the needs of all. But how does one pursue them?

I am going to present two different answers to that question, aimed at different circumstances. Each will be an answer to the question, how should a decision be made whether or not to abort a child. This is a tough question, probably the most difficult issue in gender politics, since the stakes are high and the parties are often highly polarized. My first answer will address the question of legal rights and responsibilities, what the law would say if it were just and gender balanced. The second will address the moral question of how to make a particular decision with a particular mother and father.

It took me years to work out what I think is a genuinely gender equal analysis of rights and responsibilities around abortion. Gender equality is difficult to figure in this case because the biology is highly unequal – only women get pregnant. When I did finally work it out, I published my thinking in an internet blog post, which I chose to address to women. I have reproduced that post below.

"I want to speak to women, to all women, in this post. It's about abortion. A great injustice has been perpetrated in your name and on your behalf. I hope that you will wish to correct it.

What is this injustice? The cry we hear from women on the question of abortion is usually, "My body, my choice." This slogan is designed to silence men on the issue. I want to go on record, here and now, as repudiating this campaign. Let me walk you through the argument.

"My body, my choice" says that men have no right to a place at the table when abortion is considered. This is wrong. If I am the father of a child that you are carrying, then I have a right to be part of the process that leads to a decision whether or not to abort. My right is based on three facts.

1. The child is as much mine as yours, for we both contributed equal amounts of genetic material to make it.

2. Except for the matter of the pregnancy, the future that is being contemplated is my future just as much as it is your future; the decisions made affect me hugely just as they affect you.

3. I care as much about the question of children, of whether I want or don't want to be a parent, as you do.

I acknowledge that women's bodies and not men's are the delivery vehicle by means of which children come into the world. But owning the delivery vehicle does not mean that you own the product it carries, as any commercial delivery driver knows. The "My body, my choice" slogan is designed to deny and obscure this vital distinction.

"My body, my choice" is a policy which disenfranchises fathers, steals their right to have a say in what happens to their offspring. There was a time when women were legally disenfranchised in that only men had the vote. Suffragettes campaigned for the vote for women; men considered the question and agreed with them. Men passed the legislation which gave women the vote.

Universal suffrage feels right to us these days, but let's be clear about how big a cultural change this was at the time. The culture of the time was that men were the heads of households, a role that involved authority and also duty, obligation. Men could have said, with perfect sincerity, "My household, my choice" in response to women's claims about disenfranchisement. That was undoubtedly what felt right to many of them at the time. But men didn't just go by their feelings or their fears about loss of power and control. They thought about the question, and they shared power because it was right, because it was just.

I know that women have fears about sharing power with men in this area, fears about being coerced into aborting or delivering a child against their will. But let's be realistic here. There is not the slightest chance today that we would pass a law coercing women around abortion. The days of men legally coercing women, in the west at least, are over. The days of women legally coercing men, however, as in this abortion issue, are still with us. Men's fears around abortion, of being silenced about a decision which will change their lives, are completely realistic. That is exactly what is happening throughout the western world; men are being told that on the question of abortion their concerns are irrelevant, their lives subject to women's control without the slightest accountability. That is the very definition of disenfranchisement.

What I want is that men be granted the legal right to be heard by the mother about what will happen to their unborn offspring. A place at the table, an opportunity to express their fears and their wishes. "My body, my choice" silences men's voices in a way that women would be outraged if it were done to them. It is not right, it is not just. A father has a right to be heard on what is to be done about his unborn child, a right that is absolute and not subject to a woman's agreement, not contingent on her goodwill.

There is one significant way that the disenfranchisement of women through the vote is not parallel to the disenfranchisement of men in abortion. Whatever decision is made about abortion, it is the woman's body and not the man's that is involved in completing or terminating the pregnancy. This difference is not enough to justify silencing him, but it means that his power to influence the decision should not prevail over hers. His power is limited to expressing what he wants to the mother. A woman who chooses to abort a child that a good and willing father wishes to raise, even on his own, should not be entitled to avoid knowledge of what she is doing. She must not be protected from seeing his pain as she chooses to deprive him of a choice, single parenthood, that she takes for granted, a choice that she would be outraged if anyone suggested depriving her of.

In the opposite case, where she wishes to keep the child and he does not, she must not be allowed to sue him for child support. She has the right to abandon her fetus, after conception, in three legal ways; through abortion, through leaving it at a drop-off center, or through adoption. A man must have the same right not to be forced to support a child he doesn't want, just because a woman wishes it. A woman who chooses to raise a child alone should accept the consequences of her decision, and not be able to force a man to subsidize her. Lack of the right to walk away from a fetus that he doesn't want is another way that men are disenfranchised compared to women.

I started this argument with the issue of rights, because that is the bedrock that determines what should be done. But involving the father in an abortion decision is also the best and most practical thing to do. The mother and the father are the principal stakeholders, the two whose lives are most affected by what will be decided. We should give them an opportunity to come together, to pursue a solution that works best for both of them. Sometimes two heads really are better than one. If they can't agree then the woman's choice will prevail, but at least a decent, honorable process was followed rather than a cruel exclusion of one of the parties.

Women, what will you do about this? You can go with your fears and your feelings, deny the legitimacy of my claim, and keep the sexist, coercive status quo. You have all of the power in this area of reproduction, and men have none, the same way that once men had all of the political power and women had none. You have the power to keep oppressing me, but you will not be able to shut me up about this issue. I am asking you for this, but I am also demanding it as my right and as your obligation, as you once demanded the vote, trusting you to recognize a matter of justice even when it goes against your immediate interest. This is what you demanded of men, and this is what you received from them. I know that it likely goes against the culture, against what feels right to you right now, but when faced with a similar challenge in their area of power, men trusted you by stepping aside in order to share power with you.

Will you return the compliment?"

That's what I think the law should say around abortion, the rights and responsibilities of the parties. But how should a particular decision be made, whether or not to abort in a given case?

What I am offering here is a vision of how to work difficult human issues with wisdom. I will present this in a general way, as principles and guidelines, because I want to offer it as an example of a general process for finding one's way through any issue to a fair and just resolution. Note that we are no longer looking at what the law should be around abortion, but at how to reach a good decision in a particular case, with specific individuals and circumstances. By a good decision, I mean a decision that takes into account all relevant parties and factors and helps people to recognize and move beyond coercive, manipulative or dysfunctional positions. A good decision also means a decision that is arrived at lovingly, with respect and empathy for all involved. In the process we will generate a general framework for considering difficult issues and a procedure for seeking a good solution. This process is applicable for any decision that has major life consequences, such as making child custody and financial support decisions after divorce, or deciding whether to divorce in the first place.

The process I will suggest has three parts. In the first we generate a general framework by identifying stakeholders and principles. In the second we bring in practical concerns, specific details of the particular circumstances and consider how they change things. In the third we dialogue together to seek the best outcome for all concerned. Let's begin with part one.

In any issue, the stakeholders are those whose lives will be significantly affected by the decision on the table. In the case of a potential abortion, they are not hard to identify. Clearly, the fetus is one such – it will live or die by the decision that is made; there are no higher stakes than that. The fetus' needs can be presumed to be the wish to live, although the life situation that it faces might be taken into account if it presents significant shortcomings. The mother's life is affected in two major ways, first in whether her pregnancy will continue to term or not, second by whether she will get to be a parent to the child. The father's life is affected in whether he will get to be (or be compelled to be) a parent. Finally, society may be a stakeholder in the case where the child will need public financial support (e.g. a single mother). So there are up to four stakeholders whose needs and aspirations matter and should be taken into account. Not an easy prospect, but that's the reality of the situation. Note: a doctor is not a stakeholder, but an agent. A doctor's role is to advise the stakeholders, but since his life is not significantly affected by the decision of whether or not to abort, she is not a stakeholder and does not have a direct voice in the decision.

Now let's look at the general principles. There are three. First, there are no absolutes, by which I mean there is no one principle which trumps all of the others. It is common for parties in a dispute to seek a device, a strategy to make their own concern paramount and absolute. This is simply an illustration of our lack of maturity, our lack of empathy for certain others and for concerns that aren't our own. Pro-life advocates do this by making the life of the fetus absolute, by equating abortion with murder and claiming that nothing can justify murder. But even if one accepts the assumption that a fetus is a full human being, the fact is that killing a person is not an absolute either. As columnist George Jonas observes, "All societies, religious societies included, authorize individuals, sometimes classes of individuals, to kill for certain reasons. Judges, parents, police officers, ship's captains, inquisitors, soldiers, executioners and others have been entitled to terminate human lives, provided they did so for compelling reasons." [57]

So abortion is not absolutely wrong. Neither is it morally determined by the woman's choice alone. The pro-choice position argues that the woman's choice must rule over all other issues by virtue of her absolute control over her own body. But she is not the only one affected by this decision; the lives of others are hugely impacted. The mother does not have an absolute moral right to abort.

Absolutes are wonderful things; they make decisions easier by overwhelming all competing claims. But they do not often conform with reality; like it or not, real life has a tendency to be non-absolute.

The argument I am making here is a moral, not a legal one. I have already described what I think the law should say about abortion, and it does not include coercing women to abort or to carry to term. If a woman chooses to repudiate her obligations to others in this matter, the law should permit her to do so. However, we are not considering law now. From a moral point of view, the right thing to do is for all parties to make best efforts to come together around an equitable solution, and that is what we are about.

The second principle is that no stakeholder may be silenced. Feminists often argue that men should have nothing to say about abortion because they don't get pregnant. If pregnancy were the only issue at stake, this might be appropriate. But eighteen years of child raising, or the deprival of the same, is arguably a larger stake than nine months of pregnancy. Fathers are major stakeholders in the issue of the possible abortion of their child and they must have a role in making this choice – and that role must reflect their own concerns, not just support of the mother. The fact that we have legally denied this role to fathers in all western democracies is because of the unacknowledged power of women under the current dominance of the feminine archetype.

The third principle is the prevention of coercion or manipulation via power plays. No one should be allowed a privileged power position, in which they exert influence beyond the weight of their argument. If you think back to my gender codependent power matrix in chapter five, you will see that this is easy to recognize in the case of traditional masculine power (threats of violence or economic sanctions) but very difficult to recognize in the case of feminine power (moral shaming or emotional manipulation). The difficulty in the latter case is because feminine power is still in our shadow, still not raised to consciousness, so that neither contemporary culture nor women themselves recognize these behaviors as powerful and manipulative. They just feel like what comes naturally. Indeed, the wholesale shaming of men that has proceeded from fifty years of feminism has been of this ilk; women (and many men) doing what felt right to them. As I have noted numerous times, however, feeling right doesn't make it right. At this stage, I will simply note that the principle of prevention of power plays is an important rule for effective decision making. I will have more to say later about how to work with this principle in practice.

We have now identified the stakeholders and the principles of a fair and equitable decision process, and that completes the general framework. Let's proceed now to consider how practical issues and specific circumstances modify or customize the general framework.

There are two types here. The first is primarily about modifying the weight given to the various stakeholders. If the pregnancy is the result of a rape of the mother, for instance, then the father's rights as a stakeholder are eliminated. Similarly, if the pregnancy is in an intact family that will support the baby if it is carried to term, or if it will be given up for adoption, then society's role as a stakeholder, which is predicated on having an obligation for financial support of the child and/or mother, falls to zero. If the fetus is found to have a genetic disorder which reduces its viability or its prospects for a happy life, then its "right to life" stake is reduced. If there are medical complications in which carrying the baby to term would threaten the life or health of the mother, then the decision becomes more weighted towards abortion, and only a strong determination on the part of both parents should prevail over that bias.

Additionally, participation in such a decision process is voluntary – if any party does not want to participate (such as the father), he effectively abandons any control over the process. The interests of society and of the fetus would be represented by delegates,

The second way that practical considerations modify the general framework is about practical logistics. If an abortion decision is to be made, there is strictly limited time in which to make it. Perhaps the father cannot be readily identified or found. Perhaps medical issues abbreviate the time available. Perhaps one of the parties has limited availability, or there are geographical challenges. Such complicating factors are difficult to deal with in a way that is fair to all, and it is probably impossible to say in a general way what should be done about them. As with many human issues, there is no general answer; wisdom is not formulaic. If there is limited time to reach agreement, then there is limited time, and the process that is put in place should reflect this urgency. Geographical challenges can often be reduced with technology. With good intent, adequate solutions can be found to logistics challenges.

We have now put in place most of the structure, the process to support a good decision. In part three of the process, we get to the content, which takes the form of dialogue among the stakeholders. It is ultimately up to the participants, but I suggest that a mediated dialogue, assisted and moderated by a skilled and experienced mediator, be the general rule. The mediator is not a stakeholder and does not have any personal input into the decision, his or her role is simply to assist the participants in reaching an effective and equitable, a wise decision. A particular responsibility of a mediator is to recognize and prevent the use of power plays by any participant, indeed to prevent any process that would divert or subvert a healthy dialogue.

In *The Different Drum: Community Building and Peace*, M. Scott Peck described a process by which a group can reach a place of wisdom. He called it community building, and he spent some time describing the stages. Unsurprisingly, the stages bear a resemblance to the stages of spiritual growth in my own model described in chapter six. The first stage he calls pseudocommunity. It is where people are simply being polite with each other, getting along by going along, i.e., by not saying anything difficult or potentially offensive. They are pretending to be in good relationship with each other but it's all superficial, with their differences hidden from each other. His second stage is called chaos. It's where people have abandoned the pretence of agreement and are expressing their real opinions, but in hostile and accusatory terms. It looks like a descent from pseudocommunity, since it's aggressive and judgmental, but it's actually healthier because it's more honest. In the chaos stage there is truth telling, but no reconciliation, no community. Both of these stages are related to my stage 2, denial.

Peck's third stage he calls emptiness. It's where people turn their honesty spotlight on themselves and confess their judgments, their fears, their shame and insecurity. It corresponds closely with my own stage three, recovery. It is this difficult and painful process, he says, that leads to the final stage, which he calls community. A group in community is one where respect and empathy for others is integrated with accountability and responsibility. It corresponds with my stage 4, wisdom.

Peck argues that a motivated group can move all the way from pseudocommunity to community in just hours or at most a few days. He has personally led many such groups, and he founded an organization dedicated to just such work. I can personally vouch for the power of this process, as I brought one of his community building facilitators to my own work group at a Canadian telecom company in 1992. Our group of a dozen managers reached community in three days of intense dialogue.

A group that has achieved community is a powerful, effective and wise decision making body. I can think of no better process for a small group to approach the making of high stakes decisions like whether or not to abort a fetus. With a good facilitator, and a degree of willingness in the participants, a small group (usually no more than four – the mother, the father, and the delegates for society and for the fetus) could be expected to reach a wise decision, one well considered and agreed to by all, within a day or two, three at the most. Of course, determined intransigence by any party can defeat such a process, but I believe that it is hard to remain unreasonably intransigent in the face of earnest, informed goodwill on the part of other participants. If a person who is locked into a position can be persuaded to express the fears that lie behind their intransigence, then groups can usually find ways to address those fears while also accommodating the real needs of others. This process really works.

Not only does this process work well for reaching wise, balanced decisions about difficult issues, but it also has the effect of growing us up. The subjective experience of being in community is almost always one of joy – deep and memorable joy as we surrender our individual focus, perhaps for the first time, to the wisdom of a group.

The experience of being genuinely loved within a group, of having a group care deeply about meeting our personal needs, is life-changing. I still remember the first time it happened for me, about twenty five years ago. I was in a men's group that had been meeting for a couple of years, and we were considering whether to admit two new members. We "interviewed" the two men, and then invited them to remain present in the group while we discussed whether to admit them permanently. I argued strongly against admitting them, I don't remember my reasons now, but they persuaded me fully. The group decided to accept the new members – and I felt its wisdom in this. I still felt the legitimacy of all of my individual arguments against the decision, but I somehow knew that the group was smarter, wiser than I was. It was a profound moment of transcendence, when I felt the wisdom of the group without understanding it. It was intensely exciting to me. I remember that I sent an email to the other members about how I felt, how moved I was by the experience of surrendering to the wisdom of the group. It was an experience of transcending the self/other duality, I know now, and it was my first experience of the joy, the intense rightness of that process.

The process that I have described above has this power because it is dualistically balanced itself. It is balanced on the self/other dimension, on the truth/love dimension, and on the accountability/compassion dimension. It is, in fact, a truth and reconciliation process, giving equal weight to truth telling and to loving respect for each participant. A group like this is willing to wrestle honestly with the issues, and to care genuinely about each participant, for as long as it takes to find the solution that works best for all. The process of loving each other, listening carefully and speaking thoughtfully, grounded in truth about the issues, is a process that blesses each person involved.

I recommend this process for all really tough decisions where choices need to be made that have profound effects on the lives of several people. For instance, deciding on custody, child support and alimony following a divorce would be well suited to this process, which would involve all family members, including non-infant children. We need to find ways to do better than the win/lose protocol that rules in family court and that almost always results in lasting resentment and discord. The community building process offers a means for people's fears to be heard, respected and addressed, and an opportunity for them to co-create a solution that will work for everyone.

After nine chapters, we have taken the theory about wisdom as dualistic balance about as far as I can go at this stage of my own development. We have considered, in this chapter, how to apply it to one of the thorniest real world problems there is, one that has divided ideologues in our society for forty years. We are going to change direction now, and consider for the next few chapters the results of extreme dualistic imbalance. What happens when a whole political movement is unbalanced, when the movement politics come out of stage 2 victimhood and denial? How does this manifest in society, and what happens when imbalance around particular issues takes militant, coercive form? Can a whole society get lost in the perceptual distortions and denial that is characteristic of this stage? We will begin by considering times in history when this has happened.

Chapter 10 – Evil Among Us

"He who passively accepts evil is as much involved in it as he who helps to perpetrate it. He who accepts evil without protesting against it is really cooperating with it." – Martin Luther King, Jr.

"It is a man's own mind, not his enemy or foe, that lures him to evil ways." – Buddha

"Virtue cannot separate itself from reality without becoming a principle of evil." – Albert Camus

"Understanding does not cure evil, but it is a definite help, inasmuch as one can cope with a comprehensible darkness." – Carl Jung

"The idea of evil is always subject to denial as a coping mechanism." – John Bradshaw

"In [the play Medea], evil appears as the incapacity to take any distance – through reason – from the primal force of feeling, so that all strong emotion becomes automatically self-justifying." – Michael Ignatieff

I regret the necessity to explore the question of evil in this book. However, as I understand it, evil is the most extreme form of stage 2 dualistic imbalance, when a person or a group becomes so totally biased or prejudiced that they become willing to do violence (physical or psychological) in the name of their unbalanced worldview, and supported by their *feeling* of righteousness. Usually, it is a highly exaggerated feeling of victimhood that enrages them to the extent that they feel entitled to commit extreme acts against others. Terrorists are a good example of this perception of desperate and entitled victimhood. However, terrorists are usually marginal groups that occupy the fringes of most societies. Of greater concern is when evil moves to center stage in a culture and engages the majority of its citizens.

So a presentation of wisdom as dualistic balance would be incomplete without a discussion of how imbalance can manifest as evil, and how the human psyche accommodates and justifies evil. In this chapter we will explore a new definition and understanding of evil, and validate the description with historical examples.

I am aware that evil is a dangerous word. Much evil can and has been done in the name of fighting evil (in fact, this is the usual cover story) and I do not want to add to it. I begin, therefore, with some cautionary words. Evil is here defined as a psychosocial (or, if you prefer, a spiritual) disease. My intent is to name it and describe its nature so that we might begin to study it and take effective action to heal it. For evil is comprehensible; its origins, the pattern of its development and the forms that it takes are all subject to rational analysis. Evil people are victims as well as they are perpetrators; polarizing the world into evil perpetrators and innocent victims is to oversimplify matters and is a symptom of the disease, not of its cure. If you become righteously outraged at evildoers, then you undermine your ability to combat it, and self-examination is called for.

In recent years, with the general decline of religious convictions in the west, we have become confused about evil. Indeed, modern new age and secular humanistic thinking is that evil has no existence, is all shadow projection. I once shared this notion, but I have now concluded that such thinking is dangerously naïve. M. Scott Peck wrote in *The Road Less Travelled*, "I have to conclude that evil is real. It is not the figment of the imagination of a primitive religious mind feebly attempting to explain the unknown. There really are people, and institutions made up of people, who respond with hatred in the presence of goodness and would destroy the good insofar as it is in their power to do so. They do this not with conscious malice, but blindly, lacking awareness of their own evil – indeed, seeking to avoid any such awareness." [58] And from Alice Miller, "The Jungian notion of the shadow, and the notion that evil is the reverse of good, are aimed at denying the reality of evil. But evil is real. It is not innate but acquired, and it is never the reverse of good, but rather its destroyer. ... It is not true that evil, destructiveness and perversion inevitably form part of human existence, no matter how often this is maintained. But it is true that evil is always engaged in producing more evil and, with it, an ocean of suffering for millions that is similarly avoidable." [59]

In this chapter I will focus on and define ideological evil of the kind that can capture the psyche of entire societies. Our amazing technological progress since the industrial revolution has persuaded us that we are enlightened, that we have moved beyond the kind of major, systemic evil that we know about from history: the Inquisition or the witch-burnings, for example. That is why the horrors of Nazism were so shocking; we saw that evil could take over a modern, liberal democracy.

But we no longer like to use the word itself. It seems primitive, too harsh for modern sensibilities. I think that this is a serious error. In his book *The Death of Satan; How Americans Have Lost the Sense of Evil*, Andrew Delbanco writes,

> "A gulf has opened up between the visibility of evil and the intellectual resources for coping with it. Never before have images of horror been so widely disseminated and so appalling – from organized death camps to children starving in famines that might have been averted. … The repertoire of evil has never been richer. Yet never have our responses been so weak. … Few people still believe in what British writer Ian McEwan has recently called a 'malign principle, a force in human affairs that periodically advances to dominate and destroy the lives of individuals or nations, then retreats to await the next occasion.'[60]… Yet something that feels like that force still invades our experience, and we still discover in ourselves the capacity to inflict it on others. Since this is true, we have an inescapable problem: we feel something that our culture no longer gives us the vocabulary to express." [61]

Delbanco concludes, "… if evil, with all of the insidious complexity which Augustine attributed to it, escapes the reach of our imagination, it will have established dominion over us." [62]

We must face the fact that our technology and democracy are mere surface wrappings over our deeper psychic reality that is not yet free of dark, feeling-driven irrationality. We are still vulnerable to project our fears and insecurities onto convenient scapegoats and to pursue and punish those we have made repositories of our judgments with all the power at our disposal. Paul Oppenheimer, in his *Evil and the Demonic; A New Theory of Monstrous Behaviors*, described how this happened in historical times.

> "The accused and persecuted group, whether witches or heretics

or Satanists, seemed to become the repository of the larger society's nightmares about itself. Its own feelings of inferiority, its own socially unacceptable desires, … its discreet convictions of its own evil, its impulsive superstitions and superstitious impulses, its immolating sorrows, its bruising frustrations and misdirected violence – all swarmed like angry bees around flowers of imaginary evil, those about to be sequestered and murdered as a distraction from the society's incapacity for what Pascal calls self-investigation." [63]

The last comment is the key, for the deepest motivation of evil is the wish to avoid looking honestly at oneself. In *People of the Lie; the Hope for Healing Human Evil*, M. Scott Peck makes this point plainly. "As has been noted, it is characteristic of those who are evil to judge others as evil. Unable to acknowledge their own imperfections, they must explain away their flaws by blaming others. And, if necessary, they will even destroy others in the name of righteousness." [64]

What *is* evil? We need a definition. The most basic answer is that evil is anti-life. If, as Jung claimed, the purpose of life is to develop ourselves fully, to realize our potential as human beings and to become all that we can be, then evil strives to reverse this process, to diminish and attenuate people's humanity, to regress them towards infantilism. It does this for its own survival, because fully developed, wise people are both able to discern and recognize evil, and powerful to withstand and oppose it. Psychologically undeveloped people, on the other hand, lack the ability either to recognize or to stand against evil, and in fact are readily recruited to its cause.

How does this work in practice? I said in chapter five that good parents guide and assist the maturation of their children. Evil parents do the opposite; they actively inhibit and reverse this process. Consider a child who observes an inconsistency in her mother. She might speak up and say, "Yesterday you said you would always listen to me if I said it was important, and now you are ignoring me." If her mother, out of the wish to avoid examining her own faults or errors, abuses her authority over her daughter and says, "I'll teach you to be so disrespectful" and sends her to her room, is that an evil act? Yes, for she has squelched an honest observation through an abuse of power. She has taken the growing skill of her daughter to discern inconsistencies, a valuable life skill, and punished her for her honesty, for her accuracy. The mother's implicit message is, "My image of blamelessness is more important than truth, and I will force you through my power over you to subordinate truth to my image of innocence." In this way, she attempts to stop her daughter from growing into independent and accurate understanding, in order to preserve her own false image of innocence.

Evil acts do not an evil person make. Many of us occasionally do things of this type. So, as Peck says in *People of the Lie*,

> "If evil people cannot be defined by the illegality of their deeds or the magnitude of their sins, then how are we to define them? The answer is by the consistency of their sins. While usually subtle, their destructiveness is remarkably consistent. This is because those who have 'crossed over the line' are characterized by their absolute refusal to tolerate the sense of their own sinfulness." [65]

He continues a few pages later,

> "A predominant characteristic ... of the behavior of those I call evil is scapegoating. Because in their hearts they consider themselves above reproach, they must lash out at anyone who does reproach them. They sacrifice others to preserve their self-image of perfection. ...

> "Evil, then, is most often committed in order to scapegoat, and the people I label as evil are chronic scapegoaters. In *The Road Less Travelled* I defined evil as 'the exercise of political power – that is, the imposition of one's will on others by overt or covert coercion – in order to avoid ... spiritual growth.' In other words, the evil attack others in order to avoid facing their own failures. Spiritual growth requires the acknowledgement of one's need to grow. If we cannot make that acknowledgement, we have no option except to attempt to eradicate the evidence of our imperfection.

> "Strangely enough, evil people are often destructive because they are attempting to destroy evil. The problem is that they misplace the locus of the evil. Instead of destroying others they should be destroying the sickness within themselves. As life often threatens

their self-image of perfection, they are often busily engaged in hating and destroying that life – usually in the name of righteousness." [66]

I have reprinted an extensive excerpt from Peck's discussion of evil because of its relevance to our own exploration, and because I wish to give him credit for his pioneering work in this area. My own interest and the focus of this chapter is not so much on evil individuals, however, as on those times when evil manifests in society in a way that attracts the majority of people together under a particular, coherent set of ideas, an ideology. I call this ideological evil, and I will now proceed towards my own definition of this phenomenon. My definition keeps the coercive component that Peck identified, makes the 'righteous image' part of the definition, and alters the terms in which the ontological or motivational component is described.

Evil is a distortion, a retrogression at the foundations of the process of living. We have seen that evil operates by scapegoating others, in order to defend against finding fault in oneself – but this is the focus of the whole of stage 2, as described in chapter six. The evil go beyond this, however, by actively coercing or abusing those scapegoated others, and whitewashing this behavior as righteous. Why do they do this? What is in it for them? We find our answer when we ask ourselves what is the most basic business, the economy of life. For living things to survive, they must find or produce more than they consume. Any living unit, whether a plant or an animal, a human individual, a family or a society, must produce or acquire at least as much as it needs to consume, or it will decline towards death. Since some members of a family or a society (mainly children) are not able to produce as much as they consume, the deficit must be made up by others, the adults. Indeed, a useful working definition of an adult is that it is a person who is a net producer.

This production is not solely material, it's also emotional or psychological. A parent who, out of love or empathy for their child, confronts anger without returning it is working against the emotional flow, is producing love and psychological peace – a work requiring just as much disciplined effort, practice and competence as does material production. Healthy individuals and healthy societies do this work naturally and without resentment, rightly seeing it as the basic, foundational economy of life.

But production is effortful, it requires discipline, and the nature of laziness (which Peck offers as the genesis of human evil) is the wish to avoid discipline and effort. It is easy and pleasant to consume, but production requires the postponement of gratification. So the temptation has existed throughout history for people to undermine this natural economy, to find a way to consume without producing. For this to succeed, others must be found who can be made to produce for your consumption. An evil ideology provides the purported justification for enslaving or otherwise forcing those others to yield the fruits of their labor. Evil is inextricably bound up with power over others and ideas of elitist entitlement to consume what those others produce.

Putting all of this together, we arrive at my definition of ideological evil. It has three necessary components. Ideological evil is:

1. The desire for unearned consumption or privilege

2. The overt or covert coercion of others in order to achieve it

3. The insistent and consistent, formalized rationalization of this behavior as moral and righteous.

Enjoying unearned consumption is essentially the role of an infant or child. A child is unique before the law in enjoying rights without responsibilities, whereas adulthood is the state of having rights *and* responsibilities. Traditionally, men's responsibility/production has been physical, economic and political, as noted in the codependent power over matrix of chapter five. Exerting themselves against the entropic forces of decay and randomness, they have created order and organization, resulting in food on the table and laws in the land. Women's responsibility/production area has historically been moral, emotional and sexual (*re*production). In their relationships with their families, especially their children, their emotional exertion returned comfort for pain, peace for anger, security for fear. The quality and sustainability of any society is based entirely on the quality and quantity of production in these areas. In a healthy society, individuals and institutions trade their production for that of others in conscious, consensual, non-coercive, non-deceptive contracts.

Traditional marriage is the basic example of this trade, where the man's external production of food and shelter is traded for the woman's 'internal' reproduction of children and production of the moral and emotional development of children and domestic relationship harmony. Both are work, in that they require the disciplined exercise of effort towards a goal.

If some are to enjoy unearned consumption, others must produce more and/or consume less. Where this is not offered willingly, as it is to children and to welfare recipients for example, some will seek to take it by force or deception. An example of taking by force is robbery, or by deception, fraud. However, robbers and defrauders are not evil unless they meet the third criterion and attempt to justify their actions to themselves and others as morally righteous. It is this last feature of evil which makes it so pernicious, for the attack on reality, on logic and reason that comes with moralizing the enslavement and coercion of others can be utterly confusing and make the destructive nature of evil actions difficult to recognize.

An evil ideology contains within its formal arguments such a disguised attack on reason, in the form of claimed moral justifications for unearned privilege for the favored group, extracted coercively from others, the scapegoat group(s). In the case of the ideology which is today regarded as emblematic of evil, Nazism, those others were the Jews, whose property was confiscated and who were methodically exterminated, and the surrounding nations, whose lands were regarded as forfeit to the German need for *Lebensraum* (living room), whose peoples were enslaved (coerced production without right of consumption) and whose property was seized, all by force and justified by self-serving moral arguments. These entitlement arguments were built, as they must be, on the notion of the superiority of the German people as the master race, the *Ubermenschen*, while the Jews were a subhuman race, the *Untermenschen*, unfit for survival.

For an example of ideological evil in North America, consider the period of public lynchings in the USA. During the late 19th and early 20th century, lynching, meaning a killing committed without legal sanction or due process by a mob seeking vengeance for an offense, was usually approved of by the public. Under a cover story that the lynch mob was acting in the name of justice, incredibly violent killings were seen as necessary and appropriate. Lynchings often included tortures such as burning, dismemberment and castration. Crowds of hundreds or even thousands gathered to watch victims being whipped and doused in coal tar before being set on fire.

"How could ordinary people participate in such brutality? The answer lies in the psychological processes of persuasion and propaganda. ... The atmosphere of a racist caste system, perpetrated by the traditions and culture of the South, provided the background for lynch mobs. Although slaves were freed in 1863 by Lincoln's Emancipation Proclamation, white domination of blacks, on every social, economic and legal level, continued. ... Lynching became a vital tactic that was utilized by whites to intimidate and control African Americans. In order to justify the practice, justice was used as an excuse for vigilantism. ... People were lynched for 'crimes' such as registering to vote, arguing with a white man, disrespect to a white woman, shoplifting, drunkenness, elopement, insults and refusing to give evidence." [67]

"... The press usually added to the sense of lawlessness by suggesting that all things considered, most civilized men recognized that the races are divided as this *Mobile Register* editorial did on June 19, 1897: 'There is a feeling in the white man's mind that whoever of the race not his own who attempts to defy this race instinct, and violently upset the physical line which nature has established, does by that act take his life in hand.' Of course, the editorial neglected to mention that African Americans were being murdered by blood thirsty mobs that killed for transgressions like "demanding respect" [68] and in doing so, share at least part of the blame for the frenzy of lynching that took place in the South during those decades." [69]

In *A Festival of Violence: An Analysis of Southern Lynchings, 1882-1930,* Stewart E. Tolnay and E.M. Beck write that there are:

"2805 [documented] victims of lynch mobs killed between 1882 and 1930 in ten southern states. Although mobs murdered almost 300 white men and women, the vast majority – almost 2,500 – of lynch victims were African-American. Of these black victims, 94 percent died in the hands of white lynch mobs. The scale of this carnage means that, on the average, a black man, woman, or child was murdered nearly once a week, every week, between 1882 and

1930 by a hate-driven white mob." [70]

"In addition to the punishment of specific criminal offenders, lynching in the American South had three entwined functions: *first,* to maintain social order over the black population through terrorism; *second,* to suppress or eliminate black competitors for economic, political, or social rewards; *third,* to stabilize the white class structure and preserve the privileged status of the white aristocracy." [71]

It is clear that this fully meets the definition of ideological evil:

1. The desire for unearned consumption or privilege

2. The overt or covert coercion of others in order to achieve it

3. The insistent and consistent, formalized rationalization of this behavior as moral and righteous.

With hindsight we can feel, with horror, the brutality and savagery of this behavior, but the key lesson it has for us today is contained in the fact that these people saw themselves as good, law-abiding, civilized, churchgoing folk. They took their children to the lynchings, they sent photographs of the event to friends and family, some of them even collected body parts as souvenirs! These activities somehow did not disturb their good opinion of themselves as moral and upstanding. It is vital that we understand what creates this state of mind, for these weren't criminals or any kind of social deviants; they were regular people not unlike you and me. This was a whole society gone off the rails into evil behavior, but in just one area and with respect to just one issue. How does this happen?

In chapter three, I described the condition of dualistic imbalance where feeling, what feels right to a person, dominates their psyche. After much reflection, it seems to me that this is the essential precondition for this kind of self-deception. In his book *The Lesser Evil: Political Ethics in an Age of Terror,* in a section considering in what state of mind a terrorist could justify terrorism, Canadian intellectual Michael Ignatieff writes, "In [the play *Medea*], evil appears as the incapacity to take any distance – through reason – from the primal force of feeling, so that all strong emotion becomes automatically self-justifying." [72]

Mr. Ignatieff is here describing the extreme of a total imbalance between feeling and thinking, where thinking is a slave to whatever feels right, employed simply to produce rationalizations that support the feeling. He goes further than I have so far, in describing this as evil, but I think that he is right. If we are completely unbalanced on one of these psychological dichotomies, then we are literally mentally unbalanced. The behavior that flows from our imbalance will be harmful to us and to others. Our good intentions will not excuse us from responsibility for the evil that we perpetrate.

I think that the ideological evil that I am defining and exploring here has its genesis in this imbalance, which manifests as a total one-sidedness in empathy. The evil experience the world not as it is, but through the filter of their ideology, and their ideology tells the ideologue that there is a good group, for whom they have empathy, and a bad group for whom they have little to none. They do not experience those that they coerce as fully human. Indeed, the felt perception of the lesser humanity of their victims is essential to their worldview, and is formally built into the evil ideology with which they justify their actions. They truly believe that their victims deserve what is being done to them. But this stance, although sincere at a conscious level, is a cover story designed to conceal a deep unconscious fear. In the case of the lynchings,

> "Many whites, after Reconstruction and during the first four decades of the twentieth century, feared that the Negro was 'getting out of his place' and that the white man's social status was threatened and was in need of protection. Lynching was seen as the method to defend white domination and keep the Negroes from becoming 'uppity'. Therefore, lynching was more the expression of white American fear of Black social and economic advancement than of Negro crime. W. E. B. DuBois[73] was correct when he stated: '... the white South feared more than Negro dishonesty, ignorance and incompetency, Negro honesty, knowledge, and efficiency.'"[74]

In other words, the belief in the subhumanity of the Negro was a defense against the possibility of his equality – or superiority. You will recall that in chapter six we saw that stage 2 on the map of spiritual growth is the stage at which people project out their shame, their sense of inferiority, creating classes of people that they can feel superior to. Ideological evil, then, is simply the most intense and socially virulent form of this sociopathy, where for a time a particular cover story gains sway in a society and provides the purported moral justification for acts of extreme oppression, cruelty and discrimination against particular, identified scapegoats – oppression and discrimination that is often both legally and socially sanctioned through the widespread acceptance of that same cover story.

There is one more feature, or symptom if you prefer, that seems to be uniquely associated with ideological evil when it takes possession of a whole society. We have seen that the willingness to perform horrific acts against identified scapegoats is grounded in a lack of balance, a complete one-sidedness of empathy, and that this one-sidedness is an extreme form of stage 2 – denial – on the four stage journey of psychological growth. It is grounded, in other words, in the soil of human collective immaturity. Furthermore, it manifests when a particular group is identified as scapegoats for a society's unconscious fears, so that extreme acts against members of that group can feel justified and necessary. But what does it feel like in such a society? Can we identify a particular cultural feature that is always seen when ideological evil is present and operating? There is such a feature, and sociologists have labeled it 'moral panic'.

Wikipedia defines moral panic as "an intense feeling expressed in a population about an issue that appears to threaten the social order.[75] Moral panic is a necessary but not a sufficient symptom of an evil ideology. In other words, all evil ideologies will feature moral panic, but not all moral panics will be expressions of evil ideology in a society. The key feature of moral panic is that it is a disproportionate, an exaggerated fear focused on a particular group in society. Historically, we have seen moral panic focused on (purported) witches (the witch burnings) or religious heretics (the Inquisition). More recently, Negroes (the lynchings) and Jews (the Holocaust) have been the objects of moral panic, where they were seen as urgent and powerful threats to the social order, to the moral underpinnings of society.

What is the difference between ideological evil and moral panic? It is the ideology. Moral panic is pure feeling. Ideological evil incorporates the feeling, but includes a justifying ideology to support the feeling, to give it a purported rational justification. This ideology will necessarily be false to fact, will be founded on lies, but in the grip of the feeling, few will notice. Rather, the ideology will be taken as true *because* it supports and justifies the feeling, while the feeling itself needs no more justification than the fact that it *feels* true. Once again we are confronted with the fact that only thinking – critical, analytical thinking that is independent of feeling – can possibly offer a check on the veracity of what is felt to be true.

Note that ideological evil is not a conspiracy. In a conspiracy, the conspirators are conscious of their deceptions, of the fact that they are attempting to mislead others. The great danger of ideological evil is that it is an unconscious process; the people caught up in it are entirely unaware of the harm that they are doing – indeed, they are convinced that they are doing good. In ideological evil, the human psyche misleads and deceives *itself* and remains unaware, at a conscious level, of the distortions and lies in its ideology.

In the next chapter, we will begin considering whether ideological evil could be a major part of our *contemporary* society. This is a distressing notion. It is not comfortably distant in historical time and cultural evolution like the lynchings we considered above. In chapter one, I argued that the primary force arrayed against a seeker of truth is that it will seem to convict her. That is certainly the case here. If ideological evil is operating in current society as it has in the past, then virtually all of us are implicated in it and this is very difficult to contemplate. We react viscerally against the idea that we could be allied to an evil ideology. I think that we have demonized evil, made it monstrous, made it into something done only by exceptional others, perverts and deviants, never by people like us. I think that we have done this in order to distance and insulate ourselves from this distress.

Evil *is* monstrous, in that it can make us blind and insensitive, indeed, deluded about the effects of our actions on others. But it is also banal and ordinary. When it is part of our society and culture, it feels completely normal and appropriate – even righteous – and it is essential that we really get, really *feel* the truth of this point. To help us to see this, I will include an extensive quote from *The Quest for the Nazi Personality; a Psychological Investigation of Nazi War Criminals*. Nazism is today regarded as emblematic of ideological evil. You may be surprised at what was found when psychologists had the opportunity to examine a Nazi leader, Adolf Eichmann, the very individual directly responsible for implementing the project that exterminated six million Jews.

Eichmann was the German SS colonel who was head of the 'Jewish desk' (Judenreferat) in the Reich Security Main Office. His responsibility was to assemble the Jews of Europe under German control. He organized the deportation of Jews to extermination camps in Poland. The Israeli secret service captured him in 1960 in Argentina. He stood trial in Tel Aviv, Israel and was condemned to death on December 15, 1961. He was executed in June, 1962.

"During his trial, Eichmann was portrayed in the media as a depraved killer responsible for the deaths of millions. But the Rorschach protocol did not fit. Where was the depravity? Or, perhaps, an overwhelming sense of guilt? Sadism? Bigotry? Hatred? None of these seemed apparent in the psychological profile. Just the opposite; the psychological protocol seemed to indicate an ordinary, rather untroubled person who, although likely to be somewhat distant and inflexible in interpersonal relationships, was not bent on the destruction of whole populations of human beings.

"The Eichmann Rorschach begins to make more sense when examining the work of Arendt, the noted political philosopher. Arendt, who had been assigned by *The New Yorker* to cover the Eichmann trial, was among the spectators in the converted auditorium of Jerusalem's municipal cultural center. After observing the trial of Eichmann and drawing from interview information (including some knowledge of the psychological test data collected during the trial), she proposed that the actions of Eichmann and of other Nazis were not related to significant psychological derangement in those men, but were a result of a lack of personality substance, that is, banality. Arendt argued that Eichmann was not a sadist or even an aggressive individual intent on doing harm to others for depraved satisfaction, but just an ordinary, conscientious, moderately ambitious bureaucrat who was more interested in simply obeying orders than he was in sending millions of people to their deaths in the camps. …

"Arendt's proposition seems neat and simple. Most Nazis, she suggested, were not the swaggering sadists of the 'B' movie genre, but stultifyingly ordinary men who were just doing their jobs or 'following orders' as they claimed in the war crimes trials' defenses. … Arendt's theory … suggests that the potential for behaving like a Nazi exists in each of us. If Asch, Milgram, Zimbardo, and Arendt are correct, it may be that law-abiding men and women with conventional virtues are indeed capable of committing Nazi like crimes, once the command is given and appropriate social mechanisms are set in motion." [76]

Let's summarize what we have discovered in this chapter. The basic economy of life, for human groups and human society, is to produce enough, materially and psychologically, to sustain life. Healthy human societies share this production task, internally and externally, through conscious, consensual trading of products and services. Ideological evil subverts this process by enabling some to coerce others to produce for their consumption under a banner of purported entitlement, a rationalized moral justification. It leads to increasing exploitation of scapegoat groups, under a cover story of moral righteousness which is built on lies.

Examples of ideological evil in history include the period of lynchings in the USA and the Nazi period in Germany. Key to understanding these times is that the people who carried out these horrors, who inflicted massive suffering onto others, were normal people. They were not monsters of depravity, but saw themselves as (and were acknowledged by others to be) good and upright citizens. They, their neighbors and associates, all were deluded by their feelings which told them that what they were doing was just and righteous.

We have spent some time looking carefully at historical evil, in order to validate a definition and understand some of the psychology behind this phenomenon. In the next chapter, we will apply this understanding as we attempt to discern ideological evil in contemporary society.

Chapter 11 – Contemporary Evil

"Man's nature is not essentially evil. Brute nature has been known to yield to the influence of love. You must never despair of human nature." – Mahatma Gandhi

"There are a thousand hacking at the branches of evil to one who is striking at the root." – Henry David Thoreau

"What is objectionable, what is dangerous about extremists, is not that they are extreme, but that they are intolerant. The evil is not what they say about their cause, but what they say about their opponents." – Robert Kennedy

"All things are subject to interpretation; whichever interpretation prevails at a given time is a function of power and not truth." – Friedrich Nietzsche

We spent time in the last chapter looking at culture-wide evil in historical societies in order to understand something of its nature. We have the advantage of perspective, of sufficient remove from the culture that gave rise to those attitudes and behaviors that we can now recognize and be repelled by the horrific nature of what was done, even though that insight and that empathy were unavailable to most people of the time. On the contrary, the majority of the population felt good and righteous about the torture and lynching of black citizens in the late nineteenth and early twentieth century American South. They felt that they were doing God's work, upholding the natural order, doing what was necessary to make a better world. There was no mainstream movement against the lynchings for over fifty years.

It would thus stand to reason that, if there were a form or forms of ideological evil operating among us today, most of us would not recognize the fact. Most of us would in fact applaud the evil behavior as appropriate and necessary. Let me repeat that; it's a vital point. If there were an evil ideology in our culture, most of us would be caught up in its righteous cover story; we would strongly approve of it and see it as just and necessary and important. Since we would not be repelled by it as we are with historical evil, the only way we could recognize the behavior as evil would be by analyzing its nature. We would have to approach and recognize it through the thinking function, because our feelings would be caught up in the cultural tide. We would have unconsciously 'bought' the ideology of lies on which evil is usually based.

That is what I ask of you in this chapter. I ask you to weigh and evaluate the truth, the veracity of evidence that may *feel* very wrong to you. I ask you to apply the tests of truth – agreement with reality, logical consistency, elegant simplicity – in an attempt to discover if there might be evil lurking behind a cover story that yet *feels* entirely righteous, important and necessary; that feels, in a word, true. I ask you to be willing to admit that a lie is in fact a lie when we uncover the logical inconsistencies in a cultural cover story. The first step in correcting a problem is to acknowledge that the problem exists.

Let us look more closely at how evil could hide in plain sight, could feel righteous and worthy in today's society. It would have to be closely aligned with the cultural milieu of our time, aligned with the accepted story about who are good and who are bad, who are victims and who are perpetrators. It would have to do its work by processes that are seen as just and appropriate means of punishment and coercion. I described in chapter four how the masculine archetype, which was prominent until the middle of last century, was eclipsed in the 1960s by the feminine archetype. A consequence of this is that the overt and direct forms of coercion such as physical force or intimidation through fear and violence no longer enjoy our approval. The more feminine forms of coercion, through social pressure and legal sanctions, feel right to us now, when we feel they are justified by the behavior of those we judge to be guilty. Finally, the issues it was addressing would have to feel important, urgent, a severe and imminent threat to our very way of life, so that severe actions against those judged as guilty could be seen as just and necessary.

In short, there would be an ongoing moral panic in our culture around the behavior of a certain identified group of people (the scapegoats), a moral panic that is regularly reinforced by news of further severe, inexcusable and intolerable transgressions by members of that group. Society would be responding to those provocations with penalties of increasing harshness and a progressive reduction of the civil rights of the designated perpetrator group and especially of accused individuals. The innocence of the designated victims would be as emphasized and reinforced as the guilt of the designated perpetrators. However, when examined thoughtfully and without prejudice, the transgressions of the perpetrator group would be found to be grossly exaggerated, the guilt often presumed rather than proven, and the penalties out of proportion to the offense. Finally, there would be a formal ideology which underwrote and justified all of these processes, an ideology of unassailable innocence for the designated victim group and inexcusable guilt for the alleged perpetrator group, an ideology that felt right to just about everybody – but yet was founded and propagated through lies because it was false to fact.

That's what it is like when a society is in the grip of an evil ideology. We recognize it readily as an apt description of historical evil, where the cover story has already been exposed and our feelings no longer blind us to the truth. Is there anything in contemporary society which fits that description? Let's feel our way into it gradually.

A major news story of 2014 was the kidnapping of over 276 Nigerian schoolgirls in the town of Chibok by Boko Haram, an Islamist jihadist group.[77] The world was outraged, and the story was front page news for months as the girls remained missing. I am sure you remember the story, just about everybody does. Did you know that in February of that year, two months before the kidnapping, Boko Haram murdered 59 schoolboys in Buni Yadi?[78] If you are like most of us, you didn't know because it wasn't a big news story. These boys were killed, which is presumably more serious than kidnapping, but the story hardly made the news here in North America. What's the difference? The difference is that when it is females, girls and women, we care much more than we do when it is boys and men. We don't *feel* like we make this difference; under the influence of modern gender politics we genuinely believe that we are gender balanced, but we aren't. We are vastly more sensitive to the issues of girls and women, much more concerned to protect them from disadvantage or harm.

Rape Culture
As I have been writing this book, the issue of rape culture has been constantly in the news. The idea is that rape is pervasive and

normalized due to societal attitudes about gender and sexuality.[79] In late 2014 as I have been writing this manuscript, comedian Bill Cosby has been accused of multiple rapes and has had his public appearances protested, Canadian national radio host Jian Ghomeshi was fired from the Canadian Broadcasting Corporation because of allegations of non-consensual rough sex, and thirteen male dentistry students at Dalhousie University in Halifax, Nova Scotia were publicly excoriated for joking, rapey comments shared with each other on a private facebook page. Emilie Buchwald, author of *Transforming a Rape Culture*, defines rape culture as:

> "A complex set of beliefs that encourage male sexual aggression and supports violence against women. It is a society where violence is seen as sexy and sexuality as violent. In a rape culture, women perceive a continuum of threatened violence that ranges from sexual remarks to sexual touching to rape itself. A rape culture condones physical and emotional terrorism against women as the norm." [80]

… Condones physical and emotional terrorism against women *as the norm*! This is very scary, if it's true. On the other hand, if it isn't true, it is the kind of extreme, exaggerated description that we would expect of a moral panic. It all depends on whether it's true or grossly exaggerated. Let's find out.

Do you recall the list of comments that I quoted at the end of chapter three, taken from a news website featuring a story about a man alleged to have raped a girl? [81] The girl's father first tortured the alleged rapist (by burning off his penis) and then strangled him to death. On the first page of 42 comments under this story, by my count, only 5 expressed any kind of reservation about the father's behavior, compared to 33 which offered total approval and praise for what was done to the alleged rapist. Almost all of those commenting on this story are outraged by this rape to the point where they advocate torturing and killing the alleged perpetrator.

These comments point, in fact, to the opposite of a rape culture. They point to a moral panic, where the rape of a girl, rather than being condoned and accepted as the norm, is considered (by both men and women) so heinous a violation that brutal reprisals including both torture and murder are felt to be appropriate. Note that these people are content to presume the matter of guilt – the man was only *accused* by his alleged victim; his guilt was not tested in court. This is clear evidence that what we are dealing with is a moral panic; the man is stereotyped as a member of the perpetrator group (men), such that for most people an accusation, especially from a female, is tantamount to a conviction.

However, let us acknowledge in fairness that, while very suggestive, such comments do not comprise a representative sample. They are evidence, but not calibrated evidence, and certainly not proof. Let us look for that at the fundamental shape of society's response to female rape, and let us compare it to our response when men are raped.

In 2014 the US government Centers for Disease Control and Prevention (CDC) published their National Intimate Partner and Sexual Violence Survey (NISVS), [82] based on 12,727 telephone interviews conducted in 2011 with non-institutionalized (i.e., outside of prison) men and women from across the USA. Based on these interviews, they estimated that 1.7% of women had been raped during the past year, compared to a number of men too small to be statistically significant. This certainly sounds like a serious problem of which women are the primary victims, and in fact this is the study most often cited in support of rape culture narratives.

When you look a little deeper into the numbers, however, a different picture emerges. The CDC definition of rape is "completed or attempted forced penetration, or alcohol or drug facilitated penetration." By focusing exclusively on penetration, it is a definition biased towards female victims; since men don't have vaginas, the only way they can be raped under this definition is orally or anally, usually by another man – and this is indeed relatively rare (outside of prison). However, if you include "forced to penetrate" (which the survey listed under a separate category from rape) into the definition of rape, then the figures change to 1.7% of women and 1.6% of men were raped during 2011.

Is "forced to penetrate" rape? The central issue of rape is clearly the lack of consent, which the CDC acknowledges elsewhere. The interview questions were identical for both genders. For instance, "How many people have ever used physical force or threats to physically harm you to make you have vaginal sex?" [83] The answers from female respondents were counted as rapes. However, men's answers to the identical question were counted as instances not of rape but of "forced to penetrate." "Forced to penetrate" is the equivalent, for men, that "forced to envelop" would be for women. "Forced to envelop" is everywhere acknowledged to be rape.

What's going on, as always, is that our biased feelings are getting in the way, feelings that legitimize female victimization and male perpetration but delegitimize the reverse. Are you able to think about this in an unbiased way, to see the sexism inherent in the CDC's definition of rape, and to rise above it? If you can, then you will conclude with me that when the definition of rape is gender balanced, almost identical numbers of women and men are raped.

Further, note that the survey specifically excluded the prison population, which is almost entirely male. What are the numbers of prison rapes? It's hard to know, because there have been few formal surveys to collect that data, and the reporting rate is expected to be low because of fear of reprisals. Estimates range from 1.9% to 20%,[84] with about a fifth being perpetrated by prison staff.

Finally, note the gender imbalance in the second part of the CDC's definition of rape, "alcohol or drug facilitated penetration." If both parties are drinking or taking drugs (by far the most common scenario), presumably neither the male nor the female are in a condition to give informed consent. So who was raped? It's clearly impossible to say in most cases, and so the fair thing would be to include either both or neither, but the CDC, with its focus always on "penetration" counted all of these instances as a rape of the female, but not of the male (again, except for anal or oral penetration).

This is the grossest sexism. How is it that when a man and a woman are both intoxicated or both high, and have unforced sex, he is a rapist and she is a victim? If we believe in gender equality, why should he get all of the responsibility and she none of it? There was no category, and so no data collected, for "alcohol or drug facilitated envelopment," which would be the gender-reversed equivalent to "alcohol or drug facilitated penetration," and would be a category almost exclusively occupied by male victims, in the same way that the CDC's definition selects out female victims. But collecting such data would make woman into rapists, and that wouldn't feel right.

What do we get if we include the whole population and a gender-balanced definition of rape? The 1.7% figure for female rape in the previous 12 months was broken down into 1% "completed or attempted forced penetration" and 0.7% "alcohol or drug facilitated penetration." Let's assume that most of the latter figure related to male-female sex where both parties were drinking or drugging (not precise, I admit, but the best we can do since the survey didn't collect the data we need), which would mean that a similar amount of men experienced what we might call "drug or alcohol facilitated envelopment." Let's, in fact, reduce the figure for men from 0.7% to 0.5% to allow for this imprecision. Then if we say that such intoxicated but unforced sex represents both parties being raped, we get final annual rape figures of 1.7% for women and 2.1% for men. Or if we say that intoxicated sex isn't rape for either party, then our final annual rape figures become 1.0% for women and 1.6% for men. And these figures don't include prison rapes, in which male victims greatly outnumber female victims.

In all cases, when we use a gender balanced definition of rape we find that significantly more men than women are raped every year. Yet we have endless, exaggerated media, police and political attention to rape against women.

The conclusion is clear. There is no rape culture against women. Rape of women is severely criminalized, and the population is hyper-sensitized to female victims and against male perpetrators – which is a moral panic, the opposite of a rape culture. On the other hand, most rape of men (made to penetrate, the type perpetrated predominantly by women) is not classified as rape, and there is little attention paid to it or to prison rape. If rape culture is the condoning of rape as a social norm, then we have no rape culture of women, but we *do* have a rape culture of men.

I encourage readers to do their own research into these questions. There is a massive amount of data available on the internet and in libraries. The majority of it, of course, promotes the cultural narrative about these issues, which means that it avoids dealing with the questions in a gender balanced way and instead plays to people's unbalanced feelings, their sensitivity to women-as-victims and their expectations that men will be perpetrators. But by digging into the data with careful analysis based on a disciplined, gender balanced focus, as I have demonstrated above, a researcher can see past these biases and discover the less known and less comfortable truth.

We have looked in some detail at the rape culture narrative, but this is just one part of a wider overall narrative about women as victims and men as perpetrators, the whole of which I am arguing is grossly unbalanced and driven by a moral panic. For another example, consider violence against women, a major feminist initiative from the earliest days of feminism. Google "violence against women," and compare the number of hits you get with "violence against men." When I did so on 7 February 2015, I got 15.2 million hits for the former compared to 269,000 for the latter. That's 56 times as many references to violence against women.

Let me put that another way. On the internet, violence against women gets 98.2% of the attention, violence against men just 1.8%. That's a whole lot of attention to when women are victims, compared to when men are. Is this a proportional response? Are women victims of violence far more than men? Is violence against women *the* major violence issue in society? Or is it a moral panic, out of all proportion to the facts simply because we care far more about female victims? Let's find out. What are the facts?

Let's start with the most serious violence, intentional homicide. Wikipedia reports that "According to the data given by the United Nations Office on Drugs and Crime, worldwide, 78.7% of homicide victims are male ..." [85] In the USA, the figure is 79%,[86] and in Canada, 74%.[87] So for the most serious form of violence – murder – male victims outnumber female by between 4 and 5 times.

What about lesser crimes? For all violent criminal assaults, including rape and other sexual assaults, I failed to find any aggregated gender figures for the whole world, but in the USA the victims were 56% male and 44% female in 2011,[88] and 49% male and 51% female in Canada in 2008.[89] In other words, men are 75 to 80% of the victims of homicide, and around 50% of the victims of all violent crime. Yet an internet search revealed not a single government program specifically addressing "violence against men," while there are too many to count, and at every level of government, focusing on violence against women. Furthermore, we have hundreds of women's shelters in North America, and not a single men's shelter. Yet all studies that are gender balanced in structure (i.e., that ask women and men the same questions) find similar rates of domestic violence perpetration by women as by men, and similar rates of victimization between women and men.

What we have is once again a moral panic, driven by our extreme concern to protect women from harm. Yet the violence statistics show that women are already more protected from violence than men. Our attention to violence against women is out of all proportion to the rate of such violence. Ask yourself why we are content to have so many "violence against women" programs, and a federal "Violence Against Women Act" in the USA. The project is inherently sexist on its face. How would you feel about "violence against whites" programs that focused only on white victims? I suspect we would both recognize the racism inherent in such a project.

The issue is violence, pure and simple, and violence against any social subgroup should be considered under that inclusive rubric. That is what racial equality looks like, and that is what gender equality looks like. Separating out violence against women for special focus is an expression of our sexism against men, our chivalrous need to provide special protection to women. If we are honest with ourselves we will admit that and end such biased projects.

It is worth pausing to consider carefully and seriously how society can get these issues so wrong. How can it be that we are convinced there is a rape culture, i.e., a condoning of female rape, when there really is the opposite; an exaggerated moral panic about female rape? How can it be that we give virtually no attention to the rape of males, even distorting the definition to exclude the most common form of male rape – a situation that actually *meets* the definition of rape culture? How can it be that violence against women is perceived as a horrific plague, but no one is talking about violence against men, who are equal if not greater victims of violence? How can perceptions be so false to fact; indeed, opposite to fact?

We are back, of course, to the power of feeling. When feeling rules the psyche, as it does for the majority of citizens, then facts are of virtually no account. In this case, our feelings are strongly gender biased, such that when a man and a woman have intoxicated sex together, for instance, we want to release the woman from responsibility for her actions, but not the man. It *feels* like he raped her. That's what feels right, so that's what the survey measured. But it isn't right, it is actually sexism, sexist prejudice, and if we really do want to treat the genders equally, then we need to own up to such prejudices and remove them from our psyches and our culture.

To see the sexism, consider how we treat drunk driving. We hold a driver criminally responsible for their intoxicated state – as indeed we should – whether they are a man or a woman. So why the difference when it comes to drunk sex? Why do we wish to exonerate the woman, find a way to see her as innocent and hold the male accountable? There is no logical reason, the reason is all in our feelings, and those feelings kick in most strongly when *both genders* are involved, as they are in heterosexual sex. The same for violence against women, our sexist feelings get engaged for *male* violence against *women*, not for male violence against men or female violence against women, where gender isn't central. We rationalize those feelings, of course, to come up with purported reasons for the difference, but those reasons don't hold water if we think critically about them. Unfortunately, few of us actually do this.

This bias isn't our fault, but it is our responsibility. We used to be more honest about it, we used to admit that we wished to protect women more than men, telling ourselves that they had "finer sensibilities," but that changed in the sixties. Feminism changed it. Now we are telling ourselves that women are the equal of any man, but our feelings, reinforced by feminist initiatives like violence against women, are still driving us to protect them much more than men. Now we are lying to ourselves about our actions and about reality itself.

We have established that there is currently a moral panic around gender which is driving rape culture and violence against women narratives. This same moral panic is behind every single feminist initiative these days; each one is built on a distortion of facts and plays to our eagerness to see women as victims and men as perpetrators. There isn't room in this book to make the case for the many other feminist initiatives. If you have any doubts, I encourage you to do your own research (see Appendix A for a list of useful resources).

We have seen that there is a moral panic around feminist issues, but that is only one of the symptoms of ideological evil. What about the other symptoms? One is that we would systematically reduce the legal rights and protections for the alleged perpetrator group, the group that we are scapegoating, under the influence of our presumption of guilt, and expand the rights and protections for the designated victim group. Are we doing that?

On April 4, 2011, Assistant Secretary for Civil Rights Russlynn Ali, head of the US Department of Education's Office for Civil Rights (OCR), distributed a 19-page "Dear Colleague" letter [90] to all colleges and universities in the USA. At the risk of losing federal funding, on which most institutions of higher learning have become dependent, they must now, under "Title IX" of the Civil Rights Act (which prohibits discrimination on the basis of sex), curtail the due process rights of those accused of sexual violence or harassment – overwhelmingly men. In particular, OCR's new interpretation of the law requires universities to "strongly discourage" permitting the accused to "question or cross examine the accuser." If an appeals process is offered, it must be available to both parties, which subjects the accused to double jeopardy. Finally, and most egregiously, rather than a presumption of innocence which requires proof of guilt "beyond a reasonable doubt," the burden of proof is to be shifted to the lowest "preponderance of the evidence" standard – in other words, whom do you believe more? In a moral panic situation, where we are oversensitive to the need to protect women and inclined to see them as innocent victims, and suspicious of the motives and truthfulness of men, whom is that likely to be? Such a process amounts, in practice, to a presumption of guilt for the accused.

As Stanford senior fellow Peter Berkowitz remarks,

> "On campus, where casual sex is celebrated and is frequently fueled by alcohol, the ambiguity that often attends sexual encounters is heightened and the risk of error in rape cases is increased. The consequences for a wrongly convicted student are devastating: Not only is he likely to be expelled, but he may well be barred from graduate or professional school and certain government agencies, suffer irreparable damage to his reputation, and still be exposed to criminal prosecution." [91]

These are severe reductions in due process rights for the accused (almost always male), with corresponding expansions of the rights of the alleged victim (almost always female) and they are enforced by the threat of loss of funds for colleges that fail to go along. The vast majority of US colleges and universities have complied without protest. This is the second symptom of a society infected with ideological evil.

The third is the presence of a formal ideology which underwrites and justifies all of these processes, an ideology of unassailable innocence for the designated victim group and inexcusable guilt for the alleged perpetrator group, an ideology that feels right to almost everyone – but yet is founded on lies and propagated through lies. That ideology is feminism.

Feminism

Firstly, it is important to say to what I refer with the name feminism. A standard defense against any criticism of feminism is that it is no one thing, but many shades of beliefs and affiliations, such as liberal feminism, socialist or Marxist feminism, radical feminism, ecofeminism, etc. Of course these branches exist, but this is irrelevant. Any ideology is identified by its basic tenets, which remain unchanged across all its variations since it is they that unite the varieties under the one name. In the case of feminism, all branches share the same basic belief that history has been a story of general oppression of women by men. Indeed, this is acknowledged by feminists as the essential, defining principle, for example, by Alison M. Jaggar and Paula Rothenberg Struhl in their book *Feminist Frameworks,* where they say, "... the conservative view of women's situation in society is not feminist, because it denies that women are oppressed." [92]

A related objection to criticisms of feminism is that it is continuously evolving, and indeed this is true; in the period that I focus on in this book, from the 1960s to the present, we have seen both second and third wave feminism. However, the changes that have occurred under these evolutions have been changes of focus and style rather than of substance. In the foundational area that we are examining, the prejudice that offers only compassion for women and only accountability for men, there has been no change at all. No mainstream feminist branch or subgroup has ever acknowledged the symmetry of male and female disadvantage, and none have ever advocated for the correction or amelioration of even one of the many gender issues that affect men and not women.[xi]

Secondly, I want to be very clear that it is not my intention, nor would I consider it valid, to indict feminism based on the words or actions of any radical elements or "lunatic fringe". Only the consistent messages of its major, acknowledged spokespersons and the major policies that it has pursued will be used here to build a case. My focus is on *modern, mainstream* feminism, which for brevity I will refer to simply as feminism. While my research suggests that the same phenomenon is operating throughout the Western world, I will confine my examples to North American feminism, since this is the area that I know best.

Is feminism founded on and propagated through lies? We saw with the story of the Titanic at the end of chapter four that the notion that men have oppressed women won't hold water (no pun intended). Oppressors have never died to save the oppressed, and never will. The claim that men have oppressed women is one lie. Another is that feminism is about pursuing equality between men and women. When I suggest that feminism is actually about women's advantage, feminists swiftly cite the dictionary definition of feminism, "The doctrine advocating social, political, and all other rights of women equal to those of men." [93] Something similar to this is indeed the formal definition of feminism in every dictionary I know.

The problem with the dictionary definition, in the case of feminism, is that it overlooks the effect of our gender biased feelings that focus on women as victims and men as perpetrators. If we are under the influence of an evil ideology that is preying on us by means of those biased feelings, then that will include society-wide self-deception about the nature of that ideology. In short, we cannot trust what is said, written and believed about feminism. We cannot trust our definitions, since they will represent our cover story rather than the

---

[xi] There are people who call themselves feminists who pursue real gender equality and advocate for men's issues; for instance Christina Hoff Sommers who calls herself "the factual feminist," and Camille Paglia, a self-described dissident feminist. However they are vehemently repudiated as anti-feminist by all mainstream feminists and feminist organizations. People may name themselves as they wish, but I too argue that their gender balanced politics are more accurately described as anti-feminist.

truth. Instead, we have to determine the true nature of feminism by looking below the surface at what it is actually *doing*, the way we looked earlier into the nature of the CDC survey of sexual violence, which presented and believed itself to be gender neutral but was actually very gender biased.

Let's do that. The first thing to note is that the definition of feminism is gender biased even on its face. It wants women to have equal rights to men, but says nothing about men having equal rights to women. Furthermore, it says nothing about women having equal *responsibilities* to men. If it were true, as feminists believe, that men have oppressed women, that men have had many more rights than women, then such a focus might be appropriate, at least at first. But what if the truth is that men and women have had differentiated gender roles, originating of course in their different biology, and that out of those different roles have evolved different rights and different responsibilities? Then feminism, according to its definition, wants women to have all the rights that men have, but cares nothing about men having all the rights that women have, and wants nothing to do with the responsibilities that come with those rights. Clearly, this won't lead toward equality, even on its face.

But let's look deeper, below the surface into the practical politics. Feminism presents itself as the whole answer, as all that is needed to achieve full equality between women and men. It claims that the men's human rights movement (MHRM), men advocating for their own issues, is mistaken and misogynist. It has pursued many policies aimed at the ways that women have been disadvantaged by their gender roles, which is good and necessary, but has it ever, even once, pursued a policy aimed at correcting a uniquely male gender disadvantage; for instance, male homelessness, suicide or incarceration rates – all many times higher than the female equivalents? Has it spoken out against the male military draft, in support of disenfranchised fathers, or against lower funding for research into men's health issues like prostate cancer (funded at ¼ the rate of breast cancer)? Or, shifting from rights to responsibilities, have feminists ever suggested that women should be subject to military conscription the way that men are? No, because this is a male *responsibility*, not a right. They want no part of it.

In years of looking, I have not found a single instance of mainstream feminist concern with any of these major issues affecting men's lives. What I have found, rather, is that when feminists mention men's issues it is only to delegitimize them as false, inflated or trivial, as backlash against feminism, or as all men's fault anyway. At the level of basic policy, feminism has proven in fifty years that it is not at all about gender equality. The claim that it is, is another lie.

Let us pause for a moment; this is a heavy chapter. My goal here is not judgmental but explanatory, to help my readers to see what is real and true so that each of us might be better able to decide what to do and how to do it. We are in a difficult time, one featuring a lot of unconsciousness and distortions of truth leading to great amounts of avoidable harm and suffering. I also believe that we can learn from history and that we can help each other to see clearly and to choose wisely. We can check the accuracy of our feelings by thinking carefully, independently about these questions. We can look at the evidence, discover our biases and correct them. The process is difficult, it requires some discipline, but it is also immensely rewarding.

Growing into wisdom is like gaining one's sight after being blind for a lifetime; it is hugely exciting and fulfilling. The "bliss" of ignorance and conformity offers no attraction to one who has woken up. But before that, before one awakens, there can seem to be great comfort in holding to an ideology of simple black and white, of guilt and innocence, of victims and perpetrators. I remember the eleven year old boy I was fifty years ago, sitting in school wishing that the truth were self-evident and obvious. I remember when I first woke up myself, in December of 1990, and realized that the reason it is so difficult is that it seems that the truth must convict us – and realized still later that that is an error. The truth frees us; after it convicts us, it pardons us.

Feminism is seen by most of our citizens as the hope of our culture, the vision of equality between men and women that will save us from the injustice and oppression of history. To consider that, on the contrary, it might be the very worst thing in our contemporary society, a manifestation of ideological evil that is doing massive harm – this is an almost impossible reversal. How can we take it in, how can we contemplate that we might have in our midst something similar to the Inquisition, the lynchings, or that icon of evil, Nazism? How could reality possibly be so opposite to what we have believed?

I have laid out the theory and it is all there; the explanation is sufficient to the problem. But that is an intellectual statement, and what we are struggling with here is an emotional reaction. I know about the problem of coming to terms with such a difficult conclusion from my own experience. The realization that feminism is an evil ideology, along with much of the theory about ideological evil, came to me in 1998, almost twenty years ago. I published an essay about it, but the reaction against it from every one of my friends and all of the men in my men's group was so severe that I spent years struggling with the concept. Could it possibly be true, when no one else could contemplate it even for a moment?

I was like Freud, discoverer of a theory that no one could accept – but at least I wasn't faced with losing fame and livelihood as he was. It took me fifteen years to check my thinking completely and conclude that the theory was true, that I really was right and all of my friends were wrong. I spent most of those years feeling lonely and sorry for myself, stuck in a victim place around the inability or unwillingness of others to think about this issue.

Today, I have come to peace with the conclusion that feminism is an evil ideology. Our age is not special; we are not so enlightened that we are free of the taint of evil that blighted past societies. It is in the nature of ideological evil that it should hide in plain sight, fooling just about everybody into thinking that it is a righteous movement for the good of everyone. Mahatma Gandhi said, "Many people, especially ignorant people, want to punish you for speaking the truth, for being correct, for being you. Never apologize for being correct, or for being years ahead of your time. If you're right and you know it, speak your mind. Speak your mind. Even if you are a minority of one, the truth is still the truth."

Today, I embrace this advice. But I know the difficulty of that journey, and I empathize with those who still have it before them. A great deal of grief is involved in revising one's worldview so fundamentally. But the alternative is worse. I recognize the wisdom of Soren Kierkegaard when he said, "He who dares, loses his footing for a time. He who dares not, loses himself."

I felt the need for this interlude as I wrote, but I am a little ahead of myself. I have not yet shown that feminism is an evil ideology, only that it is driving a moral panic and is founded on lies, which are just two of the symptoms. What of the formal definition that I offered:

1. The desire for unearned consumption or privilege,

2. The overt or covert coercion of others in order to achieve it,

3. The insistent and consistent, formalized rationalization of this behavior as moral and righteous.

Does feminism fully meet all of these criteria?

Firstly, does feminism seek *unearned* privilege—rights without responsibilities? A major plank of modern feminism from the beginning has been female reproductive rights; specifically, a woman's right to abort an unwanted child. We explored the issue of abortion in some depth in chapter nine; here I want to simply highlight one aspect. (Note that this is a brand new right, not one that men ever had.) So we have the iniquitous situation that the father has no say in whether his offspring lives or dies, is not even required to be notified of the pregnancy, yet is legally obliged to support the child if the woman chooses to keep it, and whether he intended or wishes to be a father or not. Saying to a woman, "If you didn't want a child, you shouldn't have had sex" is met by feminists with howls of outrage and accusations of sexism – yet this is exactly what those same feminists say to men in the same situation. Their hypocrisy is blatant.

Similarly, in the matter of parenting, feminism has not sought equality between fathers and mothers, but has argued strenuously for a presumption in favor of the "primary caregiver" (usually the mother) in contested divorce cases.[94] In 2001, Canadian women's groups refused to sit at the same table with fathers' groups seeking a presumption of shared parenting after divorce.[95] It is worth noting that equal shared parenting would mean that no child support money would need to change hands, whereas a primary caregiver presumption leads to child support court orders in which men provide money to both mother and child, and hope that the mother allows them to "visit" their children.

Clearly, in women's area of traditional responsibility, reproduction, feminism wants no gender equality, but rather has sought and won rights for women and responsibilities for men.

What about in other areas? In men's areas of traditional responsibility, the real equality issues – the right to vote, laws against gender discrimination in employment, in salary, in housing, in access to professional roles – were addressed years ago. Today, all feminist initiatives, every single one, are about giving women rights over men, and men responsibility for women. Thus we have employment equity (affirmative action) legislation for jobs where men predominate, but not for those where women are in the majority. We have ever more punitive enforcement of child support after divorce, but no enforcement at all for access by fathers to their children. We have zero tolerance (i.e., arrest the man on the woman's word) against *male* violence against *women* based on feminist advocacy studies that model all domestic violence in terms of male oppression of female victims, and deny the reality of women's equal initiation of violence in the home. We have redefined sexual assault, in Canada, so that a man is guilty of rape if a woman consents to sex but, unknown to the man, does so out of fear.[96] We have sexual harassment laws addressing the ways that men might abuse women's sexuality in the workplace, but no laws addressing (or even acknowledging) women's use of their sexuality to unfairly advance their careers. We have even defined obscenity, here in Canada, in terms of what harms women![97] All of these laws and policies were direct results of feminist initiatives.

All of these feminist initiatives seek women's advantage *coercively,* which is the second criterion describing an evil ideology. They have insisted (and have been granted) that these rights be given the coercive force of law. In doing so, they employ their own, archetypally feminine forms of coercion: deception and shame. Deception appears in the creation and use of false and distorted statistics (such as the many studies showing that women continue to earn less than men, but which ignore differences between men and women in hours worked, years of experience, overtime, credentials and the like, which when factored in account *entirely* for the differences in apparent earnings).[98] Shame is coercive in a similar way to blackmail, in that the ability of legislators, academics, judges and voters to consider the issues dispassionately and make free, sensible choices is virtually eliminated by their need to avoid their denied but still devastating feelings of shame if they ever see themselves as abusive to women.

In Canada, a major feminist initiative was pay equity within the federal government. A Human Rights Tribunal ordered the government to pay approximately five billion dollars to (mostly) female government workers, because their work was "undervalued" with respect to that of men. This argument is totally false. Unequal pay in the same job and discrimination in hiring (the real equality issues) have been illegal in Canada for many years. Any woman who wanted the higher paying 'male' job could have applied for it. The fact is, salaries are set by market demand; where many people desire a particular kind of work (such as clerical or secretarial duties), the oversupply forces salaries down. That's as it should be, since the price of production then represents the real costs. Communist Russia went bankrupt trying to make the market serve ideological goals.

What the pay equity advocates really want is the cushy, convenient, attractive office work, but at the higher salaries of the less attractive (hence higher paid) jobs that tend to be held more by men. They want to be subsidized on the backs of men. They want to increase their consumption without any increase in their production. They want a legal entitlement to it. In our dysfunctional society, they're getting it.

The third aspect of an evil ideology is the maintenance of an image of total and perpetual moral righteousness. In *People of the Lie,* M. Scott Peck describes this aspect as follows:

> "Utterly dedicated to preserving their self-image of perfection, [the evil] are unceasingly engaged in the effort to maintain the appearance of moral purity. They worry about this a great deal. They are acutely sensitive to social norms and what others might think of them. … [T]hey dress well, go to work on time, pay their taxes, and outwardly seem to live lives that are above reproach.

> "The words 'image,' 'appearance,' and 'outwardly' are crucial to understanding the morality of the evil. While they seem to lack any motivation to *be* good, they intensely desire to appear good.

> Their 'goodness' is all on a level of pretense. It is, in effect, a lie. This is why they are the 'people of the lie.'" [99]

No adult in our society today could have escaped exposure to this aspect of feminism: *every* argument that it makes is based in this appeal to moral righteousness and justice, and many of the examples already discussed have already made this apparent, so I will confine myself to exposing the basic strategies employed to maintain the image of righteousness when the reality is quite different.

If one is pursuing goals (women's advantage at men's expense) which must be disguised, then it is vital to have devices by which meaningful dialogue, which might lead to exposure of the truth, can be avoided or deflected. Feminism has three basic strategies for this:

1. Where there is a difference in society between men's and women's roles, ignore the real causes and present the difference always as evidence of male oppression and discrimination against women, and demand compensatory programs (e.g., abortion on demand, sexual harassment, pay equity, rape culture, etc.).

2. Where there is no difference between men's and women's roles, or such differences as do exist already favor women, create biased studies and statistics to argue that women are disadvantaged. Claim that difference as evidence of male oppression and demand compensatory programs (e.g., women's health, violence against women). If necessary, introduce "violence against women and children" as an emotional trump card to shut down debate of the real issues. (e.g., allege child or wife abuse in family court).

3. If anyone opposes or criticizes feminist claims, silence or isolate them through shame, by accusing them of "misogyny" or "backlash", i.e., of being opposed the equality of women in order to maintain their own selfish or oppressive behavior. Note that this also works against women, who are said to be "colonized" by the patriarchy.

Summary: Never, under any circumstances, yield the moral high ground. Consider, for example, the contortions that feminists performed as they rationalized their support for feminist President Bill Clinton in the face of behavior that, in anyone else, they would condemn as sexual exploitation.

We have been analyzing at a high level, looking at the lies built into overall feminist programs, and this is important, but it doesn't give a flavor of the real ugliness of what is going on. For that, let's return to rape culture for a moment, and look at some specific details of how it is defined and interpreted. You will remember that I said that the basic, underlying, hidden motivation of feminism is to regress women toward infants, people with rights but no responsibilities, and to regress men toward slaves, people with responsibilities but no rights. It still astonishes me that such a thing can be done under a banner of gender equality, but it can and is being done.

For some insight into how it is done in practice, consider some questions from a survey conducted in late 2014 by the Ottawa University "Task Force on Respect and Equality." In their report, *"Ending Sexual Violence at the University of Ottawa,"* the task force wrote,

> "Our survey highlighted a number of concerns with respect to attitudes and behaviors among the student population.

> Harmful beliefs about women and rape were measured by 16 questions, each containing five possible responses, ranging from "strongly disagree" to "strongly agree," to statements that minimize harassment and hold women responsible for sexual violence. Although the majority of students disagreed with the statements, substantial proportions agreed with or were neutral (which may suggest a level of ambivalence) toward them. For example,

> 25% agreed (21% were neutral) that interpreting harmless gestures as "sexual harassment" is unfair to men.
> 15% agreed (11% were neutral) that women who put themselves in risky situations are partly responsible if they are raped.
> 14% agreed (15% were neutral) that when women wear low-cut tops or short skirts, they are sending men mixed messages." [100]

These healthy responses were categorized as the problem, as symptoms of rape culture! What a shame that we have been indoctrinated to the extent that only 15% of students agree that "women who put themselves in risky situations are partly responsible if they are raped." Of course women who put themselves in risky situations bear some responsibility if the risks turn against them. To deny this, to absolve them of any responsibility for their own choices, turns them into infants and makes men responsible for them no matter what they do, like a parent with a child. We all have a part to play in defending ourselves against crime, and if we take risks, a healthy society assigns some responsibility to us for our actions. However, the feminist rape culture narrative interprets this healthy perspective as *part of rape culture*, part of the problem.

The rape culture moral panic is propelling a process in which female responsibility is progressively eroded and male responsibility is progressively expanded. This is actually explicit in parts of the document, for instance where it says, "A clear message emerged from these conversations: the University needs to protect survivors and *privilege their voices* during discussions of sexual violence on campus." [101] [Emphasis added]

What does "privilege their voices" really mean? It means that there should be no level playing field when sexual violence is discussed. Men's descriptions of their feelings, their motivations and their understanding of the situation are to be dismissed. The sexism against men has become so accepted, it feels so right to us in our moral panic, that it can be openly named and enforced. The goal is clear; what is seen as ideal is that women should have no responsibility at all, and men should have it all. This while claiming to be seeking gender equality! The ugliness of this, the perversion of truth and justice under a banner of truth and justice is appalling. It is, indeed, evil. Yet it is invisible to most of us; we are caught up in the feeling that it is good and right and just.

In the last chapter we saw that the real reason for the judgment of Negros as inferior to whites was as a defense against the possibility of their superiority. Is it the same for feminism; is the real reason for the judgment of men as morally inferior to women as a defense against their possible superiority? Yes, of course; whenever guilt is projected onto another party, it is an attempt to deny the guilt of the projecting party.

It is not hard to imagine why women might feel inferior to men; their historical role has been far less prominent. Men have been most of the pioneers, the discoverers, the scientists, the architects, the builders and designers, the lawyers, judges and politicians, even the poets and artists. But men's prowess in the external world has been a role driven, partly if not mostly, by their need to impress women, to compete for and secure a place in the world where they can have a family, where they can love and be loved. Women's role has been less prominent but perhaps more central, more foundational. In any event, there is no difference that matters in moral terms between the characters, the natures of men and women. We are truly equal, and the notion of essential guilt on the part of either of us is an error. We can let it go and relax into equality.

Can I put this thesis in simpler terms for a moment, so that we can get a clear feeling for how this could happen? Human nature is wired for tribal thinking so that until we have done a lot of personal growth, until we have matured ourselves considerably, we tend to see the world in terms of us and them. "We are good and they are not" is a comforting notion for a still insecure soul. The result of making this moral judgment is that we find it difficult to empathize with the other. More than that, it feels unnecessary and inappropriate to empathize with them. For examples of this, consider religion (the saved and the damned in Christian terms, or the followers of the Prophet and the infidels). So this is one factor – moral judgment.

The presence of a visible biological difference as in race or gender makes it even easier to slip into us-and-them prejudice. Gender, because of the unrecognized moral power of women and the visible and psychological differences between men and women, meets both criteria. At times when the psychosocial circumstances favor it, that prejudice gains popular cachet and slips still further, into moral panic and ideological evil, where we come to believe that coercion and violence are justified to defend the good guys against the badness of the scapegoated group. This is what has happened in contemporary society, and feminism is the vehicle that has formed around this tribal prejudice, to justify and propagate it. It is an expression of the primitive, tribal forces of the psyche. It is very dangerous.

This is dark indeed. Evil ideology manifests as lack of empathy combined with moral panic. To justify denying their rights and wrecking their lives, men must be seen as contemptible. Is this what is happening? Consider some of feminism's major slogans. When a man complains about receiving mixed sexual signals from a woman, he is asked, "What part of 'no' don't you understand?" Can you feel the moral indictment that this question implies? No nuances, not the slightest interest in considering whether there might have been any miscommunication on her part, just judgment, hostility and contempt for him. Consider another. "Why do men rape [or beat, or abuse] women? *Because they can.*" Can you feel the contempt built into this question and answer? Men have no conscience, no redeeming features, no moral compunction at all; only external force can possibly restrain them from violent behavior. This is how feminism sees men. This is how it wants us all to see them. This is why it must be named and recognized as evil.

In writing this book I have been careful to come from stage 4 understanding. I can see and empathize with the fear that is behind feminist rhetoric and self-righteousness. My interest is to heal feminism, not accuse and judge it. But I do not want that balance, that lack of angry judgment on my part to excuse or diminish the facts. The hate, the contempt for men that motivates feminism is very, very dark. It fully deserves the name of evil, and we will not begin to correct the damage it is doing until we realize just what we have in our midst. We must diagnose it accurately and we must oppose it effectively. It is not only men who are injured by it, but women and children as well. Our whole social fabric is under attack.

I have brought almost to a close my argument that we are facing, in the rise of feminism, an evil ideology that is tapping into and exploiting our biased, sexist feelings about men and women, and that this is analogous to periods in history when an evil ideology gained sway in a population. But this has of necessity been largely an intellectual exercise, and even if it has been successful and raised a doubt in your mind about feminism, I imagine that it is still virtually impossible to believe that feminism could truly be as harmful as those monstrous periods in our history with which I have compared it. In the next chapter, I will look more deeply at consequences in the world; at how feminism is propagating and how it is affecting people's lives.

Chapter 12 – How Evil Propagates

"Although images of perfection in people's personal lives can cause unhappiness, images of perfect societies - utopian images - can cause monstrous evil. In fact, forcefully changing society to conform to societal images was the greatest cause of evil in the twentieth century." – Dennis Prager

"There is no crueler tyranny than that which is perpetuated under the shield of law and in the name of justice." – Charles de Montesquieu

"Propaganda requires a permanent network of communication so that it can systematically stifle reflection with emotive or utopian slogans. Its pace is usually fast." – John Berger

"When we forgive evil we do not excuse it, we do not tolerate it, we do not smother it. We look the evil full in the face, call it what it is, let its horror shock and stun and enrage us, and only then do we forgive it." – Lewis B. Smedes

In the last chapter I argued that feminism matches the criteria and the definition of ideological evil. I know that this goes against the passionately held convictions of the vast majority of our society. More than that, it is a horrific conclusion. Our attachment to seeing women as innocent victims in all but minor exceptions is virtually total. Considering that the women's movement might be evil in the way that Nazism was evil feels abhorrent – yet this can only be our sexism, our unwillingness to see women as truly equal to men. We have no trouble acknowledging that men are capable of evil, but we want women to be better than this, morally superior, special. This is, in fact, female chauvinism.

There is little doubt that many will judge *me* as evil for asserting that feminism is evil. Nevertheless, I have presented a coherent theory and enough evidence in support of that theory that the case I have made cannot be legitimately dismissed out of hand. Those of my readers who really want to know the truth of this matter will test what I have said by doing their own research, and from that research will draw their own conclusions. That is all that I seek with my writing.

But one area of the case remains to be made. If feminism really is comparable in form and severity to those massively harmful projects of history that we now name as evil, where is the fallout? Where is the great damage that we would expect to see? I have hinted at this in previous chapters; now it is time to make it plain.

First, let us be clear what we are looking for. Extreme examples of evil behavior do not need to be universal or even widespread for the overall effects to be massive. There were only some 4,743 lynchings in the USA from 1882-1968, a period of 86 years. Of these, 27.3% were of whites, usually for helping blacks or for being anti-lynching.[102] The 3446 blacks lynched is a tiny proportion of the total black population – but it represents the extreme tip of the iceberg in terms of generic racial discrimination against Negroes. The function of the lynchings was to keep the blacks subordinate despite their legal equality – subordinate socially, morally, economically and politically. It was this massive, systemic but more subtle and less visible denial of equality rights that carried the major consequences for the whole black population; the lynchings were just the most extreme, relatively rare form.

Similarly, historians estimate that a total of approximately 150,000 people were tried by Inquisitional courts, of which 3000 were executed,[103] over the 600 years from their beginning in 1184 until the mid nineteenth century, an average of about 5 executions a year across the whole of Europe. Again, these numbers are small compared to the whole population of Europe; they were again the extreme tip of the iceberg of religious intolerance and lack of religious freedom enforced by the church under its ideology against hereticism that all of Europe suffered under. Although not formally part of the Inquisition, the Church's intolerance of Protestant "hereticism" led to several religious wars that together almost halved the population of Europe.

We conclude, then, that an evil ideology may result in relatively few extreme examples of completely destroyed lives; its hallmark is the systemic eroding of basic freedom and justice for a scapegoated group across a whole population. However, and this is a key symptom to identify it as evil, even the extreme events are seen as appropriate and righteously justified under the ideology.

With this in mind, let us seek to discover, first, how ideological evil propagates in civil society, and make comparisons between history and current time. There are two difficulties we must overcome to do this. Firstly, we are still caught up in this one, so it's much harder to 'get' it in a way that feels the same as when we consider historical evil. We are aware these days (indeed, overly aware) of the shadow of the masculine, so we can feel the horror of Nazi brutality, of the Negro lynchings, of the witch burnings. But we have no place in our psyches, yet, to put horror of the shadow feminine, since we continue to deny its existence as a major player in the world. We feel that feminine excess is an exception, a minor factor; it is masculine excess that has been the source of evil in the world. When unmistakably confronted with feminine abuses, we tend to make excuses, trivialize or rationalize them away. We still use the word "motherhood" to mean that which is beyond question or debate. Consider what Patricia Pearson reports in her groundbreaking book, *When She Was Bad: Violent Women and the Myth of Innocence:*

> "Female serial killers, according to Eric Hickey, actually average a greater number of victims than their male counterparts, even though the deaths occur right under their communities' noses. Since authorities have no framework of suspicion for multiple murders in a family or hospital, they often don't even suspect there is a killer to pursue. They have on their hands, instead, a series of abrupt natural deaths or unexplained disappearances. It is lack of suspicion, nothing more complex, that enabled a woman like Nannie Doss, of Oklahoma, to kill four husbands, two children, her mother, two of her sisters, and her nephew in the 1930s and 1940s; Marybeth Tinning to destroy her children; Genene Jones to murder an estimated forty infants and small children; and British nurse Beverly Allitt to kill at least four children in a Lincolnshire hospital." [104]

Secondly, the fact that feminine power is archetypally indirect and covert means that it is by nature more hidden, less visible, harder to discern and identify. Especially, it is more difficult to connect effects to causes. More than that, because of our deep attachment to seeing women as powerless, it is difficult for us to feel the reality of female power, to actually realize that their power is the equal of that of men. It just doesn't feel like women could have prevailed over men in men's traditional arena of political power. We tend to vastly underestimate the potency of the moral power that women have always wielded, and that was specifically acknowledged[105] in the very first feminist event at Seneca Falls almost 170 years ago.

Patricia Pearson explains this difference clearly:

> "In a 1993 survey of Ontario high school girls, the community psychologist Fred Mathews put the following question to them: Defining violence as broadly as they wished, who were they most afraid of? Overwhelmingly, they responded, 'Other girls'.

> Ask women what they did in childhood to disrupt the status quo – engaging in subversion – while their brothers, for instance, were running around stealing hubcaps, blowing up frogs, or throwing eggs at the neighbors, and their answers also reveal ingenious forms of indirect aggression. 'My father was an obsessive-compulsive type,' says Karen, a twenty-four-year-old from Seattle. Everything had to be in its place. So I spent a lot of time fucking with his head, moving his stuff around, scratching his car with a penknife, so that if he asked me if I'd driven the car, I could honestly say no, just driving him nuts.' Shelly, a twenty-nine-year-old actress, ruined the confidence of her little brother once, by telling him that, although he thought he was eight years old, he was actually twelve. He was retarded. His parents hadn't wanted him to know.

> What qualitative measures do we posses in our culture to understand injurious behavior that isn't masculine in style? Would Shelly's 'retarded' brother have suffered more if she'd struck him on the head? Would Allison's father have been more damaged if she'd crashed his car instead of tormenting him psychologically? … Because we have developed a male-centered measure of aggression, we have blinded ourselves to the ways in which girls develop and utilize power." [106]

Can we contemplate that there could be a whole realm of feminine aggression and manipulation, deception and intimidation that is virtually invisible to us in our focus on more direct, masculine forms of violence? Pearson acknowledges another difficulty that this poses a few pages later:

> "What is clearly discomfiting about indirect strategies of aggression is that they bestow upon women ignoble traits:

hysteria, duplicitousness, manipulation, cunning. At least, we think, a male villain is straightforward. His aggression mirrors that which is valorous in other arenas, such as in war. Female aggressive strategies are never valorous, for they are by necessity underhanded, and partly because of that, they run completely counter to the way women want to view themselves. We cringe when we hear a man deriding our sex as sneaky and two-faced. As a result, our inclination is to deny the intention as well as the strategy – to adamantly insist on the absence of feminine malice."[107]

Patricia Pearson is a woman willing to talk honestly about the shadow feminine, to acknowledge its power in the world and also to admit to women's role in concealing and denying it. She has my thanks for her courageous honesty.

Thirdly, the most obvious victims of feminist policies are men, and we have already noted the fact that our empathy for men is greatly attenuated compared to our empathy for women. This bias, when added to the fact that men tend to conceal their pain, is another factor making it hard for us to see the harm that feminism is doing.

In summary, moving ourselves to the place where we 'get' that feminism is a modern ideological evil, where we feel the truth of that, is a difficult accomplishment. It is difficult firstly because we are still under its sway and thus have no psychological distance, no perspective; secondly because its archetypally feminine form means that its processes are indirect, and thirdly because our ability to empathize with men is very weak. When processes are indirect and denied and also align with our prejudices, it becomes hard indeed to perceive them accurately. However, given those three handicaps, let's see what we can do to discover how evil might be propagating in modern society.

First, let's look at the process that was used in Nazi Germany, the process that is now acknowledged to be the prime vehicle by which the German public became emotionally and ideologically engaged with the Nazi program. Albert Speer, one of Hitler's chief war Ministers, writing from prison after being convicted at Nuremberg, described the way that Hitler and Goebbels were able to find and exploit a deep well of psychological passion and create a moral panic in the German people. Describing an early speech by Hitler, he writes,

"He spoke urgently and with hypnotic persuasiveness. The mood he cast was much deeper than the speech itself, most of which I did not remember for very long. Moreover, I was carried on the wave of the enthusiasm which, one could almost feel this physically, bore the speaker along from sentence to sentence. It swept away any skepticism, any reservations. Opponents were given no chance to speak. This furthered the illusion, at least momentarily, of unanimity. Finally, Hitler no longer seemed to be speaking to convince; rather, he seemed to feel that he was expressing what the audience, by now transformed into a single mass, expected of him. It was as if it were the most natural thing in the world to lead students and part of the faculty of the two greatest academies in Germany submissively by a leash. Yet that evening he was not yet the absolute ruler, immune from all criticism, but was still exposed to attacks from all directions. ... Both Goebbels and Hitler had understood how to unleash mass instincts, how to play on the passions that underlay the veneer of ordinary respectable life. Practiced demagogues, they succeeded in fusing the assembled workers, petits bourgeois, and students into a homogeneous mob whose opinions they could mold as they pleased. ... but as I see it today, these politicians in particular were in fact molded by the mob itself, guided by its yearnings and its daydreams. Of course Goebbels and Hitler knew how to penetrate through to the instincts of their audiences; but in the deeper sense they derived their whole existence from these audiences. Certainly the masses roared to the beat set by Hitler's and Goebbels' baton; yet they were not the true conductors. The mob determined the theme. To compensate for misery, insecurity, unemployment, and hopelessness, this anonymous assemblage wallowed for hours at a time in obsessions, savagery, licence. This was no ardent nationalism. Rather, for a few short hours the personal unhappiness ... was replaced by a frenzy that demanded victims. And Hitler and Goebbels threw them the victims. By lashing out at their opponents and vilifying the Jews they gave expression and direction to fierce, primal passions." [108]

This is a wonderful, candid description of what it looks and feels like when archetypal energies are tapped and exploited. The result is a kind of mass psychosis, as the godlike possessive powers of psychological archetypes bedazzle and subvert the superficially civilized psyche.

The whipping up of crowds into angry mobs by political leaders is not something that we see today. That is a hierarchical, more masculine form; the feminine archetype does things differently. I have found only a few references to the kind of virulently angry, irrational crowds that were characteristic of Nazi Germany. Camille Paglia, a crusading US *dissident* feminist, wrote, "While lecturing at major American universities this year, I have come into direct contact with the politically correct establishment. ... Following my lecture at Brown, I was screamed at by soft, inexperienced, but seethingly neurotic middle-class white girls, whose [feminist] party-line views on rape I have rejected in my writings. Rational discourse is not possible in an atmosphere of such mob derangement." [109]

If this form of mob manifestation is rare, where is the moral panic surfacing? How is it being tapped and exploited? How could this be happening under our noses, as it were, and we remain unaware of it?

Let us remember that it will take a form that is ostensibly about solving social problems. The Nazi rallies all took as their surface theme an exploration of and purported solutions to problems that faced Germany at that time. However, it will be more environmental, more background than overt, due to the more indirect and covert nature of feminine archetypal power. It will imply, without stating directly, the moral superiority of women over men, the responsibility of men for everything bad in the world and the virtuous innocence of women, the way that Nazism emphasized the virtuous superiority of Aryan Germans. And it will be done in a way that reaches virtually everyone.

In *Spreading Misandry; The Teaching of Contempt for Men in Popular Culture,* [the word misandry means the hatred of men, as misogyny means the hatred of women], Paul Nathanson and Katherine K. Young write:

> "The venue par excellence for those who want confirmation of
> the notion that women are superior to men is surely television,

especially daytime talk shows (which are addressed primarily to women) and prime-time news-magazine shows (addressed to the wider public). …

"Even though talk shows often try to disseminate information by way of 'experts,' usually the authors of books on pop-psychology or other forms of self-help for the masses, intellectual analysis of the information presented is seldom high on the list of priorities. *Immediate emotional reaction* [emphasis in original] by members of the studio audience, on the other hand, is high on that list. In fact, it is the only thing that really matters. This state of affairs was not invented by talk show hosts and psychologists, pop or otherwise. Its ultimate origin is in a romanticism that can be traced back long before the period normally referred to by that name. Its immediate origin, however, is a popularized version of psychoanalysis."[110]

After discussing a particular talk show, ostensibly about the problems of men, in which the female studio audience are encouraged to shame and discredit the five male guests, Nathanson and Young observe,

"Talk shows have been likened to the public square, but they are much more like therapeutic encounter sessions. What takes place is not the moral discourse on which democracy depends, but the abreactions and peer solidarity on which group therapy depends. … The five men on *Donahue* are straw men, there to be knocked down by members of the audience or, if necessary, by Donahue himself. … Participating in this symbolic battle either directly or vicariously, women are 'empowered' to feel righteous without ever having to take seriously what the men are saying." [111]

Spreading Misandry: The Teaching of Contempt for Men in Popular Culture is in fact a 250 page discourse on how the whole of popular media, from movies, novels, print journalism, the internet and especially television, participate in this process of discrediting, demeaning and shaming men and building the rage of women over their innocent victimhood, which is all perceived as the fault of men. I am not saying that this sexist shaming is the whole of the media message. I am simply saying that this is where the feminist story is principally propagated, with the internet becoming more prominent in this media list in recent years. The subtext is that women are intrinsically morally superior to men, and that men are undeserving of empathy of any kind. In their conclusion, Nathanson and Young observe,

> "The worldview of ideological feminism, like that of every other religion or movement, is all inclusive; nothing is beyond its purview. From that perspective, it would seem that men could best be understood through its lens. The trouble is that this form of feminism has no philosophical or moral framework for the notion that women, like men, can succumb to sexism or that men, like women, can be seriously damaged by hatred. To the extent that feminists refuse to focus much attention on their own gains (mainly because doing so would undermine their call for continuing political action), and to the extent that they refuse to acknowledge the problems of men (including misandry as the intentional or unintentional fallout from ideological feminism), they are morally implicated in the problem. That perspective leaves women largely unaccountable for their own behavior." [112]

Is this ubiquitous message of inherent moral righteousness for women and contempt for men in popular culture the psychosocial equivalent of the Nazi rallies described by Albert Speer? I think so. It is not focused and hierarchical in the way the masculine archetype requires, but rather omnipresent, enveloping and environmental in the feminine way that that archetype calls forth. Its purported solution, which for the Nazis took the masculine form of social improvement through military action and political hegemony, takes instead the feminine form of social healing; reforming men and protecting women through community action, one-sided laws and policies like zero-tolerance, no-means-no sexual consent laws, women's shelters which emphasize women's victimhood and justify their rage, and programs 'for' men like "Confronting Abusive Beliefs" that we examined in chapter seven. The fact that these programs and laws are inherently abusive and misandric of themselves is overlooked (more precisely, is unconsciously required by the fact that what is being acted out is the archetypal psychic energy of feminine ideological evil, rather than any attempt at real healing).

Can there be any doubt that the ostensible leaders of this popular culture, the talk show producers and hosts, the print media publishers and editors, are in practice *following* the direction set by the consuming public, in the same way that Speer observed when he wrote, "… as I see it today, these politicians were in fact molded by the mob itself, guided by its yearnings and its daydreams." [113]   The influence of TV ratings and media sales on content is hard to overstate; it is popular appeal that both directs these media and legitimizes their misandric content. The competitive selection and promotion pressures that surface and sink talk show hosts and media personalities would bring forward and maintain in the public eye just those individuals who can best mirror to the public the unconscious patterns that are moving the whole population. Is it an accident that the most successful TV personality of all time, talk-show host Oprah Winfrey, is a black woman who emphasizes feminist politics? [xii]

We saw how strongly talk-shows can silence any real dialogue about gender when we considered what happened to Fred Hayward, founder of Men's Rights Inc. in Sacramento, CA, who was invited to appear on *Oprah.* Fred's comment, after he was thrown off the show, is key. "They don't play devil's advocate to women, but they do to men because they're trying to cater to the women who are watching." That sounds innocuous, but consider it carefully. Why should talk shows have to play devil's advocate to men in order to appeal to women viewers? There can be only one answer. Clearly, those viewers don't *want* the truth about men, or about women. They want, instead, a reassuring cover story that consistently distorts reality in ways that don't require women to ever examine themselves with any humility, or men with any empathy.

What is being packaged and served up in a thousand ways is a consistent message about gender, one that claims and pretends to be true and honest, but is actually carefully managed to conceal its massive bias. Our popular media are teaching prejudice, are teaching inherent righteousness for women and essential contempt for men. They are doing this by a process of selection, emphasis, value

---

[xii] If you consider it carefully, Oprah's success virtually disproves all on its own the feminist notion of the glass ceiling, the idea that the top roles in the mainstream business world are barred from women because of sexist prejudice. She – black, female and from a poor sharecropper family – rose to the very peak of the TV world on talent alone.

interpretation and censorship; real information about men's victimhood or women's culpability is simply filtered out. This is not a conscious conspiracy but something much darker. These people sincerely believe in what they are doing; they are as much caught up in the fantasy as are their consumers.

The distortion, the perversion of reality can become amazingly gross without being recognized. Consider a story told by Camille Paglia in her book *Sex, Art and American Culture*:

> "One of the main reasons that I am so angry is that last year at the University of Pennsylvania I went to a lecture … [by] … Diana Fuss of Princeton, a very prominent feminist theorist. She seems to be a very nice woman. … [W]hat she did was show a series of slides that she had made of contemporary ads and pictorials from *Harper's Bazaar* and so on.

> "Let me tell you the full story of what happened that night. … [I]t was *torture* to me, because she was showing these *gorgeous* pictures up on the screen, beautiful pictures that were stimulating the mind, stimulating the imagination, you understand? And at the same time she was *trashing* these pictures with this horrible Lacan, labyrinthine thing. … Let me give you an example. There was a Revlon ad of a woman in a blue pool of water, and she was beautifully made up, and there was obviously a reflector being used to shine the sunlight especially intensely on her face. This was a beautiful ad. And Diana Fuss was going, 'Decapitation – mutilation.'

> "Then there was a beautiful picture from *Harper's Bazaar,* I think, of a black woman wearing a crimson turtleneck. But instead of the collar turned over, you know, it was up like this, around the chin. It was very beautiful. It was like a flower. And she was wearing aviator glasses that I recognized, from the 1930s! Now Diana Fuss said, 'She's blinded!' *I* would have said, 'She has mystic vision.' Anyway, with the turtleneck, what do you think? 'Strangulation, bondage!' It went on like this, picture after picture after picture. I thought, 'This is *psychotic.'* Such radical misinterpretation of reality is psychotic. But it's a whole system. People within that system feel it's very rational.

> "Now, what I hated about this was you had two hundred young

women, who didn't understand a *word* of what she was saying – it was all that Lacan gibberish – and they're all going, 'Ohhh, *wow*! The woman from Princeton – a big woman from Princeton. She's so brilliant!' And I thought, 'This is *evil.*' Diana Fuss is not evil. She's a nice woman. But if what you're *doing* is evil, I'm sorry, it has to *stop.* This is perverted. It really is perverted. When you destroy young people's ability to take pleasure in beauty, you are a pervert!" [114]

What is the effect of this subtle, omnipresent, continuous onslaught? It works on our beliefs and our feelings, as did Hitler and Goebbels in their speeches and rallies. It continually erodes our ability to empathize with men or to see their value, their contribution, anything positive about them. It continually erodes our ability (already constrained by chivalry) to hold women accountable, to see their power or anything except their victimhood and innocence.

The movie *In the Company of Men* is a good example illustrating this bias. Here is an excerpt from a review by author Warren Farrell:

"The credits are rolling and my stomach is churning. Not a single woman exiting *In the Company of Men* is speaking with even a trace of warmth toward her male partner. Women in all-female groups are laying into men-as-bastards in voices easy to hear, in a way no one would with Jews, blacks or women.

"I seek some female perspectives. I find myself unable to approach any woman; each seems surrounded with an energy field saying, 'You are man … stay back.' In the lobby, I notice two women whose energy seems softer. They stop to read the movie review. I read it with them. As they finish, I gently ask what they thought of the movie. Their bodies shudder in disgust; they mumble, 'Men.' Then they look up, eyes registering me, and without embarrassment they turn their backs and leave.

"I am shaken. I decide to walk it off. After a light bite, I wander into a bookstore. There are the same two women. My first thought: 'Maybe now's a better time,' is cancelled by a deeper fear: 'Stalker.' I leave. I feel like a black man approaching the wrong restroom at the turn of the century in the Deep South.

"The film packs this wallop by portraying two men filled with hatred toward women ('Women … they're meat, gristle, hatred

— they're all the same.'), each hurt by a woman. They conspire for revenge. So far, it's *The First Wives' Club,* but in the company of men. But *The First Wives; Club* drew half of all the opening weekend moviegoers in [the USA] to cheer the 'vaporization' of the husbands-as-bastards. In *In the Company of Men,* no one cheers the men on to hurt the woman; rather, they fear a woman being hurt.

"In *In the Company of Men,* the target is Christine, the personification of vulnerability: deaf, innocent, beautiful, young, female. Her deafness has made men neglect her romantically, so the men plan to separately but simultaneously court her, send her flowers, confess love, then coldly drop her and laugh as she 'reaches for the sleeping pills.' Christine's sweetness courts the audience and … uh oh, … even the men. We watch even Chad, the ringleader who has thus far come across as the worst of Iago and Manson soften, weaken, and fall in love. Christine returns Chad's love. And then Chad grabs her face, mockingly tells her it's all a game, he just wanted to hurt her. He haughtily exits the bedroom. The audience realizes that it, like Christine, has been sucked in by Chad's pretense.

"Women in the audience, who have just heard virtually every loving assurance a man ever gave them, and now see that they were duped, cannot help but recall their most blistering pangs of rejection. It is the feeling of having been sucked in again that emotionally seals their feelings of identity with Christine as victim and Chad as Evil Personified (or is it Man Personified?). …

"So what's the point of the movie? When a man says he's been hurt, be suspicious. His pleas for compassion are the bait and you are just the fish. Proof? Men love fishing. Motivation? It gives them a thrill to exercise their power. In the film's words, he does it because he can. Because he has the power. That's it. So don't even listen to men. …

"It is the unconsciousness of our anti-male sexism that makes it so dangerous." [115]

How far does this biased, distorted, fairy-tale worldview extend? Are there any institutions of our society where it has not penetrated?

It seems not. The academy (universities, education system), the judiciary, the legislatures, government administration, the media, the church, private corporations have all been submerged in the propaganda onslaught and proven themselves entirely unable to resist it or to see through it. Here and there an individual speaks out, but the effect is like shouting in a windstorm: few hear and fewer still take note. The world's most prestigious newspaper, *The New York Times,* is completely besotted. Warren Farrell, in an interview with Steven Svoboda, said, "… regarding the places like the *New York Times* in which I had published every single thing I had written when I was a feminist, since I have questioned feminism nothing I have written has been published. I was on the *Donahue* show seven times as a feminist. I was on once where I deviated from the feminist position, and I was never invited back." [116]

What are the consequences that flow from this subtle (and not-so-subtle but still unrecognized) tide of reality-distorted propaganda? What effect does it have in the lives of the populations that it influences? Note, as I ask this, that I am not putting the media into the role of prime cause, and consumers as effect. As I have already described, this is a dance of enmeshment, and we the public are more leaders than followers in this dance, as Speer observed of the Nazi 'leaders'.

What this media misandry does is to legitimize for us the expression and manifestation of our own sexist prejudice. Its practical effects are that, thousands of times a day, repeated in millions, indeed billions of human lives, we are ever quicker to judge men and to see them as guilty, ever quicker to excuse women and to see them as innocent. In millions of marriages, wives become less tolerant of their husbands' little differences, more contemptuous of their advice, more controlling of their behavior, and feel ever more entitled to their support and devotion. Their empathy for their husbands' or sons' or brothers' pains and efforts erodes towards the vanishing point of pure contempt.

Eventually, for example, it becomes first thinkable, and then doable, for her to make a phone call to the police, accusing him of "domestic violence" because he raised his voice and she felt some momentary fear, or just because she thought he needed 'teaching a lesson'. And then the feminist zero tolerance law kicks in, and he is removed from his home for six or ten months, without compensation, barred from seeing his children or his wife, forced to take a room somewhere – and all of this is justified, in his wife's mind and in ours, by *his* behavior.

What has really happened is that her empathy for him has been eroded almost to zero, so that she has indeed become 'zero tolerant' – intolerant of the nature of daily life with a man who, no matter how subservient he may try to be, forever challenges her inflating sense of entitlement.

Can this really be true, we wonder? Can contempt for men be so common? Warren Farrell relates that "… even female-positive therapists are often surprised at women's anger towards men. For example, Dan Kiley, author of *The Peter Pan Syndrome* and *Wendy's Dilemma,* startled himself when, to an audience of several hundred Midwestern women, he was explaining research showing that men who are excessively self-involved are six times more likely to die of coronary heart disease than men who are not, *and four hundred women erupted into applause and cheers.*" [117]

The forms, the details, the ways in which this anger and contempt will manifest in peoples' lives will differ in a million ways. It is the basic pattern that I point to here. Consider one man's story of his marriage:

> "The woman I married was an active, intelligent and growing feminist. I considered myself to be an egalitarian, and I believed that humankind had wasted much of its potential by keeping women in relative subservience. … The amount of material that one finds in the media supporting feminist claims is staggering. It seems that one cannot listen to the radio without being told of the many women that seek shelter every day from abusive men, one cannot watch television without being reminded of the self-serving and selfish nature of men and of their propensity for violence. Surely, I thought, there must be a strong reflection of the truth in all of this. Men are violent, opportunistic and manipulative, and they must change.
>
> Being a gentle man did not seem to free me from the sense of guilt for being part of such a group. Responsibilities go further than the self, and I found myself starting to intervene when it

seemed appropriate. I participated in rallies, interrupted sexist jokes at work, and began to isolate myself from those 'beer-bellied, foul-mouthed' guys that gather at break time. Slowly, my feminist convictions led me to turn my back on my own kind. I started disrespecting men. … By the time I woke up, it was too late. No longer happy to be a man and rejected by the radical feminists whose ideas I generally endorsed, I was a man without a home.

"By then, goddess religion had entered our home. On the premise that women were sacred life bearers, the flagships for a more pacifist society, the key to a better future, altars were appearing in every corner of our home. … Our last year together was a series of ideological arguments, financial upsets and emotional battles. New age feminism had entered our home, and Kali was burning it down. …

"Radical feminists have taken a healthy discussion and turned it into a fight from which there has to be a loser. Armed with retributive arguments, legislative powers and the sour taste of revenge, they have failed to understand that a world without strong men, without strong fathers, will be just as poor as it was without strong women. … As a divorced father, I saw my role eliminated by the powers given to a retributive wife to simply portray me as a 'typical male.' That was enough to have the system take my child away from me, to transform a loving father into a visitor. … As a man and a father, I am told to pay and to be happy to have the right to visit my child. As a man, my emotions are discarded as unfounded, my goals reduced to dreams, my powerful intellect interpreted as arrogance, my strength reduced to bestial violence. No longer an individual, I am made the symbol and probable cause of our failure as a family.

After a period of unsuccessful attempts to reason with my ex-wife and with the system, I took the hardest decision I have ever made. I appealed directly to my ex-mate for moral justice, for shared custody of our child, for my right to be a father. When that was denied me, I decided that I would not see my daughter as a visitor. …

"I end my testimony with the words of my five-year-old daughter. She said it best when I announced my terrible decision to her, that it might be a very long time before we would see each other again. As tears were falling on my cheeks, she said, "I understand, Papa. You let mommy be my mommy, and she won't let you be my papa." My lips broke into a smile of pride as tears brushed them." [118]

When I printed this story in *Everyman,* some readers wrote letters criticizing this man for not remaining in his daughter's life, even as a visitor. I do not. While his is indeed a terrible decision, it may be a heroic one. I acknowledge the heroism of those fathers who continue to pay child support to vengeful ex-wives who refuse to let them see their own children, purely for love of the children. Who are we to presume to say how much pain a father should suffer for the sake of his children, or what represents a wise decision for him and for them? Who are we to decide that this man took the easy way out? Perhaps accepting a subservient role as a pseudo-father is the easy way out. We must each find our own way to serve those who need us, and to fight against the progress of evil, if we choose to fight at all.

Such stories, such suffering, repeated a million times a day in the lives of our nations, are the result of this huge, unconscious process of reality erosion, of fantasy manifestation, that is progressing in our societies under the misleading banners of liberal enlightenment, of sexual equality, of feminism. I see it as directly analogous to the Nazi rallies that stirred up the beliefs in German superiority and entitlement, anti-Jewish sentiment, and that led directly to the extermination of Jews in death camps and to Germany's invasion of neighboring countries and the devastation of World War II. I name this modern process as evil for the same reasons that history has named Nazism as evil. There is no doubt that it meets the definition I offered:

1. It supports the entitlement of women to unearned privilege, rights without responsibilities;

2. It legitimizes the coercion of men to provide and pay for these rights and privileges;

3. It insistently and consistently rationalizes such behavior as moral and righteous.

In *Spreading Misandry,* Nathanson and Young even suggest why men seem unable to oppose this tide of hate against them.

> "Most men … are probably too confused to take a position specifically on misandry. They are aware at some level of consciousness that something is wrong, but they are not equipped to identify or analyze it. Even the few men who really are equipped to do so often find it difficult to say anything in public. The taboo on male vulnerability is not only experienced internally, remember, but also enforced externally. Men who admit to feeling vulnerable are attacked as cowards, and by no group more effectively than women. The ability to shame men has always been among the most useful of women's weapons. In this case, men are shamed into silence, a form of abuse that few women today would tolerate." [119]

Nathanson and Young recognize the power of women to shame men, though without identifying the key and central role of such shaming in the symmetrical power relations between men and women that I outlined in the Gender Codependent Matrix (chapter five).

What is the ultimate objective of modern feminism? Feminists believe that it is equality that they seek. But it is not. Because they are acting out an evil ideology, their unconscious goal is to regress women to the state of childhood: i.e., rights without responsibilities, consumption without production. For men, they have the opposite objective: responsibilities without rights. People with responsibilities but no rights are slaves. We are currently headed, unconsciously but steadily, for a world in which women are children and men are slaves. This represents a huge cultural subversion, a massive, coercive oversimplifying of life, a monstrous amputation of human growth and potential. This is why I have named this process as evil. It is as hugely destructive as any historical campaign that has been given that name: the Inquisition; the witch burnings, Nazism. Not until we begin to recognize the truth of this and recoil in horror as a whole culture, will we wake up from this nightmare.

The situation is grave, but it is early days yet. We are still unconsciously appeasing feminists, much as the Britain did with Hitler in 1936-39. It didn't work then and it won't work now. In fact, as then, it will lead to disaster. When British Prime Minister Neville Chamberlain returned in 1938 from appeasing Hitler by giving him Czechoslovakia to headlines of "World War Averted," a standing ovation in the House of Commons, and accolades like the *Times'* "No conqueror returning from victory on the battlefield has come adorned with nobler laurels," only one prophet saw clearly what had happened. Winston Churchill rose in Parliament and said, to hisses and boos, "We have suffered a total and unmitigated defeat." [120] History records who was right. Let us not forget how completely and disastrously mistaken popular understanding and feeling can be. The British politicians of 1938 chose to believe what they wanted to be true and to ignore or deny what was really true. Churchill was rewarded for his prescience by being given the role of Prime Minister in 1939 so that he could clean up the disaster exacerbated by those who had refused to listen to him. Let us not ignore the prophets of our own time.

Howard Schwartz, in his remarkable *Revolt of the Primitive: An Inquiry into the Roots of Political Correctness,* explores the power of feminism and political correctness to overturn rational discourse and defy reality itself. His is the only other book I know that explores the psychosocial roots of these phenomena, as I do here. Using Freudian approaches and models, Schwartz argues that what we are seeing is nothing less than a massive revolt of the primitive, pre-rational energies of the psyche against the civilized, based on a fantasy of the restoration of the primordial mother. I suspect that if my own models of the stages of spiritual growth and of the roots of evil ideology could be converted into Freudian terms (something well beyond my own limited understanding of Freudian psychology), we might be saying the same thing. Schwartz's conclusions about where all this is going may be even darker than my own.

> "[I] suggest that the social order defined by political correctness, and determined by the revolt of the primitive, may be only a way station on the road to pure chaos, to the Hobbesian 'state of nature.' This is not hyperbole, and is not to be taken lightly. ...

> "The problems that the revolt of the primitive has brought – a generation of confused and helpless male children, of women intoxicated by self-worship and victimized by their own grandiosity, decomposition of the family, destruction of the educational system, castration of the military, and many that we have not even mentioned – are monumental. Yet the worst of

these is the undermining of self-criticism. The social forces that have created these problems have rendered them beyond discussion and precluded the possibility of solution. What they need is rigorous, robust, frank and fearless discussion. They need intense commitment to the intellectual process itself, to the pursuit of truth for its own sake, to the belief that the truth will make us free. …

"How did we get to this? How did it happen that Western civilization, at the height of its greatest achievements, would give its best minds over to the task of taking itself apart? The answer is, of course, an old one. … For this turns out to be the classic material of tragedy. It is *hubris*. We pushed reality back so far that its existence became only a rumor. Then we suppressed the rumor. We said it was politically incorrect. It interfered with our grandiosity, and we chose our grandiosity.

"Of course reality will have its day. For if we have managed to make it so that the consequences of individual mistakes are mitigated, are buffered by the system, there still remains the possibility of making a mistake. All we have done is to ensure that if we make a mistake, and we will make a mistake, it will be a mistake of the whole system – a big, big, big mistake." [121]

Perhaps, as Schwartz seems to imply, this process will lead to a collapse of our civilization. I am hopeful that such might be avoided. While a civilization in the grip of ideological evil is indeed a massive tragedy and leads to monumental suffering, it is not without precedent.   Although we have rarely faced an onslaught of ideological evil from the *feminine* archetype, there are things that we can learn from our experience with the analogous *masculine* situation we found ourselves in when Nazism arose in Germany. There, the threat was at first avoided, minimized and appeased as we are doing now; but eventually faced and dealt with from the *healthy* masculine, through political and military action. Can this threat be met through the healthy *feminine*? What would that mean?

Some women's organizations, such as R.E.A.L. Women[122] in Canada, and The Independent Women's Forum[123] and The Women's Freedom Network[124] in the USA, are speaking out against feminism. It is significant that all of these organizations seem to be strongly conservative or traditionalist, more right wing than left. This is not hard to understand. After all, feminism is an ideology of the left, so its errors are more readily visible to those who are already inclined to see the left as mistaken. To put it another way, traditionalists are more (or still) in touch with the value of men, which was recognized in traditional society. But can an effective offensive be mounted from this section of society? I would love for the answer to be yes, but unfortunately I doubt it. I doubt it because there is no traditional cultural pattern of female mass protection of men or masculinity to draw on, as there was of male military protection of nations and of women and children. Women have indeed used their moral power to support men in traditional society, but this power was exercised individually, privately, domestically. It would be a huge innovation for women to step into overt cultural leadership and to defend men's honor on a national or international scale. And these are *conservatives,* people who are largely opposed to significant innovation, who see the answers to society's problems mainly in the patterns of the past. It would be very difficult for them to strongly embrace an entirely new cultural pattern.

I also have to say that the activities of these groups in opposing the feminist tide seem to have been of no more effect, so far, than have the activities of the men's movement. If there is a unique and powerful force of which these women's organizations are the vanguard, I have yet to perceive it.

Some writers have suggested that international law might be used to expose and correct systemic evil. In his *Evil and the Demonic,* Paul Oppenheimer writes:

> "What facts such as these all add up to is, at a minimum, a deduction and a prescription. The deduction is clear enough: to seize control of a society's legal system is to seize control of its intelligence. One may then do with it what one pleases. The prescription is … if evil is understood as an analyzable form of behavior, the legal systems that protect and encourage it may be analyzed as evil themselves and may be described as evil in law. It is conceivable, in other words, that they too may be indicted before courts of international law empowered to adjudicate in a new though undoubtedly controversial area of evil acts and laws, in which the specious defense of plain legality with be found to be insufficient.

> The vacuousness of the 'legal defense' can be cited in those cases in which the motifs of evil itself are shown to exist in full abundance; where hearsay evidence, police powers amounting to an inquisitorial dictatorship, the prevention of an adequate defense through cross-examination, the segregation of the accused from the rest of society, the determination of guilt solely by association with a particular group, extraordinary or cruel and unusual punishments, and the silence at the centre of the society accepting these practices and pacts for malice – the absence of defiance or the opportunity to amend or abolish them – are sprinkled as a deathly dust through the legal atmosphere." [125]

While Oppenheimer's list of the motifs of evil is weighted towards masculine forms of intimidation through fear rather than feminine forms of intimidation through shame, it nevertheless offers an approach to fighting systemic evil which seems theoretically possible. In the case that we are examining, however, it seems a vain hope. The vehicles of international law, most especially the United Nations, seem themselves to be hopelessly enmeshed and lost in feminist ideology; they too have been entirely captured and subverted and are now part of the tide pushing it forward. [126]

There is some opposition to feminism in the media, especially on the internet, but it is scattered and uncoordinated, and so far ineffective. For the most part, those who see the contradictions in feminism fail to see that these contradictions do not undermine its power. For example, in a November, 2014 *National Review* essay entitled "Modern Feminism; Appalling Stupidity Backed by Hysterical Rage," David French ends by dismissing feminism. "Feminism doesn't really have a philosophy. It's barely even an ideology. It's mostly just a series of temper tantrums thrown by a small, privileged minority. And, unless it changes, it will soon be irrelevant." [127]

French is typical of commentators who perceive the inconsistencies in feminism; most conclude that those inconsistencies render it powerless. He thinks that we will readily see through it and move on. He is quite wrong, because he has no inkling of the female power to shame men within the gender codependent matrix. We must not underestimate the power that feminism holds to distort and subvert what is healthy in society. Ideological evil grips us deep in our own psyches, deeper than the place where our rationality lives.

Restoring social health and gender balance will be neither a small nor an easy task; it will challenge us monumentally. The remaining chapters will address how we might rise to that challenge. But before we explore solutions, let us spend a moment considering how things might unfold if we do not succeed in turning this around.

In an earlier chapter, I talked about how we would do well to reframe our understanding of what is happening around gender from the judgmental moral framework of men oppressing women that feminism has promoted, to something more like a disease model, as AA did some eighty years ago. I want in this chapter to explore another dimension of this disease metaphor for society, namely, how the disease will progress.

I think that where we are at right now in our understanding of social science is about where medical science was when it was sticking leeches on people. We have little real understanding of what moves societies or of large scale interpersonal dynamics, and so we use theories, like *"Men oppress women and children, and want power and control in relationships: women are innocent victims"*, in order to explain what we see. Since the theories, like the *"Disease is in the blood, so letting out the bad blood will help"* theory behind the use of leeches, are plausible but mistaken, what we do to fix things (e.g., anger management and relationship re-education for men, women's shelters where women are reassured of their powerlessness and innocence), don't actually help much. Like leeches, they are unpleasant for all concerned and often make things worse. In our ideological attachment to our theories, however, we don't notice that these activities aren't effective, or if we do we assume, according to our theory, that men are just resisting 'losing their power and privilege,' blame them even more, and try harder. If two leeches don't work, use six or ten!

It is instructive to consider what medical researchers did to move from the feeling-driven theories behind the use of leeches, to instead discover the objective knowledge that lies behind our modern, fairly effective medical system. First, they scientifically studied anatomy and metabolism in order to discover how the body actually functions. (Leonardo da Vinci, probably the first to systematically study the human body, was criticized for his misunderstood practice of obtaining and dissecting cadavers, and had to leave the Vatican in order to avoid prosecution.) Then, they studied disease patterns to understand the mechanisms of metabolic distress and failure. Finally, they designed intervention techniques to interrupt disease and restore health. (Louis Pasteur, discoverer of the role of micro-organisms in human and animal disease, invented the powerful technique of immunization by inoculation with attenuated microbes.)

The success of these efforts was built on the application of the scientific method: open-minded study of the facts; generation of hypotheses, experimental testing of those hypotheses, and publication of results for checking through peer review in order to uncover error. In the physical world, our sophisticated technology, including medical technology, is proof of the success of this approach. In the world of sociology and societal dynamics, our primitive, pseudo-scientific theories reflect our unwillingness to take this approach.

Given that we are in this pre-scientific, superstitious stage of understanding in our relationship to human systems, what does that mean about how social disease mechanisms will play out? Well, what happened in the past? If a patient had a serious, life-threatening disease like polio or smallpox, and the physician did things like putting leeches onto their body to 'cleanse the blood,' such actions had no positive consequence, did not intervene in the disease process in any way. The only thing able to fight the disease at all was the individual's own unconscious, biologically-evolved disease antibodies. And so the disease took its natural course, which was well known and documented. The symptoms and the patient's distress (dis-ease) would increase until the 'climax' of the disease process was reached. At this point, either the patient's internal disease-fighting mechanisms would triumph and turn the tide of the affliction and he or she would begin to recover, or the patient's disease antibodies would be overwhelmed by the disease onslaught and they would die.

The same pattern plays out in our society regularly. Social disease processes like war, civil and domestic violence, etc., are observed to come in cycles, and sometimes the social organism (the society, the culture, the relationship) survives them and sometimes it does not. Certainly, the things that we are currently doing to address these problems can be classified, along with leeches, as ineffective at best and counter-effective at worst. Where was the effective, truth-based, empathy-engaged dialogue following 9/11, for instance, that might have explored the root causes for that horror in terms of US foreign policy, international hegemony, national insecurity, etc.?

I don't wish to point fingers uniquely at the USA. I use their response to 9/11 only as a typical example. American culture is no different from anyone else's in any way that is significant on the dimensions that we are exploring here. No country, no institution, no organization that I am aware of has yet developed effective social intervention tools into common societal disease processes. Indeed, we have not yet even identified such social patterns *as* disease.

Only the almost unknown science of psychohistory has even begun the scientific study of actual societal psychodynamic processes. [128] Psychohistorian Lloyd deMause writes of war, "All standard theories of war deny that it is an emotional disorder at all. War, unlike individual violence, is usually seen solely as a response to events *outside* the individual. Nations that start wars are not considered emotionally disturbed – they are either considered rational or they are 'evil,' a religious category. Although homicide and suicide are now studied as clinical disorders, war, unfortunately, is not." [129] And so our social interventions are designed and guided by pre-scientific superstitions and theories that are followed because they feel right to us, like "the best defense is a good offense" and "women are only violent in self-defense."

Why are we unwilling to discover the real nature of overt societal disease processes like war, social and domestic violence, and of covert social disease processes like political correctness (i.e., ideological intimidation) and social shaming? One answer is that these questions, being essentially about our own unconscious processes, are extraordinarily difficult to penetrate, since they challenge our story about ourselves. Another is that of George Orwell, who wrote in his essay on Kipling, "We all live by robbing Asiatic coolies, and those of us who are 'enlightened' all maintain that those coolies ought to be set free; but our standard of living, and hence our 'enlightenment,' demands that the robbery shall continue." That is, we fear, at some deep, unconscious level, that we would lose something we depend upon, if we really penetrated the reality behind our social dysfunctions. But that is the addict's excuse, and it will not do.

So we return to leadership. The massive research teams of universities, corporations and governments, with their multi-billion dollar budgets, are not going to penetrate these questions. Their focus, their presumptions and their very intentions arise within the cultural mandate of political correctness and ideological rigidity; how could they discover that which they unconsciously sanction? No, it will be innovative leaders, intuitive eccentrics, Leonardo da Vincis and Louis Pasteurs of social science, who will uncover the real nature of our societal disease mechanisms and develop powerful intervention techniques. In doing so, they will give us a gift beyond price.

How are such leaders made? How do they become the powerful free thinkers that allow them to see clearly and do *effective* research? Effective research begins by asking the right questions. Asking the right questions is a result of unlearning the cultural mandate. And unlearning the cultural mandate can begin only when we discover the failure, the incorrectness of accepted social wisdom.

Some in the men's movement have made this first step: they have discovered that there is something fundamentally wrong and harmful in how we are currently dealing with gender. However, this alone does not make them into leaders. In order to become leaders, we need also to unlearn the cultural mandate. Until we do that, we can only react against the wrongness in culturally-prescribed ways, such as self-righteous protest, angry victimhood or reactive violence. These do not change the culture, since they are all expressions *of* the culture. They cannot heal the disease because they are just other symptoms *of* the disease.

To become *real* leaders, we must *unlearn* the cultural mandate, and become at least partly free of its compulsive modes of thought and behavior. Only then are we able to invent and pursue actions with *new* effect.

And, it is important to say, the personal cost might be high. Human systems are resilient and strongly resist change. Dysfunctional culture defends itself; after all, it is fighting for its life. Even (perhaps especially) the best new ideas are typically resisted for some time. For instance, Dr. Oliver Wendell Holmes, pathologist, physician and president of the Boston Society for Medical Improvement, realized through careful observation and deduction that childbed (puerperal) fever, the principal cause of death in new mothers at that time, was caused by the soiled hands of doctors. He began speaking on the subject, and in 1843 published "The Contagiousness of Puerperal Fever." [130] His essay offered eight rules for obstetricians, including hands and clothes washing and avoiding autopsies if obstetrics cases were being performed. However, his conclusions were ridiculed by his contemporaries. Charles Meigs, a prominent obstetrician, was incensed by the idea that he might himself be transmitting disease. "Doctors," he said, "are gentlemen, and gentlemen's hands are clean." [131]

Dr. Ignaz Semmelweis of Vienna, who independently in 1847 came to the same conclusion as Dr. Holmes, instituted hand sterilization practices into the Vienna Lying-In Hospital and saw the mortality rate for puerperal fever fall from 18 percent to less than three percent in just one month. Yet, he also was entirely unable to persuade other doctors to institute the same practices. Indeed, he was similarly ridiculed by many in the Viennese and wider European medical establishment.[132] It wasn't until the end of the century, fifty years later, that antiseptic practices finally became widespread in hospitals, including obstetric units.

It is easy for us now, with the advantage of hindsight, to leap to judgment of those doctors who ridiculed the pioneers among them and who continued to cause the deaths of women who came to them for childbirth services. But which group are we really like? To me, the indignant "Gentlemen's hands are clean" sounds a lot like "Women don't lie about rape" or "Women don't initiate violence." The good guy/bad guy groups have been switched around according to current fashion – 'gentlemen' have been removed from the moral pedestal and women are up there instead – but is the problem any different? Is the harm any less? More to the point, is the solution any different from what it was then? What *is* the solution?

For those great men and women who challenge us even more deeply, we have still more serious consequences to offer. Many of our best real cultural leaders (e.g., Jesus, Gandhi, Martin Luther King) were imprisoned and/or assassinated. But the call to truth, to power and to leadership always finds some who answer.

There are some things that can be said in general about how to fight – or heal – evil, to work effectively and powerfully for social change, to advocate in ways that do make a difference. We have already explored some of these ideas. The next two chapters will go into greater detail about what might be done to intervene effectively in the social epidemic that is building.

I want to end this chapter on a more positive note. On the other side of this challenge lies greater cultural maturity, social consciousness. When we become able to perceive and acknowledge the dark side of the feminine archetype as well as the dark side of the masculine, we will become more dualistically balanced, wiser as a society. We will consciously work on and recover from our shame and emotional abuse issues just as we do now with our physical and sexual abuse issues. We will begin, for the first time ever, to transact consciously rather than codependently with each other as the *general* pattern of social intercourse. What forms of government, of entertainment, of social discourse we will create and enjoy, I can hardly imagine. I probably won't be alive to see it. But I intend to live to help it come to pass.

Chapter 13 – What Can We Do?

"The whole course of human history may depend on a change of heart in one solitary and even humble individual – for it is in the solitary mind and soul of the individual that the battle between good and evil is waged and ultimately won or lost." – M. Scott Peck

 "The discovery of truth is prevented more effectively, not by the false appearance things present and which mislead into error, not directly by weakness of the reasoning powers, but by preconceived opinion, by prejudice." – Arthur Schopenhauer

"Truth will ultimately prevail where there is pains to bring it to light." – George Washington

"Those who journey from political correctness to truth often risk public disapprobation, but it is notable that most never lose their tolerance or humanity. They may question the politics of race, but not that racism is bad; they may question campaigns about women's pay, but not that women and men deserve equality of treatment."[133] – Anthony Browne.

"If only it were all so simple! If only there were evil people somewhere insidiously committing evil deeds, and it were necessary only to separate them from the rest of us and destroy them. But the line dividing good and evil cuts through the heart of every human being. And who is willing to destroy a piece of his own heart?"[134] – Alexander Solzhenitsyn

We've covered a lot of ground in a dozen chapters. Let's review what's been presented.

In chapter one, we saw that the truth about human society is hard to accept because it often seems to convict us. The solution is to be willing to endure the distress by wanting the truth more than anything else. This is difficult, and few choose this path. Chapter two introduced the concept of wisdom as dualistic balance, an integration of opposites. In chapter three we looked deeply at a particular dualistic balance, that between thinking and feeling, and saw that feeling, what feels right to us, dominates the psyches of almost everyone today. Chapter four looked at sex and gender as basic examples of dualism, and introduced the concept of archetypes.

We learned that the dominant story in our culture about gender, feminism, is built on a dualistic imbalance: compassion for women and accountability for men.

In chapter five we sought to understand the true nature of power relations between men and women, and I introduced the codependent gender power-over matrix which explains how power is equal but different between the genders, and how we could be unaware of that fact under the sway of our codependent 'cover story' of male power and female victimhood. Chapter six introduced a fundamental model of psychological growth which featured stage 2 as focusing on the reassuring side of dualistic balances (usually seeing oneself as innocent victim), stage 3 as working the other side of such dualities (embracing guilt and grieving loss), and stage 4 as integrated wisdom. We noted that the majority of the world's citizens spend most of their time in stage 2, which is a particularly stuck and intractable place from which people project moral judgments onto others.

Chapter seven looked at where we are in society with respect to dualistic balance and the progress towards balanced wisdom. We found that a number of social institutions and cultural products do display a degree of dualistic balance, but that there is still much stage 2 unconsciousness. We are most retarded in the area of social power relations, i.e., politics, and gender politics in particular seems especially dysfunctional. In chapter eight we had some fun by extending the theory of dualistic balancing in various directions, including developing definitions of love and truth as dualistic phenomena. Chapter nine presented a challenging practical illustration of balanced wisdom by exploring what a wise process would look like for determining whether or not to abort a fetus.

In chapter ten we looked at the nature of human evil, and introduced a definition of ideological evil in order to understand those periods in history when evil seemed to take over a society, resulting in scapegoating and consequent atrocities against human subgroups. We learned that this process is a kind of mass delusion, where the majority of citizens become enthusiastically aligned with the evil ideology such that they see it as good and righteous and the atrocities as just and necessary. In chapter eleven we moved our focus from history to contemporary society and discovered that feminism meets the definition of an evil ideology and that under its influence we are progressively scapegoating men and infantilizing women. Finally, in chapter twelve, we looked at how evil propagates in a society and in particular how feminism is progressing and maintaining its cover story through popular media. We ended our contemplation of feminism as evil ideology by examining the level of suffering flowing out of this process.

It has been intense, and the last three chapters have been very dark. If you have found them difficult to read, imagine how it has been to write them. Let us congratulate each other on getting to this point. The rest of the book will be more positive as we consider possibilities for action.

For an individual to contemplate changing society is a daunting prospect. Society is vast and has huge momentum. Yet who can know what the full effect of an action might be? Chaos theory tells us that in dynamic systems large consequences can flow from tiny beginnings. M. Scott Peck wrote, "The whole course of human history may depend on a change of heart in one solitary and even humble individual – for it is in the solitary mind and soul of the individual that the battle between good and evil is waged and ultimately won or lost." What is the nature of this internal battle? How does it begin, and how is it fought?

The battle of the heart cannot be fought at all in stage 2. In stage 2 our view of the world is an artifact of our own needs, our need to avoid the pain of guilt. We do not let anything in that seriously challenges our worldview because we need that worldview too much, to reassure us of our worth, our innocence. It is in stage 3 where the battle begins. In stage 3 we become willing to look for truth even though we expect that truth to convict us. In stage 3, a feminist may look at men with a wish to know their truth for the first time, and discover that she has been lying to herself, with assistance from the culture, about female intrinsic innocence and male guilt. It is in stage 3 that the battle is fought, and it is bloody, and it is glorious. We reach stage 4, for any particular issue, when the battle is won. Of course, there are always other issues, other battles.

In the end there is only one answer to how we can change the world for the better. We do it by growing ourselves up. From stage 2 we may be very active to change the world, but our actions do not come from love and are not based in truth, they come from our own need to avoid pain. Our actions from stage 2 aren't about the world at all, no matter what we believe. They are about us and they are usually based on false perceptions of the world, which we have made into a projection screen for our own guilt. Because of this, our actions often do harm rather than good. From stage 3 we can help the world through the example of our honesty and our devotion to discover truth and to act from love, but we are not yet powerful to see clearly and act confidently. From stage 4 we see clearly and act from love, and our actions are powerfully helpful, though it may not look that way to those who do not know what to look for, who do not understand that the avoidance of pain is the problem and not the goal.

What can we do to heal the world? At this basic level, the answer is simple. We can grow ourselves up, move from stage 2, denial, through stage 3, recovery, to stage 4, wisdom. That is the whole answer. It will work, and nothing else will. We do that simply by wanting it. There are endless techniques for spiritual or psychological growth offered in the world, but in the end techniques don't matter much because if we want to grow we use whatever techniques we find for that purpose, and if we don't want to grow, we use whatever techniques we find in order to avoid growing (usually while making a pretense of growth). So all that matters is whether and how much we want to grow, to recover, to find truth. How do we increase our wanting of it? I have no idea. That is a complete mystery to me. I don't know where my own wanting truth came from, and so there isn't much more I can say about that.

But for those who are on the journey, for those in stage 3 who are trying to understand the nature of the world and how to be in it, it may be that more detail about the process, information about how others have managed to influence the world in positive ways, would be useful. That is what the rest of this book is about.

Social Systems are Resilient
In 1992, I was working for a Canadian telecom company. At one point, I investigated a number of chronic problems to see why they were so difficult to change. One was why there was a company-wide hiring freeze by about the middle of every year. It seemed strange that we couldn't get our act together so that we could budget and

manage our new hire recruitment better than that. I started by going to talk to the accountants who were in charge of company wide recruitment management.

"Why do you guys force a hiring freeze by July or August of every year?" I asked? The accountants were helpful. "It's the managers," they told me. "They recruit at an astonishing rate during the first six months of the year. Over the whole company, the entire new hire budget is consumed by about July, because the rate of hiring is so high. If that rate continued, we would completely blow our budget and there would be hell to pay. We'd probably have to lay people off to get our payroll down to what we could afford again. Every year, we have no alternative but to institute a hiring freeze. We certainly don't want to."

They showed me a recruitment rate chart from the previous year. I have reproduced it roughly, from memory, below. They had a point.

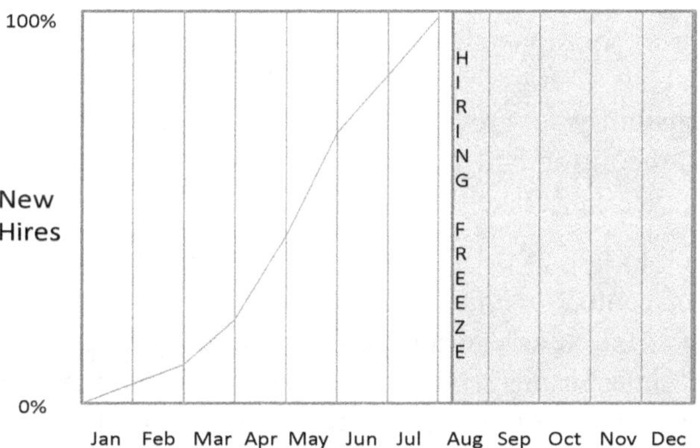

Annual Hiring Chart

Chart in hand, I went to talk to some line managers. I showed them the graph.

"Why do you recruit so fast and basically consume the entire hiring budget in the first half of the year?" I asked them.

"Are you crazy?" one of them said. "Every year, there's a company-wide hiring freeze by July or August. Look, it's there on the chart.

If we don't get our new hires in the door by then, we lose the opportunity for the whole year. It's a terrible rush, and sometimes we choose a candidate who isn't exactly who we want, just because we can't afford to wait until the hiring window opens up again next January."

I stood there with my mouth open. It was so obvious. Of course that's what they would do. Given the repetitive pattern of hiring freezes every year, what else could they do?

In a state of some excitement, I rushed back to the head office accountants. They were as surprised as I to hear what the line managers had said, and as rueful as I to realize that it was so obvious in hindsight. "So the solution is clear," I said. "Just stop calling a hiring freeze. The managers have already done all of their recruitment for the whole year by July. They're not going to hire any more people even if you don't institute a hiring freeze. In a year or two, after they realize that the hiring freezes really have gone away, they'll start spreading their recruiting into the rest of the year, which will be better for everyone."

I saw their expressions change. "We couldn't do that. What if the recruitment *did* continue and we really blew our hiring budget? It's our responsibility to prevent that. If we didn't institute a hiring freeze and the hiring budget overran, it would be worth our jobs, and rightly so. We can't take the risk."

I went back to talk to the line managers again. "Look, guys," I said. "You're in control of this. The accountants only institute a hiring freeze when the year's hiring budget is already consumed. If you took your time hiring, so that the hiring rate didn't go through the roof by July, they wouldn't slap a freeze on at all. It's your insisting on getting everyone by July that results in the hiring freeze."

"You're probably right," they said, "but we can't take that risk. For that to work, a majority of us would have to slow our hiring across the whole company. How could you get so many to do it? While that's what we'd like to do, if other managers didn't do it and a hiring freeze was called, the ones who took their time would be screwed. Would *you* take that risk?" I admitted that I wouldn't.

I learned something that day about the resilience, the resistance to change of human systems. They may end up doing things that no one really wants, and it may be entirely within our power to change them, and yet everyone, from their own perspective, has good reasons not to change.

This is a very common situation. Do you see how closely it resembles the stage 2 codependent relationship dynamics that we discussed earlier? As I see it, this is codependence on a larger scale, on a system-wide scale. Everyone involved feels that their own behavior is constrained by the actions of others; that other people have the real power in the situation, the power that matters. What is going on at a deeper level, as we have discussed, is that people's needs are being met by the system the way it is. Everybody is getting something important out of the arrangement (in this case, the security of a regular paycheck through the approval of their superiors), and they are unwilling to do anything that would jeopardize those needs.

I am not describing this situation and naming it as codependence, as an addiction dynamic, in order to criticize or judge it or the people involved – just the opposite. I describe it in these terms in order to make it *understandable,* in order to show it in a light that encourages us to empathize with it. These are good, regular people, they are like you and me. The fact that we are *all* almost completely enmeshed in this addictive culture is not something to be ashamed of. It's not wrong. It just is. We're not who we think we are in our cover story; our behaviors don't flow from the reasons that we believe, but that doesn't mean we're bad. We're just psychologically immature, and that's no crime.

Another situation that I investigated was closer to home for me. My job had been to manage a group of engineers who were designing semicustom integrated circuits (silicon chips) for the company's products. I was part of a large IC design group of perhaps a hundred engineers, designing thirty or forty silicon chips a year. One thing I had noticed was that we were almost always late to complete a design, at least as far as our customers were concerned. Since custom IC design took two or three years, the silicon was usually the longest lead-time item in the product delivery, so our lateness often made the whole product late to market. It was a very big problem.

Over the years, many sincere and serious attempts had been made to address it, and had resulted in tighter design processes, error checking, design tool enhancements, etc. Yet the late design completions had stubbornly refused to go away.

I spent several weeks meeting with silicon designers and managers, and also system designers and managers. It took some time for me to sort through the information they provided and realize what was significant. Eventually I noticed a similar pattern to the 'hiring freeze' problem. The system designers were blaming the silicon group: the silicon designers blamed the system group. I thought I knew what was going on.

Part of the answer lay in our organizational structure. Because of the highly specialized complexity of custom silicon design, a separate design group had been created, with a separate management structure all the way up to vice president level. This organizational structure interacted with the corporate culture in an interesting way.

Since custom silicon design takes so long, system product designers made sure to get it started early. The design contract with the silicon group was concluded as soon as possible, so that the silicon design could get under way as early as possible. A specification to act as the design goal for the silicon designers was developed, but since it was so early in the system design, it was necessarily somewhat speculative. A silicon design schedule was developed and agreed to, and the overall system design schedule was usually built around the silicon schedule.

However, in the course of system development, there would always be design changes from what was initially contemplated, and these system changes would inevitably alter the original silicon design specification. At this point the silicon designers would attempt to revise their own delivery schedule, arguing, with merit, that the specification changes meant doing work over again, which would extend the delivery schedule The system people, with their whole product delivery dependent on the silicon schedule, would insist that the silicon schedule could not change, or could change only minimally. The usual result was that the silicon design team would reluctantly agree to "make best efforts" to meet an unchanged design schedule, and would do so, but would end up late against that schedule (but on time based on their revised, unofficial schedule).

Are you getting a sense of how this all played out? The silicon design team was blamed by the system design customer for making the system late to market, while the system designers were blamed by the silicon guys for forcing an unavoidable delay through specification changes, while not permitting the design schedule to extend to accommodate the changes. Each group's story was familiar and made sense to its own management in its separate division. It 'felt right', and so the managers and engineers in each group were 'excused' by their executives for the poor result which was seen as the fault of the other organization. The hierarchical bridging between the silicon and system divisions, way up at the president level, was too far away for these different stories to be put up against each other and integrated, reconciled.

Once again we can see codependence in action, where each party sees the other as powerful and at fault, while their own behavior is reasonable – not perfect, perhaps, but excusable compared to those other guys. But let's not overlook the role of the corporate culture here, for it's the key piece. The unspoken though not unconscious corporate culture at this time measured and judged engineers and managers by how well they delivered against their agreed-to responsibilities. To succeed against your agreed deliverables was a brownie point, and would lead to pay raises and promotions, but a number of such brownie points were needed for a person to rise very far. However, a single significant failure to meet your deliverables, where you were personally to blame, was a career-killer, usually unrecoverable. (Let me note that this is certainly not an unusual business culture – it's probably almost universal.)

The natural, human response to this is to find ways to excuse your own failures, so that that deadly career-killer result can be avoided. That means finding ways to take credit when you succeed, but to avoid responsibility when you fail. This need to manipulate objective truth explains why codependence creates false worldviews and cover stories and avoids the truth, which it thinks will convict it. One good way to excuse yourself from failures is to have a scapegoat who can be held responsible for things that go wrong. This is what the behavior pattern between the system and silicon design groups accomplished. Each group was enabled to take credit, within their own management structure, for what was seen to have succeeded, while blaming the other group for major failures. The pattern was resilient, resistant to change (even though everyone was sincerely trying to succeed, to deliver on time) because it provided for the real needs of the participants. The ability to blame the other organization was like a drug which kept the deep anxiety of their dependence on an unknowable fate, of striving for an uncertain success, at bay. Their jobs and paychecks and social standing within the company felt more secure through this pattern, and so it remained, despite genuine and sustained attempts to solve the late delivery problem within both divisions.

Do you find this human behavior as fascinating as I do? I find it exciting to see below the surface, to discern the deeper engine of human social interaction. It makes such sense, once we see it laid out in this way. We are all just doing what we must, trying to deal with our needs and fears as best we can. As waves and tides move the water molecules of the ocean, we are moved together in a huge, coordinated, repetitive dance that few of us understand. Can you find empathy, fellow-feeling for people caught in these patterns? Can you see that the bigger and more troubling patterns, the wars and violence and such, are just similar patterns of well-meaning codependent people, doing what seems right to them in cultures they didn't invent and under forces they can't control. They're not really victims in the way that they may think they are, but they certainly don't feel the power that they have to do things differently.

When we do begin to understand, what can we do? We can work on our own recovery, of course, and that is utterly central. Without that, things change only by unconscious evolution. But as, or after, we work on ourselves, what can be done to change the larger system?

For large human systems to change, it often takes heroic action from some individuals. Some people, often just one, have to decide to take the risk, and at that level the risk is high, the personal consequences can be severe. The situation isn't helped by the fact that, while people in positions of power are best placed to initiate such changes, the behavior that has got them into those positions, for which they have been recognized and promoted, has not usually been heroic risk-taking. Society more often rewards those who play it safe, who take smaller, carefully calibrated risks and succeed in pulling them off, and find ways to duck the blame for any failures as I have described.

However, there are exceptions. I saw one during my time at the telecom company. A senior engineering executive was responsible for a large product development group, some three or four hundred engineers. His group was awarded a major development project in the usual way, funded by the factory that would eventually make the new product. However, the first year's design budget that was offered was not enough, in this executive's opinion, to pay for the design work that was required. The market window was short, and the money offered would only pay for a design team half the size of what was needed to design the product in the available time. The executive announced that he was not willing to plan for failure, and he launched a design project involving double the budgeted number of engineers, whose combined salaries would exhaust the year's funding by July. The executive was completely up front with his customer and his engineering team about this: the designers all knew that they were taking a major risk, and that there might be no money to pay them by mid year. The engineers and managers trusted their executive, and plowed ahead.

This leader was basically betting his career that the client factory would see the wisdom of his approach, or at least trust his judgment, by the time the money ran out, and would find a way to increase the budget. So it turned out; the executive's credibility was good and the project budget was doubled in order to meet the burn rate that had been judged necessary to achieve the market window.

This is high stakes stuff. If the factory had not come forward with the extra money, that executive's career would have been toast. A lot of people may have been laid off, and probably no client factory (not to mention engineering team) would ever trust him to lead a design project for them again. Few of us are willing to take such risks, and fewer still are in positions of authority where we can make such a large difference. Yet, such are the actions by which the world is positively changed through human agency, rather than the more usual process of slow, unconscious cultural evolution. Such heroic human actions are not always so spectacular, or even noticed, but they are real, the personal risks are real, and the heroism is real. I give honor here to the men and women who accept such risks for the sake of truth and justice and healing, for the sake of us all. I especially include in this group those who risked in this way and failed, the dead-ended or career restarted managers and others whom most regard as failures. They have my respect and my admiration.

How do we get ourselves to the place where we can make such choices? First, we have to be genuinely confident in our judgment; we have to deeply believe that we know the *truth* about a situation. We have to trust ourselves to see clearly what right action in this circumstance is. Secondly, we have to genuinely love ourselves. This means knowing that our identity is secure. To take a major risk, we have to be willing to fail, to lose the bet, with all that that implies – the loss of status, the negative judgments of our peers, the potential loss of income and prospects. We have to know that even if these things come to pass, even if we lose, it was still worth it, because we were true to ourselves. What this means is that we have to love truth and right action more than we love the image of success and status. We have to desire the reality of truth more than the image of truth. We have to be, in short, dedicated to reality at all costs.

We are back to where we started in chapter one, where I argued that what matters is what we really want. If we really want truth, we really do find it. As a result we grow up, our lives change, we become powerful. Let me confess right here that I am not a good example of this maxim. I have wanted truth, and I have found some, but for a long time I have not had the courage to step forward fully with that truth. For fifteen years I have hung back, unsure of myself and unwilling to trust my judgment fully. I think that with this book, I am finally stepping forward in power in service of truth, taking the risk of naming a great evil in our society. It's not a small thing, but it is time. I have hidden for long enough.

I imagine that one of the main groups who could have an interest in this book would be the Men's Human Rights Movement (MHRM), the movement that is seeking to bring balance to the gender debate by opposing feminist one-sided analysis and identifying the ways that men are also victims, and women are also powerful. Unfortunately, this movement tends to be misperceived as backlash to feminism, principally because the advocates, mainly men, are angry. They have good reasons for their anger given that many of them have lost children in family court or suffered from anti-male prejudice in other major ways. Still, it isn't working well for them, principally because most people associate anger in men with violence and aggression. So most MHRM advocates are seen as misogynist, an inaccurate perception since what they are opposed to is feminism, not women, but one that they find difficult to repudiate since most people see no difference between opposition to feminism and opposition to women. We aren't comfortable with the notion of men as victims; it doesn't feel right and so we judge their anger as inappropriate.

I spoke to this in an editorial I wrote for the magazine *Everyman* in 2000:

> In the last few weeks, the question of how to work effectively and powerfully for social change has occupied me. From the panel discussion on this topic at the 2000 Everyman Gathering to conversations with leaders in the movement, I have noticed myself taking a position which is often not well understood by others. In essence, this position is, "Let's be, ourselves, the way we want others to be. Let's live our vision of a better world in our own lives."
>
> Here's what I mean by this. We want our politicians, lawyers and judges to listen to us respectfully, and to be willing to hear and accept views that are socially unpopular and challenging to them. We want them to be open to our position, rather than sure that they already have the right of the issue, already see it correctly. Well, are *we* like that? Do we listen to *them* with open minds; are we willing to have them change our mind? When they speak of their difficulties, do we hear them with understanding or with judgment? Are we already convinced that we have the right answer and that they are wrong?
>
> Let's be honest; the issues of prejudice against men and injustice in family court are not issues that will make them winners in the eyes of their constituencies. They know — and we should too — that if they champion these causes, it will cost them support or votes, and quite possibly their job in the next election. The feminist lobby is very powerful, as we know first hand. So we are asking them to do the right thing on *principle*, to voluntarily take a stand against their own interests for the sake of what is right. Let's realize that that is what we are doing and stop being so self-righteous, so strident, so shaming in our demands that they do so. Frankly, we are being hypocritical. For that's not what we

did. We are in this battle, almost all of us who are politically active, because the system hurt us, took from us our role as parents or our money or both. We are fighting *entirely* in our own interest, to change a system that injured us personally. So let us have the humility, the integrity, to acknowledge that we are asking politicians, lawyers, judges, etc. to do things of much greater integrity and selflessness than we are doing ourselves. We are asking them to go *against* their self-interest, just because it's right. Well, fair enough. Let's ask for that. But feeling and claiming that they *should?* That they *owe* it to us? That's arrogant in the extreme and hypocritical as well. Our self-righteousness is an affront to them, and I'm not surprised that many of them don't want to give us the time of day. We are at least partly responsible for their reaction against us.

What do you think the reaction would be if, instead, it felt right to us (that's important, I'm not asking us to fake it) to say: "Sir, I know that you have good and sufficient reasons for the position and the stand that you are currently taking on this issue. I know that what I will ask of you is currently politically unpopular, and may well cost you credibility and votes, so I will understand if you choose not support the position that I am advocating, even if I should convince you that it has merit. I ask only that you hear me out and consider what I will say. I commit to you that I will do the same: I will keep an open mind as you explain the constraints and expectations that are placed upon you in the important role that you play, and I will not jump to hasty conclusions in the event that you do not see the same need for action on these issues that I do."

I suggest to you that a politician, a judge, a lawyer, an academic approached sincerely in this way, would recognize a difference in us, a maturity that is rare among advocates, and would pay greater attention to a presentation that was introduced in this fashion.

How does one get to this place? How do we put away the anger, the pain, and the need for instant solutions and change *RIGHT NOW?* How do we move to a place where we can hear and empathize with those who don't agree with us, and not just expect them to do that for us? My answer is simple to say, but difficult to do. We forgive them. We forgive the lawyers and the judges and the politicians and the feminists and the ex-spouses.

Let me be clear here. Forgiveness doesn't mean that what happened to us was OK; that it wasn't wrong. It doesn't mean that we excuse those who hurt us or that we tolerate or forget what they did. Nor does it mean that we stop advocating for change. It means that *we stop letting our past hurts dominate our present lives.* Psychologists generally define forgiveness as a conscious, deliberate decision to release feelings of resentment or vengeance toward a person or group who has harmed you, whether they actually deserve your forgiveness or not. This is what we need. With the chip off our shoulders, we advocate for change with equanimity, from a sense of peace with those whose minds we seek to change, rather than from righteous, injured judgment.

How do we forgive? By accepting the reality of our pain, our injuries, and grieving them, and thus letting them go. Our attitude of righteous innocence is really a way of holding our pain at a distance by loading it, in our mind, onto those that we hold responsible. I acknowledge, pain truly *is* fearsome, and it is no small task to decide to feel it deeply again. If, however, we accept our pain in the knowledge that it is ours, then we can move through it and out the other side. Find trusted associates to do this work with. I did mine in men's groups; some do it in therapy; some with friends or family. Be sure that I, for one, do not presume to judge that you *should* do it, or to know the size of the blocks or constraints that might keep you from it. You are free, as I am, and it is in a relationship of equals that I, as a friend, invite you to choose this path.

In 2002, I developed my ideas further about how to advocate effectively, and introduced a metaphor as a parable, to help people to feel their way into what I was saying. Here is the editorial I wrote for issue #55 of *Everyman,* June/July 2002:

In my address to the 2002 Everyman Gathering, I said something like, "If I have had one good idea, it is this. We can best change the world from vision, not outrage; from faith and not need."

What do I mean?

A good metaphor bridges from something we already know and understand to something that is new to us, in a way that allows us to extend our existing understanding to the new. Perhaps the best metaphor for healthy advocacy work is healthy parenting. For I think that most of us already understand that parenting done from need, from outrage, is neither healthy nor effective. If I *need* my child to follow in my footsteps, for example, or to succeed where I feel I have failed, or to realize some of my dreams, or (insert your own need here), then I will exert myself to make this happen. I may be subtle or aggressive, manipulative or directive depending on my personality, but I will communicate my need. In doing so, I will damage my child; undermine her/his own dreams. Even worse, my expectations for my child may be completely inappropriate or impossible. To take a silly example, if I, as a father, want my child to excel in calculus by the time she is three years old, then it is clear who has the problem.

Now let's bridge to advocacy work. The key is to see society as an immature child. It may be a stretch at first, but work at it. Like a child who is not yet old enough to do calculus, our society is not yet mature enough to deal with gender appropriately. We are still caught up in chivalry, which was about species survival, and only able to pay lip service to equality, which is about human fulfillment. So in family court, in business, in government, in all aspects of public and private life, we are not yet mature enough to overcome ... our internalized feelings of shame and guilt when we try to hold women to account. What feels right to us is still to protect them, to make them special and to expect men to sacrifice for them.

What we are seeing happening in family court, in sexual harassment and date rape and domestic violence legislation is *age appropriate behavior*. We need to really *get* this insight. Think of it like a two-year-old's tantrum. Yes, we need to stand up to it and confront it, but not because it's wrong. It's not wrong. It's harmful and counter-effective, but not wrong. It's age-appropriate acting out.

It's hard to get to that place in our relationship to society, where we see it as an immature child, but it's so valuable. Because once we do, we can let go of our outrage. A child is *supposed* to be immature; there would be something wrong if they weren't. Likewise, our society is *supposed* to be immature at this time.

Believing that we *should* be more mature than we are today, that we *should* be able to do family court without gender bias, without chivalry, is like believing a three-year-old *should* be able to do calculus. It's *our* problem.

When we try to change the world from outrage, from our need to have it conform to our picture of how we think it should be, we are like dysfunctional parents, passing on our own wounds and issues to our offspring. We need to change if we want the world to change. We need to become loving parents. I'm not saying it's easy. It's not. It's quite a challenge. I'm saying it's important; it's the only way that our advocacy, our efforts towards change, can be effective. Because once we change in this way, we are able to *respect* the world, to deal with it with dignity, with honor. We stop seeing conspiracy and corruption everywhere, and instead see honest people trying to do right as they see it. With that respect replacing our outrage, is it hard to imagine that we might get a better hearing, that those we seek to convert might be more open to our point of view?

Can we do this? Can we come from vision and not from judgment, from faith and not from need. For that is what healthy parenting is about. We hold a vision of a mature and healthy, happy adult, and we work to help our child grow towards that vision. Not because they are wrong as they are – they are not, of course. Not because they need to be fixed – they don't. In the same way, the world is not wrong as it is, and does not need to be fixed. It needs to be guided forward by those who have the maturity to act as loving parents, who hold a positive vision of what it could become, and not a righteous judgment of how it is wrong right now.

Are you one who is willing to step up to this challenge? Are you inspired by this notion of working with the world from vision rather than from need, from faith rather than from outrage? Hold yourself gently while you do the work. Outrage isn't wrong; it's just age appropriate behavior. It's just a stage on the path of human growth. Create a vision of yourself as a person free of such needs, working with the world from faith in what it could become and respect for where it is now. Hold that vision carefully, and seek ways to move towards it in your own life. From the way you experience yourself doing this, you will gain a real appreciation for the greater power that vision holds compared to judgment.

How do we actually put aside our judgment, what is the process? It is the work of stage 3 on the journey of psychological growth. We grieve the losses that we experienced, the injuries we suffered, until we come to the point where we can let them go and forgive those who hurt us. Not excuse them – there is no making what was done ok, or excusable. No, we hold them to account, and then we forgive. We do it not for them, but to set ourselves free of our anger and resentment, to set ourselves free to choose to trust again, if and when we wish to do so. We do it, in short, to heal ourselves.

Is this approach to social change effective? Probably the two most successful non-violent movements for social and political change in the last hundred years were Gandhi's movement to free India from British colonial rule, and Martin Luther King's movement for racial equality in America. Both took the repudiation of anger as a central plank of their advocacy, both sought to campaign from a vision of change motivated by love rather than by outrage (see MLK's "I Have a Dream" speech for an inspiring example of this approach). It is because their personal leadership was so powerful in inspiring their movements, based on this approach through love and truth, that both of these movement leaders were assassinated by those who opposed their goals. Yes, it is effective.

Let us review what we have covered in this chapter about how to heal the world. We began by acknowledging that we can heal the world only by healing ourselves, by growing ourselves up through the growth model stages 3 and 4, recovery and wisdom. We explored how human systems are resilient because they are meeting people needs (conscious or unconscious). Because of this, it often takes heroic action on the part of individuals to make significant change. In the case of advocates for social change such as the MHRM, we observed that anger is counter-productive, and I suggested that treating others as we would wish to be treated, coming from vision rather than judgment, and regarding the world as a child that needs good parenting are useful tools or concepts in social advocacy work.

Is this enough? In this book we have identified feminism as an evil ideology that is riding and driving a moral panic in our society. What is involved in combating something as dark and dangerous as that? That is the subject of the next chapter.

Chapter 14 – Working with the Dark

"In a time of universal deceit - telling the truth is a revolutionary act." - George Orwell

"Human progress is neither automatic nor inevitable. ... Every step toward the goal of justice requires sacrifice, suffering, and struggle; the tireless exertions and passionate concern of dedicated individuals." – Martin Luther King, Jr.

"Throughout history, it has been the inaction of those who could have acted; the indifference of those who should have known better; the silence of the voice of justice when it mattered most; that has made it possible for evil to triumph." – Haile Selassie

"I believe that unarmed truth and unconditional love will have the final word in reality. This is why right, temporarily defeated, is stronger than evil triumphant." – Martin Luther King, Jr.

When I began thinking about gender politics, I thought that the need was for public education. I imagined that the primary task was that of articulating the issues clearly and presenting them persuasively. However, as my life with gender issues unfolded (some of it shared in these pages), I discovered that things are not so simple. I now believe that the essential nature of gender relations is addictive. This means that, while we think we want equality and freedom and responsibility between men and women, for many of us that is just a denial mechanism, a story to cover the fact that we are still addicted to the codependent dance between the genders, to getting our security and other needs met through traditional cultural patterns, and by not rocking the boat.

How does this addictive process start? I think it starts with our need for approval and our consequent fear of guilt. As children, we quickly discover that when something goes well, we want to be responsible. But when something goes wrong, we want to be innocent, to have someone else take the fall. However, it is usually impossible to know in advance whether something will turn out well or ill. We start to play games with the truth, to try to set things up so that we can claim the credit for things that succeed, but avoid the blame for things that fail. As you can imagine, that's difficult to do, and we end up creating a totally confusing world of half-truths and hedged bets and cover stories. Finally, in order to make our act convincing, we have to lie to ourselves as well as everyone else.

Think about two children caught fighting by a parent. The parent might ask, "Who started it?" I am sure that, like me, you expect that each child will claim that the fight was started by the other. Neither child is very interested in the objective truth, especially if it might convict them. This is simply human nature, and it continues throughout our lives, unless we change and become interested in what is really true.

By the time we are adults, such a crazy, mixed-up world has come to seem natural, especially since just about everyone else is doing the same dance. That game, that dance of cover up and "creative accounting" is the root of codependency, founded on our very human need for love and approval.

Thus there is a tension in the world between those who desire to live "in the light" – who want to be responsible for their decisions even when they are wrong, who want the truth even when it convicts them – and those who want the appearance and thus the rewards of responsibility without the risks.

I came to realize that addictions are not usually penetrated by "working in the light," by consensual education and explanation. Different techniques must be used to "work with the dark" energies of codependence and denial. Such techniques focus on creative confrontation and self-sacrifice, and have been articulated by leaders such as Jesus, Gandhi and Martin Luther King, Jr.

"Working with the dark" is challenging. It requires powerful individuals willing to take real risks in order to make social injustice visible. It takes little character to shout loudly when one's rights are abused. It takes more character to creatively (rather than angrily) identify potential solutions, and it takes a great deal of character to endure being scapegoated and yet choose to suffer and accept the injustice for the sake of bringing it into view.

Let me be clear here. To restore justice and equality between men and women will take great sacrifice on the part of many individuals. Such gender warriors must have done the work of self-purification, of soul-searching to ensure that they are moved by love of truth and justice, love of others and not self-serving avoidance of pain. Rather, they will walk into pain and injustice in order to expose its presence and effect. Such people, using what Gandhi called "soul-force", will be the means by which the current direction of rights for women and responsibilities for men will eventually be turned around and restored to balance: rights *and* responsibilities for men *and* women. Such people will be genuine heroes.

What I have outlined here, the attitudes and the approach, are a good start. However, there is a lot further to go in terms of working effectively with the dark energies, with those who are deeply caught in denial. I have studied the lives and teachings of some noted spiritual leaders, especially Jesus of Nazareth and Mahatma Gandhi. Each in his own way addressed this issue of social shadow, of stage 2 denial and dysfunction. Each had some wisdom that they wished to communicate to people who certainly found it threatening to their worldview.

One tool that Jesus used often was parables. As I see it, a parable is a tool for circumventing denial. What Jesus would do was tell a story in familiar, homely terms, such that everyone could immediately identify with it, and for which the conclusion had the property of *feeling* right to people. For instance, he said, "Would any of you who are fathers give your son a stone when he asks for bread? Or would you give him a snake when he asks for a fish?" [135] Of course, people would feel, that's right. Such a story connects us to a strong and good part of us: our natural love for our children.

This homely story would then be connected to a spiritual lesson. "As bad as you are, you know how to give good things to your children. How much more, then, will your Father in heaven give good things to those who ask him?" [136] Now, this is a more challenging message. People at that time believed strongly in a vengeful God who visited sickness and accident on people as punishment for their sins. Now that they have the complete parable, they face a problem. In order to keep their view of a vengeful God, they must either repudiate the homely story of human love for their children (difficult to do since it *feels* so right), or they must repudiate the connection between the story and the lesson about God (also difficult to do since they already think of God as their father, and their religion names him as such).

They have been maneuvered by the parable into serious, unanticipated self-questioning.

What Jesus did, over and over again with his parables, was to exploit the lack of internal rigor and consistency in most people's worldview, in a way that made his new ideas very hard for them to refute. If he had simply approached the issue directly, he would have run straight into their denial, their familiar defenses against being shown that their ideas were mistaken or inconsistent. But by first covertly engaging their feelings of rightness on his own side of his argument, and only then revealing where he was going to take the argument, he recruited their feelings in support of his point. This is powerful indeed, and it is unsurprising that he was despised by many people. Most people do not take kindly to having the inconsistencies in their beliefs pointed out to them in ways that are difficult to refute.

This is also extremely advanced spiritually and psychologically. It speaks to a deep understanding of human nature, and also to a deep, non-judgmental empathy with that nature. It demonstrates a person operating from well into stage 4 of spiritual development.

Many of his parables still have great relevance today. For instance, one of the themes of this book is how to move towards gender equality. But what does equality really mean? What *is* equality? The world is full of people demanding their rights in the name of equality. With this level of societal interest, one might think that we would have got around to agreeing what it is. Not so. Actually, once you admit that equal doesn't mean identical, then what it *does* mean becomes quite difficult to say.

This difficulty isn't new. For a 2000-year-old illustration, consider a parable that Jesus told:

> "The Kingdom of heaven is like this. Once there was a man who went out early in the morning to hire some men to work in his vineyard. He agreed to pay them the regular wage, a silver coin a day, and sent them to work in his vineyard. He went out again to the market place at nine o'clock and saw some men standing there doing nothing, so he told them, 'You also go and work in the vineyard, and I will pay you a fair wage.' So they went. Then at twelve o'clock and again at three o'clock he did the same thing. It was nearly five o'clock when he went to the market place and

saw some other men still standing there. 'Why are you wasting the whole day here doing nothing?' he asked them. 'No one hired us,' they answered. 'Well, then, you also go and work in the vineyard,' he told them.

"When evening came, the owner told his foreman, 'Call the workers and pay them their wages, starting with those who were hired last and ending with those who were hired first.' The men who had begun to work at five o'clock were paid and silver coin each. So when the men who were the first to be hired came to be paid, they thought they would get more; but they too were given a silver coin each. They took their money and started grumbling against the employer. 'These men who were hired last worked only one hour,' they said, 'while we put up with a whole day's work in the hot sun — yet you paid them the same as you paid us!'

"'Listen, friend,' the owner answered one of them. 'I have not cheated you. After all, you agreed to do a day's work for one silver coin. Now take your pay and go home. I want to give this man who was hired last as much as I have given you. Don't I have the right to do as I wish with my own money? Or are you jealous because I am generous?" [137]

The power of parables like these lies in the fact that one can empathize with both sides. It's not hard to share the angst of the first workers hired, after a long, hot day's work, at being given the same remuneration (is that being treated equally or unequally?) to those who worked only an hour. Yet one can certainly see the owner's point; he honored his agreement with each of his workers, and what right did they have to expect or claim more than they had already agreed to work for?

Actually, great public interest in a topic is no guarantee of reaching agreement. After all, hundreds of Christian religions and sects claim the Bible as their doctrinal source. The Bible is the same for each of them. Clearly, they differ in the matter of interpretation, of determining what, in any particular case, is relevant, and how it should be applied. The same is true of the question of equality. Is there one 'correct' or 'best' interpretation of what equality means? To be honest, I'm not sure. I *am* sure that there isn't a formula you can write down that will always yield the right answer. However, I can point to some things that should be born in mind, to help frame the debate.

There is an aspect of equality that *does* mean identicality. For instance, the constitutional principle of "equality before the law" means that people's treatment by the law and the courts should not differ because of their sex, or their social status, or their race, etc. I call this people's *intrinsic status,* and I hold that the intrinsic status of all people is equal (by which I mean identical) as human beings.

However, people differ in many ways, including talent, skill, experience and other factors that affect their ability to work and add value to society. An important value in our culture is that people should be rewarded for these achievements. Indeed, rewards such as salaries and social status are often the primary motivators to achieve. In this area, we have been content to set lower limits (e.g., minimum wage, welfare) and let the marketplace determine the rewards, based on its estimation of the value of the achievements. To summarize, if we want people to be motivated by societal rewards, in order to treat them equally, we must *not* treat them identically, but must discriminate between them in order to reward them for merit.

Beyond that, to confound the situation more, lie our personal freedoms, which if they are to mean anything at all, must include the freedom to associate with whom we choose, to enter consensual contracts with whom we choose, and to spend our money as we choose. Thus our personal freedom seems to entitle us to discriminate, for reasons that need make sense only to us, between people – i.e., to treat them unequally.

For any particular situation, it is in the dynamic balance between these three opposing values or principles that the meaning of equality lies. Indeed, all three are involved in the parable I began with, which is why I used it to illustrate these issues. It is often a major task to resolve these opposing tensions and interpret what equality means and requires of us in any particular situation. One thing that *is* clear is that, as a society, we are not currently doing well in our impassioned attempts to treat people 'equally.'

Perhaps the most impressive psychological reframing that Jesus achieved was when he was brought a woman taken in the act of adultery. The story is found in chapter eight of the Gospel of John.

"Early the next morning [Jesus] went back to the Temple. All the people gathered around him, and he sat down and began to teach them. The teachers of the Law and the Pharisees brought in a woman who had been caught committing adultery, and they made her stand before them all. 'Teacher,' they said to Jesus, 'this woman was caught in the very act of committing adultery. In our Law Moses commanded that such a woman must be stoned to death. Now, what do you say?' They said this to trap Jesus, so that they could accuse him. But he bent over and wrote on the ground with his finger. As they stood there asking him questions, he straightened up and said to them, 'Whichever one of you has committed no sin may throw the first stone at her.'" [138]

Consider the situation that Jesus faced here. This was clearly a trap; every one of those teachers and Pharisees was hostile to Jesus, seeking a way to discredit him publicly and convict him through his own words and actions. They certainly were not open to having their own minds changed.

Jesus responded, "Whichever one of you has committed no sin may throw the first stone at her." This is a masterpiece of human psychology. Look how deeply it works its magic. Jesus clearly saw and understood that the fundamental human dynamic in play was the stage 2 projection of guilt and shame out onto the woman. The Teachers and Pharisees were alleviating their own shame wound by feeling superior to the woman because she was guilty of breaking the Mosaic Law, while they were not. But Jesus found a way to speak directly to this projection, by forcing a comparison on them, by requiring them to examine the roots of their presumed moral superiority. Are you without sin? he asked in effect. If not, on what basis are you entitled to judge her and take her life?

This is an inconsistency in their moral foundation that the Teachers had never looked at before, and they didn't know how to resolve it. But that wasn't all that was built into this one, masterful sentence. "Whichever one of you has committed no sin may throw the *first* stone at her." This is remarkable. For Jesus turned the projection back on the priests in yet another way. His words made it such that any priest who took up the challenge and stepped forward would be saying by his action, in front of all the others and in front of the onlookers, that he is without sin and thus superior to all the other priests. By making them inferior to him, he would trigger their own inferiority issues and become their target. But he would know that he could not support a case that he was different in kind from them, that he was free of sin while they were not. Jesus actually found a way to employ the power dynamics of the group of hostile Teachers and Pharisees in service of a reframing of the question, in service of the spiritual lesson he sought to offer. They couldn't do what he was requiring them to do, but couldn't argue either that his injunction to them was illegitimate. They were forced to either acknowledge the inconsistency in their beliefs, or lose face in front of the very public that they had thought to impress. Utterly amazing! I am truly in awe of the power and sophistication of this man's wisdom.

The story continues,

> "When they heard this, they all left, one by one, the older ones first. Jesus was left alone, with the woman still standing there. He straightened up and said to her, 'Where are they? Is there no one left to condemn you?' 'No one, sir,' she answered. 'Well then,' Jesus said, 'I do not condemn you either. Go, but do not sin again.'" [139]

It is sad that not one of the religious leaders present was able to acknowledge this gift, at least at that moment, but all slunk away without a word. Jesus turned then to the woman, and said that he didn't condemn her either. He didn't make himself superior to her, even while not avoiding naming her actions as sinful, as had the Pharisees as well. He was clearly coming fully from stage 4.

A spiritual war is always a war about *meaning,* and what is deeply at issue for us is the meaning of gender in society today, whether women have been oppressed and deserve compensation, to what extent men are responsible, etc. Only from stage 4 do we see such meanings clearly: in stages 2 and 3 we contaminate them with value loadings which are entirely our own artifacts and have no independent reality. Only from stage 4 can we actually fight well as spiritual warriors.

Fighting evil is perhaps the most horrific battle there is. In his study of evil, *People of the Lie; The Hope for Healing Human Evil,* psychiatrist M. Scott Peck wrote:

> "Let me stress that authority over the power of evil does not come

easily. It is gained by enormous exertion in addition to knowledge. Such exertion can be born only of love. … Genuine love is always ultimately sacrificial. There are no words strong enough to describe the matter. … I know now that he or she who would do true battle with evil must expect to be depleted beyond imagination – perhaps even beyond recovery." [140]

One who knew the meaning of love and self-sacrifice was Mohandas K. Gandhi, later known as Mahatma (Great Soul). He was a leader in the non-violent war over British Colonialism, first in South Africa, and later in India. Was it oppressive, as Gandhi claimed, or beneficial to African and Indian subjects, as the British believed? Gandhi's strategy was to highlight the nature of Indian suffering by voluntarily taking it upon himself and his associates in visible ways. In this, he followed the advice of Jesus, who said, "You have heard that it was said, 'An eye for an eye, and a tooth for a tooth.' But now I tell you, do not take revenge on someone who wrongs you. If anyone slaps you on the right cheek, let him slap your left cheek too. And if someone takes you to court to sue you for your shirt, let him have your coat as well. And if one of the occupation troops forces you to carry his pack one mile, carry it two miles." [141]

Gandhi spoke of the practical wisdom contained in this message. He coined the word 'Satyagraha,' meaning 'soul force' to stand for the kind of non-violent resistance that he pioneered in the world of politics.

"'Satyagraha,' Gandhi wrote, 'is the vindication of truth not by the infliction of suffering on the opponent but on one's self.' The opponent must be 'weaned from error by patience and sympathy.' Weaned, not crushed. Satyagraha assumes a constant, beneficent interaction between contestants with a view to their ultimate reconciliation. Violence, insults and superheated propaganda obstruct this end. … Satyagraha reverses the eye-for-an-eye-for-an-eye-for-an-eye policy which ends in making everybody blind or blind with fury. It returns good for evil until the evildoer tires of evil." [142]

There is little doubt that this approach was largely responsible for the effectiveness of Gandhi's advocacy for more equality and dignity for immigrant Indian laborers in South Africa, resulting ultimately in the 'Indian Relief Bill' of 1914. The bill eliminated the tax on indentured laborers, declared Hindu, Moslem and Parsi marriages valid (they had been invalidated when a Justice of the Supreme Court declared only Christian marriages to be valid), and provided other remedies and dignities for Indian immigrants. At the time, the South African head of state was General Smuts.

> "His mission accomplished, tired but happy, Gandhi … sent General Smuts a gift of a pair of leather sandals he had made in prison. Smuts wore them on his farm near Pretoria until 1939 when, as a gesture of friendship, he returned them to Gandhi in India, saying, 'I have worn these sandals for many a summer since then, even though I may feel that I am not worthy to stand in the shoes of so great a man.' Such humor and generosity proved him worthy of Gandhi's mettle. Gandhi had not won a victory over Smuts, he had won Smuts over. The settlement came not when Smuts had no more strength to fight but when he had no more heart to fight. …
>
> Writing in 1939, in a gracious contribution to a fat seventieth-birthday Gandhi memorial volume, Smuts, by then a world-famous statesman, said men like Gandhi 'redeem us from a sense of commonplace and futility, and are an inspiration to us not to weary in well-doing. … It was my fate to be the antagonist of a man for whom even then I had the highest respect. … [H]e never forgot the human background of the situation, never lost his temper or succumbed to hate, and preserved his gentle humor in the most trying situations. His manner and spirit, even then, as well as later, contrasted markedly with the ruthless and brutal forcefulness which is in vogue in our day.'" [143]

And is still in vogue almost a hundred years later, I add with some sadness. Writing about Gandhi's campaign twenty-five years later, Smuts said,

> "I must frankly admit that his activities at the time were very trying to me. … Gandhi showed a new technique. … His method was deliberately to break the law, and to organize his followers into a mass movement. [Many of these were imprisoned, and] Gandhi himself received – what no doubt he desired – a period of rest and quiet in jail. For him everything went according to plan. For me – the defender of law and order – there was the usual trying situation, the odium of carrying out a law which had not

strong popular support, and finally the discomfiture when the law was repealed." [144]

I have described above the results of Soul Force, of Satyagraha, but what of the methods? The methods are anything but easy, and as I read about the action at the Dharsana Salt Works in 1930 led by Gandhi supporters (the Mahatma was in jail at the time), I marvel that so many people found such self-sacrificing courage.

"Several days before his arrest, Gandhi had informed the Viceroy that, 'God willing,' he would, with some companions, raid the Dharsana Salt Works, 150 miles north of Bombay. God, it developed, was not willing. Mrs. Sarojini Naidu, the poet, substituted as leader of the raid. Twenty-five hundred volunteers participated. Before proceeding Mrs. Naidu warned them that they would be beaten 'but,' she said, 'you must not resist; you must not even raise a hand or ward off a blow.'

"Webb Miller, the well-known correspondent of the United Press … was on the scene and described the event first in dispatches and then in his book, *I Found No Peace.* Manilal Gandhi, second son of the Mahatma, advanced at the head of the marchers and approached the great salt pans which were surrounded by ditches and barbed wire and guarded by four hundred Surat policemen under the command of six British officers. 'In complete silence,' Miller writes, 'the Gandhi men drew up and halted a hundred yards from the stockade. A picked column advanced from the crowd, waded the ditches, and approached the barbed-wire stockade.' The officers ordered them to retreat but they continued to step forward. 'Suddenly,' the report reads, 'at a word of command, scores of native policemen rushed upon the advancing marchers and rained blows on their heads with their steel-shod lathis [staves]. Not one of the marchers even raised an arm to fend off the blows. They went down like ten-pins. From where I stood I heard the sickening whack of the clubs on unprotected skulls. The waiting crowd of marchers groaned and sucked in their breath in sympathetic pain at every blow. Those struck down fell sprawling, unconscious or writhing with fractured skulls or broken shoulders. … The survivors, without breaking ranks, silently and doggedly marched on until struck down.' When the first column was laid low, another advanced.

'Although everyone knew,' Webb Miller writes, 'that within a few minutes he would be beaten down, perhaps killed, I could detect no sign of wavering or fear. They marched steadily, with their heads up, without the encouragement of music or cheering or any possibility that they might escape injury or death. The police rushed out and methodically and mechanically beat down the second column. There was no fight, no struggle, the marchers simply walked forward until struck down.' Another group of twenty-five advanced and sat down. 'The police,' Miller testifies, 'commenced savagely kicking the seated men in the abdomen and testicles.' Another column presented itself. Enraged, the police dragged them by their arms and threw them into the ditches. 'One was dragged to a ditch where I stood,' Miller recorded; 'the splash of his body doused me with muddy water. Another policeman dragged a Gandhi man to the ditch, threw him in, and belabored him over the head with his lathi. Hour after hour stretcher-bearers carried back a stream of inert, bleeding men.' ...

"India was now free. Legally, technically, nothing had changed. India was still a British colony. But there was a difference and Rabindranath Tagore explained it. He told the *Manchester Guardian* of May 17, 1930, that 'Europe has completely lost her former moral prestige in Asia. She is no longer regarded as the champion throughout the world of fair dealing and the exponent of high principle, but as the upholder of Western race supremacy and the exploiter of those outside her own borders. For Europe this is, in actual fact, a great moral defeat that has happened. Even though Asia is physically weak and unable to protect herself from aggression where her vital interests are menaced, nevertheless she can now afford to look down on Europe where before she looked up.' Tagore attributed the achievement in India to Gandhi.

"The Salt March and its aftermath did two things: it gave the Indians the conviction that they could lift the foreign yoke from their shoulders; it made the British aware that they were subjugating India. It was inevitable, after 1930, that India would some day refuse to be ruled, and, more importantly, that England would some day refuse to rule. When the Indians allowed themselves to be beaten with batons and rifle butts and did not cringe they showed that England was powerless and India invincible. The rest was merely a matter of time." [145]

What can we say about these methods? Why do they work so well?

First, they are *efficient.* They lead to the absolute minimum of violence and suffering that must be borne in order to achieve the objective, for two reasons. Firstly, the non-violent resister contributes no violence of his own; only the violence of the adversary actually takes form in the world. Secondly, the lack of hatred toward the antagonist, the lack of personal condemnation of the opponent, minimizes the risk of escalation.

> "'Turn the searchlight inward,' [Gandhi] repeatedly urged; 'perhaps the fault is partly yours. Adjudicate, negotiate, arbitrate,' he begged, 'otherwise one interreligious brawl or one race riot will immediately create fuel for another, and one war will generate the venoms, fears and military designs which make a second and third more likely.'" [146]

Second, Satyagraha, by emphasizing freedom from passion, from reactivity, enables accurate, realistic strategizing. Rather than feeling compelled toward ill-considered or rationalized action by rage or pain, the non-violent warrior takes the time and effort to consider every option, and carefully chooses only those designed to achieve his goal with minimum suffering and damage. Moreover, in such calculations his analysis includes *all* such suffering and damage: he gives equal or greater weight to the suffering and losses of his opponents as he does to his own. In this way, his evaluations minimize *total* suffering and loss, rather than the more usual approach in which the suffering of the opponent is seen as of little account, or even as desirable.

Third and most powerful of all, enlightened non-violence directly addresses the moral and emotional issues and fears that often lie behind conflict. Its intent is to raise unconscious issues to awareness, without shaming or humiliating anyone, simply so that the wrongs can be corrected. As Gandhi wrote in a letter to the Indian Viceroy, "My ambition is no less than to convert the British people through nonviolence, and thus make them see the wrong they have done to India." [147] It is founded on deep respect for the humanity of all players, including the adversary. Satyagraha thus leads towards permanent solutions to violence and oppression, since it avoids all coercion and instead seeks a change of *heart and mind* in the adversary, so that a new relationship can be entered into *voluntarily.* In modern parlance, its aim is a win-win.

I have spent some time outlining the methods and the effectiveness of stage 4 social advocacy, of stage 4 spiritual warriorship, of Satyagraha, soul force, enlightened non-violence – all of these are closely related. I have acknowledged that they are psychologically advanced: I am by no means sure that I am ready to step up to such a challenge myself. But what is the process by which one works towards this level of wisdom, of spiritual competence, of psychological maturity? I have already described briefly how to work with my model of the stages of spiritual growth: reclaiming one's projections, grieving one's guilt, forgiving oneself. But I also want to say something about how to support oneself in this work, how to create enough safety in one's life to step confidently forward and to experiment with changed behavior and new paradigms.

The end goal is stage 4 wisdom; integration of duality, balance of opposites. Consider this description of Gandhi by Louis Fischer, one who knew and admired him:

> "[Gandhi] was fastidiously clean, studiously economical, and very kind. The capacity for suffering and identification, his spinning and nonviolence probably contained elements of the feminine. He liked to tend the sick and nurse the weak but spurned such care himself. He looked very male and had a man's steel strength of body and will, yet he was also sweetly gentle and softly tender; firm yet caressing, adamant yet yielding, brave yet meek. He had the might of a dictator but the mind of a democrat and therefore preferred to conquer with affection rather than power. What he won with iron he wrapped in down. Intuition was the ally of his intellect, indeed sometimes guided or superseded it. This combination of masculine and feminine qualities seamlessly, harmoniously welded together made Gandhi intricate and attractive, and supplies an important clue to his personal life and public work." [148]

How do we move towards such mature integration? I have outlined the basic process in terms of moving through my model of spiritual growth, but are there structures, techniques that can help us? Indeed, there are many. One way that has worked for me is men's groups. I have been in a total of three men's groups, more or less sequentially, over the last twenty five years. Each has, to differing degrees, provided support and safety for my life journey. In this respect, men's groups – and women's groups and all personal growth and support groups – can be seen as developmental, as safe way-stations on the road to adult maturity. They are places where we can create an environment of emotional safety, by means of conscious agreements about what we *won't* do to each other. In essence, we promise not to inflict on each other those behaviors by which our authenticity was hammered into submission in the first place, when we were children. We promise not to attack each other physically or emotionally, we promise to respect confidences and honor personal boundaries. In this environment of externally managed safety, we try to grow the maturity, the strength to carry our safety with us, so that we won't forever need the artificial safety that the group provides.

Of course, such support groups are only one way of providing greater safety for spiritual/psychological experimentation in one's life. I know people who have used personal growth workshops, or therapy, or even friendships, to the same effect. The key to finding real safety is to find a place where one is loved, and to make a conscious agreement that a part of the purpose of the relationship will be personal growth. Such space needs to be 'bracketed' from one's regular life, so that one's growth work does not undermine the life tasks of making a living, caring for children, etc.

It is important to keep in mind that the final goal of such processes is to have the group members transcend the need for externally managed safety and so need them no longer. If this is not remembered, the comfort of the safety can become a crutch. Like a child who eventually grows able to take care of itself in a dangerous world and no longer needs the structural safety of a "child-proofed" home, so we aspire to grow the emotional and spiritual strength to go beyond our need for the formal safety of support groups in order to be our authentic selves. To be sure, being authentic in the secular world, where most people are still addicted to self-serving cover stories and are strenuously avoiding truth, is no small task. History shows clearly that those who choose to confront secular powers for spiritual reasons can expect to be persecuted. From the Old Testament prophets to the early Christians, and in modern times from

Mahatma Gandhi to Martin Luther King, Jr., the pattern is unmistakable.

To walk as an *adult* in the world – honest, authentic, real, *and wise* – is perhaps the highest human calling. Support groups and other similar structures are the schools, the preparation for this life work. In such groups, we practice living authentically in an environment where the risks of authenticity are artificially reduced. But as long as we can be authentic only within the sacred boundaries of the group's protection, we are still children. Let us aspire to authentic *adulthood,* where we become able to retain our integrity, our authenticity, even in the midst of human evil.

I end this chapter with the story of a man who lived up to this ideal. He changed the world for the better, entirely through the strength of his personal convictions, through his spiritual *empowerment* rather than through the exercise of any formal power or wealth.

John Woolman, 1720-1772, was a New England colonial Quaker whose life was outwardly quiet and uneventful. He mastered the craft of a tailor and practiced it all his life. At the age of twenty three, he was "recorded" by his meeting as a minister, and he remained a "Minister among Friends" for the rest of his life. He died of smallpox during a trip to London, England.

The influence of Woolman's life was only slowly recognized after his death, and even today his name is not well known. Yet it was he who, through thirty years of quiet, sustained labor, operating virtually alone, persuaded *every Quaker in what is now the United States to cease keeping slaves – fifty years before the Civil War!*

How did he do it? I quote from an introduction by Frederick B. Tolles to his journal, published posthumously.

> "His most momentous social insight came to him in the very year he commenced his public ministry, when he was called upon as a conveyancer to write out a bill of sale for a Negro slave.
> Suddenly it flashed upon his conscience that the whole institution of slavery was inconsistent with the religious testimony for equality. If, to our enlightened minds, this hardly seems revolutionary, it is well to realize that in 1743 scarcely a man in Christendom – a white man, that is – saw the injustice of slavery.
> ... Travelling in the ministry throughout the southern colonies in

1746 and again in 1757, he saw slavery at first hand, and it seemed to him a "dark gloominess hanging over the land," whose consequences would be "grievous to posterity." His *Journal* contains the record of his actions, how he labored earnestly with the plantation owners of the South, how he galvanized his fellow Quakers into purging themselves of the evil with a stirring message in the Philadelphia Yearly Meeting in 1758. What is most essential to remark is how, hating the evil and loving the slave, he never ceased to embrace the evildoer, the slave owner, in his love. In time, the Friends, having eliminated slaveholding within the household of the faith, would pass on the concern to others like William Lloyd Garriston, who galvanized the whole country; but they could not pass on the loving spirit of John Woolman, and the consequences of that failure have been grievous to posterity." [149]

John Woolman labored quietly, consistently, earnestly and lovingly. His spirit, not his ego, was engaged in his actions. His journal tells movingly of his constant efforts to look inside and chasten himself, to base his words and actions always on a loving humility and respect for all. It is this passion of his for pure and perfect love that lies at the heart of his success. He had that rare combination that moves mountains: a surrendered will that accepted and loved people where they were, without expectation that they *should* change – and, simultaneously, a passionate vision of a world free from slavery, poverty and war. The combination of these two, acceptance and vision is supremely charismatic. This is the source of John Woolman's remarkable influence and success.

His is not an easy path to follow. As G. K. Chesterton said, speaking of this kind of love, "The Christian ideal has not been tried and found wanting. It has been found difficult, and left untried." [150] Few indeed seem able to walk this path, but those who do find that they become powerful in the world. Not in terms that we usually think of power, such as wealth, or fame, or authority over others. John Woolman had none of these. What he had, rather, was a quiet, respectful earnestness that touched people's hearts and persuaded them to listen carefully to him, combined with a carefully worked out and passionately articulated vision of a better world. As a result of these qualities, Woolman became that luckiest of men who saw, in his own lifetime, the world make visible progress towards his vision as a result of his own efforts. I salute him as a remarkable man and a model for our emulation.

Chapter 15 – A Message to Men

"The truth is found when men are free to pursue it." – Franklin D. Roosevelt

"All men who have turned out worth anything have had the chief hand in their own education." – Walter Scott

"This was not guilt: guilt is what you feel when you have done something wrong. What I felt was shame: I was what was wrong." – Atul Gawande

"Shame corrodes the very part of us that believes we are capable of change." – Brené Brown

"To be shame-bound means that whenever you feel any feeling, need or drive, you immediately feel ashamed. The dynamic core of your human life is grounded in your feelings, needs and drives. When these are bound by shame, you are shamed to the core." – John Bradshaw

In the early 1990s I attended a gender conference in Toronto led by American poet Robert Bly and Canadian Jungian analyst Marion Woodman. These two offered the best work available on gender understanding and reconciliation at that time. There were about 150 women and 50 men, and it was an intense, three-day event.

At one point, the conference became mired in judgment and accusation between women and men. To address this energy, the conference leaders asked for three male and three female volunteers to speak to the conference participants, to express their thoughts and feelings about the issue. The men who spoke seemed confused or inarticulate; I don't remember anything they said. But the women were clear and passionate. They spoke of looking into history and society and seeing only men, only male leaders and male actors. As they spoke, I felt their pain, the pain of absence, of lack of visibility and agency. The following week, back in my home town of Ottawa, I happened to see in a store window a picture of the signatories to the American Declaration of Independence, and I wept there in the street at the absence of any women from this pivotal event. Women have articulated their grievances about historical gender imbalance in a dramatic way that society has been able to feel, to empathize with, and the result has been the many feminist programs and policies attempting to redress this problem. Men, who clearly have issues of equal gravity, have not yet articulated their perspectives in a way that society can appreciate, and none of their issues are yet being addressed. Why this imbalance?

We have looked at the moral power that women have used to shame men into silence, and how this power has been able to insist on a one-sided view of gender history; female victimization and male perpetration. But in this chapter, speaking specifically to men, I want to look at what it is in us that makes us unable to stand in the face of this attack. Why are men so weak when it comes to standing up to women, and what can we do about it?

A part of the answer is illustrated by another event at the same conference. We men went away with the male leaders for a couple of hours of single gender conversation, and the women with the female leaders. As the time came for us to come back together, we heard the women, somewhere else in the building, practicing a song that they clearly intended to sing to mark our return to a mixed conference. We considered what we might do to celebrate this same return. Robert Bly suggested a chant that he knew, and we practiced it for a few minutes. It was strong and fierce, a celebration of masculine warrior energy. Then we moved into the main hall where the women already were, chanting our chant as they sang their love song. It was a powerful moment, with two very different energies – the men's chant raucous, staccato and percussive, the women's song sweet and gentle and melodious. I looked at the women's faces as they circled around, holding hands and singing. They were smiling and welcoming, there was no judgment there at that moment.

I remember wondering how we could reconcile these very different energies, what possible union might come from them. But almost immediately, the men began to falter. The male chant faded away, and my brothers began singing the women's song. I was appalled. Yet I felt what I am sure they did, some shame at our raucous, warrior chant which seemed so much less appropriate than the women's loving welcome. I felt the shame, but I knew that it, the shame was what was inappropriate, and I stayed with the chant as the men around me stopped. I think that I was the last man in that room still trying to keep the chant going. Then I too stopped; it was too much to carry, to be the last holdout against the capitulation of the men to the feminine energy. I couldn't fight both my inner shame and the outer dynamic as well. Rather than join in the song, I lapsed into a sullen silence, feeling the bitterness of lost opportunity. What might we have discovered if we had held both energies, searching for a creative resolution, honoring both the masculine and the feminine and holding the tension? The energies were very different, but that is the challenge of dualistic opposites, and the secret, as I have explained and as Marion Woodman herself emphasized at the conference and in her books, is to sustain and maintain the energy of difference until a natural accommodation is found; not to let one subsume the other.

It is noteworthy that this capitulation of the masculine to the feminine was not remarked upon by the conference leaders – it went completely undiscussed. It's just how things are for men and women these days, and how they have been for over fifty years now. Men are ashamed, and both men and women feel that they should be. Perhaps, after more than fifty years of living under a feminist worldview built on this notion of male guilt and female innocence, it is time for a new balance to emerge. If so, men will have a prime role to play in repudiating their shame, redeeming their male pride and asserting their equality to women.

How will we do this? As I see it, there are two stages. The first is to really get that our shame is inappropriate. This work begins with an intellectual analysis. Does it really make sense that one gender should be uniquely guilty and the other innocent? In your experience, does this black-and-white picture show up in the men and women that you know? Are the women *really* more innocent than the men, in general? In order to know the truth about gender, we have to ask real questions and examine them honestly. We have to put our feelings about the issue aside for a time, and think carefully about what is true and what is just spin, image, illusion. This takes courage, not least because our lives will surely change if we alter our understanding of gender. It is disquieting to see more deeply than the popular culture, for one becomes out of step with one's contemporaries. Relationships change when one party sees more clearly than the other.

At some point in this thinking process, we confront our shame explicitly. We realize that we have a wound in our psyche and that it is our responsibility to heal it. This is a hugely painful realization. We are tempted to turn away from it, deny it, and avoid dealing with it. This choice does nothing but waste time. Many men, probably most, turn away for a lifetime and so live lives of unconscious denial and self-deceit. But if we can find the courage to tolerate the pain, the key here is to tell the truth about our wound, our shame, to acknowledge that we have judged ourselves to be unworthy, guilty, bad. If we acknowledge our shame, then for the first time we can actually evaluate it, look at it with an eye to its accuracy. Maybe quickly, maybe slowly, we discover that it is in fact a mistake. We are not damaged, we are not broken, and we are not guilty and bad in our essence. We are actually what we have pretended to be, wanted to be all the time, but didn't really believe. We are actually good men, with nothing to be ashamed of. This discovery is our first inkling of stage 4 wisdom.

This shame recovery work begins in contemplation, but as we heal we move to action. Knowing more than our contemporaries about a particular issue calls us to leadership. If the current story about gender, the story of female innocence and male guilt is wrong, what can we do to correct this error and advance a better understanding? What are the factors that have caused this error to become so widely believed? How do we speak of this issue in a way that is memorable, a way that can be received? The female story about historical powerlessness and invisibility is dramatic and memorable. What is the equivalent male story? What is the story that will touch the heart and the mind? How can we help our brothers to discover and then to heal their own shame?

We need to get creative about this. What the angry men of the Men's Human Rights Movement (MHRM) are doing may be dramatic but, for the most part, it is not memorable. It is too easily dismissed under the feminist cover story as just angry guys, unable to deal with loss of their privilege. The task of an advocate for social change is to be recognizably different than the stereotype that people hold about you. Some people, those open to the possibility that they could be mistaken, will notice that difference and will look more closely. When that happens, you have created an opportunity for a real dialog, one that can result in changed minds.

My personal attempt to answer these questions about how to connect with society about real gender equality is expressed in what I have written in this book – but I am aware that I could be missing the mark. My own journey to come to willingness to write and publish these words has been long and difficult. I feel ready now, but it is certainly possible that I am mistaken, that I am not as healed as I think, that there are shadow issues of which I remain unaware. I do not underestimate the challenge facing us as men in redeeming our masculinity.

Let me describe a part of my journey. The realization that feminism is evil came to me in 1998. I had been considering for months how to understand the fact that the foundational ideas of feminism – male oppression of women, gendered inequality of women and men – were false, and yet universally accepted as true. As I considered the consequences of the acceptance of that lie, I realized that there was a redistribution of resources going on, from men to women. Financial resources, emotional resources (both primarily through family court) and moral status were all flowing to women from men. I saw that this flow was seen as just compensation for past and present inequity, as female victims being compensated for longstanding disadvantage.

I realized, suddenly, just why certain aspects of feminist ideology were defended so vigorously – the idea of female disadvantage, of female innocence (never blame the victim), the idea of male patriarchal conspiracy (i.e., male essential guilt, a kind of 'original sin' uniquely for men), the idea that men had oppressed women throughout history. It was because these were essential premises in the argument to keep the compensation flowing. And one morning in 1998 I awoke at about 3am with the urge to write, and I went to my computer and wrote an essay entitled "Feminism is Evil." By 8am I had finished it, including my definition of evil ideology and an analysis of feminism as developed in Chapter eleven.

It was a scary idea. Frankly, it terrified me. I hadn't before considered that evil might be present in major form in the modern world. But it felt true, and I spent weeks examining every proposition, every logical deduction and inference for error. I found none, as I have found none in the years since that time. I published the essay in the January 1999 issue of *Everyman; A Men's Journal*, the gender magazine I was editing and publishing at the time. I considered what I wanted to do with this terrible insight.

I took it to my men's group and asked their advice. To a man, they told me that the idea was inappropriate, that it would be misunderstood and would do harm. They told me to find another word, that evil was too strong, too dark. None of them seemed very interested in the thinking behind it, in testing whether it could be true, though I didn't notice that immediately. I spoke to other friends about it. All had the same advice – don't suggest that feminism is evil. Find a different word. The idea itself seemed to be too much for people to contemplate.

It shook me. I was alone with my theory, and alone as well in the belief that what really mattered was whether it was *true*. If it was true, then I had a responsibility to share it, to publish it so that people would at least have the chance to understand what was really happening in the world of gender politics. But I was totally alone with it; every friend I had, every person I knew opposed me on it. If it wasn't true, if it was my own stuff, my childhood wounds projected out into the world as my friends seemed to think, then clearly I should heal myself.

I entered a mild depression that lasted for about ten years. I researched and expanded my theory, and even wrote a book manuscript but I couldn't publish it. How could I be sure that it was true? I worried about it, in a background sort of way, for years, and during those years I suffered a chronic sense of loneliness.

In February 2013, something changed. It was time to stop worrying about whether I was right. By some deep unconscious process I had concluded that enough was enough. The theory checked out in every way and it was time to put it out into the world. I had decided to trust my own judgment over that of my friends. I had done enough self-doubting. The theory was true, and not a projection of my own woundedness onto women. I began writing this book.

I have told this story to illustrate that the personal process by which we put aside our shame, by which we discover what is true in the psychosocial realm, is still quite mysterious to me. The only thing that I can say about it for sure is that it hangs primarily on what we want. If we want to recover, if we want to know what is true in ourselves and in the world, then eventually we find it and recognize it as real, as something to be trusted. The journey can be long but it is not endless, and the destination is worth the difficulty of the process. We come at last to a degree of wisdom, and recognize that that is where we have arrived.

One of the ways that some men come to awareness of the truth about gender issues is through experiencing the gender bias in family court. During the years of 1994-2006, when I was involved in writing for and later editing and publishing a gender issues magazine in Canada, I got in touch with a lot of such men. Most were men who wanted to be good fathers but had been forced into a diminished if not absent role in the lives of their children by a family court judgment which gave primary custody of their children to their ex wife, and the lack of enforcement of court-ordered access.

They were hurting and they were looking for help. I studied them and I studied the court system, how it worked and how the gender bias operated. Unfortunately, not many such men were interested in my advice – it was too difficult. Their experience had opened their eyes to gender bias, but it had not grown them up and they remained in a stage 2, victim space. As far as I can see, little has changed today. My advice remains the same.

Here is a typical example of a conversation that I have with depressing regularity, either by email or phone. I receive a request for help from a distraught father who has had sole custody given to his ex wife, and she is denying his court-ordered access. He writes something like: "I have every intention to keep on fighting for my children. I am not whining; I am just frustrated. If you think I am crying foul then you are right. My children mean the world to me just as I am sure the children of other fathers mean the world to them. To say the system is unfair is an understatement. My ex wife knows that I am no threat to the children or to her; why she is not held accountable for her actions and I am is beyond comprehension. … I intend to do whatever is necessary to regain access to my children. I am going to keep fighting regardless of the time spent doing it."

To this man, I responded, "As long as [what is done by our justice system] is 'beyond comprehension' to you, then you are fighting an enemy whom you do not begin to understand, and this is a recipe for failure. You will know that you understand when you cease to be outraged. As long as you are outraged, you are expecting the world to be different than it is, and that speaks to your own fantasies and misconceptions about the world – all of which compromise your ability to be effective in your fight. I am blunt because I am tired of seeing brave, determined, *naive* men waste their lifeblood fighting without studying the nature of the enemy – and, of course, lose. They get to keep their outrage. I hope it comforts them in their bankrupt solitude."

The basic issue is our relationship to power. If we feel we *must* fight against something, if we feel *compelled* to it, then we are making that thing more powerful than us and so at some level we *expect* to lose. A fighter who expects to lose is already beaten.

What is it about gender bias in family court that so knocks us for a loop? We men are used to the odds being against us. We know how to come back from three goals down in a hockey game, and even how to deal with an unfair referee without letting it get to us. We would know instantly that a general who said, "I am outraged that the enemy tricked us and occupied the high ground – he didn't play fair, and it shouldn't be allowed," was not in touch with the realities of his job. "Deal with it," we would say to him.

But in this issue of systemic gender bias against men, it is as if something sacred, something central to our worldview is threatened, and we lose our heads. We get angry, and we react from outrage – sometimes for years! Like flies attempting to escape through a window glass, we batter ourselves against the 'justice system' again and again, futilely hoping that maybe this time they'll see their bias and be more fair.

The fly analogy is actually quite apt, though a little undignified. In the natural world of the fly, there is nothing resembling glass. Anything that a fly can see through, he can fly through. Flies just don't 'get it' when they meet window glass. Their instincts, what 'feels right' to them, lead them to fly towards the light. In the few days of their life, they fly against every square inch of the window and die bravely, still trying to fly or crawl through it.

Can you imagine a kind of 'super fly' with perhaps the intelligence of a mouse? A fly like that might spend an hour checking out a single window and note that there didn't seem to be a way through the glass anywhere. Then he might take a look at all the fly corpses littered on the windowsill and think to himself, "Hmm, if all those guys died here without finding a way through, then there probably isn't one. I need to do something different if I hope to succeed."

His difficulty then would be that to do that something different, he would have to go against what felt right to him. Millions of years of evolution have given him the instinct to fly towards the light if he is trying to escape. There is no glass in the natural world where this instinct evolved, so that strategy works pretty well. Doing something different involves turning away from the window and looking elsewhere for a way out. Can he do it? Can he overcome the power of his instincts and his illusion that glass 'should' be intangible? Can he get past his outrage that something that he can't see or understand still has the power to defeat him?

If he can, he still hasn't solved his problem. He still isn't outside. He has to look elsewhere for a way out, and it may not even exist. But he *has* at least begun to look, rather than being fixated on what cannot work, and so he has a chance.

I imagine you see the relevance of the analogy. The 'glass' in the court system that just won't let you through is chivalry; it's thousands of years of biological and cultural evolution that has taught us that when the concerns of men and women come into conflict in a major way, men must sacrifice and women and children must be saved. This is why, when there aren't enough lifeboats, men go down with the ship in order to save women and children. This was functional (it enhanced our survival) for all those years when men alone held social power roles.

That chivalrous duty is now virtually hard-wired, like an instinct. It goes much deeper than our new ideas of gender equality – after all, it goes deeper than the individual survival instinct. Almost all family court judges, lawyers, social workers and psychologists, male and female, still have those unconscious blinders on; they feel they are doing right by expecting and enforcing a provider role onto men and a dependent, child-care role onto women. When the court case doesn't come out that way (for a mother who wants it) they *feel bad,* they feel that something isn't right and they quickly close the loophole. In short, it's a rigged game. Don't keep playing it and expecting fairness as if it weren't rigged, and don't waste your time shouting that it shouldn't be that way. That just won't work. It *is* that way, that's reality, my friend! The glass is *there*, the window is *closed!* We men are able to deal with reality in sports, war or business. Can we extend ourselves to do so in this realm as well?

It's different in sports or business or war, of course, because there we are fighting other *men,* not women. When we fight women, we fight our own chivalrous instincts as well as those of everyone else. There are only two ways to do it. One is to get so angry that your outrage overcomes your chivalry. That's the way most of the fathers I talk to have gone, and it doesn't work. It doesn't work because the system is used to dealing with angry men; it stereotypes them instantly as a danger to women and children, and acts accordingly. Theirs are the 'corpses' littering the windowsill, the 'deadbeat dads' you keep hearing about. The other way is to overcome your own chivalry through personal growth so that you don't need to be angry to fight; you fight then from choice, not compulsion. You become able to back away from the 'glass' of chivalry and find new and creative ways to fight for justice and for your children.

I am not saying this is easy; it is anything but. However, for each man who does his own grief work, his own recovery from his outrage, he becomes able to think with all cylinders firing. Here is the test: as long as you feel *compelled* to fight, that you *must* fight for the sake of your kids or for justice or for (fill in the blank), you are *reacting* rather than choosing. A man who fights because he must is a gladiator, not a warrior. He does not choose his battles or plan his strategy (though he may deceive himself that he does) and his life is one of continuous desperation. His status as a gladiator may not be his *fault,* but it *is* his responsibility.

In contrast, a man free of compulsion can pick his battles, and of course he picks battles where he has some chance of winning rather than being forced to fight where his enemy chooses, where his enemy controls the high ground and has all the superior weapons, as is undoubtedly the case in family court.

Are you still with me, men? Is this message too hard to hear? Most divorced fathers and MRAs didn't want to hear what I wrote in this and other essays, and they let their subscriptions lapse. *Everyman* failed for lack of subscribers in 2006.

I remember attempting to start a group for divorced dads. I invited several to my home for a first meeting. I said that they could do whatever they wanted for most of the evening, but that if I was going to be involved, I would insist that every meeting include a short process to help the men get past their anger. One man refused in no uncertain terms, telling me that he "needed his anger to fuel his advocacy work." That man was dead within a year from cancer. Coincidence? I don't know. But the group never met again, the men didn't want what I had to offer.

What is so fearful about looking inside at the source of our anger? Why do we need our anger "to fuel our advocacy work"? The answer is that anger can carry us past our shame. What comes up for us when we confront women about their behavior is shame. It doesn't feel right, we have been shaped by evolution to protect women, not to accuse and attack them. Anger can carry us past that feeling, can let us do it anyway. But it doesn't really work well, because anger is weak, it's about compulsion rather than choice. Not only that, but the system is well defended against angry men – they are readily dismissed and disregarded.

What is needed for us to become powerful is that we work through our shame; that we move from stage 2 through the grief of stage 3 to the empowerment of stage 4. From stage 4 we can speak truth to power, and it makes no difference whether that power is female or male. Here is an editorial I wrote for *Everyman* #40, Nov/Dec 1999, to highlight this issue in dramatic form.

Taking Mothers off the Pedestal

Mothers! This is the big one, boys. The feminists may rail about male power and Patriarchy and men oppressing women, but let me tell you, no one has more moxie these days, more power in the psyche (public and private) than Momma. Poppa has been dethroned and humiliated, but Momma is still up there, and she ain't kidding around. Men may kill your body, but Momma – she can kill your soul!

In particular, the various aspects of the gender movement are all currently stuck on mother issues. The feminists and pro-feminists, who have the power today, don't *feel* like they have it because they are caught in *victim* – a shadow form of the feminine archetype. They want power but not accountability, and that's a real problem because the two belong together and are hard to separate. But, as Warren Farrell pointed out in the last issue, it's something that *mothers* – and *only* mothers – were granted in the past. "In the past, lack of permission for divorce kept the woman from being 'fired' from her role. If a child stole something, we did not fire the mother for failing in her role. In contrast, if a man coached a team that failed, he would expect to get fired."

Feminism is following this same pattern, trying to get power for women while having only men held accountable. (Check it out for yourself: consider the implications of *any* modern feminist initiative.) This approach will fail in the long term, of course, but the moral and social harm that such distorted ideology, laws and policies cause to our psyches and our societies will have major consequences for years to come.

In contrast, the men's movement is split into two halves, each of which is currently blocked by the power of the mother. The men's (and fathers') rights movement [now the MHRM] has the political issues right – it really is about genuine equality between men and women (for the most part). However, it's not making much headway because it's filled with outrage, with angry men. What is the anger about? We are angry because *women* have betrayed us. We can't get over the fact that women, whom we trusted and married and loved, have turned out not to be the nurturing, gentle, longsuffering, *noble* creatures that we needed them to be. Rather, they have all of the dark, manipulative, hypocritical, destructive sides to them that men have. It's an outrage!

We must get over it. We must stop putting women on a pedestal and let them be fully human. Indeed, we must hold them accountable and *require* them to be fully human. It will take a lot of work. The grief underneath the anger is immense. In particular, we will have to discover how to redeem ourselves as men, rather than going to women for moral support. Guys, most women don't do that trick any more. In fact, many of them are doing the opposite, shaming and humiliating us. It's time we grew up and stopped needing *mother* to tell us we are good enough. We can learn to do that for ourselves.

The other half of the men's movement is focused, not on the outer world, but on men's inner lives, on men healing their wounds and recovering from gender stereotypes in their individual lives. The biggest visible group is the mythopoets. These men have done a lot of work on their father issues, and done it well for the most part. But having done that work, they now face the mother issues. Those wounds, being deeper and about 'other' rather than 'self,' are scarier. What's more, the techniques men have used to work with the masculine energies: men's groups, men's retreats, drumming and dancing and truth-speaking with other men don't get at the mother issues very well. Those energies tend to come up in men's relationships with women and in the wider society. Most men doing their inner work are currently avoiding the mother issues. …

How will we work our way through the mother issues? To be honest, I don't really know. I tell of my own journey with these issues [in chapter five]. I think that we have to do it with women. Our defensiveness, our anger in the face of the modern attack on manhood or in the face of personal attacks by ex-wives or girlfriends is because, deep down, we don't *know* that we are ok – unless women approve of us. That is the heart of the mother wound, the last major, universal wound in our psyches. It is shame, and the only way forward is for us to recover from it.

One trap we must avoid. You may have noticed that I have not included organizations like the Promise Keepers in my descriptions of the men's movement. This is because these organizations are offering the false hope of a return to a form of traditional gender roles. They are regressive rather than progressive, nostalgic rather than visionary. They wish to avoid taking women off the pedestal, and instead to re-install men back on their own pedestal. We have much to learn about gender from our traditional patterns, but I do not believe we can return to them, and attempts to do so will not succeed in creating healthy relationships or a healthy society. The new can be avoided, for a time, but it cannot be denied without penalty. Ultimately, it must be discovered and embraced."

I still like that editorial, which is why I have included it here. Fifteen years after I wrote it, little has changed. The men's rights movement has gained an acronym, the MHRM; the mythopoetic movement has morphed into the ManKind Project and similar organizations, but the whole movement is still stuck on shame. It still falls to individual men, in therapy, personal growth workshops, retreats and men's groups, to do their emotional work and gain the strength to claim their own moral power. I hope that we will soon begin to step out of these protected spaces and acknowledge our gender truth in the public arena. When we do, we can expect to be shamed. We will be called backlash, misogynist; the privileged seeking to continue their oppression of others. To stand against such shame attacks, we will need to know, to *really* know, that they are not true. To know this, we will need to have examined our souls as deeply as we can.

The real gender revolution will involve breaking denial and doing this hard recovery work, one man and one woman at a time. This work is painful and fearful, which of course is why we avoid it. It involves acknowledging our wounds from the past and the dysfunctional, codependent ways we have used to avoid feeling and owning them. Most importantly, it involves grieving the loss in order to discover (recover) our intrinsic worthiness. This work takes different forms for men and for women. Women, in general, are in denial of their power, which they fear as guilt. Men, in general, are in denial of their powerlessness, which they fear as failure or weakness. We do not break denial patterns "because we should" (a shame attack) but only when we want to.

This issue can feel overwhelming. It is so massive, so universal, and so invisible. And how does one recover from loss of oneself? Once, because of shame, one has substituted a false self, an image that is more appropriate, more acceptable, more 'politically correct, then the road back to authenticity is so difficult. For, no matter how much approval I gain for my 'act', for my false self, I can never get enough, because approval of my false self, my image, isn't approval of me but just the opposite. No, filled with fear and trembling, I must risk showing my real self to the world, knowing that when I did that as a child, I was usually punished or shamed. What a task lies before us as we start to untangle this web!

I see this as the last great universal challenge facing us as adults and as parents. The archetypically masculine – overt, direct or physical – abuses are easy to recognize today, and universally known to be harmful. It is the indirect, the covert, the deceptive, the shaming, the manipulative abuse that is the great destroyer of our children's souls today. Can we, who were not loved for who we were as children ourselves, yet offer to our children that vital soul-food – respect and valuing of their essence, of their real nature – even as we help them shape their behaviors in ways that will work for them in society? If we can, it will be the greatest gift that can be given, the gift of authentic life itself.

To do that, we have to heal our own essential shame. The critical first step on that road is to break the cover story, the denial, and to begin instead to tell the truth about one's inner life, one's wounds and fears. That is an act of pure courage, for most will not understand and will be threatened by such truth telling. But until we accept responsibility and the pain of the shame that comes with it, we cannot forgive ourselves, for without responsibility there is nothing to forgive. The shame, projected out onto others, remains with us. I have lived that way. I don't recommend it.

Our essential shame keeps a part of us locked away in a kind of cage as long as it remains unhealed and unconscious. Robert Bly, in his book *Iron John* – that basically launched the mythopoetic men's movement and that remained on the bestseller list for almost a year – suggests that it is our "Wild Man" that is locked up, the earthy, uncivilized but radiantly alive part of us, our soul as it were. "The kind of wildness, or un-niceness, implied by the Wild Man image," writes Bly, "is not the same as macho energy, which men already know enough about. Wild Man energy, by contrast, leads to forceful action undertaken, not with cruelty, but with resolve." [151]

The king's son loses his golden ball into the Wild Man's cage, and asks him for it back. The Wild Man says he will give the ball back if the prince sets him free from the cage. The key to the cage containing the Wild Man, it turns out, is under the boy's mother's pillow. Why? Because "when the King locked up the Wild Man, he gave the key into the keeping of the Queen."

This speaks to me of the codependence I have been describing, of the way a man and a woman typically transact to cement their relationship, and of the hidden losses from this transaction: that something essentially masculine is locked up, and this affects the children as well.

Bly says,

> "… the key is under our mother's pillow – just where Freud said it would be.

> "Getting the key back from under the mother's pillow is a troublesome task. Freud, taking advice from a Greek play, says that a man should not skip over the mutual attraction between himself and his mother if he wants a long life. … Michael Meade, the myth teller, once remarked to me that the pillow is also the place where the mother stores all her expectations for you. She dreams: 'My son the doctor.' 'My son the Jungian analyst.' 'My son the Wall Street genius.' But very few mothers dream: 'My son the Wild Man.'

> "On the son's side, he isn't sure he wants to take the key. Simply transferring the key from the mother's to a guru's pillow won't help. Forgetting that the mother possesses it is a bad mistake. A mother's job is, after all, to civilize the boy, and so it is natural for her to keep the key. All families behave alike: on this planet, 'The King gives the key into the keeping of the Queen.'

> Attacking the mother, confronting her, shouting at her, which some Freudians are prone to urge on us, probably does not accomplish much – she may just smile and talk to you with her elbow on the pillow. Oedipus' conversations with Jocasta never did much good, nor did Hamlet's shouting.

> "A friend mentioned that it's wise to steal the key some day when your mother and father are gone. 'My mother and father are away today' implies a day when the head is free of parental inhibitions. That's the day to steal the key. …

> "And the key has to be *stolen*. … No mother worth her salt would give the key anyway. If a son can't steal it, he doesn't deserve it.

> 'I want to let the Wild Man out!'

> 'Come over and give Mommy a kiss.'

> "Mothers are intuitively aware of what would happen if he got the

key: they would lose their boys. The possessiveness that mothers typically exercise on sons … can never be underestimated." [152]

Later in the book, Bly uses a different metaphor:

"We know that more that one American man today needs a sword to cut his adult soul away from his mother-bound soul. Australian aboriginal initiators use that sword precisely to cut that psychic umbilical cord. The sword has the edge that cuts clinging away from love, cuts boyish bravado away from manly firmness, and cuts passive-aggression away from fierceness. The Tibetans refer to such a sharp interior sword as 'the Vajra sword.' Without it, they say, no spiritual life is possible, and no adult life." [153]

I don't know to what extent what Bly is describing here corresponds to the shame wound that I describe. There is some degree of overlap, I am sure. Certainly my own experience of 'killing my mother' at the experiential workshop I described in chapter five was largely about repudiating my (internalized) mother's expectations about what I 'should' be like, and setting myself free of her moral power over me. It was the start of healing my shame wound.

It is probably no coincidence that the men's movement that feminists find of greatest concern is the mythopoetic movement. In *Women Respond to the Men's Movement: A Feminist Collection,* [154] virtually none of the contributors can find a good thing to say about the men's movement, (actually, their message throughout the book, in a thousand different forms of words, is "Shame on you, men, shame, shame, shame"), and the movement they are shaming is the mythopoetic, as seen through the lens of *Iron John.* What's more, the part that seems to really burn them the most is this bit about the key and the mother's pillow. I interpret this as an accurate fear on their part that if men actually do this shame wound work, if they really do steal the key, then they will become strong and independent men, no longer able to be controlled and silenced through the use of shame.

At the end of "The Maiden Tsar," The Russian folk tale analyzed by Robert Bly and Marion Woodman in *The Maiden King; The Reunion of Masculine and Feminine,* the hero, Ivan, finds the love of his betrothed for him buried inside an egg inside a duck inside a hare inside a coffer inside an oak tree. That's pretty deeply buried. This resonates mythologically with the state of the world today – the love of women for men and masculinity has indeed been deeply buried, and in its place we have a ubiquitous feminist shaming of men and all things male. Through long struggles leading to strength and wisdom, Ivan finds the egg and returns it to his beloved. She eats the egg, and thus re-assimilates and rediscovers her love for Ivan.[155]

This suggests to me that men have a vital role to play in healing the loss of love for men that feminism represents. That role is for men to recover from their essential shame so that they can stand proudly as men, strong and independent and unashamed. Doesn't this make sense – isn't such a man much more admirable, more lovable than one wounded and crippled by self-doubt, by shame, no matter how well he hides that shame behind an image of assurance or respectability? We know that we are crippled because we cannot stand against the shame attack that feminism has put into the world. We have capitulated, we have faltered, we have not spoken up to point out the flaws of logic and the failures of empathy. Although it is built on lies, we have not been able to say so with power, and therein lays our indictment and proof of our codependent wounds.

Yet, as always, there is another side. It has not just been women's moral power to shame us that has pushed women's issues forward in society. Men have also supported them, just about universally, because it was right. Women's issues are real, and deserve to be redressed. There is no good reason why women should not be politicians, corporate executives, indeed why they should not compete for any job they want. We have granted them equality in the workplace because it is right. We see the justice of their claims, and we have passed laws to support them. We can be proud of that.

Indeed, we are owed for it, and what we are owed is a corresponding equality in the homeplace. We are owed reproductive rights of the kind that women already have and parenting rights equal to those of women. But to seek those, we will have to ask for them – indeed, to demand them. Again, because it is right, it is just. To do this, to ask for what is owed to us under the other side of gender equality, the side that benefits men and asks women to share their traditional world as men have shared their own, we will need to recover from our shame and learn how to stand up proudly rather than angrily for our own gender, something we have never done before.

This is my ultimate message to men. There is a journey set before us, a journey that calls to us all, but each one of us must take that first step alone, in fear and trembling. It is the journey of freedom from the compulsion of evolutionary conditioning and until we begin it we are not fully alive. I hope that we may be on the verge of beginning that journey as a whole society, significant numbers of us moving into recovery, perhaps within a single generation. We will need leaders who have healed their own shame wound to point the way and welcome the journeyers. You have read this chapter through to the end. Are you ready to take the first step? Or a next step?

I offer you the question with which I challenge myself: "If not me, then who? If not now, when?"

Chapter 16 – A Message to Women

"A woman is like a tea bag - you can't tell how strong she is until you put her in hot water." – Eleanor Roosevelt

"The test of civilization is its estimate of women." – George William Curtis

"Women don't realize how powerful they are." – Judith Light

In Honor of the True Love of Women

I find that some books or movies can move me greatly, but that the affect, the emotion is fragile. Conversation, even innocent questions about what I am feeling and what in the movie affected me, seem to break the spell. This short piece is my first attempt to withdraw into silence after watching a movie, and to write from that affected space.

What can be said to capture a mood, an emotion? Many have tried. Even to hold it within myself, after a powerful, touching movie like *The English Patient* is difficult. Emotions seem so ephemeral, so fragile.

Who was the woman? I don't remember her name. The French Canadian nurse who looked after the English patient, and swung high in the church to see the paintings. She represents for me those women, those many good and honest women, who have loved men truly. What a gift that was. My heart is full of gratitude to the women who have loved men. Loved them as she loved the Seik bomb disposer, with her body and her heart. Loved them as she loved the English patient, with her heart and her mind. Loved truly, in wisdom, so that she could honor his final wish to die, and help him to do so, even as it brought her pain and sorrow. How I wish to honor such women, who know how to love men. Like Katherine Maddox, dying alone in a cave, trusting her man that he had done all he could to get back to her, and so avoiding sinking into resentment and recrimination even as all she feared closed in on her in the dark, and she died alone. No wonder that he so treasured her diary.

I wish to die with praise on my lips for women like these, who love well and truly. I wish them to hear from my mouth and my pen that their love is much valued, is esteemed and honored. In these times of shame and anger, of fear of men, I wish to say to women that this is what most men live and die for. Love of this kind is what men move mountains for. There is nothing between men and women that can inspire a man to greater heights of heroism or of dedication than this.

And yet, love of this kind is not drawn forth by arguments like this, as though it were to be purchased by the heroism of a man. No, love like this is given freely, because the true heart of its author would have it no other way. I do not write to reward women for their true love. No payment is possible, or necessary. I write only to honor them, to speak from the depths of my own feeling in gratitude and in praise. There is no exchange of value here, no trade. My gift is free, as is theirs.

May such love never die in the world. And may men never cease to honor it. It is women's form of heroism, and it is worthy of its own medals, its own ribbons and rituals of celebration.

I give honor, and bend the knee in homage to women who love well.

As we approach the end of this book together, I want to tell you something of what it is like to be a man these days. As I watch the beauty of love between good women and good men in movies like *The English Patient*, *The Time Traveler's Wife* or *The Adjustment Bureau*, I feel blessed to be alive, to share the world with women, to be loved myself by a good woman. As I look more widely and see the poisonous judgment of men spread by feminism into every corner of our world, as I see the erosion of goodwill that it causes, the undermining of trust, the suspicion, the exaggerated fear on the part of women, I feel much sadness. As I listen to men, some angry, some confused, some just unaware, I see the diminishment of what we could be. I see some women struggling under the propaganda of victimhood, of moral superiority, wondering whether they should claim their responsibility or whether things in their lives really are a man's fault. I see other women who are totally caught up in feminist ideology, hateful and self righteous.

There are as yet relatively small numbers of extreme cases where lives have been completely destroyed by sexist prejudice, but the more subtle and more widespread damage is insidious. It seeps into our communities and families like water into fabric, growing slowly more saturated with invisible and poisonous lies. I see no solution to it until more of us grow up and become able to see and to speak the truth, and to do so with love in our hearts. For feminism is riding on our immaturity, our biased feelings, our codependent blindness, and will continue to do so until we find the strength to change.

At this time in history, with respect to this particular issue, women are more powerful than men. The evil of feminism is being propagated through women's moral power over men – but that power can be employed for good as readily as for evil. When men speak out against feminism, they are easily silenced or disregarded, both because of women's power to shame them and also because they are easily dismissed as self-interested, as defending patriarchal privilege. It's usually a lie, but a powerful one.

Women are more difficult to dismiss. Good men, most men, have protected women with their bodies and their lives throughout history; can women now step forward to protect men, to defend them from this most unjust assault upon their character and their lives? Will you? We men are suffering, we really need your help, and I for one humbly request it.

For women who have believed the feminist story about oppression and victimhood, a wonderful discovery awaits you. You are as powerful as men and always have been. You don't have to fight for power or step into power roles; you have only to open your eyes.

But there is a difficulty. It is the difficulty that has kept many women from doing this for a long time. With power comes responsibility, and with responsibility comes guilt, the knowledge of having done harm. There is no getting around this, it must be accepted. The biggest guilt that must be accepted is that feminism, the movement that has been launched and propagated in your name, is built on lies and has done much damage. It hasn't been about equality at all, but about women's advantage. I am sorrier than I can say that this is true, but it *is* true and it must be acknowledged.

What does that look like when women own their own power and accept responsibility for it? More than twenty years ago, while I was working at a Canadian telecom company, I happened to see a sign that a female employee had posted in her cubicle. It read, "In this cubicle, sexual harassment will not be reported – but it will be graded!" That's it. That's exactly it. This woman was repudiating generic female victimhood and stating unambiguously that she had the power to handle male overtures that the culture regarded as oppressive. I regret to this day that I did not then have the awareness or confidence to step up to that woman and congratulate her on her personal attitude of empowerment. But her sign made an impression on me; even then I knew that it was admirable, and I never forgot it.

I know that men have done a lot of harm. One of the gifts of feminism has been for men to learn humility. Back in the fifties and before, men were "up on the pedestal" of social adulation. Now we're in the basement of social contempt. But neither place is where we belong. We belong in the middle, in dualistic balance; neither worshipped nor scorned, just human. Imperfect, but worthy.

Women belong there too, right beside us, just as imperfect but just as worthy. That is real equality. But in the last fifty years, women have been up on the pedestal themselves. Perhaps it's hard to hear coming from a man, but as feminism has been blaming men for the state of the world, women have been able to feel morally superior. Men have helped with this project, but it has primarily been driven by women's power to shame men into silence and to control moral discourse in the public sphere. It will be necessary for women to own up to this power and to the fact that they have employed it abusively.

Now, no woman is responsible for what others have done, so let me speak to my female readers as individuals. Feminism is not your fault. It is not your fault, unless you are actively feminist, and even then you have an excuse, for you did not know what you were doing. You were sincere in your belief about men's power and women's victimization. Your blindness was willful; you denied and dismissed all the evidence that you were mistaken because it didn't feel right, but it was still blindness. Feminism is not your fault.

However, it is your responsibility. Not exclusively; men bear some responsibility for it as well, for taking the easy path of compliance and appeasement rather than growing ourselves up to where we can stand up for what is true in the face of female shame attacks. But the primary responsibility, and the primary power to fix the problem, lies with women.

I do not underestimate the difficulty of hearing this message. Perhaps a gender reversal would make the situation more accessible, if no less painful. Feminism is propelled through an abuse of women's moral power over men. The analogous male power is men's physical power to coerce women through fear. The gender reversed equivalent to feminism, then, would be if men en mass, as a political program purporting to be about gender equality, had progressively disenfranchised women, eroded their equality rights, frequently stolen their children, confiscated some of their property, and threatened women with extreme violence if they spoke out against this program in any way. Spend a moment considering how that would feel – that is what feminism is like to men.

There is one difference, of course; such a masculine program would be consciously intimidating, while feminism's intimidation is usually unconscious to both women and men. No less powerful, but we have been unaware of, in denial of its power. But surely, after reading this far, you cannot remain completely unconscious. Even if you disagree with my thesis, you can see that it is a plausible alternative to the feminist cover story. The theory hangs together; it makes sense even if it still doesn't feel right. You have the opportunity now to check it out, to do your own research, to think carefully and reach your own conclusions. If you choose instead to dismiss the argument I have made and to turn away, you do so knowing the risk – that what you continue to support may be an evil ideology.

It may be difficult for you, as a woman, to realize how powerful your ability to shame men is. It is fully as big in men's psyches as is your own fear of violence and murder. When women shame men, it feels like emasculation, it feels like death. It is utterly terrifying. Yet we men hide our pain and our terror, because that is how we have been taught to be true men, to be good men, to be worthy of a good woman. We hide it even from ourselves. Men have been complicit in hiding and denying women's power; we carry some responsibility for your lack of awareness of it, but the larger measure belongs to women, for it has been used massively and destructively in your name in the last fifty years.

Here's the heart of the problem. Women must come to acknowledge that their first major foray into public policy, into practical politics, has been a disaster. It has been founded on lies and propagated through intimidation using a power that most women don't consciously realize they possess. It has done and is still doing immense harm. It is ideologically evil. I know that it is harder for women to acknowledge such responsibility than it is for men, for women's codependent moral power is built on a foundation of innocence. Acknowledging this responsibility means giving up moral power, moral superiority, and embracing guilt for a time. It will hurt a lot.

But it must be done. For each woman who does it, there is the reward of a relationship of genuine equality with men, and the ability to see men for who they truly are; flawed and beautiful, honorable and human and worthy of full equality with women. For each woman who does it, it means the end of the "no good men" refrain which is built on an erroneous contempt for masculinity. For each woman who does it, it means the beginning of a new life of non-addictive, non-codependent relationships with others in the world. For each woman who does it, it means becoming progressively able to see clearly, to discern truth, and to manage your life successfully. For each woman who does it, the world is a little more healed, a little less wounded, and a little happier.

The choice is yours. You can be a leader, one who chooses early to embrace wisdom, or a follower, one who takes a path only when it is well trod by others. I do not say what you should do, because I cannot know your circumstance, your history, the issues that keep you stuck or your access to courage to overcome them. I do say that you can, if you desire it enough, because I believe this to be true for us all. In the end we are responsible for the shape of our lives because we all have the power to grow ourselves up if we choose.

Who am I to say these things to you, to speak in this way? I am a man who has done some personal growth work to get free of my own gender codependence, to become able to speak even in the face of female shame attacks. I related some of that journey in chapter five. It was not easy, and it isn't finished yet, but it has given me the ability and the will to speak with authority about these matters, to see them clearly and to know what is so and what is not so. You don't have to believe me – in fact, I prefer if you look for yourself, discover the truth about gender and power and wisdom yourself. Then act, powerfully and decisively, to change your own life.

One of the saddest aspects of the moral polarization that feminism has wrought is the loss of masculine wisdom from the world. Women have become isolated, left with just their own half of dualistic wisdom and frequently unable even to understand the loss that this represents. Let's look at rape to explore this issue.

Feminine wisdom about rape is that it is devastating, life-changing. Real, forcible rape undermines the innocence that women feel within the gender codependent matrix, so that they now feel dirty, shameful, unworthy. One of their most basic powers and rights, the power and right of sexual choice, has been ripped from them, possibly with major consequences – disease or an unwanted pregnancy. All of these feelings are appropriate – but they are also unbalanced, and men hold the balancing piece, the piece that is missing.

Masculine wisdom is the wisdom of choice, of will. Men know that where there is no choice, there is nothing to forgive. They *feel* the truth of this. Good men will reassure a woman who has been raped that she is not dirty or shameful, she is not unworthy because of the actions of another. The rapist carries the guilt and the shame, whether he acknowledges it or not. For a woman who can let it in, this wisdom is healing; it restores her feeling of innocence and moral purity, as indeed it should. It is a blessing from the sacred masculine. But today, the contempt for male wisdom and the feminist insistence that men have no right to speak on the question of rape, isolates women from the healing that men can offer.

It is the same in all areas of gender politics. Consider women's shelters. They usually prohibit men from even entering the building, ostensibly to alleviate women's fears. But what is needed for women who have been victims of male violence is to learn that there are good men, non-violent men, and how to tell the difference between them. Abused women need, above all, to recognize and heal whatever it is in themselves that attracts them into abusive relationships. Isolating women from good, positive masculinity is a recipe for protracted fear and insecurity. It inhibits or prevents full healing, which cannot be completed in isolation from men.

The healing of gender issues, for both men and women, requires both single gender and mixed gender processes. I have found this to be true for me personally, and I am convinced that it is a general rule. I have found it inexpressibly sad at those times when a woman, hurting because of what some man has done, has been righteously indignant when I have offered a perspective which could empower her out of victimhood. Powerless victimhood, whether in the case of rape or domestic violence, can appear attractive to women in that it preserves moral innocence – but at what horrific cost! Masculine wisdom sees the downside of victimhood; it is a perspective that is sorely needed in today's world, but it is a perspective that is shamed as abusive, as "blaming the victim.' In pushing masculine wisdom away, in using women's moral power to shame it as abusive, women have lost access to a vital, healing component of our human heritage.

I am struggling to imagine, as I write, what might be the stumbling blocks for you, what might stand in the way of seeing yourself as an owner/operator of moral power over men. I know that it is difficult for women to *feel* the power that they have over men, to actually experience it as power. Perhaps it would help if I said something about how I think this balance of gender power came to be.

For thousands of years, men have mostly held societal power roles, and women have mostly not. During those years, we evolved cultural forces to restrain the abuses of power that men tend towards. Indeed, chivalry itself is a way of requiring men to internalize and accept the *responsibility* of power, to serve others even at the cost of their lives. We have grown accustomed to holding men accountable and holding women blameless; these things now feel right to us.

The widespread modern movement of women into social and economic power roles traditionally held by men is brand new in evolutionary terms, less than a hundred years old, and none of these evolved restraint mechanisms work effectively against abuses of power by women. Neither the internal mechanisms such as chivalry (there is no cultural 'honor code' instilled into women obliging them to protect men), nor the external social control mechanisms such as courts and legislation. These institutions still operate mainly to protect women, and seem unable to find the will to hold them accountable. So women today are exerting great power in our society, and there is no cultural mechanism yet evolved to restrain their abuse of this power. As they do what feels right to them, some of their actions are doing massive harm.

If it is the case that women have forms of power that balance the more overt forms possessed by men, then we have to ask ourselves how such an arrangement might have originated. I am not an anthropologist, nor have I attempted to research this area. However, I wish to offer, purely as plausible speculation, a scenario describing how this might have happened.

My scenario begins with violence. Consider that in prehistoric society there was an unavoidable need for either aggressive or defensive fighting.[xiii] Such wars arise naturally from the competition between tribes for resources, or for any number of more complex reasons. (The modern notion that primitive societies were peaceful and harmonious is a nostalgic fantasy; most, like Native Americans, were warlike long before they encountered Europeans.[156]) Given the biological differences between men and women which lead naturally to women being engaged in child rearing and men in hunting (a division of labor also common in the animal kingdom), this task of war would naturally have fallen to men, and that would create a problem. For once men organize themselves as a fighting force, what is to prevent them from taking over the society, enslaving women and taking what they wish from them?

The answer is that nature abhors a vacuum, including a power vacuum, and always finds a balance. The balance in this case was provided by an honor code. Such a code remains the chief way that societies guard against military excess to this day. In elegantly simple fashion, men held the physical power and women the moral power. Each had a power over the other, and each had something the other needed. Men had the physical power but needed the moral affirmation of women in order to achieve social recognition as good men, not to mention a wife and children. Women had the moral power but needed the physical protection and often also the provision of food and shelter from men. So men had the power to destroy women's bodies and women had the power to destroy men's souls

---

[xiii] In his book *War Before Civilization*, archeology professor Lawrence H. Keeley concludes that casualty rates in prehistoric tribal conflicts were on average 20 times those of 20th century warfare.

and a kind of detente, a balance of power, was struck. All of this was unconscious social evolution, where things that work persist *because* they work, because they have survival value. We don't need to know *why* we feel a certain way in order to feel that way: fear, shame or pride spring from within us and are shaped in us by physical and cultural evolution without us knowing or caring how it is done.

Perhaps at first there were tribes where the men enslaved the women. What must have happened is that such tribes were less effective, less able to compete with those where a gender balance of power was invented and men and women were able to work cooperatively, and so over time evolution favored those with an honor code restraining the force of the warrior men. We are their descendants.

This is simply plausible speculation; I do not present it as factual. Whatever its anthropological roots, however, there is little doubt that this honor code exists today and has taken many forms over time, from the ritual chivalry of the middle ages or the heroic "counting coup" of Native American tribal culture to the exaggerated Puritanism of the Victorians, but it has usually been focused on and controlled by women. Its deepest root is, of course, the power that women have to grant or withhold sexual favors, and so to cut off a 'dishonorable' man from access to sex, marriage, progeny and a normal community life.

This honor code is deeply and fundamentally alive in men today, and it is still society's greatest defense against both individual and collective male perfidy and violence. This is where the urgency of our present situation is apparent, for feminism has, for the first time in history, turned women from shaming individual men who are judged dishonorable, which had an important function in service of social order, to shaming men in general and masculinity as an institution. The very real danger is that if men come to perceive that there is no way for them to achieve honor, to be recognized publicly and privately as 'good' men, then they may sense that they have little to lose by taking what they want, since they have little to gain by restraining themselves. I very much fear that if we do not turn aside from our still-growing, wholesale shaming of men and all things male, that our future may contain civil violence of a degree we have never seen.

Let us not underestimate the power that feminism holds. The deepest, most deadly power given to women by tribal evolution is the power to shame. It had to be powerful, because it balanced the most deadly power given to men; the power to kill. That power to shame the deep souls of men is the power that feminism is using today to silence most of the men (and women) who would otherwise shout its errors and biases aloud. It is not easy for a man to grow out of his dependence on women for his essential honor. This is deep masculine stuff: "death before dishonor" is not a trivial male soul-cry. History has proven that regular, ordinary men will charge from trenches directly into machine gun fire, as we have seen in numerous battles. They will stand on the deck of a sinking ship as they did on the Titanic, watching lifeboats filled with women and children pull away and leave them to die. They will choose certain death rather than face the shame that they experience when they see themselves as dishonorable, as cowards. That's how big the honor code is in men: bigger than the fear of death, bigger than the survival instinct.

Women, until men grow themselves up, you hold the strings of that power. It is a huge responsibility. You carry this power simply by virtue of being female, and I hope that you will choose to step up and take the lead in acknowledging that power and learning to use it well again. The distortions that we see in society today around gender – programs that address only women's fears and ignore men's issues – have succeeded *only* because of that female moral power to shame good, civilized men into compliant silence.

The feminist movement has used the unconscious honor code of chivalry, resident in all good men, to overcome men's evolved wisdom about correct use of social power and instead install hugely harmful, oppressive and abusive one-sided rights-for-women-and-responsibilities-for-men laws and policies – even as it has simultaneously shamed that whole honor code and wisdom as patriarchally abusive and oppressive. It is a feat of unprecedented, though unconscious, hypocrisy. The very best in men, their self-sacrificing code of honor, has been co-opted to bind them while the very thing that their honor code was designed to prevent – widespread abuse of social and political power – is put into place to serve the interests of women alone.

Remember the balance of power: men can kill women's bodies; women can kill men's souls. What does it look like when men's souls are being killed, even as they are shamed into silence about it? Look around you. The evidence is huge: it requires only a glimmer of consciousness and a lick of courage to perceive. Yet, most of us do not yet perceive it. Such is the blindness of addictive denial. Addiction recovery workers are not kidding when they say that a dysfunctional family (or society) is like having an elephant in the living room, that no one ever points to or consciously acknowledges is there.

My hope is that women will choose to move into recovery around their gender codependence and own their half of the dance of power. As an individual woman, you have the choice to step into full awareness around these gender issues, and to acknowledge the hidden half of the gender codependent matrix – women's power over men, especially moral power, and men's victimhood. I hope that you will find the courage to own up to the power, the responsibility, and feel the pain of your previous blindness. With that will come a deep grief, which will be the process by which you will heal yourself and let go of the image of innocence and moral superiority. Do not forget, as you do your grief work, that you are worthy and loved by men, by good men, by most men, and certainly by this man.

On the other side of this personal journey of recovery and growth toward enlightenment lies a different kind of power, an empowerment based in truth and love that you will employ in wisdom to help heal the world. On the other side, as well, lies a new kind of relationship with men, a relationship of respect and of genuine love, a relationship solidly founded in the truth that men and women are equal and always have been. In that place, you will *feel* the truth and the glory of that essential equality, you will feel men to be good and worthy partners for the journey of life.

Chapter 17 – I, Too, Have a Dream

"The books that help you most are those which make you think the most." – Pablo Neruda

"Vision is the art of seeing what is invisible to others." – Jonathan Swift

"A dream is your creative vision for your life in the future. You must break out of your current comfort zone and become comfortable with the unfamiliar and the unknown." – Denis Waitley

"A dream doesn't become reality through magic; it takes sweat, determination and hard work." – Colin Powell

The writing of this book has been motivated by two goals. One is to provide insight into how to discover what is true in the realm of human society and culture, as a foundation on which more might be built by others and in the hope that some might be assisted in their personal journey of growth and discovery. The other is to explore the puzzle of gender, how feminism is so powerful under a banner of powerlessness, and to end by naming and understanding a major evil that is yet unrecognized in the world, in the hope that it might be sooner perceived and dispelled.

These two distinct themes have been woven together throughout the course of the book because it seems to me that the latter depends upon the former. Our current cultural fairy story of a victim class of innocent women and a perpetrator class of patriarchal men is one that cannot be recognized and transcended unless the largely unconscious feelings that support it are critically examined, carefully thought about. To do that, we have to shake free of the power of those feelings, and the best way for that to happen is as an act of will, a choice to seek truth and grow ourselves up. I have described the case and the process for that in earlier chapters.

I have also worked hard to craft the book itself as an example of the dualistic balance that I am advocating. I have balanced careful analysis (head) with personal stories (heart). I have held feminism accountable for its lies, but with genuine compassion. I have talked extensively about the outer, objective world, but also the inner world of emotion and thoughtful reflection. I hope that these balances have made the book more accessible, more interesting, more holistic, more personal and above all, more helpful, more useful.

The truth about gender is both simple and beautiful. Women and men are equal in power and in powerlessness, and always have been. The advantages and disadvantages balance out for both genders. This is hard to see as long as we are enmeshed in society's codependent cover story about male power and female victimhood, but it is true nonetheless. That cover story is simply an example of dualistic imbalance, stage 2 cultural immaturity, where the power of women and the victimhood of men are denied because they don't feel right.

The problem that we face is not about practical law and policy. We could draft gender equal laws tomorrow, if we chose. The problem we face is that we don't want to, even though we sincerely believe that we do. The problem is in us, in our biased feelings. That is why this book has been about human meta-psychology, the basic processes by which we give meaning to our lives. That is why I have exhorted you, my reader, to grow yourself as an individual in wisdom and insight, to break denial and move into gender recovery.

Let me demonstrate my claim that it is not difficult to draft gender equal law and policy. Can I offer a practical vision that could be implemented promptly, that would represent a major step towards equal rights and equal responsibilities between men and women? In 1998, I organized and hosted the first of a series of annual national gender conferences in Canada. At that first conference, attended by about fifty men and women, we spent much of our time crafting a document to represent our vision of gender justice and practical political equality. At the end of the conference, we all signed the document. It wasn't easy to come together around every detail, but we worked hard and we succeeded. The document is a bit dated now, but I include it as an example of a practical first step toward gender justice. Since the last fifty years have seen feminism advance women's issues but not men's, it necessarily focuses on introducing rights for men, but I hope you will see that the goal is a reasonable and workable balance of rights and responsibilities between women and men.

Here is the document:

"Vision for Gender Equality, Everyman Gathering, May 3, 1998

Introduction

This document begins to articulate a vision of gender equality and gender justice inside the larger context of establishing authentic equality for all members of our society. It seeks not to repudiate the achievements that women have made, nor the work left to do, but rather, wishes to advance an awareness of the important areas of systemic discrimination against men.

This vision represents our clearest statement of the unique value and contribution men have made and can continue to make to society.

Reproductive Rights and Responsibilities

Where we are now: Men have no reproductive rights at all, but full reproductive responsibilities. After conception, mothers have the right to abort or not, or to put their child up for adoption or not, as they choose. In most places, fathers have no say in any of these decisions about their child, but their legal responsibility to support the child if the woman decides to keep it is strongly enforced. This responsibility continues even when they are given no access to the child or influence in its upbringing.

What we want: A pregnant woman has the legal responsibility to promptly inform the father of her pregnancy and her intentions. A father will enjoy equal power with the mother to give up his parental rights *and* responsibilities through the legal adoption of his child.

Parenting

Where we are now: In the past 30 years, we have witnessed dramatic changes affecting the family, structure and parenting, including very high divorce rates with a rise in single parent families, traumatic custody battles, breakdown of the extended family, and even changes in the definition of the family. Family law has not kept pace with the above present day reality. The legal framework used to resolve conflicts between estranged parents is seen to systematically discriminate against men and to be deeply flawed, awarding custody of the children overwhelmingly to mothers. The divorce industry itself is a significant obstacle to positive reform. Society appears to have forgotten the value of fatherhood resulting in negative impacts on the lives of our children. Kids need both parents.

What we want: The gender bias in family court will be eliminated, and fathers will be known, in law and in practice, to be caring, effective and entitled parents, fully equal to mothers in all respects, and entitled in law to full access to their children. Shared parenting arrangements following separation will the norm.

Sexuality

Where we are now: Traditional promulgation and commercialization of sexual stereotypes emphasize the differences rather than the similarities between people and are harmful to men, women, and children.

Ineffective communication in talking about sex between partners leads to a lack of negotiated consent between parties, the loss of respect for the sexual act, and a separation from authentic feelings. While some of women's unique sexual vulnerabilities have been addressed with legislation and judicial protection dealing with consent, harassment, rape shield, date rape, and censorship legislation and judgments, men's unique sexual vulnerabilities have scarcely begun to be socially recognized or protected.

What we want: We want women and men to share equally in taking responsibility and in the task of negotiating consent in dating and intimate sexual relationships. Abuse and false allegations of abuse are equally serious and should carry equal penalties.

Work

Where we are now: Men still work longer hours and overwhelmingly make up the "death professions" - firefighters, loggers, heavy truckers, construction workers, miners and combat troops. Ninety-six percent of Canadian workplace fatalities are men.

What we want: Men are seen as fully competent and equal to women in the important role of caregiver. Men will have the same rights and opportunities to care-giving professions including full time parenting. Social pressures on men to be successful providers that oblige them to take unattractive, often dangerous jobs will be a thing of the past. Workplaces will recognize and support the equally valuable nurturing role of fathers.

Health

Where we are now: Approximately equal in the early years of the century, Canadian women's life expectancy has increased twice as fast as men's to the current gap of almost six years. Male death rates are 23% higher for cancers, 96% higher for heart disease, 127% higher for accidents, and 350% higher for suicide. Yet not one major Canadian government commission or study has been dedicated to male health or mortality.

Among the many largely-invisible men's health issues are:
• the limited range of acceptable emotional expression for males
• men's and boy's covert depression
• higher rates of addiction and risk-taking behavior
• sexual and physical abuse of boys and men
• under-recognition of the father's importance in child development
• routine newborn male circumcision
• the epidemic of male suicide
• men's shorter life-spans
• an insufficient awareness of and funding for male-specific cancers (prostate and testicular)
• men's reluctance to seek help for psychological and physiological symptoms

What we want: Raised visibility among men and society of each area of male health issues, ongoing education of health professionals as to men's real health needs, medical research into and provision of focused services for men's health, and accessible information for men on resources in each of these areas.

Violence

Where we are now: The current valid focus on violence against women obscures both the reality of violence against men, and the dependence on systemic violence within society.

Most Canadian provinces have an explicit "arrest the male" zero tolerance policy when called to domestic disputes.

What we want: Violence in society will be recognized not as a war against women but as a systemic social dysfunction that causes grievous harm to both sexes. Society's social, health and penal systems will address the needs and responsibilities of all victims and perpetrators regardless of gender. Zero tolerance policies with regard to *male* violence or to violence against *women* will be recognized as sexist and eliminated."

It is important to consider practical as well as theoretical issues in the quest for gender justice. The document above stands as proof, not only that a realistic practical vision can be articulated, but also that a group of some fifty people, men and women, can come together in consensus around such a vision. The negotiation was strenuous (I remember because I was the principal facilitator), but it was successful after just two days. It is not the difficulty of the task of articulating gender justice that defeats us, but our unwillingness to address men's gender issues as we have addressed those of women.

Does it strike you as outrageous that we might pass laws to make reproductive rights equal by eliminating women's reproductive dominance, or to enforce equality of opportunity in parenting? If so, allow me to suggest that this is simply sexism, sexist prejudice. We have passed laws enforcing strict gender equality in every area of men's traditional roles – the workplace, governance, and the military. What is different about passing laws to enforce gender equality in women's traditional areas?

We are back, aren't we, to what I have been going on about for the whole of this book – the power of feeling. What is different is that it doesn't feel right. Women are sacred, women own children; we can't do that to them! These feelings that lead us to protect women and children and hold men accountable were functional for a long time in that they aided our survival, but the world has changed and they're dysfunctional now. Now we really need equality between men and women.

To make these personal changes, we begin by softening our hearts to let the pain of injustice in. We do that naturally for female pain, but male pain is more difficult. Are you able to empathize with my pain at the lack of real gender equality, at the injustice of feminist hypocrisy? Let me share a story.

Every year I go to Blue Skies music festival in Ontario, and most years I sing in the choir that forms, just for the weekend, from 60 or 70 interested participants. We learn six songs, in four part harmony, in about four practice sessions, and perform them on the main stage on Sunday evening. It's an intense experience, with about eighty singers striving to master challenging harmonies, timing and even lyrics in other languages. We work hard, we have inspired and dedicated choir leaders, and we have a lot of fun. At the end of the weekend, we put on a magnificent show for the 3000 strong audience.

In 2013, something unexpected happened for me. We were in a practice session and our choir leader was speaking to us about the differences between male and female voices and achieving balance between them, and suddenly a lot of emotion welled up in me and I found tears in my eyes. I knew what it was about. The choir represents a vision of real gender equality in action, without dysfunction, without blame, exactly how I wish it was in the outside world. Let me explain.

In the choir, male and female voices are different, but both are equally valued, both add a vital dimension to the sound of the music, and the two in harmony are truly glorious. There is no sense in which one group is suspect, or blamed, or distrusted. The deeper male voice, the higher female voice are good, are both already perfect. The task for each group, for female sopranos and altos and for male tenors and bases, is to strive to bring their best to the joint project, and we do. We work together to build a worthy mutual creation, and we succeed every year. We enjoy each other, we enjoy and appreciate the differences, we blend our different contributions in the discipline of musical harmony, and we have a huge amount of fun. The equality, the equal worth of the male and female contribution is a given from the start, it is never in question. That is real gender equality, that is what it looks and feels like, and I love it. My emotion when that equality came to my attention was an expression of how much I love it, and how much I wish we could do gender work that way in the wider world.

Instead, we have concocted a story of one-sided historical oppression that poisons the relationship between women and men. Instead of an inspiring vision of mutual cooperation and valuing of difference, instead of an attitude of appreciation for the historical legacy of men and of women, instead of trust and mutual goodwill we have created a climate of distrust, resentment, blame and enforcement. We have destroyed so much in this way, so much of the potential for love and creativity and fun and mutual trust. We told ourselves that it was necessary – but we were wrong. We projected our own dysfunctions onto something beautiful, and I am so sorry that we did. We have wounded ourselves where we could have been celebrating each other even as we worked together toward a joint vision of crafting something new, a greater balance between the roles of men and women, a harmonious sharing of the work and the joy of the world.

Is it too late? For the wider world of public space, corporations and institutions, I think that it is. We have crafted so many gender biased laws and policies that the very sense of equality has been deeply undermined. We abandoned wisdom, dualistic balance without even trying to reach it. We made the error that outer is better than inner, that overt power is greater than covert, direct more valuable than indirect, leaders more important than followers. We focused so much on women as victims and men as perpetrators that we lost sight of our inherent equality. We became so intent on fixing things that we failed to see that most of them aren't actually broken. We will need to somehow recognize our errors, forgive ourselves and grieve the losses before we can come to a better space.

But in small groups, in workshops and courses, we can aspire to what I will call the choir experience, where we celebrate and value the differences between men and women and let go of our distrust and suspicion of ulterior motives. We can strive to recognize our inherent equality and to meet each other, to see each other anew. To do this, we must soften our hearts to let the new in, the truth that we have been denying. When we do, the result is a glorious affirmation of our gendered differences, and we make beautiful music together.

If we can give ourselves such an inspiring joint achievement, a powerful recognition of our essential equality even for a short while and in a small group, I suspect that that experience, more than anything else, can lead us toward our vision of more balanced and equal roles for women and men.

Look at what moves us, what brings tears to our eyes, as in the story above where I was moved to tears by an experience of genuine equality, of respect for both genders. What moves us speaks to the deep humanity in us, to our longing for justice and freedom and equality. I don't think that anyone's heart was ever opened by angry finger pointing, blame, revenge or criticism of the kind that has come from feminists towards men, and in more recent years from Men's Rights Advocates (MRAs) towards feminists.

Directors and authors of literary, radio, TV or movie dramas know that the dramatic moment comes when someone softens, when they yield courageously to a resisted reality or a fearful necessity. We are moved by human courage, by loving sacrifice and by dedication to truth and justice. We are moved to tears when we see people come together in love, in harmony, in service, in forgiveness, in devotion, not when they break apart in fear or anger or blame.

How can we, how can I encourage the emergence of such transformative events and processes? I earnestly hope that this book is such a catalyst, that it will assist and encourage tears in place of anger, courage rather than avoidance, hope instead of despair, and loving forgiveness rather than righteous judgment. We will live through this, we will come together as conscious equals in the end, and we will be wiser for having passed through such pain. Evil is a temporary dysfunction, very dark and damaging but ultimately not what really matters.

What really matters is this. Women and men have travelled a long way together. We have lived together for thousands of years; we have shared homes, beds and lives together. We have raised money and food and flowers and children together. We have shared dreams and heartbreaks and joys and losses together. We have lived and loved and suffered and died together. Indeed, we have frequently lived and died *for* each other. What a cheap and ugly thing is this modern idea that one of us has oppressed the other throughout all of that time. We can do better than this if we wish, if we choose.

We can reach for the truth that I have outlined in these pages; we can see the noble, glorious equality that has been the imprint of every one of those thousands of years. Men and women have had different roles, developed through evolution from our different sex roles, and having nothing at all to do with oppression. Both have been worthy, and I wish to say that, all things considered, we have done well. Our path has been one of ascending freedom, increasing justice, improving livelihoods, expanding culture and enhancing happiness. We have done these things, men and women, together. We have no reason to feel ashamed of our record as a species.

A worthy gender transition movement, one we could be proud of, would be a movement that turned away from finger pointing, from bitter judgment, from resentment and envy, and looked instead to celebrate all that we have been to and for each other. A worthy gender transition movement would seek to empathize with and to understand our past, our unconsciousness, to acknowledge our mistakes and failures to each other and to forgive each other for the pains we have caused. Instead of blame and recrimination, we would focus on truth and reconciliation. We need to grieve together the losses of unconsciousness, the errors of immaturity. Even evil can be forgiven, after it is acknowledged and grieved.

Let us turn away from delusions of smallness, of shame, of failure and especially of moral judgment. We have real challenges to face, global challenges of limits to growth, of population and pollution, challenges that we have never faced before. Let us face them as men and women together, united in our love and respect for each other, united in our determination to see through and beyond the illusions of immature ideology, of dualistic imbalance.

You are seeing here my vision of human maturity; it is about versatility. It is about dualistic balance and equality. It is about leading but also surrendering; it is about love of self and also love of other. It is about accepting ourselves exactly as we are and also challenging ourselves to become more and greater, wiser. This is advanced, this is mature; this is what I aspire to for myself and for us all. Let us find the courage to step out of our stuck, one-sided victim patterns and reach for the other side, for genuine dualistic balance. We will do it one by one, as individuals, but it will get ever easier as more of us wake up and help to guide and welcome others. Who knows what the future holds if we step into it with the courage to seek wisdom, with true love and love of truth?

We can predict what the future holds, however, if we do not change. More and greater infantilizing of women and enslaving of men. More gender fear and injustice. More evil. Changing is difficult, but things will likely get worse until we do. Evil is among us and we need to wake up to it. Not in outrage, not in anger, but in wisdom and compassion. Men are not the enemy; nor are women or feminists. It is hate that we must put aside. I have a vision of feminist women and men weeping in remorse, apologizing for the way that their movement, begun with such good intentions, became a monster. That's all it would take to go forward again in good heart and companionship; just to acknowledge responsibility, feel genuine remorse, and start afresh.

When I think of all of the beauty of love between men and women, of the sacrifices, how men have died to protect women and children, the idea that feminism is built on – that men have oppressed women, that they make war on women – seems too ridiculous to imagine that it could be taken seriously. It is quite insane. It genuinely *is* insane, but it is a collective insanity and it has almost all of us in its grip, in a way that is insulated from reality and almost impervious to reason. I hope that we begin to awaken soon.

I want to end this book with a story about faith that I wrote twenty years ago. I am not a religious man; in fact I am an atheist, but I think that faith is a fundamental human quality that can sometimes sustain us when little else can.

The year was 1994. With my friend Andrew, I had started the Ottawa Men's Wisdom Council, an open circle of men that met monthly in a downtown hall. For the first three months, Andrew and I had led the group process. We offered some simple rituals of opening and closing and a confidentiality agreement to create the safety for personal sharing. But our hope for the group was that leadership would be shared among the members, and so at the third meeting we confirmed that we wanted to step back, and asked for volunteers to lead the next meeting. Two young men took this task on themselves.

A month later, as the fourth meeting opened, I did not feel good. It had been a year since I left my career as an engineering manager, and I still didn't know what I wanted to do, and I still had no income at all. With my mortgage and taxes running at $1300 a month, my savings were practically gone and I was already dipping into my retirement fund. Within another year that too would be exhausted. I felt that I had "trusted the Universe" in walking away from work that paid well but was draining me spiritually, and now the Universe owed me. What was going to happen to me? Would I lose my house as well, that I had designed and built myself? It didn't look good, and I didn't feel good.

The two young men had brought a large, fat candle to the meeting, and they placed it in the centre of the circle of men, in a bowl filled with sand. They gave out long, thin, tapered candles, the kind that can be held in the hand, one to each man. For the opening ritual, they suggested that each man light his candle at the end of his check-in, and push it into the sand around the large candle, so that it would stand upright.

I was the last to check in, and I spoke of my sense of approaching doom. Of the major support structures in my life: my marriage, my career, my money, my house—all except my house had fallen to nothing, to ashes—and it looked very much as if I would lose my house also. As I lit my candle and pushed it into the sand, I noticed that the first ones lit were already half consumed. These will all go out before the end of the meeting, I thought.

As the sun dimmed outside the meeting room, so too the candles dimmed and died inside the room, and the descending gloom fitted my mood exactly. By the time most of the candles had died, I could not see the faces of the men across the circle. Still no one spoke of this; no one turned on the room lights or lit more candles. I couldn't stand it. What is the matter with these two young men? I asked myself. They took the responsibility for leading this circle, but they didn't plan it well, they didn't consider that the candles wouldn't last till the end of the meeting. Now they're compounding their error by ignoring and avoiding dealing with it as we all slide into darkness.

I know what to do when I am feeling so intensely. I shared with the men how I was feeling in my life, and how the growing darkness was an exact metaphor for what seemed to be happening to me financially. I acknowledged that I was full of fear. I had had work that paid me well, and I had given it up, let go the control and stepped, in faith, into the unknown. In the same way, I had given up control of the group to the two young men. In both cases, I felt let down, I felt like it wasn't working out the way I wanted and needed. The fading light exactly matched my sense of fading control in my life, fading financial viability, fading prospects, fading faith.

I asked if I could light another small, taper candle, and the leaders agreed and gave me one. I lit it, I don't remember what I said as I did so, and stuck it into the sand with the others. As I did, the next-to-last remaining candle went out. Only the one I had lit during my check in, and my new one, remained alight. It wasn't enough, even the new candle I had lit gave only a tiny light, the room was filled with darkness and I was filled with despair.

I watched my first, check-in candle as it burned down into the sand, feeling like my life was dying with it. By chance, I had placed it close to the large centre candle and as it burned low, the flame began to melt the side of the larger candle. The wax ran down and into the sand, which became wet with melted wax, just where my candle was burning down to nothing. But before the little candle died, it ignited the wax in the sand around it and the flame began to grow. The sand acted like a wick for the molten wax, and as the flame grew, it melted more of the large candle. As more wax melted and ran down into the sand, the flame grew still larger. It was astonishing; totally unexpected and profoundly meaningful to me. The process of gathering darkness was reversed; now the light was growing.

I shared with the men in the circle that this was a miracle for me. I had been shown that it is not possible to anticipate how the Universe will solve the problems that it faces; that my fears were because of my attachment to conventional thinking. I acknowledged that that was stupid, because I was consciously and intentionally walking away from conventional thinking in my life and choosing instead a spiritual path. How ironic, to expect spirit to be limited to conventional solutions.

By the end of the meeting, half of the fat candle had melted and run down into the sand, and the flame from the burning wax was six inches wide at the base, and over a foot high. It looked more like a campfire than a candle. For me, that evening, the universe had worked a miracle, and I determined not to forget it.

Perhaps the best lesson I learned that evening was that I don't have to be perfect. I don't have to have perfect faith, or to be perfectly fearless. I know this because my fears didn't prevent the miracle. The Universe gave me what I needed, even though I was in a dim and sulky, victim place. Even my faithless attempt to fix things by lighting the extra candle didn't defeat the miracle.

I guess you'd like to know what happened to me after that, to my finances and my house. Although my faith continued to waver from time to time, I never again got myself into such a dark, despairing place. As I approached the end of my retirement fund, I considered putting my house up for sale. I even had real estate agents come and value it, but selling it didn't feel right, so I chose not to put it on the market. And yet, I had no alternative, no way to carry it. Without the miracle of the candle, I think I would have panicked completely. Instead, I was able to trust that somehow, a solution would appear.

With only a few thousand dollars left in my account, I decided, knowing I might never have the money to do so again, to visit my family in New Zealand. I knew that I would return to an empty bank account, and so I consulted my bank manager to find out what happens when one defaults on a mortgage. I felt very strange, embarrassed to be talking about defaulting. I had never defaulted on a bill in my life, and here I was risking my home! At a deeper level, it still felt right.

In February, 1995, I left Canada. In March, a couple of weeks before I was to return, I received a telephone call. A woman with five children who had visited my house a few times had tracked me down in New Zealand. She said, "I want to rent your house." I said, "Wow, that's interesting, and it could suit me well. How much rent did you have in mind?" "I was thinking of $750 a month," she said. "Well," I replied, "I have no idea what is appropriate for a house like mine; that could be a very fair rent. However, my situation is this. I have no income, and my expenses on the house total $1300 per month, so if you can't pay that amount, then I can't make a deal with you." "Let me think about that," she replied. By the time I returned to Canada in April, she had decided to pay the $1300, and I moved into an apartment with my girlfriend, Christine.

Within another year or so, Christine had decided that she loved my house so much that she wanted to buy into it and live there with me. In 1996, she paid down the mortgage by about 50%, which put the monthly premium into a range that she could afford from her salary, and in 1997 we moved in, and we have lived here since. Christine, bless her heart, has been so supportive of my gender work that she was willing to pay the greater amount of our living expenses, for a time, so that I could continue with work which does not pay enough to live on.

The miracle correctly foretold the future, and I learned that it is not always necessary for us to solve our own problems. Sometimes life asks us to wait and trust, and to be willing to receive. For men, taught to get out and make it happen, to pull our own weight, it can be a difficult lesson. I am grateful that I was given it in such a memorable form.

Today, I think that 'miracles,' like coincidences, are commonplace. They are not usually spectacular, not even as spectacular as the flame in the men's circle that wouldn't die. They are those sublime moments when grace gives us an insight, when the universe touches us just so and restores our faith, and we see a little deeper into the mysteries of life. The universe, which birthed our planet with its abundant and varied life forms, is not hostile to us.

Faith is not rational, yet sometimes it is wise. It is faith that tells me that real gender equality can be achieved and recognized in society, is worth striving for, and that what is happening today between men and women is not wrong, but simply part of the process, the path by which we will move towards equality. It will be a difficult path, full of seeming darkness and suffering, yet it is the right path. I have speculated in the privacy of my own thoughts that perhaps chivalry, the male need to give special protection to women and children, is so deeply wired that only the virulent hatred for men that is coming from feminism could possibly correct that programming.

Let us have faith to trust the process, even as it seems to move us into the darkness, even as the last remaining light of political rationality or reasonable communication about gender seems to be dying. These things are necessary. The miracle will come when we least expect it, and in a way that we cannot anticipate. Let us have faith, let us choose to believe that opportunities exist to make a difference; that our lives can be powerful agents for change. Let us fight for the gender freedom and gender equality that we desire.

I think that life offers us opportunities to make miracles happen, if we are up for it. I think of miracles as times when we take unexpected action, perceive new insights, change things by the power of our will and our courage. The sense of hope and potential for change that this offers to us is important in preventing us from becoming lost in despair. It is easy to undermine our own creative potential by seeing the world as too big to influence, almost predestined to follow a particular track. I see the power of evil in the world, but I also see opportunities. I don't know what form those opportunities might take, just as I didn't know what was going to happen with the candles in the story I told above. I want to be ready for opportunities, and creative to imagine and develop them. I think that's important.

What form might this take, what might it look and feel like? What I hope is that a healthy movement for gender equality might take powerful shape in society, composed of individuals who have done their own gender healing work and are willing to stand strongly in support of balanced equality, neither for feminism nor masculism, but for equalism. Society, biased in favor of feminism, would project misogyny, backlash, etc. onto such a movement. However, since it was false to fact some people would recognize that the projection didn't fit. Such people would look more closely, seeking to discover what is really going on, and a dialog would begin – a real dialog dedicated to discovering the truth about the situation. Some of those people, their eyes newly opened to real gender equality, would join the ranks of this fledgling movement and it would grow. This is how I think Gandhi's movement for Indian independence grew, and Martin Luther King's movement for racial equality.

But that is not enough. The movement needs to gather mainstream attention, and this may happen suddenly. In the case of the movement for racial equality, things seemed stuck for a long time; nothing significant appeared to be happening. Then an unknown black woman named Rosa Parks refused to give up her bus seat to a white passenger in Montgomery, Alabama. A bus boycott by African Americans ensued, and suddenly the issue of racial prejudice became front page news and the movement for racial equality gained real traction. A major new leader (MLK) rose to prominence and the movement gathered new energy around him.

I hope for something similar in the movement for gender equality – some event triggering a new focus on societal sexism against men and showing it in a new way, a way that catches society's interest and imagination. Such an event might happen by chance, or it might be created by advocates seizing an opportunity, creating an opening. But a seed crystal of genuine equalist advocates needs to be already in place, prepared to take advantage and run with the new insight.

I hope that this book might serve in two ways – first as a stimulus, a catalyst by which some people will be moved to prepare themselves, to grow themselves into the powerful, unbiased individuals that such a movement needs, and second as a bible for an equalist movement, a guide for healthy, stage 4 advocacy for real gender equality. I earnestly hope that some of my readers might be assisted and encouraged to choose that journey towards human maturity, stage 4 wisdom.

Our touchstones for the journey are love and truth, the highest values of the feminine and masculine archetypes respectively. Love provides the motivation for the long effort. Truth provides the map, the guide for the journey. Both are vital, and both are available to us if we reach for them. It comes down to just one thing; what do we really want? We need courage to follow the path of love and truth in an immature society, for most will not understand and many will judge us and oppose us. It was ever thus – we can take inspiration from those in history who did the right thing anyway.

What do *you* want, my reader? We have come to the end of this journey that we have taken together, you and I. Are you inspired to go further, to dig deeper and to discover more? Perhaps our paths will cross again. I wish you well.

Appendix A – Research Resources

The following is a list of recommended resources for research into balanced gender equality, where both women's and men's issues are seen as fully legitimate.

Goldich, Tim, *Loving Men, Respecting Women; The Future of Gender Politics,* Anima-Animus Publishing, Chicago, USA, 2011. ISBN 978-0-9827948-0-7.

Sommers, Christina Hoff, *Who Stole Feminism; How Women Have Betrayed Women,* Simon & Schuster, 1994. ISBN 0-684-80156-6.

Farrell, Warren, Ph.D., *The Myth of Male Power*, Berkley, NY, 1993. ISBN 0-425-18144-8.

Farrell, Warren, Ph.D., *Father and Child Reunion: How to Bring the Dads We Need to the Children We Love*, Tarcher/Putnam, NY, 2001. ISBN 1-58542-075-1.

Farrell, Warren, Ph.D., *Why Men Earn More; The Startling Truth Behind the Pay Gap – And What Women Can Do About It*, Amacom, NY, 2005. ISBN 0-8144-7210-9.

Sommers, Christina Hoff, *The War Against Boys; How Misguided Feminism is Harming Our Young Men*, Simon & Schuster, NY, 2000. ISBN 0-684-84956-9.

Bly, Robert and Woodman, Marion, *The Maiden King; The Reunion of Masculine and Feminine*, Henry Holt & Co., NY, 1998. ISBN 0-8050-5777-3.

Nathanson, Paul and Young, Katherine K., *Spreading Misandry; The Teaching of Contempt for Men in Popular Culture*, McGill-Queens University Press, Montreal, QC, 2001. ISBN 0-7735-3099-1.

Young, Cathy, *Ceasefire! Why Women and Men Must Join Forces to Achieve True Gender Equality*, Free Press, NY, 1999. ISBN 0-684-83442-1.

Index

Notes

1 http://www.brainyquote.com/quotes/authors/j/james_hillman.html #ZRxIQfWokTbLmHIj.99

2 Sigmund Freud, *The Standard Edition of the Complete Psychological Works*. Translated from the German under the general editorship of James Strachey. In collaboration with Anna Freud. Assisted by Alix Strachey and Alan Tyson. Volume III (1893-99), p.215.

3 Alice Miller, *Thou Shalt Not Be Aware: Society's Betrayal of the Child*, Meridian, NY, 1984, p.117.

4 Jacob Needleman, *Why Can't We Be Good?* Penguin, NY, 2007, p.42.

5 ibid

6 ibid, p.43.

7 ibid, pp.43-45.

8 Ibid, p.53.

9 Mathew 13:44

10 Jacob Needleman, *Why Can't We Be Good?* Penguin, NY, 2007, p.55-56.

11 Kabir, version by Robert Bly, *The Kabir Book*, pp.24-25. Cited from Robert Bly and Marion Woodman, *The Maiden Tsar; The Reunion of Masculine and Feminine*, Henry Holt & Co., NY, 1998, pp.89-90.

12 Robert Bly, *Iron John; A Book About Men*, Addison-Wesley, 1990, p167.

13 www.carolcarnes.com, cited May 2013.

14 See Wikipedia article at http://en.wikipedia.org/wiki/Law_of_attraction_(New_Thought)

15 Taken from http://en.wikipedia.org/wiki/The_Secret_(book) on August 7, 2014.

16 Hume 1969/1739-40, p.462.

17 Jonathan Haidt, The *Righteous Mind; Why Good People are Divided by Politics and Religion*, Pantheon Books, NY, 2012, p14-15.

18 Charles Paul Freund, "Free Market Culture Gives People the Liberty They Crave." In *Culture Wars; Opposing Viewpoints*. Thompson Gale, Detroit, 2008, p.180.

19 From the Snopes website at www.snopes.com, 27 April 2014. Read more at http://www.snopes.com/travel/airline/obnoxious.asp#jMTzAsX68igSeAxg.99

20 http://fox40.com/2014/11/02/dad-invites-young-daughters-alleged-rapist-to-dinner-then-tortures-him-to-death/

21 http://dictionary.reference.com/browse/archetype

22 Robert Moore and Douglas Gillette, *King, Warrior, Magician, Lover*, Harper Collins, 1990, 9.

23 Carl Gustav Jung, *Collected Works #9*, Bollinger, paragraph 99.

24 George Monbiot, "Ghost Psyche", in *Prospect* magazine, June 2013. See also http://www.monbiot.com/2013/07/02/ghost-psyche/

25 Carl Gustav Jung, "Introduction to M. Esther Harding," Women's Mysteries, in *Collected Works #18*, Bollinger.

26 James Hillman, *A Blue Fire: Selected Writings*, Harper Collins, N.Y. 1991, 24.

27 Carl Gustav Jung, The Psychology of the Unconscious, 1916, in *Collected Works #7*, Bollinger, 60, 74.

28 Tim Goldich, *Loving Men, Respecting Women: The Future of Gender Politics*, Chicago, 2011.

29 Fred Hayward. "A Warrior for Equality," interview with Jeffrey Seeman, *Everyman: A Men's Journal, #33*, Sept/Oct 1998, Ottawa, ON, Canada, p.8.

30 Warren Farrell, Ph.D., *Why Men Are the Way They Are: The Male-Female Dynamic*, McGraw Hill, NY, 1986.

31 Alexis de Tocqueville, "Democracy in America," 1834. Quoted from reprint, ed. Phillips Bradley, Vintage Books, NY, 1945, vol.1, pp.315-8.

32 "Resolved, That inasmuch as man, while claiming for himself intellectual superiority, does accord to woman moral superiority, it is pre-eminently his duty to encourage her to speak, and teach, as she has an opportunity, in all religious assemblies." Declaration of Sentiments and Resolutions, Women's Rights Convention, Seneca Falls, 1848. Cited from http://ecssba.rutgers.edu/docs/seneca.html on February 20, 2015.

33 Howard S. Schwartz, *The Revolt of the Primitive: An Inquiry into the Roots of Political Correctness*, Praeger, Westport, CONN, 2001, p.152.

34 See Shiela Rotham, "Women's Proper Place." cited from Ferrel M. Christensen, *Pornography: The Other Side*, Praeger, NY, 1990, p.53.

35 Howard S. Schwartz, *The Revolt of the Primitive: An Inquiry into the Roots of Political Correctness*, Praeger, Westport, CONN, 2001, p.158-9.

36 Robert Bly, *Iron John: A Book About Men*, Addison-Wesley, Reading, MASS, 1990, p.135.

37 Camille Paglia, "Homosexuality at the Fin de Siècle," *Sex, Art, and American Culture: Essays*, Random House, NY, 1992, p.24.

38 *The New LexiconWebster's Encyclopedic Dictionary of the English Language*, Canadian Edition, , Lexicon, NY, 1988, p.645.

39 Solomon Asch, "Studies of Independence and Conformity: I. A Minority of One against a Unanimous Majority," *Psychological Monographs*, 70, 1956, pp.1-70.

40 Thomas J. Scheff, *Microsocialogy: Discourse, Emotion and Social Structure*, University of Chicago Press, Chicago, IL, 1990.

41 Howard S. Schwartz, *The Revolt of the Primitive: An Inquiry into the Roots of Political Correctness*, Praeger, Westport, CONN, 2001, pp.155-6.

42 Robert Bly and Marion Woodman, *The Maiden King; The Reunion of Masculine and Feminine*, Henry Holt & Co, NY, 1998.

43 https://www.aadnc-aandc.gc.ca/eng/1100100015644/1100100015649

44 Schedule N of the Indian Residential Schools Settlement Agreement, 1998, taken from the Truth and Reconciliation Commission of Canada website at http://www.trc.ca/websites/trcinstitution/index.php?p=7

45 http://www.trc.ca/websites/trcinstitution/index.php?p=10

46 http://www.robertsrules.com/

47 Robert M. Pirsig, *Lila; An Inquiry Into Morals*. Bantam, NY, 1991, p.255.

48 M. Scott Peck, *The Road Less Travelled; A New Psychology of Love, Traditional Values and Spiritual Growth*. Simon and Schuster, NY, 1978.

49 Jacob Needleman, *Why Can't We Be Good?* Penguin, NY, 2007.

50 as reported in the March 1996 edition of the newsletter *Making Waves* of the organization "Battered Women's Support Services" of Vancouver, BC. Program tenets submitted to Family Service Canada for validation.

51 Camille Paglia, "The Rape Debate, Continued," *Sex, Art, and American Culture,: Essays*, Random House, NY, 1992, p 57.

52 Private correspondence from Maggie Feitz, CEO, Family Service Canada, Ottawa, ON, dated April 11, 1996.

53 M. Scott Peck, *People of the Lie: The Hope for Healing Human Evil,* Simon and Schuster, NY, 1983, p. 267.

54 David Shackleton, "Seeking Sanity, Loving the World," *Everyman: A Men's Journal, #39*, Sept/Oct. 1999, Ottawa, ON, p.2.

55 Quoted by Keith Thompson in "What Men Really Want: A New Age Interview with Robert Bly," p32

56 ibid, p 33.

57 George Jonas, "Abortion is a Parent's Decision, not the Government's," *National Post*, Canada, Feb. 15, 2014.

58 M. Scott Peck, *The Road Less Travelled: A New Psychology of Love, Traditional Values and Spiritual Growth* (Simon & Schuster, NY, 1978), p.277-8.

59 Alice Miller, *Banished Knowledge: Facing Childhood Injuries* (Doubleday, NY, 1988), p.142-3.

60 Ian McEwan, *Black Dogs*, Doubleday, NY, 1992, p.xxi.

61 Andrew Delbanco, *The Death of Satan; How Americans Have Lost the Sense of Evil*, Farrar, Straus and Giroux, NY, 1995, p3,9.

62 Ibid, p.234.

63 Oppenheimer, Paul, *Evil and the Demonic; A New Theory of Monstrous Behaviour* (Duckworth, London, 1996), p.100.

64 Peck, M. Scott, *People of the Lie: The Hope for Healing Human Evil* (Simon & Schuster, NY, 1983), p.255.

65 Ibid, p.71.

66 Ibid, p.74.

67 Stewart E. Tolnay and E.M. Beck, *Festival of Violence* Chicago (University of Illinois Press, ILL, 1995), p.47.

68 ibid, p.47.

69 Mark Gado, "Carnival of Death: Lynching in America," in online Crime Library: Criminal Minds and Methods,
http://www.crimelibrary.com/notorious_murders/mass/lynching/index_1.html

70 Stewart E. Tolnay and E.M. Beck, *Festival of Violence* Chicago (University of Illinois Press, ILL, 1995), p.IX.

71 Ibid, p.18-19.

72 Michael Ignatieff, *The Lesser Evil: Political Ethics in an Age of Terror* (Penguin Canada, 2004), p.14

73 Walter White, *Rope and Faggot* (NY, 1929), p. 97.

74 Robert A. Gibson, "The Negro Holocaust: Lynching and Race Riots in the United States, 1880-1950" (Yale-New Haven Teachers Institute course curriculum for course 79.02.04). See
http://www.yale.edu/ynhti/curriculum/units/1979/2/79.02.04.x.html

75 From Wikipedia, http://en.wikipedia.org/wiki/Moral_panic, on Jan 25, 2015. Wikipedia references "M. Jones, and E. Jones (1999) Mass Media, London, Macmillan Press" as the source for this definition.

76 Eric A. Zillmer, Molly Harrower, Barry A. Ritzler, and Robert P. Archer, *The Quest for the Nazi Personality: A Psychological Investigation of Nazi War Criminals.* Routledge, Oct 31, 2013. P. 9-11.

77 http://en.wikipedia.org/wiki/Chibok_schoolgirls_kidnapping, cited on 31 January, 2105.

78 http://en.wikipedia.org/wiki/Federal_Government_College_attack, cited on 31 January 2015.

79 Definition from Wikipedia http://en.wikipedia.org/wiki/Rape_culture cited on 29 January 2015. Wikipedia references: (1) Sharna Olfman, (2009), *The Sexualization of Childhood*. ABC-CLIO. p. 9. and (2) Rebecca Flintoft, (October 2001). John Nicoletti, Sally Spencer-Thomas, Christopher M. Bollinger, ed. *Violence Goes to College: The Authoritative Guide to Prevention and Intervention*. Charles C Thomas. p.134. ISBN 978-0398071912.

80 Emilie Buchwald, Pamela Fletcher, and Martha Roth (eds), *Transforming a Rape Culture*, Milkweed Editions, 1993.

81 http://fox40.com/2014/11/02/dad-invites-young-daughters-alleged-rapist-to-dinner-then-tortures-him-to-death/

82 Mathew J. Breiding, PhD, Sharon G. Smith, PhD, Kathleen C. Basile, PhD, Mikel L. Walters, PhD, Jieru Chen, MS, Melissa T. Merrick, PhD. "Prevalence and Characteristics of Sexual Violence, Stalking, and Intimate Partner Violence Victimization" — *National Intimate Partner and Sexual Violence Survey,* Division of Violence Prevention, National Center for Injury Prevention and Control, CDC, USA, 2011. http://www.cdc.gov/mmwr/preview/mmwrhtml/ss6308a1.htm

83 Ibid, "Appendix C: Victimization Questions," p.106.

84 http://en.wikipedia.org/wiki/Prison_rape_in_the_United_States, data cited on 30 January, 2015.

85 http://en.wikipedia.org/wiki/Sex_differences_in_crime, cited 7 February, 2015.

86 http://en.wikipedia.org/wiki/Crime_in_the_United_States, cited 7 Feb, 2015.

87 http://www.statcan.gc.ca/pub/85f0033m/2010024/aftertoc-aprestdm1-eng.htm, cited on 7 February, 2015.

88 Jennifer L. Truman, PhD and Michael Planty, PhD, *Criminal Victimization*, 2011, Bureau of Justice Statistics, Office of Justice Programs, US Dept. of Justice, p.5. http://www.bjs.gov/content/pub/pdf/cv11.pdf, cited on 7 February 2015.

89 Roxan Vaillancourt, *Gender Differences in Police-Reported Violent Crime in Canada,* 2008. Canadian Centre for Justice Statistics Profile Series, Statistics Canada, p.6. http://www.statcan.gc.ca/pub/85f0033m/85f0033m2010024-eng.pdf, cited on 7 February 2015.

90 http://www2.ed.gov/about/offices/list/ocr/letters/colleague-201104.html, referenced 31 January, 2015.

91 Peter Berkowitz, "College Rape Accusations and the Presumption of Male Guilt," *The Wall Street Journal,* August 20, 2011. http://www.wsj.com/articles/SB10001424053111903596904576516232905230642 cited 31 January, 2015.

92 Alison M. Jaggar and Paula Rothenbert Struhl, *Feminist Frameworks,: Alternative Theoretical Accounts of the Relations between Women and Men,* McGraw-Hill, NY, 1978, p.69.

93 Definition taken from online Dictionary.com, http://dictionary.reference.com/browse/feminism?s=t cited 1 February 2015.

94 National Organization of Women (NOW) New York State Oppose Memo on Presumption of Joint Custody/Shared Parenting for Minor Children, July 2005. Cited from http://www.nownys.org/archives/leg_memos/oppose_a00330.html on March 23, 2015

95 "Feminists Might be Granted Own Hearing on Divorce Law," Chris Cobb, *National Post,* July 5, 2001. See http://www.nationalpost.com/news/national/story.html?f=/stories/20010705/609951.html

96 Canadian Supreme Court "Ewanchuk" decision, 1999.

97 Canadian Supreme Court "Butler" decision, 1992.

98 See Warren Farrell, PhD., *Why Men Earn More.* Also publications of The Independent Women's Forum, http://www.iwf.org/publications/2787462/The-%E2%80%9CEqual-Pay-Day%E2%80%9D-Myth

99 M. Scott Peck, *People of the Lie: The Hope for Healing Human Evil,* Simon and Schuster, New York, 1983, p.75.

100 *Report of the Task Force on Respect and Equality: Ending Sexual Violence at the University of Ottawa*, University of Ottawa, January 2015, p.11. http://www.uottawa.ca/president/sites/www.uottawa.ca.president/files/report-of-the-task-force-on-respect-and-equality.pdf

101 Ibid, p.18.

102 Numbers from http://www.chesnuttarchive.org/classroom/lynchingstat.html, cited on 23 March, 2015.

103 http://en.wikipedia.org/wiki/Inquisition, referenced on February 22, 2015.

104 Patricia Pearson, *When She Was Bad: Violent Women and the Myth of Innocence,* Random House of Canada, Toronto, ON, 1997, pp.160-161.

105 "Resolved, that inasmuch as man, while claiming for himself intellectual superiority, does accord to woman moral superiority, it is pre-eminently his duty to encourage her to speak, and teach, as she has an opportunity, in all religious assemblies." Declaration of Sentiments and Resolutions, Women's Rights Convention, Seneca Falls, 1848. Cited from http://ecssba.rutgers.edu/docs/seneca.html on February 20, 2015.

106 Patricia Pearson, *When She Was Bad: Violent Women and the Myth of Innocence,* Random House of Canada, Toronto, ON, 1997, pp18-19.

107 Ibid, p21.

108 Albert Speer, *Inside the Third Reich.* Avon Books, NY, 1970, pp.44-46

109 Camille Paglia, "The Nursery-School Campus: The Corrupting of the Humanities in the USA," *Vamps and Tramps: New Essays*, Vintage Books, Random House, NY, 1994, p.100.

110 Paul Nathanson and Katherine K. Young, *Spreading Misandry: The Teaching of Contempt for Men in Popular Culture.* McGill-Queens University Press, Montreal, QC and Kingston, ON, 2001, p.62-63.

111 ibid, p.67.

112 ibid, p.246-7.

113 Albert Speer, *Inside the Third Reich.* Avon Books, New York, NY, 1970, pp.45-6

114 Camille Paglia, "The M.I.T. Lecture," *Sex, Art, and American Culture: Essays,* Random House, NY, 1992, pp.260-1.

115 Warren Farrell, Ph.D., movie review in *Everyman: A Men's Journal, #35,* Jan/Feb 1999, Ottawa, ON, p.57. Also in his *Women Can't Hear What Men Don't Say: Destroying myths, creating love,* Tarcher/Putnam, NY, 1999, pp.186-7.

116 Warren Farrell, Ph.D., "A Clear Male Voice," interview with J. Steven Svoboda, *Everyman: A Men's Journal, #29,* Jan/Feb 1998, Ottawa, ON, p.49.

117 Dan Kiley, *Living Together, Feeling Alone: Healing Your Hidden Loneliness,* Pawcett Book Group, 1991, pp5-6 of the hardcover version. Cited from Warren Farrell, Ph.D., *Women Can't Hear What Men Don't Say: Destroying myths, creating love,* Tarcher/Putnam, NY, 1999, p.183.

118 Charles J.P. Domingue, "Reclaiming Manhood: Testimony of a Recovering Feminist," *Everyman: A Men's Journal, #35,* Jan/Feb. 1999, Ottawa, ON, pp.14-15.

119 Paul Nathanson and Katherine K. Young, *Spreading Misandry: The Teaching of Contempt for Men in Popular Culture.* McGill-Queens University Press, Montreal, QC and Kingston, ON, 2001, p247-8

120 Quotes and summary from William L. Shirer, *The Rise and Fall of the Third Reich: A History of Nazi Germany,* Fawcett, Greenwich, CONN, 1959, p.567.

121 Howard S. Schwartz, *Revolt of the Primitive: An Inquiry into the Roots of Political Correctness.* Praeger, Westport, CT, 2001, pp.212-213.

122 R.E.A.L. (Realistic, Equal, Active for Live) Women of Canada, PO Box 8813, Station 'T', Ottawa, ON K1G 3J1, (613) 236-7203, www.realwomenca.com, realwcna@on.aibn.com.

123 The Independent Women's Forum, PO Box 3058, Arlington, VA 222203-0058, USA. 1-800-224-6000, www.iwf.org, info@iwf.org.

124 The Women's Freedom Network, 4410 Massachusetts Avenue, N.W., PMB #179, Washington, DC 20016, USA. (202) 885-6245, wfn@american.edu

125 Paul Oppenheimer, *Evil and the Demonic: A New Theory of Monstrous Behavior,* Duckworth, London, UK, 1996, p.101.

126 See Warren Farrell, Ph.D., *Women Can't Hear What Men Don't Say: Destroying myths, creating love,* Tarcher, Penguin Putnam, NY, 1999, pp.87-91.

127 David French, "Modern Feminism; Appalling Stupidity Backed by Hysterical Rage," *National Review,* http://www.nationalreview.com/corner/392831/modern-feminism-appalling-stupidity-backed-hysterical-rage-david-french Cited March 7, 2015.

128 The *Journal of Psychohistory* is available from The Institute for Psychohistory, 140 Riverside Drive, Suite 14H, New York, NY 10024. www.psychohistory.com.

129 Lloyd deMause, "War as Righteous Rape and Purification," *The Journal of Psychohistory,* vol. 27, #4, Spring 2000, p.356.

130 Hoyt E.P. *The Improper Bostonian: Dr Oliver Wendell Holmes.* William Morrow, NY, 1979.

131 R.M. Wertz and D.C. Wertz, *Lying-in: a history of childbirth in America*. New York Free Press, NY, 1977.

132 Summary history taken from Caroline M. De Costa, "The contagiousness of childbed fever": a short history of puerperal sepsis and its treatment. *The Medical Journal of Australia 2002,* www.mja.com.au   ISSN: 0025-729X

133 Anthony Browne, *The Retreat of Reason: Political correctness and the corruption of political debate in modern Britain*. Civitas, 2006.

134 Alexander Solzhenitsyn, *The Gulag Archipelago*, Harper Perennial Modern Classics, 2002, p75

135 Mathew 7: 9-10. *Good News New Testament; Today's English Version*, Canadian Bible Society, Toronto, ON. Originally published as Good News for Modern Man., American Bible Society, 1966.

136 Ibid, Mathew 7: 11.

137 Ibid, Matthew 20: 1-16.

138 Ibid, John, 8: 2-7.

139 Ibid, John 8: 9-11.

140 M. Scott Peck, *People of the Lie: The Hope for Healing Human Evil*, Simon and Schuster, NY, 1983, pp.180-181.

141 Ibid,Mathew 5: 38-41.

142 Louis Fischer, *Gandhi: His Life and Message for the World*, The New American Library of Canada Ltd, Scarborough, ON, 1954, p.35.

143 ibid, p.48.

144 ibid, pp.48-49.

145 ibid, pp.100-102.

146 ibid, p.132.

147 ibid, p.97.

148 ibid, p.129.

149 John Woolman, *The Journal of John Woolman, and a Plea for the Poor.* Citadel Press, New York, 1961. From introduction by Frederick B. Tolles, pp. VII-VIII.

150 G. K. Chesterton, *What's Wrong with the World*, 1910, p.29. Cited from edition published by Sheed and Ward, NY, 1952.

151 Robert Bly, *Iron John; A Book About Men*, Addison Wesley, 1990, p.8.

152 ibid, pp.11-12.

153 ibid, p.165.

154 Kay Leigh Hagan, Ed. *Women Respond to the Men's Movement: A Feminist Collection*, HarperCollins, NY, NY, 1992.

155 Robert Bly and Marion Woodman, *The Maiden King; The Reunion of Masculine and Feminine*, Henry Bolt & Co., NY, 1998, p.109, 218.

156 See *War Before Civilization: The Myth of the Peaceful Savage*, by Lawrence H. Keeley, archeology prof. at the U niversity of Illinois. Oxford University Press, 1996.